ST. CHARLES COUNTY COMMUNITY

3 9835 00048480 2

P9-ASB-626

TEXAS THROUGH TIME

TEXAS THROUGH TIME

EVOLVING INTERPRETATIONS

Edited by

Walter L. Buenger and Robert A. Calvert

TEXAS A&M UNIVERSITY PRESS

COLLEGE STATION

SCCCC - LIBRARY
4601 Mid Rivers Mall Drive
St. Peters, MO 63376

Copyright © 1991 by Walter L. Buenger and Robert A. Calvert
Manufactured in the United States of America
All rights reserved
First edition

Publication of this book is made possible in part by a grant from
the Texas Committee for the Humanities, a state program of
the National Endowment for the Humanities. The views expressed herein do not necessarily represent those of the Texas
Committee for the Humanities or the National Endowment for
the Humanities.

The paper used in this book meets the minimum
requirements of the American National Standard
for Permanence of Paper for Printed Library
Materials, Z39.48-1984. Binding materials have
been chosen for durability. ∞

LIBRARY OF CONGRESS CATALOGING-IN-PUBLICATION DATA
Texas through time : evolving interpretations / edited by
    Walter L. Buenger and Robert A. Calvert. — 1st ed.
        p.   cm.
    Includes bibliographical references and index.
    ISBN 0-89096-490-4 (cloth; alk. paper);
0-89096-468-8 (paper; alk. paper)
    1. Texas — Historiography.   I. Buenger, Walter L.
(Walter Louis), 1951-   .   II. Calvert, Robert A.
III. Texas Committee for the Humanities.
F386.5.T487   1991
976.4 — dc20   90-43716
                                                    CIP

Contents

Acknowledgments

If not for the aid of the Texas Committee for the Humanities these essays would have never been written. The Committee provided funding for research and for a conference during which the original ideas for these essays were discussed. Special thanks goes to James F. Veninga for his support of the idea that Texas history needed to be nudged in new directions.

Daniel Fallon, Dean, College of Liberal Arts and Larry D. Hill, Head, Department of History at Texas A&M also assisted with the conference held in October, 1988. Their encouragement and support were crucial to its success.

More than any other person, credit for uniformity of style and accuracy of citations goes to Jude Swank, word-processor operator, copy editor, and friend. We are particularly in her debt for her aid with the index. She has our thanks and appreciation.

John B. Boles and the other members of the Houston Area Southern Historians offered valuable comments on the introductory essay. We thank them for making a difficult task a bit simpler.

Walter L. Buenger   Robert A. Calvert

 Introduction:
The Shelf Life of Truth in Texas

Walter L. Buenger and Robert A. Calvert

In theory fiction, fantasy, and myth usually stand opposite to history. To the discomfort of many historians this may not
be accurate.[1] Instead, history's major contribution to the present may
be in promoting an understanding of ourselves in cultural terms. In
many ways the historian has become the keeper of the culture in much
the same sense in which the ancients used the spoken word to pass
from generation to generation the myths of their society. The speak-
ers for each generation added to or took away from this lore what society needed or demanded be kept or discarded until the myths lay
one on top of another to create a whole cloth of accepted values and
societal norms.

Texas historians, however, have had difficulty discarding old myths.
The wiry truths of forty years ago inhibit the full development of Texas

Portions of this essay have appeared in Walter L. Buenger and Robert A. Calvert,
Texas History and the Move into the Twenty-First Century (Austin: Texas Committee for
the Humanities, 1990).

1. See, for example, the exchange between C. Vann Woodward and Gore
Vidal in the *New York Review of Books* 35 (Apr. 28, 1988): 56–58. The controversy that
prompted the disagreement over the use of fiction as compared to history in explaining the past was generated by a review of Vidal's *Lincoln: A Novel* (New York: Random House, 1984) by historian Richard N. Current in "Fiction as History: A Review
Essay," *Journal of Southern History* 52 (Feb., 1986): 77–90, and by an earlier piece by
Woodward in the *New York Review of Books* 34 (Sept. 24, 1987). On historians' pursuit
of truth and its pitfalls, see Peter Novick, *That Noble Dream: The "Objectivity Question"
and the American Historical Profession* (Cambridge, England: Cambridge University Press,
1988); James T. Kloppenberg, "Objectivity and Historicism: A Century of American
Historical Writing," *American Historical Review* (*AHR*) 94 (Oct., 1989): 1011–30; William H. McNeill, "Mythistory, or Truth, Myth, History, and Historians," *AHR* 91
(Feb., 1986): 1–10.

history and warp society's perception of its current identity. Indeed, the shelf life of those truths, of myths, in Texas should have long since run its course. C. Vann Woodward, possibly the dean of American historians, estimates the shelf life of history to be about twenty years. He means that other scholars, influenced by a changing cultural environment, new methods, and new evidence, will challenge the near-truth or the partial myth that former generations of historians advocated as the causes of events or the definitions of society.[2] Serious analysts of the past may wince at the notion that part of their contribution to understanding society and to society understanding itself may well embody the accidental creation of a partial myth: the frontier as safety valve, the Native American as either noble savage or savage beast, for example. Yet most would admit that myths are necessary for ourselves and for our culture. But myths that are destructive and untrue in light of current evidence and attitudes should not be created or sustained. Thus the revision of old myths is a natural part of the practice of history, but not always of Texas history.

No single definition of a myth suffices for all disciplines. Some scholars describe myths as archetypes that, rather than deriving from societal conditioning, reflect the universal, unconscious, primordial urges in all humankind. Using that definition, the Jeffersonian longing for a preindustrial society and the physiocrats of France who identified agriculture as the only proper source of wealth are different sides of the same coin.[3] Or to stretch the imagination somewhat, the hundreds of fantasy stories that tell of space travelers landing in bucolic societies filled with busty milkmaids and innocent shepherds differ only in their sense of exaggeration from a Jeffersonian philosophy that demanded a society of yeoman farmers to preserve freedom by defeating both monopoly and encroaching governmental power. Both represent unconscious attempts or wishes to escape from the strains of mod-

2. C. Vann Woodward, *Thinking Back: The Perils of Writing History* (Baton Rouge: Louisiana State University Press, 1986), chap. 1.

3. For a convenient brief description of theories and types of myths see Louise Cowan, "Myth in the Modern World," in *Texas Myths,* ed. Robert F. O'Connor (College Station: Texas A&M University Press, 1986), pp. 1–21. The agrarian myth is explored in A. Whitney Griswold, *Farming and Democracy* (New York: Harcourt Brace, 1948), chap. 2. For a brief overview of the physiocrats see Griswold, *Farming and Democracy,* pp. 19, 21–31; and Richard Hofstadter, *The Age of Reform* (New York: Alfred A. Knopf, 1955).

ernization. Both depicted ideal societies, and Jeffersonian republicanism at least explained what made the United States of 1790 unique
and how it could remain so.[4]

The concept of the yeoman farmer, however, changed over time
until in the twentieth century it became not so much a defense against
monopoly as an attempt to deny the validity of urban life. As such,
rural America represented purity and honesty in contrast to cities,
those centers of foreigners and sin.[5] The yeoman farmer myth of the
mid-twentieth century appealed to the psyche and increasingly resembled space fantasy rather than the radical Whig tradition that produced American republicanism. A myth evolves, becoming more or
less true as time goes by. Myth also does not embody an idea that
is necessarily false. Rather, it reflects humankind's values and in turn
influences how a community sees itself and, hence, helps shape that
society's economic, political, and social behavior.

Professional historians often see their mission as stripping away
myth and exposing unvarnished truth. Yet cultural biases bind historians just as they do society at large. As purveyors of written culture
historians may arrive at only the near-truth, a truth relevant to current problems. This should cause no dismay, for understanding what
historical truth has been releases society from the blinders of tradition. Realizing the limited shelf life of history allows for the pursuit
of a new understanding of our past and present culture.

Escaping the enfolding snares of past writings on a society requires
understanding their origin. Scholars must investigate not only the past,
but how past generations looked at the past. Practitioners of history
call this process historiography: the history of historical writings and
changing intellectual points of view. For Texas the key historiographic
question is: Why have historians not subjected the myths of the state
to rigorous cyclical examination? Certainly, different cultures inter-

4. An extensive evaluation of republicanism and its impact on North American thought can be found in Drew McCoy, *The Elusive Republic* (New York: W. W.
Norton, 1980); and Robert Shalhope, "Toward a Republican Synthesis: The Emergence of an Understanding of Republicanism in American Historiography," *William
and Mary Quarterly* 29 (spring, 1972): 49–80.

5. Paul H. Johnstone, "Old Ideas Versus New Ideas in Farm Life," in *Farmers
in a Changing World,* U.S. Department of Agriculture Yearbook (Washington, D.C.:
U.S. Government Printing Office, 1940): III–17; Robert A. Calvert, "Nineteenth-Century
Farmers, Cotton, and Prosperity," in *Texas Vistas,* ed. Ralph Wooster and Robert Calvert (Austin: Texas State Historical Association, 1987), pp. 239–41.

pret their myths of origin differently. A "diversity of Texas myths" exists based on which ethnic group describes its origins.[6] Nevertheless, the dominant culture has created and added to the myth in such a way that few openly challenge its premises. Thus the macho myth of Anglo Texas still reigns.

The Texas myth has been both a part of and separate from the older frontier myth of the Anglo United States, which was born in the Puritan heritage of the City on the Hill and honed by the Manifest Destiny advocates of the mid-nineteenth century. The North American myth celebrated the past. It assumed, at least until the Vietnam War, that the United States was invincible in wartime, magnanimous in peacetime, and destined to bring peace, prosperity, Christianity, and democracy to first the continent and then to the globe.

The Texas myth accepted the North American version, adopted it, and typically exaggerated it. The outlines of the Texas myth are well known. For all practical purposes it begins with the Alamo and ends with San Jacinto. Mythic Anglo Texan male heroes—Crockett, Bowie, and Travis—die for the nation. Women are either subservient and supportive—Susanna Dickinson carries the message of heroism to Sam Houston—or sultry and seductive—Emily Morgan gives her all to detain the dictator. A foreigner, Moses Rose, refuses to cross Travis's line and flees the battle. A loyal black slave, Joe, a noncombatant, accompanies Susanna and describes the fall of the Alamo. A Tejano, Juan Sequín, leaves the Alamo as a messenger and then serves as a scout. Later disillusioned, Sequín goes to Mexico, but still represents the "good" Mexican as compared to the barbarous Santa Anna, who is saved from the cruel death he dealt to Texas heroes by Houston, the generous Anglo victor at San Jacinto, who went on to help found a republic based on freedom. The creation of the nation—the Texas Republic—separates the Texas myth from the Anglo North American myth and gives to the culture a Texas nationalism and romantic vision that transcends geography and creates, as Willie Nelson sings, a Texas state of mind.[7]

6. James F. Veninga, "Epilogue: Prospects for a Shared Culture," in O'Connor, *Texas Myths,* p. 228.

7. The authors owe much of the description of the folk myths that reinforced racial stereotypes and a male value system to our colleague Sylvia Grider, who shared with us an unpublished paper, "The Function of Historical Legends" (delivered to the Ninth International Folk Narrative Congress, June, 1989, Budapest, Hungary),

Only recently has cyclical revisionism appeared in Texas history and the myth come under considerable criticism. Like other myths it is only partially true. The actual character of the historic individuals no doubt has little correlation to their mythic presence, but debunking them makes scant difference in the perception of the myth. Selective historical memory persists and Texas elites in particular still profess at least a limited subscription to that romantic concept of Texas.[8] The myth then creates a sense of what a Texan is that precludes many of the state's citizens from identifying themselves as Texans. Moreover, the myth also defines the presumed role of all of Texas' multicultural citizens and describes the alleged characteristics of non-Anglo males. The result is that in much the way that oral myths sustained a cultural identity and gave a society shared values and common goals, written myths and folklore have shaped the goals and perceptions of those who have governed and controlled Texas for most of the twentieth century.

In like fashion, the same myths proclaim that the Texas economy has boomed because of frontier entrepreneurship and the absence of government intervention in the marketplace. Throughout the late oil boom entrepreneurs spoke of a Texas ingenuity honed by a past frontier experience, which allowed Lone Star businessmen to succeed where those on the East Coast failed. Politicians cited a favorable business climate created by low taxes, benevolent government policies, and right-to-work laws. Texas entrepreneurs gleefully derided the decadent East and the "Rustbelt" while boasting of vibrant free enterprise in Texas. This concept of frontier self-reliance blended nicely with myths of yeoman farmers, capturing an anticity bias that has always seen the East Coast as depraved.[9] Given the economic stagnation that

---

and to subsequent discussions of folk myths with her. The origins of the legends and their impact are discussed in many sources, but a good beginning point is Susan Pendergast Schoelwer, *Alamo Images: Changing Perceptions of a Texas Experience* (Dallas: DeGoyler Library and Southern Methodist University Press, 1985); Sandra L. Myres, "Cowboys and Southern Belles," in O'Connor, *Texas Myths*, pp. 122–38. Also see Mark W. Nackman, *A Nation within a Nation: The Rise of Texas Nationalism* (Port Washington, N.Y.: Kennikat Press, 1975).

8. Myres, "Cowboys and Southern Belles," pp. 135–36. Also note in particular the listing by Professor Myres's students of the important events in Texas history on p. 123. The majority cite nineteenth-century events identified with the Anglo myth.

9. Anthony Champagne and Edward J. Harpham, "Introduction," in *Texas at the Crossroads: People, Politics and Policy,* ed. Champagne and Harpham (College Sta-

has gripped Texas since the mid-1980s, it seems more likely that the economic boom and population growth of the 1970s came from the worldwide demand for oil. Worldwide interrelated economies explain prosperity more accurately than do earlier explanations based on myths of frontier self-reliance. The economic bust and the demographic changes of the recent years reaffirm historical contentions that we cannot know ourselves at all unless we challenge the cultural heritage received from previous generations with an intellectual toughness and an honesty based on the point of view of the present one.

Demands for an inclusionary history, for intellectual toughness and honesty, however, have usually run aground on the rock of Texas provincialism. One root of this provincialism grows from the mixed perception that Texans have of their own identity. Partial responsibility for this unfocused identity rests with historians who have failed to nurture cyclical revisionism. Affected by a frontier heritage that is depicted as larger than life in both fiction and folklore, university professors translated into the official history of Texas what many citizens viewed as the unique experience of Anglo-Saxon males wresting the wilderness from savage Indians and venal Mexicans.[10] The universities were largely Anglo male preserves and research and teaching represented that bias. Further, as late as the 1950s, historians still worked within the intellectual constructs of Frederick Jackson Turner's frontier thesis. They saw the frontier as the agent that shaped and made the United States unique. In this Texas historians simply followed the lead of their teachers.

At the University of Texas, which dominated the training of professional historians interested in Texas as a field of study, the first generation of historians who came on the scene in the early twentieth century took Turner's concept and applied it to the history of the state.[11] Although judicious, some still saw a war of civilized Anglos versus barbaric cultures. George P. Garrison, for whom the building that

tion: Texas A&M University Press, 1987), pp. 6–7; Nicholas Lemann, "Power and Wealth," in O'Connor, *Texas Myths*, pp. 161–62, 173.

10. Stephen Stagner, "Epics, Science, and the Lost Frontier: Texas Historical Writing, 1836–1936," *Western Historical Quarterly* 12 (Apr. 1981): 165–81.

11. Frederick Jackson Turner, *The Frontier in American History* (New York: Henry Holt, 1920); James S. Payne, "Texas Historiography in the Twentieth Century: A Study of Eugene C. Barker, Charles W. Ramsdell, and Walter P. Webb," Ph.D. diss., University of Denver, 1972, pp. 79, 82, 103–5, 122–38.

houses the University of Texas history department is named, entitled one of his books *Texas: A Contest of Civilizations* and argued that competition on the frontier produced the superior Texas character that civilized the state and vanquished aboriginal and Spanish cultures. Garrison believed strongly in scientific history. He also believed that history demonstrated progress, and that social Darwinism caused progress. The Texas frontier represented for Garrison the movement across the North American West of the Teutonic values that gave western European culture world domination. Where Garrison left off Eugene C. Barker picked up. Although his work was highly professional and more dispassionate than most, as the subtitle of his most famous work reveals, Barker also saw a "manifest destiny" in the expansion of Anglo Texas. For him the Texas Revolution was a clash of Anglo and Hispanic cultures that was almost inevitable once Spain and Mexico invited energetic and freedom-loving Anglos into Texas. [12]

The tendency to romanticize the frontier continued into the second generation of historians working in the 1930s. Both Walter Prescott Webb, who was influenced by Garrison, and J. Frank Dobie, who was not an historian but certainly shaped intellectual life in Texas through the 1950s, saw the frontier as a source of positive values relevant to modern life. They feared that the loss of the frontier heritage of Texas would weaken the state and make it like all others. This need to glorify the past led novelist Larry McMurtry to ask if there existed an unsentimental Texas historian. [13]

A sympathy for the Confederacy and southern whites also influenced the University of Texas faculty in the early twentieth century. Charles William Ramsdell, who attended the university as an undergraduate, took a master's degree there, went to Columbia University for his doctorate, and returned to Austin to teach. While at Colum-

12. George P. Garrison, *Texas: A Contest of Civilizations* (New York: Houghton Mifflin, 1903); George P. Garrison, "The First Stage of the Movement for the Annexation of Texas," *AHR* 10 (Oct., 1904): 72–96; William C. Pool, *Eugene C. Barker: Historian* (Austin: Texas State Historical Association, 1971); Eugene C. Barker, *Life of Stephen F. Austin, Founder of Texas, 1793–1836: A Chapter in the Westward Movement of the Anglo-American People* (Nashville: Cokesbury, 1925).

13. Stagner, "Epics, Science, and the Lost Frontier," pp. 165, 177–78; Myres, "Cowboys and Southern Belles," p. 128. Critics have especially objected to Webb's *The Texas Rangers* (New York: Houghton Mifflin, 1935). Larry McMurtry, *In a Narrow Grave* (Austin: Encino, 1968), pp. 40, 43, describes Webb and Dobie as not writing about the frontier as historians but as "symbolic" frontiersmen.

bia, Ramsdell accepted the historical theories of William Archibald Dunning, a professor of history who specialized in the Reconstruction period. Dunning so dominated Reconstruction historiography that later scholars would refer to the "Dunning school" of historical interpretation. This school dwelt on the alleged tragedy of Reconstruction. Dunning's followers argued that the Radical Republicans seized control of the Republican party after Lincoln's death and used every means, including subverting the Constitution, to establish unfair and coercive rule over the South. Through the use of the United States Army and by duping and enfranchising illiterate black people, the Radicals established tyrannical and illegal governments in the southern states. White southerners rebelled against this tyranny and turned the rascals out. Dunningites insisted that the resulting white animosity toward blacks, brought on by irresponsible northern politicians, led to the disfranchisement and eventual segregation of blacks.[14]

Ramsdell wrote *Reconstruction in Texas* soon after he joined the University of Texas faculty. Although it is more evenhanded than the writings of some of the other proponents of the Dunning school, the book nevertheless followed a like pattern and explained Reconstruction in terms of the assumed innate inferiority of Afro-Americans.[15] Ramsdell directed the Littlefield Fund for Southern History that came to the department as a gift from George A. Littlefield. The fund's purpose was to collect source materials that would allow scholars to research and write in such a way as to correct the northern bias in American history. Ramsdell decided to concentrate on the study of East Texas, and he soon argued that Texas had southern moorings, which made the state socially and culturally part of the South. The historian remained decidedly prosouthern and very sympathetic to white southerners' views on race.[16]

Texas' sense of place never embraced the cult of the Confederacy with quite the enthusiasm of the rest of the ex-Confederate states. Yet in Ramsdell's era the cause still burned brightly enough to cause the state legislature to investigate the history department to determine

14. Kenneth M. Stampp, *The Era of Reconstruction, 1865–1877* (New York: Alfred A. Knopf, 1965), pp. 6–23.

15. Charles W. Ramsdell, *Reconstruction in Texas* (New York: Columbia University Press, 1910); J. Edgar Snead, "A Historiography of Reconstruction in Texas: Some Myths and Problems," *Southwestern Historical Quarterly (SHQ)* 72 (Apr., 1969): 435–48.

16. Payne, "Texas Historiography in the Twentieth Century," pp. 154–74.

if an antisouthern philosophy reigned there. The legislature discovered, of course, that the university was not pro-North. But the legislative investigation revealed subconsciously what the legislators expected from history: historians in state universities should uphold the myths of the state and support its political views.[17]

The work of Ramsdell and others unintentionally did that. They helped to affirm intellectually that the system of segregation was a sound historical principle. Given the experience of Reconstruction, their work implied, if African Americans participated in politics or had free access to public accommodations, the tyranny and misrule of the period after the Civil War would return. Furthermore, the historical implication was that the experiences of whites during Reconstruction made mandatory their heirs' allegiance to the Democratic party and political conservatism, because any change threatened the political and social status quo.

Commitment to the Lost Cause also came from cultural defensiveness. Ironically, defeat in the Civil War created a myth of the superiority of southern culture. Northern technology overwhelmed noble and brave Confederate troops, with their kind but courageous generals. The mythic Robert E. Lee emerged as a godlike figure, transcending any battlefield blunders. The Confederate soldiers were enshrined in statues in front of southern courthouses, remembered as men who defended states' rights and the Constitution against the North's overwhelming population and industrial advantages. New organizations grew to enshrine the southern heroes, the United Daughters of the Confederacy among them. New holidays emerged to support the Lost Cause, a religion in the late nineteenth-century South, one that excluded Afro-Americans and ethnic minorities.[18]

17. On the origin of the Littlefield Fund and the pressure on southern universities to hire only historians with a southern orientation see H. Y. Benedict, comp., *A Source Book Relating to the History of the University of Texas; Legislative, Legal, Bibliographical, and Statistical,* University of Texas Extension Bulletin (Austin: University of Texas, 1917), pp. 406–408; Lewis L. Gould, "The University Becomes Politicized: The War with Jim Ferguson, 1915–1918, *SHQ* 86 (Oct., 1982): 256–59; Gaines M. Foster, *Ghosts of the Confederacy: Defeat, the Lost Cause, and the Emergence of the New South, 1865 to 1913* (New York: Oxford University Press, 1987), pp. 188–91.

18. Charles Reagan Wilson, *Baptized in the Blood: The Religion of the Lost Cause* (Athens: University of Georgia Press, 1980); Thomas L. Connelly, *The Marble Man: Robert E. Lee and His Image in American Society* (Baton Rouge: Louisiana State University Press, 1977); Foster, *Ghosts of the Confederacy.*

World War II and the civil rights movement diluted some of the affinities that early twentieth-century Texans held for the Lost Cause and racial apartheid. Indeed, the Ramsdell view of Texas as a southern state began to recede after 1945.[19] Yet as a result of the frontier thesis and a southern perspective the majority of scholars of all disciplines, particularly through the 1950s, viewed the Texas past in heroic terms, and described the state in ways that implied a cultural and ethnic homogeneity that did not exist. It led most writers of the 1940s to disregard minorities. The textbook justly considered the best one for undergraduate college students, *The Lone Star State*, by Rupert Richardson, in 1956 described Reconstruction as turning the "social pyramid on its apex" and hurting "the Negro." The black person became the victim of the Radicals, because "universal Negro suffrage" came too quickly, and conservative whites decided that their only recourse to unjust radical rule was to abolish black suffrage by "indirect means."[20]

The tendency to look toward historic Texas frontiers and Anglo culture as explanations for the causes for most events also skewed the direction of historical studies. It gave Texas history a strong nineteenth-century bias that is still in effect. For example, the latest edition of Richardson, still the major college textbook on Texas history, devotes 313 of its 441 pages to pre-1900 events.[21] Until recently most historians simply did not write on twentieth-century topics. By ignoring them they were not forced to ask critical questions about cultural and economic injustices. The historians were not forced to look at the limited shelf life of history.

This avoidance of culturally relevant topics and the concentration on writings in the heroic mode was also at least partially subconsciously defensive, and this defensiveness sprang from anticolonialism, another root of Texas provincialism. In a state whose economy was clearly a colonial one and whose cultural developments were limited by its rural heritage and its commitment to a yeomanlike concept of agrarian goodness, memories of the frontier past saved the society from look-

19. Frank E. Vandiver, *The Southwest: South or West* (College Station: Texas A&M University Press, 1975), pp. 7–9, 17–19, 46–48.
20. Rupert N. Richardson, *Texas: The Lone Star State* (Englewood Cliffs, N.J.: Prentice-Hall [sixth printing], 1956), p. 286.
21. Rupert N. Richardson, Ernest Wallace, and Adrian Anderson, *Texas: The Lone Star State*, 5th ed. (Englewood Cliffs, N.J.: Prentice-Hall, 1988).

ing deeply into the bleakness and poverty of much of the historical period through the 1930s. Despite the boom of the World War II years, when the state's family incomes more than doubled, in 1950 the state's per capita income only averaged 85.2 percent of the national figure and, possibly more psychologically significant, 68 percent of the national figure if the other southern states' statistics were removed from the equation. The value added by manufacturing tripled for Texas during the same period, but six northern states accounted for more than 50 percent of the nation's industrial production. Texas lagged a distant twelfth in 1945 in value added by manufacturing, and as late as 1950, when 5.1 percent of the total U.S. population resided in Texas, the state produced only 2.3 percent of the national goods. The state was a colonial economy, and its citizens resented it.[22]

This resentment did not recede when the prosperity of World War II turned into the recently ended sustained economic growth. Expansion forced Texans to consider the issues of urban growth, outside population migrations, and a transition into an industrial economy. Texans both welcomed the changes and feared them as intellectual and cultural colonialism. Some believed that the frontier produced an expansive imagination and a concept of risk taking that would be lost if the frontier heritage were lost; others insisted that modernization would make Texas like all other states and that its folk culture and heritage should be preserved to protect Texans' sense of place.

Clearly both groups wanted a usable myth for the twentieth century. The Texas macho myth hung on—less pronounced but more damaging. Once it had given many Texans purpose and identity. Now for many it had become a "Hollywood" caricature that encouraged greed and a lack of individual responsibility for society as a whole. Others saw attacks on the Anglo Texas tradition as an elitist endeavor that would destroy the past and therefore the state's *Zeitgeist*. Historical writings became a battleground between proponents representing both parts of the state's identity crisis: modernists who welcomed change

22. A. H. Belo Corporation, *Texas Almanac and State Industrial Guide* (Dallas: Dallas Morning News, 1949), pp. 293, 302; A. H. Belo Corporation, *Texas Almanac and State Industrial Guide* (Dallas: Dallas Morning News, 1952–53), pp. 187, 236; Christopher S. Davis, "Life at the Edge: Urban and Industrial Evolution of Texas, Frontier Wilderness—Frontier Space, 1836–1986," *SHQ* 89 (Apr., 1986): 509; Walter Prescott Webb, *Divided We Stand: The Crisis of a Frontierless Democracy* (New York: Farrar and Rinehart, 1937), pp. 237–39.

and wanted to verify it historically, and traditionalists who wanted writings that preserved the perceived cultural heritage. The more numerous traditionalists glorified the historic past to deter the onslaught of technocratic and cultural vandals and proclaimed that frontier individualism explained the present economic accomplishments and social stability of the state.[23]

But why have traditionalists seemingly retained such a hold on Texas history when almost every other facet of U.S. history has undergone substantial revisionism? For example, in a recent review of a 1987 book, Carl H. Moneyhon declared that the author "rested his analysis on the same evidence that Charles W. Ramsdell used in his 1910 Reconstruction study."[24] How can eighty years go by with so little change? Why has the shelf life of truth been so much longer in Texas? A partial answer is that the family trees of many historians writing on Texas still go back in an almost straight line to Garrison, Ramsdell, Barker, Webb, and Dobie. Inbreeding ruined the vigor of the herd of Texas historians. Mentors exert a force on their students far beyond graduate school. They are parents, teachers, guides, and protectors. Students of Ramsdell, Barker, and Webb, themselves often based at the University of Texas or its western outpost at Texas Tech, taught many of the generation of historians who wrote on Texas in the 1960s and 1970s. Indeed, students and admirers of Webb have turned him into a combination saint and cottage industry by encouraging their own graduate students to focus on Webb's life and labor. Even an Australian studying at the University of Texas wrote on Webb.[25] Challenging the giants of the past would have required the killing off of their surrogate parents.

In 1981, Stephen Stagner went a step further and insisted that "the nineteenth-century universalities still hold our history and our minds

23. Veninga, "Epilogue: Prospects for a Shared Culture," in O'Connor, *Texas Myths,* p. 232; T. R. Fehrenbach, "Texas Mythology: Now and Forever," in O'Connor, *Texas Myths,* pp. 205–6, 222–26.

24. Carl H. Moneyhon, review of William L. Richter, *The Army in Texas during Reconstruction, 1865–1870,* in *SHQ* 92 (Oct., 1988): 377–78.

25. Necah Stewart Furman, *Walter Prescott Webb: His Life and Impact* (Albuquerque: University of New Mexico Press, 1976); Gregory M. Tobin, *The Making of a History: Walter Prescott Webb and the Great Plains* (Austin: University of Texas Press, 1976); Kenneth R. Philip and Elliott West, eds., *Essays on Walter Prescott Webb* (Austin: University of Texas Press, 1976).

as much as they did 130 years ago." For him Webb and Dobie were simply conduits to a nineteenth-century world view. Although Stagner believes that with few exceptions we have not moved far beyond histories of the "cowboy and the glorious revolution," as his own work demonstrates, the interests and perspectives of those writing on Texas are slowly changing. Their backgrounds have also changed. In the 1970s, historians produced at places other than the University of Texas and Texas Tech and drawn from fields other than simply "Texas history" began to write on Texas. It was far easier for them to ignore the influence of their elders; they were spared the discomfort and energy needed to write in opposition to their mentors and could move beyond the frontier, the Dunning school, and the sentimental romanticism and ethnocentrism of past historians.[26]

Before this transformation occurred national historiographical trends had to alter their course. From 1945 to the 1960s these trends helped to preserve the dominance of the traditionalists. Graduate schools grew rapidly after World War II and with their growth the number of Ph.D.s increased. Regional colleges and universities expanded graduate programs as institutions sought prestige and expanded teaching and research responsibilities. History underwent a boom period. These newly minted degree holders came to the academy with neither a romantic vision of rural America or a Great Depression fear of monopolies. They avoided the frontier as an explanation for historical causation and looked to cities and industrial expansion to explain the national character.

Progress, industrial might, and the Cold War dominated American culture and the writing of history. The national character sketched out by historians emerged as one that can be best described as representing the goals of the upper middle class. U.S. history stretched unbroken as the wheels of progress led to industrial expansion that would eventually include all of the country's dispossessed, if they waited long enough. Problems would be solved by *The Genius of American Politics*, which compromised and brought into the American political system outside groups longing to join the mainstream society. The societies or movements that failed were those composed of radical fanatics, those

26. Stagner, "Epics, Science, and the Lost Frontier," pp. 180–81, 181n. For equally valuable insight on the influence of past historians see Payne, "Texas Historiography in the Twentieth Century."

who, like the Populists, denied the American system of pragmatic compromise. Extremism in the form of Joe McCarthy or Joe Stalin denied progress. The historical answer laid in avoiding extremes. American history consequently was the story of consensus, not conflict.[27]

The historical approach was as comfortable as the 1950s themselves. It aimed at describing a national consensus. Therefore, conflicts were papered over and the unique histories or myths of minorities denied. One very good consensus historian wrote of slavery and explained his approach as one that identified Afro-Americans as "white men with black skins, nothing more, nothing less."[28] The implication, denied in later editions of the books, after the shelf life of history dumped consensus interpretations, was that Afro-Americans really wanted to emulate white culture. Capitalism served as the economic answer for this country, as long as its abuses were controlled by the state and it brought consumer culture to all. There were a few historians who refused to accept the consensus. But rather than accept their historical perspective of cultural and political pluralism, the majority of historians strove for a national myth of sameness.[29]

Consensus history denied regional history, which looked to the peculiar characteristics of an area. Young historians leaving the expanded graduate programs were told not to choose state topics for their dissertations. There was a dual provincialism in place. Not only were Texans provincial but the history profession was provincial about Texas. Scholars attempting to rewrite U.S. history typically began with the assumption that state history was not worthy of their talents, unless that history of course emanated from New England. The general disdain that academicians had for regional history and particularly the

27. Rowland Bertoff, "Consensus Pyrotechnics," a review of Daniel Boorstin, *The Americans: The Democratic Experience,* in *Reviews of American History* 2 (Mar., 1974): 25–27; Kenneth L. Kushmer, "American Social History: The Boorstin Experience," *Reviews of American History* 4 (Dec., 1976): 471–82; Daniel Boorstin, *The Genius of American Politics* (Chicago: University of Chicago Press, 1953), pp. 120, 170–89; Hofstadter, *The Age of Reform.*

28. Kenneth M. Stampp, *The Peculiar Institution: Slavery in the Ante-Bellum South* (Berkeley: University of California Press, 1955), p. viii.

29. Compare, for example, the Marxist scholar William Appleman Williams, *The Contours of American History* (New York: World Publishing, 1961), with the liberal scholar Lewis Hartz, *The Liberal Tradition in America: An Interpretation of American Political Thought Since the Revolution* (New York: Harcourt, Brace, 1955), for the sharp division between majority thought and the dissenters.

history of the West prevented many young scholars from choosing Texas topics. Indeed, the fear of being identified as narrow and unsophisticated (as well as the limits on salary and mobility attached to the tag "Texas historian") still causes most of us to identify ourselves as historians of a broader construct, of the South or the Gilded Age, rather than as historians of Texas.

Too frequently Texas history was left in the hands of those who wished to preserve the Anglo myth. Those who might have challenged it, even liberal historians such as Kenneth Stampp, would probably have designed the story of the state and its peoples to fit a single mold of progress. One of the best books written on Texas in the 1950s falls prey to this engine-of-progress concept and describes the industrialization of Texas in the late nineteenth century as an inevitable move to bigness. Those who disagreed — farm protest groups, labor unions — were simply misguided if well-meaning men. Women played no role, of course, in the story.[30]

More recently, however, national historiographic trends that once helped to preserve the Anglo Texan myth have slowly worked to erode it. The 1960s changed approaches to both regional and national history; the period witnessed possibly the most profound disillusionment of intellectuals with American society since the 1920s. Older explanations for progress failed to satisfy. The Anglo male frontier turned from a metaphor for progress and democracy to a metaphor for Vietnam.[31] Historians emerged from the maelstrom of social change with greater sensitivity to cultural diversity. Gradually the old debate between traditionalists and modernists lost meaning and the same sort of spirit that questioned segregation, male-female relations, and other tenets of the establishment also questioned conventional historical assumptions. In the 1960s, long-excluded groups refused to accept 1950s consensus historians' conclusion that North American history was a celebration of progress by a people with a homogeneous value system. The melting pot turned into a salad bowl.

But the question of how to write about those who were not of the elite produced complicated intellectual problems in both approach and concept. The traditional history — consensus history, Anglo male his-

30. John S. Spratt, *The Road to Spindletop: Economic Change in Texas, 1875–1901* (Dallas: Southern Methodist University Press, 1957).

31. Glen W. Price, *Origins of the War with Mexico: The Polk-Stockton Intrigue* (Austin: University of Texas Press, 1967).

tory—had outlived its shelf life, but it left no model to be emulated. It would not suffice to change one elite theme, such as the conquering of the frontier, for another, the emergence of the city. The lack of sources complicated the problem. Nonelites kept few records, wrote few letters, and very few occupied the largely white male domains of newspaper editorships, political offices, or important educational and literary posts. Debates over how best to mine the primary source materials in order to write about nonelites and to break away from the constraints of consensus history prompted historians of the United States to read cultural anthropology and sociology and to look at social science statistical techniques, oral history, and the computer for new methods of telling a new story.[32] Scholars looked to new models outside of American traditions. They emulated the work done by European historians, the French New Marxist scholars, and the British sociologist E. P. Thompson, among others.[33]

By the late 1960s, proponents of the methods and the viewpoint of an antiestablishment history, the "new social history," took the intellectual high ground; a position they have held ever since. New social history has assumed such an influential position in graduate education over the last twenty years that one single definition oversimplifies the intellectual substructure that supports these historical approaches.

32. The uneasiness of the profession with traditional research methods can be testified to by the publishing of such books as Edward N. Saveth, ed., *American History and the Social Sciences* (New York: Free Press, 1964); or Edward Shorter, *The Historian and the Computer: A Practical Guide* (Englewood Cliffs, N.J.: Prentice-Hall, 1971), which were designed to give historians philosophical and practical approaches to investigating the rapid changes in American society.

33. The sources of transatlantic borrowing by historians would constitute a whole essay in themselves. Interested scholars should look at the works of the great historian Fernand Braudel; for example, *The Structures of Everyday Life: The Limits of the Possible,* trans. from the French by Sian Reynolds (New York: Harper and Row, 1985); and *The Mediterranean and the Mediterranean World in the Age of Philip II,* trans. Reynolds., 2 vols. (New York: Harper and Row, 1972). There is a Fernand Braudel Center for the Study of Economies, Historical Systems, and Civilizations, which issues publications. American historians were first attracted to the seminal studies carried out by Etienne Gautier, particularly (with Louis Henry) *La population de Crulai, paroisse normande: Etude historique* (Paris: Presses Universitaires de France, 1958). E. P. Thompson, *The Making of the English Working Class* (London: V. Gollanz, 1963), influenced a number of scholars interested in radicalism. Lawrence Goodwyn cites Thompson's influence on his research, for example, in his influential *Democratic Promise: The Populist Moment in America* (New York: Oxford University Press, 1976).

Nevertheless, in general, practitioners argue that the ethnicity, culture, and actions of nonelites shape society with near equal force to that of elite groups, and that they play an equal part in determining political and economic actions. These historians tend to look at group actions and not the actions of individuals.[34]

The new social history helped to revitalize the study of regional and local history. The new approach emphasized those left out of previous histories, and therefore emphasized the dispossessed, local communities, and others absent from the landscape of consensus history. In any case, the approach dictated the use of local sources — census returns, courthouse records, and so on.[35] To use these local sources no longer necessarily branded one as a provincial historian. Consequently, by the late 1970s more historians turned to Texas topics as the idea spread that you could study localities and local groups and draw conclusions valuable in the understanding of the whole. Be they historians of Afro-Americans, women, the new economics, or a myriad of other categories, the choice of Texas signaled a decline of provincialism on the part of those writing about Texas and a like decline in the assumption that to write on Texas implied a narrow historical focus.

The application of new historical methodology to Texas topics lagged behind their application in some of the other regions. This may have been the case partly because of the remaining cultural defensiveness of the practitioners of Texas history. Anxious not to be identified with those who glorified the past, it took historians a while to notice the wealth of interesting topics in a historically heterogeneous state. Gradually scattering and delving into local sources they produced theses, articles, and books, all the while searching for new topics.

34. Robert F. Berkhofer, Jr., "The New or Old Social History?" review of Rowland Berthoff, *An Unsettled People: Social Order and Disorder in American History*, in *Reviews in American History* 1 (Mar., 1973), 21–28; Stuart M. Blumin, "The New Urban History Updated," review of Lee F. Selmore, ed., *The New Urban History: Quantitative Explorations by American Historians*, in *Reviews in American History* 3 (Sept., 1975), pp. 297–99.

35. Alwyn Barr, *Black Texans: A History of Negroes in Texas, 1528–1971* (Austin, Tex.: Jenkins, 1973); Arnoldo De León, *The Tejano Community, 1836–1900* (Albuquerque: University of New Mexico Press, 1982); Arnoldo De León, *They Called Them Greasers: Anglo Attitudes toward Mexicans in Texas, 1821–1900* (Austin: University of Texas Press, 1983); Randolph B. Campbell, *A Southern Community in Crisis: Harrison County, Texas, 1850–1880* (Austin: Texas State Historical Association, 1985), are examples of these kinds of histories in Texas.

A difficult problem faced these young and not-so-young historians: what was being done in Texas history and what needed to be done? Some assumptions were obvious. To write a new history of the state of Texas, most would turn to histories of other states for models and techniques. But this done, where within Texas and on what topics should they focus their research? And how should critiques and evaluations of former writers and writings on Texas be formulated?

Interpreting Southern History, edited by John B. Boles and Evelyn Thomas Nolen, provided one model for stimulating new history. As historiography, not bibliography, each essay in the book critically evaluated writings on southern history. They did not just list titles or attach them to a grand theme. In some cases authors went even further and pointed out what needed to be done as well as what had been done.[36]

Fortunately, the Texas Committee for the Humanities provided funds to begin work on a similar project. Long before the completion of the essays that follow, the first goal was to decide upon themes and essay topics that would allow authors to comment on emerging research trends and techniques. Chronological essays on Spanish Texas, the Republic, statehood to Reconstruction, progressivism to the New Deal, and politics since the New Deal were combined with topical essays — women, Tejanos, Afro-Americans, culture, urbanization, economic development, and agrarianism. An overall critique of Texas history — a Marxist look at Texas writings or a feminist perspective on Texas history — would have been intriguing, but there seems to be no evaluation of general literature on Texas arranged in an orderly fashion. Consequently no universal critique of all of Texas history seemed possible. Thus the essays on compelling aspects of Texas' historical literature were to be a first step toward critiques of its contents from different perspectives.

Judging from the finished essays that follow in this book, suspicions concerning the provincial quality and filiopietistic nature of most writings on Texas history were well grounded. The authors enunciated three themes that helped to explain provincialism and filiopietism: historians have avoided new perspectives, methodologies, and or-

36. John B. Boles and Evelyn Thomas Nolen, eds., *Interpreting Southern History: Historiographical Essays in Honor of Sanford W. Higginbotham* (Baton Rouge: Louisiana State University Press, 1987).

ganizational structures that might provoke a rethinking of Texas history. The hold of the last generation of Texas historians on the public mind and on the historical profession still blocks new interpretations; and the persistent identity crisis of the Texas public and its historians limit a clearer look at the myths produced by an earlier Texas.

The arrangement of the essays that follow this introduction reflects those three themes. At first glance it may seem odd to begin a work on all of Texas history with an essay on twentieth-century cultural life. Yet all of the authors write about books produced in the twentieth century, and that writing was part of the state's cultural life. Thus when Ronald Davis writes of a state caught between wanting to imitate the high culture of the East Coast and preserving the folk culture of its traditional ways he offers a compelling insight into all of Texas history. He further argues that historians have avoided cultural topics and that one possible reason is that they find the resolution of this identity crisis too difficult or painful. Partial resolution of this identity crisis may come from more squarely facing groups left out of the traditional Texas myth. The next three essays deal with Texas Mexicans, blacks, and women, and the six essays that follow them fall in chronological order and suggest revisions to be made within specific periods. The final two essays deal with topics that are often difficult for modern Texans to accept, urbanization and economic development. Each author notes the lag between historical revision on national topics and those chosen by most Texas historians.

Old methodologies shaped the old perspectives. The paucity of traditional manuscript sources available on women, minorities, and nonelites abets filiopietism. For example, no area of Texas history more clearly demonstrates its celebratory nature than does the Texas Revolution. As Paul Lack asserts, new community studies of revolutionary Texas that use quantitative methods and other methods associated with new social history can aid the history of the state in escaping "the suffocating power of its heroes." Arnoldo De León insists also that quantitative methods and community studies that examine nonelites have not been used in writings about Tejanos. Perhaps such an approach would even help to limit the influence of the macho myth that Fane Downs maintains has helped create a literary and popular image of women inimical to serious scholarship. Certainly the tools of the new social history, along with more research in traditional sources and quantitative analysis of election returns, would at least discour-

age scholars of recent political history, as Kenneth Hendrickson observes, from viewing "their subject through a special prism of emotion and pride which produced a distorted image of reality."

Questions prompted by methodology point to the lack of an acceptable synthesis to explain current histories of the state. Most historians reject elitist history—for example, generalizations based upon
the biographies of great men—but such an approach produces a historical synthesis. So, too, did history written with a message, but that
approach also distorted perceptions of the past. The methods of new
social history, which most often produces fine local studies, studies
of brief time spans, or studies of specific ethnic or class groups, make
it difficult to speculate about the whole fabric of history. For example,
as Robert Calvert points out, there has been no comprehensive history of late nineteenth- and early twentieth-century agriculture in Texas.
Consequently evaluations of the impact of tenant farming or staple
crop agriculture on the state's economic and social life have not been
attempted. A good survey of public education does not exist. How
then can such issues as taxation, teacher training, and the efficiency
of the public school system be judged with no comprehensive historical framework of progressivism? Without such how can one judge
reform movements in the early twentieth-century South? Larry Hill
wonders, given the lack of emphasis given to the social history of that
period, if any viable synthesis—any accurate definition of Progressivism—can be reached.

New methodology and new organizational structures alone will
not produce a valid synthesis. Current historians must apply new perspectives. The impact of racism on Chicano history serves as a case
in point. The triumph of Anglo-Saxon civilization was depicted in
terms of the march of the virile American frontiersman against Spain,
which played the role of the decaying empire, the doomed empire.
Romantic, mysterious, with a touch of cruelty, colonial Spain inevitably receded before the triumph of democracy and manifest destiny.
This history reserved a measure of respect and dignity for Spaniards,
who were often described as those with white skins, that was often
denied the mixed bloods who greatly outnumbered the Spanish in
Mexico. With some exceptions, as De León shows, until the 1960s this
view marked Tejanos as inferior. Chicanos sparked an historical counterrevolution that militantly attacked all Anglos as oppressors. Ro-

manticism, racism, and the counterrevolution all prevented a balanced view that would foster a compelling synthesis of Texas history.

Donald Chipman and Randolph Campbell have identified similar ethnocentric and segmented approaches as limiting historical syntheses. Chipman laments the reluctance to tell the history of colonial Spain within its imperial context. Events in Europe affected the New World and consequently Texas. In his essay Campbell points out that no one has ever considered the time period of 1845 to 1880 as a unit. Instead, history has been broken off at the start and conclusion of the Civil War. The points made by these two scholars certainly apply to most if not all writings on Texas history. Ethnocentrism and the limitations it imposes may be the single most recurring theme in all the essays in this volume. A recent comment by such a well-known historian as T. R. Fehrenbach that "the great difference between Texas and every other American state in the twentieth century was that Texas had a history," illustrates this point.[37] Even works that make laudable efforts to arrive at a synthesis, such as J. S. Spratt's *Road to Spindletop,* deal with too small a time frame.

Indeed, laudable work by giants of the past can preclude the development of a new synthesis. Again, for example, note Eugene C. Barker and his effect on the history of the Texas Revolution. Barker commendably avoided racial stereotypes, presented an evenhanded view of the revolution, and offered a counterbalance to the often negative view of Tejanos in the revolution. Still, Barker celebrated the great man, Stephen F. Austin, and saw Texas as a natural and inevitable extension of the American frontier. Not only did this tend to promote an exclusionary history, but the strength of Barker's scholarship and his reputation limited attempts to move beyond his analysis of the revolution. In fact, until recently, historians have curiously neglected the 1830s, even though, as Lack has pointed out, numerous gaps in our historical knowledge of that decade exists. Possibly they wished not to challenge the historical reputation of Barker. The Republic of Texas deserves more investigation, and we need as well a relevant synthesis that explains the revolution. But first we must step out of the shadow of past interpreters of Texas.

37. T. R. Fehrenbach, *Lone Star: A History of Texas and the Texans* (New York: MacMillan, 1968), p. 711. Also see Spratt, *The Road to Spindletop.*

Barker was not the only past giant who has slowed the emergence of new, less provincial and filiopietistic ways of looking at Texas history. In support of our earlier observations, the contributors to this volume describe George Garrison, Charles Ramsdell, Walter P. Webb, and J. Frank Dobie as barriers to modern scholarship. Alwyn Barr notes the long shadow of past giants when writing of U. B. Phillips. Barr writes that "the functioning of slavery continued to be described within the paternalistic parameters set forth by U. B. Phillips until the 1970s." Only recently have historians broken through the fifty-year stranglehold of Phillips. Popular images of slavery, if slavery is considered at all, have yet to move much beyond Phillips.[38]

Thus, to return to the central theme of this essay, even in the face of the onslaught of new social history, Texas history, especially the popular version, has been extremely conservative and slow to accept new interpretations and points of view. The power of past giants emerges as a key element in this arrested development, and the publication in 1988 of an entire issue of the *Southwestern Historical Quarterly* devoted to Webb and Dobie gives evidence that their strength has yet to wane. This forces contemporary historians to be iconoclasts on two levels. They must attack the old ideas and the older purveyors of those ideas and they must step out of the shadow of the old myths and the giants who recounted the myths. This in itself takes considerable time and energy, and that high cost may partially explain the slow rate of change.[39]

Another source of this unwillingness to rewrite Texas history and of the strength of past giants has probably been the identity crisis described by Ronald Davis. Char Miller's essay on urban Texas highlights another facet of this oft-cited problem. Besides noting the need for more extensive use of the methods of new social history, Miller focuses on the place of Texas in the Sunbelt. Eighty percent of Texans now reside in urban areas. The rapidity of this change from rural pre–World War II Texas to an urban state has left some Texans unsure of their place in the modern world. Just as the state's cities seem to rise out of nowhere for no apparent reason, urban dwellers wonder about their place in those cities. In a rush to advertise the advantages

38. See Ulrich B. Phillips, *American Negro Slavery* (New York: D. Appleton, 1918); Ulrich B. Phillips, *Life and Labor in the Old South* (Boston: Little, Brown, 1929); Ramsdell, *Reconstruction in Texas*.

39. See *SHQ* 92 (July, 1988).

of the state and to differentiate it from the decadent East Coast, "Sunbelt glitz" has been liberally sprinkled on the urban history of the state, obscuring a framework for understanding the past.

Perhaps this identity crisis also springs from the inability of Texans to place themselves within the broader region of West or South. Not knowing if Texas belongs with the slaveholding South or the cattle-ranching West has allowed Texans to ignore the more innovative scholarship in those areas and to argue that Texas has always been unique. The insistence on uniqueness, added to the persistent impact of past scholars, precluded until recently a full-scale study of Texas slavery. Just as Texans cannot place themselves in the Sunbelt, then, they cannot place their history or their identity in the analytical framework of either the South or the West. The insistence by some Texas historians on the state's uniqueness and an inability to accept an analytical framework has encouraged the provincialism of outsiders who observe the doings of Texas historians. Often deservedly, historians from outside the state minimize the work done on Texas, because it fails both to draw comparisons between Texas and other similar places and to set Texas in a larger national focus.[40]

Nowhere has this identity crisis come into sharper focus than in the economic history of the state. Historians, according to Walter Buenger, have exhibited a curious "flight from modernity." On the one hand they celebrate growth and profits. On the other they flee the implications of a modern life created by growth and profits. The ranch remains the most studied and probably least significant major aspect of the Texas economy. Besides being a traditional topic acceptable to the old masters, ranches are romantic, close to a preindustrial past, and uniquely Texan—at least in the popular view. Texas historians choose ranch histories as ideal topics, for they fit within the framework of past giants, and they fire another round at the modernists. Popular culture also supports such ventures, for, tellingly, ranch histories usually outsell all other Texas books.[41]

40. Vandiver, *The Southwest: South or West,* recounts the difficulties of placing Texas in a region. The first work on slavery in Texas was not published until 1989. See Randolph B. Campbell, *An Empire for Slavery: The Peculiar Institution in Texas, 1821–1865* (Baton Rouge: Louisiana State University Press, 1989).

41. For 1989–90 the best-selling book published by the Texas State Historical Association was an attractive photographic ranch history by Laura Wilson. *Watt Matthews of Lambshead* (Austin: Texas State Historical Association, 1989) sold over three

Moreover, most economic and business histories record a fascination with a golden age, a bygone age, where things were better and the heroes and villains were clearly discernible. In this golden era the old myth of the Anglo-Saxon male triumphing over all odds without the aid of government runs rampant. Issues of class, community, gender, and ethnicity are ignored because they conflict with the pristine past. Current legends are perfect examples of the avoidance of modern realities by editing out all complexities and subtleties. Unlike history, in legends events are resolved without contradictions. The writers often ignore the evolution of twentieth-century Texas, because its development challenges earlier legends. Ironically, then, descriptions of the business world have inherited and adapted the Anglo Texan myth, encapsulated in the Alamo. Even possibly more ironic, the part of the historical discipline most closely linked to the "dismal science" of economics and to factual data seems currently to also be the one that is most enamored with myth and chained by an identity crisis.[42]

Given this "flight from modernity," obviously the most glaring research gaps cited in the following essays existed for post-1930 Texas history. Except for a general political history of the 1930s now being written (by Norman Brown at the University of Texas) and a sociological analysis of recent politics (by Chandler Davidson at Rice) just now published, the field needs work on all topics. The lack of research on recent Texas history recalls the problems of writing about the state. The theme of the period is not that of a golden age; it is one of Texas being absorbed into the culture and society of the rest of the United States. The identity crisis becomes more complex. The force of anticolonialism becomes more subtle and powerful. Texans, proud to be no longer church mouse poor, but reluctant to abandon their romantic and individualistic past, find it difficult to write a history that integrates them into the nation. Such a history would renounce the Anglo Texas myth and define away their uniqueness.[43]

---

thousand copies its first month. See "Agenda and Director's Report to the Executive Council," Texas State Historical Association, Mar. 1, 1990.

42. Leo Marx, *The Machine in the Garden: Technology and the Pastoral Ideal in America* (New York: Oxford University Press, 1967); and Henry Nash Smith, *Virgin Land: The American West as Symbol and Myth* (Cambridge, Mass.: Harvard University Press, 1950), both deal with ideas of pastoral myths and the restrictions they have placed on facing modern technological development and historical complexities.

43. One of the best examples of anticolonialism and the slow acceptance of mo-

Faced with such ambiguity, southern or western historians often ignore the state. They write of the urban South in the New Deal without mention of Dallas and Houston.[44] The academy's provincialism remains. The subject chosen must fit into recognized national themes before most academics feel comfortable committing part of their career and reputation to the topic. The provincialism of those writing on the state also remains. The daunting task of applying new methodologies, developing a synthesis, overcoming the barrier of past giants among historians, and then grappling with an unsure identity often simply overwhelms scholars. Clinging to past ways and past ideas offers a simpler choice to those who write about Texas. They can comfortably ignore the rest of the historical profession rather than challenge the mind-set of the homefolk.

The existence of the essays in this volume suggests that such a past course may well be changing. The intellectual revolt of the 1960s that spawned new social history finally reached Texas historians, if not the public. Moreover, the current economic malaise of the state may force a new view of Texas. If it calls for introspection, for a new understanding, and for a rejection of old answers, it may prompt historians to rewrite the history of the state. Soon history may move beyond the old provincialisms, beyond the passion of the 1960s and early 1970s, toward a calmer, more balanced view of the past.

A new history would be particularly useful if it adjusted our myths and values to our current situation, if it helped to resolve the identity crisis associated with being Texan, if it demonstrated the importance of opening up new ways of looking at ourselves. For, as this preliminary survey of writings on Texas history demonstrates, Texans do not know themselves very well. The image of Texas as a homogeneous state has only recently come under attack and the critique of that image has not been widespread. The strength of earlier writings on Texas history was that they perpetuated a pride in the state, a myth of what it meant to be a Texan that could lead us to value the past and refuse to accept a second-rate status. Yet until all of the popula-

---

dernity is Walter Prescott Webb. See especially *Divided We Stand: The Crisis of a Frontierless Democracy,* rev. ed. (Austin, Tex.: Acorn, 1944). Also see Chandler Davidson, *Race and Class in Texas Politics* (Princeton, N.J.: Princeton University Press, 1990).

44. Texas is ignored in Douglas L. Smith, *The New Deal in the Urban South* (Baton Rouge: Louisiana State University Press, 1988). Fortunately this is not true of Roger Biles, "The Urban South in the Great Depression," *JSH* 56 (Feb., 1990): 71–100.

tion feel a part of the myth, excluded groups will be alienated from the state's history and potentially from the state itself.

The problem grows in seriousness. What was once a minority population may well be a majority population by 2050. Non-Anglos are most likely to not finish high school and remain mired in poverty. Ironically, they will be called upon to staff and support an economic system that is moving from a raw-material, industrial base to a more complex service and high-tech economy.[45] The myth must be reworked to include the excluded groups, to encourage the population at risk to stay in school and strive for full participation in society.

Such a reworking of myths is not only crucial, but possible. Eventually historians' ideas and evidence ease their way into the public's consciousness, into the mythic structure. Society affects historians, but historians also affect society. Inquiries from teachers and others anxious to touch an increasing minority population lead us to believe that over time scholarly critiques pass into the general body of knowledge or into the general myth.

What follows in this collection of historiographic essays is an initial step in transferring scholarly critiques to the general public. There remains the crucial decision of what to do after studying how and why the history of Texas has been written as it has. Simply using this historiographic launching pad to overrun the study of Texas with new social history is not enough. We need to move beyond new social history.

There are two difficulties with new social history. In some ways it discourages the study of state history because it ignores such political boundaries as the lines separating one state from another. Texas would be split up into geographic boundaries linked to all four directions of the compass. Thus the old identity crisis will simply continue in a new guise. Further, new social history, which studies many bits and pieces all equal to one another, makes synthesis difficult and often is written in a tedious style that makes it inaccessible to the general reader. Lacking unifying themes and an interesting narrative, such

45. Champagne and Harpham, *Texas at the Crossroads*. In particular see the excellent essays by Ronald Briggs, "The Demography of a Sunbelt State," and Donald A. Hicks, "Advanced Industrial Development." United Way of Texas, "A View to the Future" (Austin, Tex.: United Way, 1989), a broadside, details the growth of poverty in the Texas population and analyzes its impact on the economy. See in particular pp. 12–17, 20–21, 35. *Dallas Morning News,* Oct. 8, 1988, and Jan. 9, 1989, comments on the dropout rate and minority goals in the public schools and colleges.

works also lack readers. If no one reads the new interpretations of the past then no amount of historiographic sophistication will change the general knowledge of the history of the state.[46]

Calling for a new synthesis that will allow Texas to be treated as a whole and that will appeal to general readers runs the risk of returning to the days of Webb, Ramsdell, and Barker. We do not need a new straitjacket to bind future historians as the past giants have bound us. Yet, if we are fortunate, the new synthesis will stimulate even more research to prove or disprove its various points. New themes should challenge historians and the public to think about Texas in new ways; they should adjust the myth to the needs of our times. For the shelf life of truth, of myth, in Texas has been overlong and debilitating.

46. On the need for and the dangers of synthesis see Gertrude Himmelfarb, "Denigrating the Rule of Reason: The 'New History' Goes Bottom Up," *Harper's* (Apr., 1984): 84–90; Thomas Bender, "Wholes and Parts: The Need for Synthesis in American History," *Journal of American History* 73 (June, 1986): 120–36; Eric Monkkonen, "The Dangers of Synthesis," *AHR* 91 (Dec., 1986): 1146–57; *AHR* 94 (June, 1989), entire issue.

TEXAS THROUGH TIME

❧ Modernization and Distinctiveness: Twentieth-Century Cultural Life in Texas

Ronald L. Davis

In his award-winning book on the Texas centennial, Kenneth Ragsdale makes the point that 1936 was the year the rest of America discovered Texas. Much was made that year of Texas history, and the centennial celebration marked a peak of ethnocentrism in the state. But as thousands of visitors poured in, Texas made some discoveries too, and the irony is that never again would the Lone Star State be the same.[1] Within a decade Texas would cease to be predominantly rural and would grow increasingly urban. As the state's population shifted from an agricultural to an industrial or multibase economy, profound changes occurred in the way Texans lived, although many still clung to the ideologies and social forms of the countryside. Texans continued to think of themselves as a breed apart — somehow special, carrying independence, the American dream, and material success to fantastic heights. The image of Texas was drawn bigger than life — power, money, everything colossal — and the myth shows few signs of disappearing. At the state fair every October, Big Tex towers over throngs of visitors munching on foot-long hot dogs on their way to the double Ferris wheel. Television's *Dallas* is for much of the world an accurate representation of the life and values of contemporary Texas, while J. R. Ewing's greed, deceit, and flaunting of the double standard serve as latter-day examples of how the Southwest was won.

Yet Texas' population has always been mixed, as Francis Edward Abernethy aptly reveals in *The Folklore of Texan Cultures,* and the state's minorities in recent years have emerged from an anonymity spawned

---

1. Kenneth B. Ragsdale, *The Year America Discovered Texas: Centennial '36* (College Station: Texas A&M University Press, 1987).

by the myth of the melting pot.[2] The confusion is nonetheless complicated since ethnic roots have frequently been stressed to demonstrate a multiple folk culture that looms unique, as evidenced at Six Flags Over Texas and in displays of the Institute of Texan Cultures. Also, Texas' population is increasingly composed of transplants from outside the state. While in repeated instances the newcomers show a need to appear more Texan than any native, others are appalled at the state's persistent provincialism and grasp at what pockets of sophistication they find scattered about. In truth Texas has never been either ethnically or culturally homogeneous, and there has always been a conflict between those who have sought to bring in high culture from outside the state and those who have tried to preserve an indigenous folk culture. The result is a kind of dualism not unlike what underdeveloped countries have experienced in a similar struggle between Westernizers or modernizers and nativists or romanticists.

Texas' cultural life in the twentieth century reflects paradoxes rooted in the state's lingering confusion over its basic identity, a confusion shared by the outside world. Self-conscious and schizophrenic, Texas clings to its frontier heritage, viewing it in heroic terms, fearful that should the past be lost, with its courage and risk taking lifted to epic proportions, so will the state's uniqueness. Geographer Christopher Davies goes so far as to claim that Texans are prisoners of their past, wandering between two worlds — the fading memories of the frontier wilderness and a glittering urban present.[3]

This fundamental identity crisis has been captured best in Texas' writing, particularly in recent years. The decade of the state's centennial also saw coming into prominence the first generation of Texas intellectuals, headed by J. Frank Dobie, Walter Prescott Webb, and Roy Bedichek. Enough time has lapsed for two of these revered figures to receive book-length biographies. Necah Furman's *Walter Prescott Webb: His Life and Impact* depicts Webb as a product of his region, growing up on the edge of the frontier, but contributing to the transition into a more complex world. Lon Tinkle's *An American Original: The Life of J. Frank Dobie* is an affectionate, human portrait, which leaves

2. Francis Edward Abernethy, ed., *The Folklore of Texan Cultures* (Austin, Tex.: Encino, 1974).

3. Christopher S. Davies, "Life at the Edge: Urban and Industrial Evolution of Texas, Frontier Wilderness — Frontier Space, 1936–1986," *Southwestern Historical Quarterly (SHQ)* 89 (Apr., 1986): 443–554.

4

literary and historical criticism to others. During the hundredth anniversary of Dobie's and Webb's births, almost half an issue of the *Southwestern Historical Quarterly* was devoted to these two pivotal Texas intellectuals, including a lengthy reappraisal of Dobie by Don Graham and affectionate reminiscences of Webb by Joe B. Frantz.[4]

It remained for Larry McMurtry, however, in his now-famous essay, "Ever a Bridegroom: Reflections on the Failure of Texas Literature," to take an irreverent swipe at the Dobie-Webb-Bedichek triumvirate, setting off an immediate explosion within the state's literary circles. McMurtry dismissed Dobie as "a congealed mass of virtually undifferentiated anecdotage," while Bedichek he assessed as a "minor" writer who didn't have "much to say." Webb's achievement McMurtry found "genuine, but small." The younger writer went on to chide Texas authors for producing an endless stream of works on cowboys, the small town, the homefolks, and the rural experience rather than probing the less simplistic life of the city. In the face of McMurtry's accusation of literary complacency, Texas letters became a battleground of controversy: the state's frontier past versus its urban present, captured in Don Graham, James W. Lee, and William T. Pilkington's *The Texas Literary Tradition* and Clifford Craig and Tom Pilkington's *Range Wars: Heated Debates, Sober Reflections, and Other Assessments of Texas Writing.*[5]

John Graves continued to write about the country and in many ways became the heir to the Dobie-Webb-Bedichek tradition. In a lecture delivered at Southwest Texas State University in 1981, published in Robert W. Walts's *The American Southwest: Cradle of Literary Art*, Graves remarked that "most of our city writers could come from almost anywhere in modern America. . . . Frances Mossiker in Dallas has done some fine historical work of literary quality on such figures as Marie

4. Necah Stewart Furman, *Walter Prescott Webb: His Life and Impact* (Albuquerque: University of New Mexico Press, 1976); Lon Tinkle, *An American Original: The Life of J. Frank Dobie* (Boston: Little, Brown, 1978); Don Graham, "J. Frank Dobie: A Reappraisal," *SHQ* 92 (July, 1988): 1–15; Joe B. Frantz, "Remembering Walter Prescott Webb," *SHQ* 92 (July, 1988): 16–30.

5. Larry McMurtry, "Ever a Bridegroom: Reflections on the Failure of Texas Literature," *Texas Observer*, Oct. 23, 1981, pp. 1, 8–19; Don Graham, James W. Lee, and William T. Pilkington, *The Texas Literary Tradition* (Austin: University of Texas Press, 1983); Clifford Craig and Tom Pilkington, *Range Wars: Heated Debates, Sober Reflections, and Other Assessments of Texas Writing* (Dallas: Southern Methodist University Press, 1989).

Antoinette and Pocahontas and Josephine Bonaparte; there's nothing Texan there." Larry McMurtry earlier insisted in *In a Narrow Grave* that Terry Southern clearly is the best writer ever to come from Alvarado, Texas, yet doubts that the Lone Star State inspired *Candy*. Nor did McMurtry feel that Indian Creek, the birthplace of Katherine Anne Porter, had been responsible for Porter's better stories, which are often set in Mexico or Europe.[6] Certainly the Texas experience has extended beyond the frontier ethos, and by the close of World War II a sampling of Texas writers were free enough of old convictions to focus on more cosmopolitan themes. Interestingly enough, the most widely read women novelists currently writing about Texas include Beverly Lowry, Shelby Hearon, and Laura Furman, none of whom are native Texans.

Larry McMurtry claimed that in his own case he had essentially exhausted his material from his growing-up years in Archer County when he finished *The Last Picture Show*. With *In a Narrow Grave* he made a farewell to writing about the country, a theme that had dominated his first four books. Yet in 1985, after publishing his urban trilogy, McMurtry himself returned to the frontier with *Lonesome Dove*, winning the Pulitzer Prize for literature with an archetypal saga of the Cattle Kingdom, which was appropriate since the author was the son and grandson of Texas cattlemen. McMurtry, the most famous Texas author since Dobie, has already been the subject of several short books, among them Charles D. Peavy's *Larry McMurtry*, Raymond L. Neinstein's *The Ghost Country: A Study of the Novels of Larry McMurtry*, and Dorey Schmidt's *Larry McMurtry: Unredeemed Dreams*.[7] He is assessed as a writer who started out as an old-fashioned regionalist and then transformed himself into a neoregionalist, employing satire and black humor and treating Texas material, including women, in a realistic manner. McMurtry has ventured to suggest that living in Washington, D.C. has given him perspective, enabling him to write about life in his native state with deeper insight.

6. John Graves in Robert W. Walts, *The American Southwest: Cradle of Literary Art* (San Marcos: Southwest Texas State University, 1981), p. 17; Larry McMurtry, *In a Narrow Grave* (Austin, Tex.: Encino, 1968), p. 31.

7. Charles D. Peavy, *Larry McMurtry* (Boston: Twayne, 1977); Raymond L. Neinstein, *The Ghost Country: A Study of the Novels of Larry McMurtry* (Berkeley, Calif.: Creative Arts, 1976); Dorey Schmidt, *Larry McMurtry: Unredeemed Dreams* (Edinburg, Tex.: Pan American University Press, 1978).

The Texas writer to receive the most critical attention, Katherine Anne Porter, probably holds the most secure place in American letters of anyone to come out of the state. Porter's life and works have been analyzed repeatedly, with attempts made to separate truth from fiction. Many of the Porter myths the author herself carefully cultivated throughout her life, but she does emerge from recent scholarship as a Texas writer who became a citizen of the world, in many respects a loner, who is determined to write in her own voice. Among the best studies are John Edward Hardy's *Katherine Anne Porter*, Joan Givner's *Katherine Anne Porter: A Life*, Jane Krause DeMouy's *Katherine Anne Porter's Women*, Darlene Harbour Unrue's *Truth and Vision in Katherine Anne Porter's Fiction*, Harold Bloom's *Katherine Anne Porter*, and Willene and George Hendrick's *Katherine Anne Porter*.[8] What emerges clearly is that Porter was a highly personal writer and that the unity in her work came from deep within her own life.

What rural Texans read during the first decades of the twentieth century is vividly suggested in Carl Wright's "Prairie Trails in Literature," based on Wright's own childhood. He and his brothers found such classics as *Robinson Crusoe*, the novels of Horatio Alger and Zane Grey, and pulp magazines a welcome antidote for the toil and heat of the Central Texas cotton fields. Rarely, however, did they read about farm life. Most editors of early twentieth-century literary magazines, as Imogene Bentley Dickey has shown, appear to have been as dedicated to the perpetuation of southern ideals as to the elevation of literary tastes.[9]

Despite the recent controversy over the direction of Texas letters, historians have been timid about entering the fray, just as they have been afraid of most cultural topics in Texas history, preferring to let what the historical profession privately considers the more effete dis-

---

8. John Edward Hardy, *Katherine Anne Porter* (New York: Ungar, 1973); Joan Givner, *Katherine Anne Porter: A Life* (New York: Simon and Schuster, 1982); Jane Krause DeMouy, *Katherine Anne Porter's Women* (Austin: University of Texas Press, 1983); Darlene Harbour Unrue, *Truth and Vision in Katherine Anne Porter's Fiction* (Athens: University of Georgia Press, 1985); Harold Bloom, *Katherine Anne Porter* (New York: Chelsea, 1986); Willene Hendrick and George Hendrick, *Katherine Anne Porter* (Boston: Twayne, 1988).

9. Carl C. Wright, "Prairie Trails in Literature," *SHQ* 82 (Oct., 1978): 143–48; Imogene Bentley Dickey, *Early Literary Magazines of Texas* (Austin, Tex.: Steck-Vaughn, 1970).

ciplines take the risks of pioneering. One of the obvious results is that writing on Texas culture remains fragmented, and the need for an overall synthesis is perhaps the most glaring deficiency.

While Pauline A. Pinckney's *Painting in Texas: The Nineteenth Century* attempted to pull together the contribution of the state's noteworthy frontier artists, nothing of comparable scope exists for the twentieth century. The art conceived for the Texas Capitol proved didactic and provided support for such dominant Anglo-American values as individualism, Manifest Destiny, and historical progress. Certainly it helped to perpetuate a fundamental Texas mythology, as Emily Fourmy Cutrer has demonstrated. Elisabet Ney's statues of Stephen F. Austin and Sam Houston are clearly wrapped in ideas of natural nobility, furthering the concept of the sturdy, stalwart Texan.[10]

James Patrick McGuire's *Julius Stockfleth: Gulf Coast Marine and Landscape Painter* is an excellent volume on Stockfleth's visual record of ships, harbor scenes, and homes of the Texas coast, particularly Galveston. Although Stockfleth was not a polished painter, he felt an obligation to depict faithfully the exact shape and correct rigging of the vessels he observed in the late nineteenth and early twentieth centuries, making the artist's work historically significant. Cecilia Steinfeldt's *The Onderdonks: A Family of Texas Painters* is a solid treatment of the state's foremost artistic family that examines their role in formulating an art consciousness in Texas during the late nineteenth and early twentieth centuries. Centered in San Antonio, the Onderdonks bridged the gap between European traditions of painting and what would become hailed as an American school.[11]

But it remained for the Dallas Nine, a group of local artists who came to national prominence during the Great Depression, to forge an artistic expression based on regional values, character, and traditions. Drawing on the state's multicultural past, the Dallas Nine tried to fuse the Hispano-Indian heritage with that from the Old South and

10. Pauline A. Pinckney, *Painting in Texas: The Nineteenth Century* (Austin: University of Texas Press, 1967); Emily Fourmy Cutrer, "'The Hardy, Stalwart Son of Texas'": Art and Mythology at the Capitol," *SHQ* 92 (Oct., 1988): 288–322; Emily Fourmy Cutrer, *The Art of Woman: The Life and Work of Elisabet Ney* (Lincoln: University of Nebraska Press, 1988).

11. James Patrick McGuire, *Julius Stockfleth: Gulf Coast Marine and Landscape Painter* (San Antonio, Tex.: Trinity University Press, 1976); Cecilia Steinfeldt, *The Onderdonks: A Family of Texas Painters* (San Antonio, Tex.: Trinity University Press, 1976).

the midwestern plains, forming an amalgam that would capture Texas' true nature. Striving to be eclectic rather than provincial in their art, these artists evolved their individual styles, yet adopted a fairly unified aesthetic outlook and created a new regionalism in painting that came to fruition during the state's centennial celebration. Rick Stewart's *Lone Star Regionalism: The Dallas Nine and Their Circle, 1928-1945* details the significance of this group of painters, describing how they collectively shunned shallow nativism and yet dissolved by the end of World War II, moving on to new challenges as postwar conditions altered old ways forever.[12]

Texas' contribution to post office and public art during the 1930s is included in both Marlene Park and Gerald Markowitz's *Democratic Vistas* and Karal Ann Marling's *Wall-to-Wall America: A Cultural History of Post Office Murals in the Great Depression.* Marling particularly stresses the compromise between aesthetic and institutional considerations, using Barse Miller's *Texas* mural at Goose Creek, in which Texas is pictured as a giant, muscular deity, as a blatant example of myth-making embedded in pioneer trappings. Susie Kalil's *The Texas Landscape, 1900-1986* reflects the unique and sometimes eccentric ways in which artists have responded to living and working in the Lone Star State, delving into the psychological responses to Texas' varied landscapes and the ways in which Texans have or have not coexisted with their environment. Jerry Bywaters's *Seventy-Five Years of Art in Dallas* is a serviceable history of the Dallas Art Association and the Dallas Museum of Fine Arts, while Tom Lea's *A Picture Gallery* serves as an attractive record of Lea's murals, paintings, and pen and ink drawings of Texas Rangers, cowboys, Indians, and farm life around the state.[13]

Texas has been less celebrated in art than other areas of the West, in part because the state does not measure up geographically to east-

12. Rick Stewart, *Lone Star Regionalism: The Dallas Nine and Their Circle, 1928-1945* (Austin: Texas Monthly Press, 1985).

13. Marlene Park and Gerald E. Markowitz, *Democratic Vistas* (Philadelphia, Pa.: Temple University Press, 1984); Karal Ann Marling, *Wall-to-Wall America: A Cultural History of Post Office Murals in the Great Depression* (Minneapolis: University of Minnesota Press, 1982), pp. 139-40; Susie Kalil, *The Texas Landscape, 1900-1986* (Houston: Museum of Fine Arts, 1986); Jerry Bywaters, *Seventy-Five Years of Art in Dallas* (Dallas: Dallas Museum of Fine Arts, 1978); Tom Lea, *A Picture Gallery* (Boston: Little, Brown, 1968).

erners' vision of the idyllic American garden. While Texas' frontier past, ethnically segmented though it might be, gave earlier Texas art some semblance of uniqueness and cohesion, many artists after World War II began to interpret the life around them in a multiplicity of styles and to use new materials, so that Texas art became less readily identifiable and often only arbitrarily separate from modern trends. Certainly regionalism became a less distinctive theme in American culture as mobility accelerated nationally, as Americans grew increasingly cosmopolitan through travel and media exposure, and as the country, including Texas, became more urban and less tied to the land. While rootlessness has created a longing for identification with place, the impact on Texas art has been superficial, except in the more commercial forms.

If pockets of regionalism have continued in painting, architecture in Texas moved overwhelmingly toward the international style and more recently toward postmodernism. Much of the writing on the state's architecture has been restricted to the nineteenth century. As Willard B. Robinson points out in *The People's Architecture: Texas Courthouses, Jails, and Municipal Buildings,* public buildings have fulfilled a fundamental need as monuments assuring permanence and stability and reflecting governmental ideals, but their classical styles have also provided communities with psychological security. Edifices dedicated to higher learning communicate a devotion to college education through their magnitude and opulence, generally following national trends. Railroad stations in the early twentieth century served as major symbols of the urbanization process. As Keith Bryant has pointed out, the depot became a social center where a town's residents often gathered to witness the arrival and departure of passenger trains; in our own time, however, this architectural heritage appears doomed.[14] By 1930, public architecture in Texas was moving toward a modern image, and the modern buildings coordinated by George Dahl for the centennial exposition, formal yet efficient, appeared to symbolize progress.

Earlier Alfred Giles, a San Antonio architect transplanted from

14. Willard B. Robinson, *The People's Architecture: Texas Courthouses, Jails, and Municipal Buildings* (Austin: Texas State Historical Association, 1983); Willard B. Robinson, "Temples of Knowledge: Historic Mains of Texas Colleges and Universities," *SHQ* 77 (Apr., 1974): 445–80; Keith L. Bryant, Jr., "Railway Stations of Texas: A Disappearing Architectural Heritage," *SHQ* 79 (Apr., 1976): 417–40.

England who also did work in northern Mexico, had employed the Italian villa style before moving on to Richardsonian Romanesque, and by 1910 showed the influence of Frank Lloyd Wright in his more advanced domestic designs. Mary Carolyn Hollers Jutson's *Alfred Giles: An English Architect in Texas and Mexico* is an engaging account of this eclectic turn-of-the-century architect who steered a course between late Victorian designs and modernism, avoiding either extreme. Henry C. Trost, on the other hand, who dominated the architectural scene of far West Texas, New Mexico, and Arizona for the first three decades of this century, mastered virtually every building style current in the United States from the 1880s through the 1930s, from the mansarded style of his youth to the art deco skyscrapers of the 1920s. Trost, whose work is ably chronicled by Lloyd C. and June-Marie F. Englebrecht in *Henry C. Trost, Architect of the Southwest,* created a prodigious number of buildings that were conscious of the special environment he called "arid America." During the last thirty years of his career he designed some two hundred structures in El Paso alone, making that city the headquarters for his regional practice.[15]

By 1928, Dallas architect David R. Williams had begun publishing articles on indigenous Texas architecture, with drawings by O'Neil Ford. Both Williams and Ford would develop original styles based on a study of local forms, becoming the founding fathers of a regional architecture. Muriel McCarthy's *David R. Williams: Pioneer Architect* graphically reveals how Williams influenced the direction of architecture in the Southwest during the 1930s and 1940s.[16]

Since Dallas reached maturity with the automobile, it has paid the price in urban sprawl and fragmentation. Architecturally the city only recently reached the sophisticated level its civic leaders had envisioned. Doug Tomlinson and David Dillon's *Dallas Architecture, 1936–1986* contends that the tremendous growth in the city's skyline since 1965 represents a positive expression of municipal and private will in the wake of the Kennedy assassination in 1963. Historic preservation, however, was a movement Dallas joined hesitantly and in repeated

15. Mary Carolyn Hollers Jutson, *Alfred Giles: An English Architect in Texas and Mexico* (San Antonio, Tex.: Trinity University Press, 1972); Lloyd C. Englebrecht and June-Marie F. Englebrecht, *Henry C. Trost, Architect of the Southwest* (El Paso, Tex.: El Paso Library Association, 1981).

16. Muriel Quest McCarthy, *David R. Williams: Pioneer Architect* (Dallas: Southern Methodist University Press, 1984).

instances too late to save major landmarks. Galveston recognized the importance of preservation earlier and has served as a model for much of the state. Richard Payne and Geoffrey Leavenworth's *Historic Galveston* is lavishly illustrated, although less than a third of the book's contents deals with the period since the storm of 1900.[17]

As life in Texas changed dramatically after World War II, tastes in architecture shifted as well. The state's cities through the 1960s and 1970s were dominated by functionalist designs, which implied an acceptance of technology as art, while economically minded entrepreneurs concerned themselves mainly with costs and maximum usage of space. By the early 1980s, tired of glass and chrome, architects began to move — then rush — toward postmodernism, abandoning the "less is more" contention of the functionalists and accepting that with endless repetition less might indeed become a bore. Chippendale-style ornamentation began to top Texas buildings, as it did buildings throughout the rest of urban America, along with decorative columns, oval windows, and French detail.

As with other areas of Texas culture, landscape architecture in the latter twentieth century clearly reflects the dualism that exists between preserving the native and importing varieties better suited to the Northeast. Sally Wasowski and Julie Ryan's *Landscaping with Native Texas Plants* urges an expansion of a trend that has grown since the early 1970s, a revolt against English garden designs and the use of plants adapted to the local environment. As Texas becomes increasingly urban, nostalgia for the land as it once was has been in part responsible for this recent move toward native flora, in sharp contrast with any of the editions of the River Oaks Garden Club's *Garden Book for Houston.* Don Riddel's *River Oaks: A Pictorial Presentation of Houston's Residential Park,* for instance, emphasizes stretches of "marching green acres," graceful curves through "woodland acres," and terraced lawns, "where every modern improvement of the most enduring character has been installed."[18]

17. Doug Tomlinson and David Dillon, *Dallas Architecture, 1936–1986* (Austin: Texas Monthly Press, 1985); Richard Payne and Geoffrey Leavenworth, *Historic Galveston* (Houston: Herring, 1985).

18. Sally Wasowski and Julie Ryan, *Landscaping with Native Texas Plants* (Austin: Texas Monthly Press, 1985); Don Riddle, *River Oaks: A Pictorial Presentation of Houston's Residential Park* (Houston: River Oaks Corporation, 1929). Also see The Forum of Civics, *A Garden Book for Houston* (Houston: Rein, 1929).

If Texas historians have been fearful of tackling topics in literature, painting, and architecture, they seem positively terrified of theater and serious music, largely surrendering both domains to local critics. A number of biographies (for example, of Joan Crawford, Jayne Mansfield, Larry Hagman, and Sissy Spacek) and autobiographies (among them Mary Martin's, King Vidor's, Carol Burnett's, Ann Miller's, Cyd Charisse's, and Debbie Reynolds's) already exist for Texas performers and directors. Of particular interest is Don Graham's recent book on Audie Murphy.[19] Linda Darnell's story is on the way. The lives of Zachary Scott, Ann Sheridan, and Rip Torn remain to be written, although Ginger Rogers is presently at work on her story, and others will follow in due course. As yet, however, there is no biography of the Dallas critic John Rosenfield, whose influence was felt all across the state and whose work was nationally recognized, nor is there an adequate study of Nina Vance, the force behind Houston's Alley Theatre. Much needed is an in-depth study of playwright Horton Foote, a regionalist who draws inspiration from his hometown of Wharton, Texas, yet shapes his material into universal themes rather than relying on vernacular speech and local quaintness to establish atmosphere. Foote's reputation is even more substantial out of his native state than it is within it, although he continues to draw on Texas sources.

What is sorely missing in the writing on Texas culture is an overview of the state's contribution to drama, set in an artistic and historical perspective. C. Richard King's "Sarah Bernhardt in Texas" is an engaging account of the great French actress's two tours through the state, the latter (in 1906) for the Shubert brothers, which were successful despite staunch opposition from the Theatrical Syndicate that then controlled most American theaters. Sue Dauphin's *Houston by Stages: A History of Theatre in Houston* is a beginning for one of the state's major theater centers, surveying as it does the Houston Little Theatre, the Alley Theatre, college drama in that city, as well as dinner theaters, ethnic drama, and musical shows. No study of similar scope exists for Dallas, although Margo Jones's book *Theatre-in-the-Round* is valuable in its comments on an important segment of Dallas's theatrical history, and the SMU Press has recently published the first full-

19. Don Graham, *No Name on the Bullet: A Biography of Audie Murphy* (New York: Viking, 1989).

length biography of Margo Jones herself, who was both a local and national figure.[20] No published study has yet reached print of the Dallas Little Theatre, three-time winner of the Belasco Cup in a national competition held in New York, or the thirty-year-old Dallas Theatre Center, although both are ripe topics.

Mark Busby's *Preston Jones* is a brief treatment of the actor-playwright responsible for *A Texas Trilogy*, which met with good success in Dallas and at the Kennedy Center in Washington but closed after five weeks on Broadway, New York critics having dismissed them as regional plays. For Preston Jones the tragedy of the Southwest stems from a rupture caused by the wrenching away from old values that inevitably comes with the passage of time. Jones realized that the frontier ethos represented impossible ideals, yet he remained ambivalent about abandoning the traditional attitudes of his native state.[21]

Nicolas Kanellos's *Mexican American Theater: Legacy and Reality* includes Texas, particularly San Antonio, but his work is highly abbreviated.[22] Far more remains to be done on ethnic theater, and as yet no study of black theater in Texas has been written. Basically the major deficiency in the writing on drama in Texas is an urgent need for more work, both general and specific, preferably by writers who can synthesize and bring a national and historical focus to the state's theatrical accomplishments.

The same deficiency characterizes writing on music. *The Houston Symphony Orchestra, 1913–1971,* by the Houston critic Hubert Roussel, stands almost as an island in terms of monographs on symphonic music in Texas. Roussel attempted to combine music criticism, anecdotes, and social history, delineating how the Houston orchestra developed into one of the finest in the nation under such internationally distinguished conductors as Sir Thomas Beecham, Leopold Stokowski, Sir John Barbirolli, and Andre Previn. But no comparable volume can be found for Dallas, San Antonio, Austin, or Fort Worth. Robert Gins-

20. C. Richard King, "Sarah Bernhardt in Texas," *SHQ* 68 (Oct., 1964): 196–206; Sue Dauphin, *Houston by Stages: A History of Theatre in Houston* (Austin, Tex.: Eakin, 1981); Margo Jones, *Theatre-in-the-Round* (New York: Rinehart, 1951); Helen Sheehy, *Margo: The Life and Theatre of Margo Jones* (Dallas: Southern Methodist University Press, 1989).

21. Mark Busby, *Preston Jones* (Boise, Idaho: Boise State University Press, 1983).

22. Nicolas Kanellos, *Mexican American Theater: Legacy and Reality* (Pittsburgh, Pa.: Latin American Literary Review Press, 1987).

berg's *Houston Grand Opera: A History* is a start in another direction, and I myself am slated to write a volume on opera in Dallas for the SMU Press sometime within the next three years. Meanwhile, my own *A History of Opera in the American West* includes frequent sections on opera in Texas, but there is definitely room for additional work, especially on the San Antonio Festival, which was unique and is no longer functioning, and the Fort Worth Opera, which reflects many of the problems of a grass-roots company.[23]

Robert Stevenson's *Music in El Paso, 1919–1939* takes an essentially biographical approach, focusing mainly on local composers, with some attention given to touring artists, while Dormon Winfrey's *Arturo Toscanini in Texas* chronicles the 1950 NBC Symphony Orchestra's tour of Houston, Austin, and Dallas.[24] Still, art music in Texas generally is unexplored territory for historians and offers rich possibilities both from a social and cultural viewpoint.

Commercial music in the state has fared better at the hands of professional historians, particularly the country and western genre. Bill Malone's *Country Music U.S.A.* has rightly become a classic, rich in historical context and showing the transition from southern hillbilly music to a western emphasis full of cowboy images. Texas' role in this evolution has been strategic and remains so to the present day, even though the country music industry is centered in Nashville. Following Malone's lead, Charles Townsend's *San Antonio Rose: The Life and Music of Bob Wills* appeared as the definitive biography of one of the giants both in the country and popular music fields who was the innovator of what became known as "western swing." Townsend's book is the product of many years of research and is enhanced by an impressive number of oral histories, including several with Wills's musicians, fondly remembered as "the Texas Playboys." Willie Nelson has recently written his autobiography, entitled simply *Willie,* and similar memoirs are bound to be forthcoming.[25]

23. Hubert Roussel, *The Houston Symphony Orchestra, 1913–1971* (Austin: University of Texas Press, 1972); Robert I. Ginsberg, *Houston Grand Opera: A History* (Houston: Houston Grand Opera Guild, 1981); Ronald L. Davis, *A History of Opera in the American West* (New York: Prentice-Hall, 1965).

24. Robert M. Stevenson, *Music in El Paso, 1919–1939* (El Paso: University of Texas at El Paso Press, 1970); Dormon Winfrey, *Arturo Toscanini in Texas* (Austin, Tex.: Encino, 1967).

25. Bill C. Malone, *Country Music U.S.A.,* rev. ed. (Austin: University of Texas

Texas' folk music has been well covered, beginning with John Lomax's *Cowboy Songs and Other Frontier Ballads*, which cataloged the preservation of British ballads as well as the creation of frontier songs. Mody Boatright's *Mexican Border Ballads and Other Lore* focuses on the balladry of the common man, the laborer, and the ranch hand, a form of expression that has since given way to more modern forms. William Owens's *Texas Folk Songs* concentrates on the place of Anglo-American folk music in the state's country life, while the author's later work, *Tell Me a Story, Sing Me a Song*, reveals a more contemporary interest in Texas's ethnic diversity, including songs from the state's French, Mexican, German, Czech, Italian, Swedish, and black populations.[26] Owens concluded that he discovered no homogeneity that could be called purely Texan. Instead he found separateness, but a separateness always on the edge of amalgamation.

Popular culture in Texas has received endless attention, all the more so with the prolonged success of television's *Dallas* series, but the tone has rarely been what historians would like, as most of the writing has perpetuated the Texas myth rather than shedding light on reality. Don Graham's *Cowboys and Cadillacs: How Hollywood Looks at Texas*, which treats movies from the silent era through *The Texas Chainsaw Massacre* (1974), shows how durable mythic Texas, with its larger-than-life image, still is. Graham's article "Remembering the Alamo: The Story of the Texas Revolution in Popular Culture" discusses repeated attempts by popular writers and filmmakers to capture the excitement and meaning of Anglo Texas' struggle for freedom, most frequently centered on the Alamo. The first epic version of the saga on film was *The Martyrs of the Alamo*, supervised by D. W. Griffith in 1915, but the story has been retold in variants ranging from *Davy Crockett and the Fall of the Alamo* (1926) to John Wayne's *The Alamo* (1960) through the revisionist *Seguin* (1979), which emphasized the Tejano contribution.[27]

Press, 1985); Charles Townsend, *San Antonio Rose: The Life and Music of Bob Wills* (Urbana: University of Illinois Press, 1976); Willie Nelson with Bud Shrake, *Willie* (New York: Simon and Schuster, 1988).

26. John A. Lomax, *Cowboy Songs and Other Frontier Ballads* (New York: Sturgis and Walton, 1910); Mody C. Boatright, ed., *Mexican Border Ballads and Other Lore* (Dallas: Southern Methodist University Press, 1946); William A. Owens, *Texas Folk Songs* (Dallas: Southern Methodist University Press, 1950); William A. Owens, *Tell Me a Story, Sing Me a Song* (Austin: University of Texas Press, 1983).

27. Don Graham, *Cowboys and Cadillacs: How Hollywood Looks at Texas* (Austin:

Somehow the Dallas Cowboys and Houston Oilers contribute to the Texas stereotype, particularly when either is on a winning streak, even though many of the players for both teams are imported from outside the state. Almost forgotten, however, is the fact that black boxer Jack Johnson, who held the heavyweight championship from 1908 until 1915, spent his early life in Galveston, where he was molded into a rebellious, defiant man. Randy Roberts points out in "Galveston's Jack Johnson: Flourishing in the Dark" that Johnson dared to marry white women and defeat white fighters, maintaining that in so doing the boxer exerted as much influence on his era as Booker T. Washington or W. E. B. DuBois.[28]

James Pohl's "The Bible Decade and the Origin of National Athletic Prominence" analyzes how the coach D. X. Bible laid the foundation for what became a football dynasty at the University of Texas, but far more research could be done on the Southwest's fascination for spectator sports, viewing the phenomenon, one hopes, with maturity and even sensitivity. Lance Rentzel pointed the way with his *When All the Laughter Died in Sorrow,* but fans prefer a more heroic look at their sports figures, which brings us back to the much-abused frontier ethos.[29]

So long as writers persist in viewing the Texas experience as grandiosely unique, any examination of the state's cultural heritage is bound to be limited and will probably be lightweight. Observers must first come to terms with the reality of twentieth-century Texas, with its ethnic diversity, and should recognize that much of the state's recent cultural life has been shaped by international standards. "Some day we shall realize that we have been trying to escape the necessity for coming to terms with the facts of our environment by using business and superficial amusements and perfunctory art as opiates," Henry Nash Smith wrote for the *Southwest Review* in 1928; "and then, perhaps, we shall set about adjusting ourselves to the actual conditions of our

Texas Monthly Press, 1983); Don Graham, "Remembering the Alamo: The Story of the Texas Revolution in Popular Culture," *SHQ* 89 (July, 1985): 35–66.

28. Randy Roberts, "Galveston's Jack Johnson: Flourishing in the Dark," *SHQ* 87 (July, 1983): 37–56.

29. James W. Pohl, "The Bible Decade and the Origin of National Athletic Prominence," *SHQ* 86 (Oct., 1982): 299–320; Lance Rentzel, *When All the Laughter Died in Sorrow* (New York: Saturday Review Press, 1972).

life."[30] Obviously, over sixty years later, the identity problem in Texas still persists.

In part, how Texans view culture depends on where they live. Dallas and Houston have led the struggle to modernize and import art forms from Europe and around the globe. Austin, San Antonio, and to some extent Fort Worth have been more inclined to promote native culture, although even the state's small towns have broadened their perspectives in recent decades, largely as a result of movies, radio, and television. Yet at this point too little of a serious historical nature has been written on the state's cultural life during the present century. I would be the first to acknowledge that my own slim volume, entitled *Twentieth-Century Cultural Life in Texas,* is uneven and badly in need of revision.[31]

Several factors work against an immediate improvement in this complex area of scholarship. First, a great many monographic post-holes need to be dug before an overall synthesis can be solidly constructed. Unfortunately most historians seem afraid of cultural topics. Their fears are not without reason, since cultural historians are likely to encounter fierce criticism from spokesmen for the arts and often fail to win proper acceptance within their own discipline. Crossing established professional lines can prove dangerous in today's segmented corporate world. Then, too, professional historians seem increasingly reluctant to devote themselves to local topics, not wanting to appear provincial in an academic climate increasingly dominated by Ivy League elitism.

While cultural history has made vast progress toward acceptance within recent decades, its advances on the local and state levels have been less remarkable, except for an increase in antiquarian endeavors. Since Texas offers few American studies programs, aside from the one headed by William Goetzmann at the University of Texas at Austin, and even fewer courses of quality in popular culture, the problems are compounded. Those brave enough to write on local cultural topics may well encounter difficulty in getting their manuscripts published, since presses are fearful of narrow topics with too restricted a readership, a reluctance that grows as production costs soar.

30. Henry Nash Smith, "Culture," *Southwest Review* 13 (Jan., 1928): 255.
31. Ronald L. Davis, *Twentieth-Century Cultural Life in Texas* (Boston: American Press, 1981).

How can Texas culture receive adequate attention unless well-trained professionals are encouraged to write about it? Why should a promising young historian with a tenure decision hanging over his or her head risk writing on a local topic that may not even be published, or may not win sufficient professional recognition if it is? The problems in writing Texas cultural history are many, although the need remains great. Amateur historians and M.A. thesis writers with less at stake can afford to be adventuresome. Yet a vacuum on the professional level persists, offering real challenges to those stalwart enough to brave the hazards and flexible enough to bridge several fields.

ᓚ Texas Mexicans:
Twentieth-Century Interpretations
Arnoldo De León

While it may be argued that only recently have students made genuine efforts to integrate Mexican Americans into the pages of Texas history, the fact is that the literature has always addressed the experience of Tejanos.[1] Their portrayal has not always been consistent, however; indeed, writings in the years before the 1960s presented Texas Mexicans in a light less flattering and accurate than the works of recent authors.

From about 1930 to the present four distinct generations have interpreted Mexican-American history: those who wrote from about the 1930s to the early 1950s; those who advanced Mexican-American history a bit further, from the early 1950s to the late 1960s; those who began the process of revision in the late 1960s and wrote in the 1980s from the perspective of their era; and the contemporary writers who have probed far beyond the earliest revisionist themes and brought Tejano history in step with modern Texas historiography. Obviously, unevenness and overlapping exists in the periodization.

Early Tejano History: 1930s–1950

Several features characterized the phase of writing beginning with the 1930s. The few historians that took up the topic were inclined to see Mexicans in much the same way as their academic predeces-

I wish to thank the following scholars for their helpful suggestions: Roberto R. Calderón of the University of California at Los Angeles; Roberto R. Treviño of Stanford University; David J. Weber of Southern Methodist University; and Richard Griswold del Castillo of San Diego State University.

1. I use the term *Tejano* in reference to persons of Mexican descent who lived in Texas, whether they were native or foreign born.

sors. In the nineteenth century, Texas historians had written roman-tically about the state's past, stressing Anglo-Saxon progress, and more specifically, the state's pioneer and revolutionary heritage.[2] This tone persisted until well into the twentieth century even as professionally trained historians committed to objectivity assumed the writing of Texas history.

But scholars seldom operate outside of a cultural context, and those writing in the 1930s and 1940s (and thereafter, for that matter) were products of a conditioning with deep roots in the state's experience. They believed, as the historian T. R. Fehrenbach commented later, that "the great difference between Texas and every other American state in the twentieth century was that Texas had a history." For them, the Texas chronicle involved the story of Anglo-Saxons who had res-cued the province from Santa Anna's hordes, from northern carpet-baggers, and from savage Indians who had stood in the way of rugged pioneers. Until the 1960s, at least, these writers could hardly escape the racist tenor of their times (a fact that Walter Prescott Webb con-ceded before his death). They lived in a time of institutionalized Jim Crowism, when attitudes attributed traits of genetic inferiority to people of color. Lastly, until the 1950s, Texas retained a rural flavor; thus, while the problems of the urban centers influenced the Progressive historians to accept new views on the writing of history, the general absence of similar problems failed to prompt Texas writers to move away from familiar themes.[3]

To these historians, the sweeping themes in Texas history were those that included Stephen F. Austin, Sam Houston, the Texas Rang-ers, the Mier expedition, Bigfoot Wallace, Cynthia Ann Parker, the cattle drives, and other aspects of the winning of the West.[4] Expect-edly, any tangential mention of Tejanos was related to their roles in the war for independence and as bandits doing battle with cattlemen, frontiersmen, and the Texas Rangers. Seldom were they portrayed as

2. Stephen Stagner, "Epics, Science, and the Lost Frontier: Texas Historical Writing, 1836–1936," *Western Historical Quarterly* 12 (Apr., 1981): 173, 176–79, 181.

3. Fehrenbach quoted in ibid., p. 165. On racism, see José A. Hernández, *Mu-tual Aid for Survival: The Case of the Mexican American* (Malabar, Fla.: Robert E. Krieger, 1983), p. 64. For an example of the criticism leveled at the new history of the Pro-gressive historians by Eugene C. Barker, see Stagner, "Epics, Science, and the Lost Frontier," p. 176.

4. Stagner, "Epics, Science, and the Lost Frontier," pp. 173, 176–79, 181.

actors in the historical process; even when mentioned as laborers in the twentieth century, they were cast as passive peons contributing little to the state's majesty. Mainstream writers deemed Texas Mexican history insignificant and undeserving of research in the primary documents. Loyalty to the tradition of nineteenth-century scholarship — cocky, self-assured, and racist — barred any other depiction. No Mexican-American historian lived during the era to posit an alternative viewpoint. Carlos E. Castañeda, the eminent scholar from South Texas, was primarily interested in the state's Spanish colonial era rather than its Mexican minority.[5]

While it is debatable that any of the above was done intentionally, the group writing in the 1930s and 1940s tended to link the Tejano heritage with the failure of Spain and Mexico to populate and control Texas — the "successful failure" or "Santa Anna at the Alamo" syndromes. J. Frank Dobie, for one, was inclined toward painting Texas Mexicans as quaint and colorful people, and the first edition of Rupert N. Richardson's durable survey *Texas: The Lone Star State* treated Tejanos as ahistoric: it mentioned the cattle rustling of Juan Cortina, certain confrontations with the heroic Texas Rangers, and the Tejano presence in the state in the 1940s as a laboring class.[6] Cortina in these early writings attracted more notoriety than any other nineteenth-century Tejano personality, but mainstream writers seldom described him in flattering terms. One biographer described the Brownsville *ranchero* as the "number one Mexican border bandit of all time" who disrupted life in the 1850s through the 1870s in South Texas by his marauding and cattle rustling. It is, of course, common knowledge that the Mexicans who entered the pages of Walter Prescott Webb's *The Texas Rangers: A Century of Frontier Defense* (1935) were brigands who lost at every turn in their encounters with his "quiet, deliberate, gentle

5. Félix D. Almaráz, Jr., has covered Castañeda's academic career in "Carlos E. Castañeda and *Our Catholic Heritage:* The Initial Volumes, 1933–1943," *Social Science Journal* 13 (Apr., 1976): 27–37; "Carlos E. Castañeda, Mexican American Historian: The Formative Years, 1896–1927," *Pacific Historical Review* 42 (Aug., 1973): 319–34; "Carlos E. Castañeda's Rendezvous with a Library: The Latin American Collection, 1920–1927 — The Final Phase," *Journal of Library History* 16 (spring, 1981): 315–28; "The Making of a Boltonian: Carlos E. Castañeda of Texas — The Early Years," *Red River Valley Historical Review* 1 (winter, 1974): 329–50.

6. See for example, J. Frank Dobie, *Vaquero of the Brush Country* (Dallas: Southwest Press, 1929). Also see Rupert N. Richardson, *Texas: The Lone Star State* (New York: Prentice-Hall, 1943).

men." His well-known quip about Texas Mexican heritage made the connection between Tejanos and decadent Spaniards/Mexicans: "There is a cruel streak in the Mexican nature, or so the history of Texas would lead one to believe. This cruelty may be a heritage from the Spanish of the Inquisition; it may, and doubtless should, be attributed to their Indian blood."[7] For this coterie of writers, Texas Mexicans contributed little of consequence and merit to the state's political and social life.

But Texas Mexicans were not without their defenders during that era. Essentially responding to the portrayal as drawn by the detractors of Tejanos, those sympathizing with Mexicans necessarily touched on the same themes. Seldom did they go beyond those subjects to deal with Tejanos as movers of history. Instead, they wrote in defense of a people being acted upon by Anglo society.

Primary defenders included members of the "Mexican-American generation" (discussed below) who, in the 1930s through the 1950s, were the political spokespersons for Texas Mexicans. Essentially from the professional class — businesspersons, lawyers, doctors, and the like — they either wrote or collected works of a nonscholarly nature designed to offset the image of the Mexicans as apathetic citizens without a positive role in Texas history. In a 1930 master's thesis, for example, Jovita González tried to explain something of Mexican culture in the lower border, although in many ways her descriptions of lower-class Tejanos were as condescending as Anglo portrayals. Three years later, J. Luz Saenz wrote *Los México Americanos en la gran guerra* to emphasize the Mexican-American contribution to World War I.[8] Expectedly, the state's centennial produced a literature from these "revisionists," the most significant being a book by Rubén Rendón Lozano entitled *Viva Tejas,* which described the participation of Tejanos in several battles and presented brief biographical sketches of the most significant participants. Writing in the same vein during the era before 1950 were two "giants" of that generation: J. T. Canales and Alonso Perales. Canales, a lawyer, businessman, and Texas lesislator (1907–11, 1917–21) sought to defend Juan Cortina and highlight the contributions of Te-

---

7. Lyman L. Woodman, *Cortina: Rogue of the Rio Grande* (San Antonio: Naylor, 1950); Walter Prescott Webb, *The Texas Rangers: A Century of Frontier Defense* (Boston: Houghton Mifflin, 1935), p. 14.

8. Jovita González, "Social Life in Cameron, Starr, and Zapata Counties," M.A. thesis, University of Texas, 1930; J. Luz Saenz, *Los México Americanos en la gran guerra* (San Antonio: Artes Gráficas, 1933).

ARNOLDO DE LEÓN

janos to the War for Independence era. Alonso Perales, also an attorney, was more concerned with civil rights in the 1930s and 1940s and documented numerous examples of social injustice in several historically valuable books.[9]

Also coming to the rescue of Texas Mexicans were Anglo writers, one of whom was Eugene C. Barker. The University of Texas historian's principal interest was Mexican Texas, and not the post-1836 Mexican experience. But in an essay he presented to the League of United Latin American Citizens (LULAC) convention in Harlingen, Texas in 1935, Barker lauded the patriotism of the native Mexicans of Texas for their "truly heroic resolution" in staking their fate with the Texas colonists in the Texas Revolution of 1836.[10] Perhaps the staunchest defender was the journalist Carey McWilliams, whose overview of Mexican-American history touched on the impact Tejanos had made on the state's economy and cultural milieu. Paul S. Taylor wrote meticulous studies on Texas Mexican laborers in Nueces and Dimmit counties, while Stuart Jamieson unearthed numerous cases of Texas Mexican efforts at labor organizing in the first half of the twentieth century. Also portraying Tejanos more positively was Charles W. Goldfinch, who in 1949 attempted a revisionist biography of Juan Cortina.[11]

9. Rubén Rendón Lozano, *Viva Tejas: The Story of the Mexican-Born Patriots of the Republic of Texas* (San Antonio: Southern Literary Institute, 1936); J. T. Canales, *Juan Cortina Presents His Motion for a New Trial* (San Antonio: Artes Gráficas, 1951); J. T. Canales, *Bits of Texas History in the Melting Pot of America*, 2 vols. (San Antonio: Artes Gráficas, 1950, 1957); Alonso Perales, *El México Americano y la politica del sur de Tejas* (San Antonio: Artes Gráficas, 1931); Alonso Perales, *En Defensa de Mi Raza*, 2 vols. (San Antonio: Artes Gráficas, 1937); Alonso Perales, *Are We Good Neighbors?* (San Antonio: Artes Gráficas, 1948). Another book of interest written during the 1930s is J. Montiel Olvera, *Year Book of the Mexican Population of Texas* (San Antonio: Privately printed, 1939).

10. The essay was published as Eugene C. Barker, "Native Latin American Contribution to the Colonization and Independence of Texas," *Southwestern Historical Quarterly (SHQ)* 46 (Jan., 1943): 317–35.

11. Carey McWilliams, *North from Mexico: The Spanish Speaking People of the United States* (Philadelphia: J. B. Lippincott, 1949); Paul S. Taylor, *An American-Mexican Frontier: Nueces County, Texas* (Chapel Hill: University of North Carolina Press, 1934); Paul S. Taylor, *Mexican Labor in the United States: Dimmit County, Winter Garden, South Texas* (Berkeley: Publications in Economics, University of California, 1930); Stuart Jamieson, *Labor Unionism in American Agriculture* (Washington, D.C.: U.S. Department of Labor, 1945); Charles W. Goldfinch, "Juan N. Cortina, 1824–1892: A Re-appraisal," M.A. thesis, University of Chicago, 1949. But not all those who wrote on Mexican

Thus, the historiography on the Texas Mexicans from the 1930s to about 1950 revolved around old themes traceable to the writings of the nineteenth century. That mainstream writers portrayed Tejanos as disloyal or inclined to crime and brigandry does not seem to be extraordinary given the cultural context in which they wrote. Since Mexicans' un-Americanism had been a key component of the nineteenth century's stable of conquest myths, the notion was not too difficult to perpetuate by those steeped in the tradition of that writing.

Defenders of Tejanos faced formidable obstacles in debunking such fabrications, for those leveling the charges had the backing of institutional resources and perhaps even a state-sanctioned view of Texas history that made heroes of the Alamo defenders and rugged frontiersmen and villains of Santa Anna's hordes and Mexican cattle rustlers. Middle-class defenders, who within their communities faced the real political and economic limits of being stigmatized as un-American, wrote at a decidedly structural and noninstitutional disadvantage, lacking access to libraries, primary documents, research funds, and the like. Their energies, along with those of Anglo sympathizers, were consumed primarily in formulating rebuttals to the image of the disloyal Mexican or in highlighting the social injustice that kept the Mexicans from making meaningful progress. The result was that the image of Tejanos as bearers of a static homogeneous culture was not challenged during this period.

Tejano Historiography, 1950–66

Sometime in the early 1950s, the writings on Texas Mexicans took a slight turn. In many ways, the characteristic portrayal of Te-

---

Americans during this period had an historical consciousness; instead they were part of a cadre of social scientists and concerned writers throughout the United States who took an interest in what they labeled the "Mexican problem"—that is, the problem of Mexican illiteracy, unemployment, poverty, disease, and crime. Among these writers were Selden C. Menefee and Orin C. Cassmore, *The Pecan Shellers of San Antonio: The Problem of Underpaid and Unemployed Mexican Labor* (Washington, D.C.: Works Projects Administration, 1940); Selden C. Menefee, *Mexican Migratory Workers of South Texas* (Washington, D.C.: Works Projects Administration, 1941); Pauline Kibbe, *Latin Americans in Texas* (Albuquerque: University of New Mexico Press, 1946). These concerned people pointed to the social forces that partly accounted for the Mexican problem. Some implied that Mexicans were themselves responsible for their conditions.

janos as marginal persons persisted, and indeed, it may be argued that this era in the evolution of historical writings on Tejanos belongs with the first phase I have identified. For one thing, historians were still influenced by the same cultural context that had so determined the direction that writings on Tejanos took up to midcentury. The conservative political atmosphere of the postwar era in Texas, furthermore, hardly promoted a reevaluation of stock understandings of the Tejano experience. Lastly, the consensus interpretation so prevalent among American historians in the 1950s in many ways endorsed old historiographical thinking. Texas history was that of a relatively homogeneous Anglo people who had lived harmoniously: such issues as racial conflict, bloody confrontations between whites and minorities, and radical dissent from mainstream views seemed to be outside the stable Texas experience, just as the consensus historians argued was the case for U.S. history.

For another thing, the old themes continued to be the subject of attention.[12] The portrayal of *Mexicanos* as antagonists, for example, prevailed. Rupert Richardson, thus, had practically no new literature to draw on for his second revision of *Texas: The Lone Star State* (1958); the result was a recycling of what he had said of *Mexicanos* in the original 1943 publication. In fact, this time appears to have been a "low point" in Texas history in several ways and one when little advances occurred in the field. No Mexican-American historian could yet be found to propose a counterportrayal although, as before, Texas Mexicans did have their defenders, some of whom were themselves young Tejano writers who wrote in a mold reminiscent of that of Perales, Lozano, and Canales.

But certain features do stand out to distinguish this second era. Ethnocentric interpretations (written by Anglo historians) of Texas Mexicans faded in the literature during the era. The themes of the

12. Among them was the old issue of the "Mexican problem." Studies that addressed the topic at midcentury were Ozzie G. Simmons, "Anglo-Americans and Mexican-Americans in South Texas," Ph.D. diss., Harvard University, 1952; Everett Ross Clinchy, Jr., "Equality of Opportunity for Latin Americans in Texas," Ph.D. diss., Columbia University, 1954. In the 1960s, the interest of social scientists in the problems of Mexican-Americans was carried on by William Madsen, *The Mexican-Americans of South Texas* (New York: Holt, Rinehart, and Winston, 1964); Arthur J. Rubel, *Across the Tracks: Mexican-Americans in a Texas City* (Austin: University of Texas Press, 1966).

Texas War for Independence and banditry lost their former appeal, perhaps because Texas history writing itself was in the doldrums (and the Tejano defenders of the 1930s and 1940s, in turn, were aging). Instead, labor and politics emerged as new themes as Mexican Americans attracted the attention of more professionally trained writers. Unfortunately, most of these were graduate students writing theses and dissertations and many of the works that composed the historiography of the era were unpublished.

Those who turned to labor as their subject of study were not trailblazers; Taylor and Jamieson, as already indicated, could claim that distinction. But the number of works produced from the early 1950s to the mid-1960s does indicate labor as being more intriguing to scholars than ever before, perhaps because poor working conditions for Tejanos remained a blot on the Texas escutcheon. Two academicians, Lyle Saunders and Olen E. Leonard, launched these probes, producing in 1951 a sociological study of the conditions of wetbacks in the lower Rio Grande Valley; the report won the endorsement of LULAC and the American G. I. Forum. Two years later, the G. I. Forum published a followup exposé; it intended to alert society to the harm wetback labor inflicted on Tejano workers. Appearing alongside such reports in the 1950s, however, were several scholarly treatments of Texas Mexican labor.[13]

The new interest in Mexican-American labor continued into the next decade. Yet, though these works on the historiography of Texas marked advances, they had their own flaws and limitations. Most were primarily concerned with labor in urban areas, especially in San Antonio, and they continued to depict the Texas Mexican workers as exploited objects unable to do much for themselves. Indeed, failure to force improvement in the workplace was in part attributed to a Mexican-

---

13. Lyle Saunders and Olen E. Leonard, "The Wetback in the Lower Rio Grande Valley of Texas," *Inter-American Education Occasional Papers* 7 (July, 1951); G.I. Forum, *What Price Wetbacks?* (Austin: G.I. Forum, 1953). The *Southwestern Social Science Quarterly* 32 (Mar., 1952): 229–44, issued Harold A. Shapiro's work on pecan shellers who worked in San Antonio during the 1930s; this study was apparently a topic that he had touched upon earlier in "The Workers of San Antonio, Texas, 1900–1940," Ph.D. diss., University of Texas, Austin, 1952. In the middle of the decade, George O. Coalson turned to migratory Mexican-American agricultural labor in "The Development of the Migratory Farm Labor System in Texas, 1900–1954," Ph.D. diss., University of Oklahoma, 1955.

American inability to cope with modernity. One study, for example, partially placed the causes for the lack of union involvement in Austin on Mexican-American clannishness, on their satisfaction with their lot and their distrust of unions. Not until their "acculturation" in the 1960s did Tejanos display a greater interest in unions, the study suggested.[14]

The subject of politics and Tejanos during the 1950s and early 1960s had scholarly antecedents as did that of labor, although the studies of the 1940s did not look approvingly on the role of Tejanos in the political arena. For example, one of them depicted a South Texas riddled with corruption and the Texas Mexican voters therein as pawns in a feudal system of political bosses.[15] But spurred by the example of the G.I. generation in the postwar era, writers began their initial probes into the subject of Mexican-American political leadership, organization, and participation. In 1951, a thesis appeared on LULAC, and in 1965, another focused on one of the leading Texas Mexican figures of the age — Henry B. González.[16] Such studies were the predecessors of the spate of works on the subject that appeared after the mid-1960s.

Standing completely alone in the historiography of the 1950s and early 1960s was the book by Américo Paredes entitled *"With His Pistol in His Hand": A Border Ballad and Its Hero* (1958).[17] Although it was mainly a study of folklore on the *corrido* of Gregorio Cortez, the book contained some incisive chapters on Texas Mexican society during the early twentieth century. In its topic and treatment the book did not fit into the writings of the age. Indeed, it was at least a decade ahead

14. Kenneth P. Walker wrote "The Pecan Shellers of San Antonio and Mechanization," *SHQ* 69 (July, 1965), and doctoral studies of labor were done. Among the latter were Sam F. Parigi, "A Case Study of Latin American Unionization in Austin, Texas," Ph.D. diss., University of Texas, Austin, 1964; Lamar B. Jones, "Mexican Labor Problems in Texas," Ph.D. diss., University of Texas, Austin, 1964; Robert Garland Landolt, "The Mexican-American Workers of San Antonio, Texas," Ph.D. diss., University of Texas, Austin, 1965.

15. Edgar Greer Shelton, Jr., "Political Conditions among Texas-Mexicans along the Rio Grande," M.A. thesis, University of Texas, Austin, 1946. See further Sebron S. Wilcox, "The Laredo City Election and Riot of April, 1886," *SHQ* 45 (July, 1941): 1–23.

16. Edward D. Garza, "LULAC: League of United Latin American Citizens," M.A. thesis, Southwest Texas State University, 1951; Eugene Rodríguez, Jr., "Henry B. González: A Political Profile," M.A. thesis, St. Mary's University, 1965.

17. Américo Paredes, *"With His Pistol in His Hand": A Border Ballad and Its Hero* (Austin: University of Texas Press, 1958).

of its historiographical time and would influence the direction of Mexican-American historical scholarship in the 1960s and 1970s.

Despite these several studies surfacing in the 1950s through the mid-1960s, the fundamental assumption remained that Tejanos lacked a history worthy of comment and serious study. Excepting Paredes's work, the literature of that era was defensive and lean on creativity. Researchers lent credence to the notion of a marginal people; the writings on politics, for example, dismissed common folks as contributing forces only to the Tejano political tradition, while labor historians borrowing paradigms from the social sciences continued to look for traits within the Tejano community for an explanation of Mexican Americans' failure to succeed economically. These traditional writings left the impression of a quaint and static Tejano community burdened by lethargy and a reluctance to join the mainstream.

"Chicano" Historiography, 1966 to the Early 1980s

Historians identify the beginnings of the "Chicano movement" in Texas with the farm workers' strike and march in the lower Rio Grande Valley during the summer of 1966 (the *movimiento*, as it was called in Spanish, lasted until the mid-1970s). That event sparked a protest movement which, in its extreme, stressed the themes of cultural nationalism and ethnic pride. Youthful activists took a stand against assimilation and assailed white society for its racist practices. Further, a call went out for the writing of more "relevant" history—a demand was most pronounced at universities and high schools.[18]

In response to this groundswell, scholars took a more serious look at the history of Tejanos as part of what came to be labeled "Chicano history."[19] Innovation came to be the trademark of the new scholar-

18. According to one suggestion, the *movimiento* in Texas can be said to have started and ended with farm worker marches. The Texas Farm Workers Union march to Austin in the spring of 1977, and thence from there to Washington, D.C. via the Deep South, was a symbolic end of the movement. Letter of Roberto R. Calderón to the author, Nov. 22, 1988.

19. Surveys include Rodolfo Acuña, *Occupied America: A History of Chicanos*, 3rd ed. (New York: Harper and Row, 1987); Matt Meier and Feliciano Rivera, *The Chicanos: A History of Mexican Americans* (New York: Hill and Wang, 1972); David J. Weber, ed., *Foreigners in Their Native Land* (Albuquerque: University of New Mexico, 1973); Arnoldo De León, "Los Tejanos: An Overview of Their History," in *The Texas Heri-*

ship.[20] Several factors accounted for such trends and perspectives. Most significantly, the tumult of the 1960s and the years that followed influenced historians in the discipline to reconsider the older themes, issues, and developments that had produced the consensus interpretations of the placid 1950s. In fact, New Left writings challenged older perceptions, and disciples of these fresh approaches probed into topics previously ignored as insignificant: they were the ones writing the new labor history, the new urban history, the new social history, and so on. More and more, historians of Texas turned to these approaches, influenced by their training and by the texture of the changing times: by civil rights demonstrations from black Texans and Tejanos, by the dismantling of the Jim Crow system of segregation, and by the liberal ideas emanating from the urban regions. In the process, they began taking Texas history in directions not considered by Webb, Barker, and Richardson (by the 1970s, indeed, the influence of these giant Texas historians of yesteryear was on the wane). The unique insights brought to the field by Mexican Americans, who were the major practitioners of Chicano history, furthered the new Tejano history. Many consciously set out to take umbrage with Webb, Barker, Richardson, and others. Others were never affected by their writings, having received their graduate education in out-of-state universities (mainly California) or having found these writings irrelevant to an accurate understanding of Texas Mexican history. This cadre of Chicanoists was assisted by only a few Anglo-American scholars. They thus formed a curious lot in ethnic history, for while Native American Indian history and Afro-American history were done by mainstream Anglo-American historians joined by a handful of Native American or black scholars respectively, Chicano history remained largely the intellectual enterprise of Mexican-American historians.

Among the more visible attempts at revision were ones designed to rectify the image of the ahistoric Mexican: one genre of publications attempted such a task by turning to some readily available top-

---

tage, ed. Ben H. Procter and Archie P. McDonald (St. Louis: Forum, 1980); Rodolfo Rocha, "The Tejanos of Texas," in *Texas: A Sesquicentennial Celebration,* ed. Donald W. Whisenhunt (Austin, Tex.: Eakin, 1984).

20. A recent historiographical piece on Chicano history is Alex M. Saragoza, "The Significance of Recent Chicano-Related Historical Writing: An Appraisal," *Ethnic Affairs* 1 (fall, 1987): 24–62. A comprehensive bibliography is Matt Meier, *Bibliography of Mexican-American History* (Westport, Conn.: Greenwood, 1984).

ics, resurrecting the old Texas Revolution participants and holding them up as examples of Tejano involvement in the historical process.[21] Confederate sympathizers, too, were acclaimed as being among the major contributors to the grandeur of the Lone State State. As the author of a biography of the Laredoan Santos Benavides put it in the parlance of the 1970s: "Benavides is described by certain militant Mexican-American intellectuals [among them the author of this essay] as a traitor to his race, a 'tio taco' or Uncle Tom." Benavides, in the biographer's estimation, ranked alongside any other Texan fighting for the southern cause.[22]

But such flattering representations provoked a counterresponse from scholars who were more in tune with the nationalistic posture of Chicanos of the era. More and more, Mexican-American students entered colleges in the 1960s, and the early writings of those in the graduate schools, reflecting the antiestablishment and antigringo feelings of the time, began seeing publication by the 1970s. Unlike the scattered Mexican intellectuals who up to the 1950s wrote defensively of the misrepresentations of mainstream historiography, the younger set of scholars took the offense. Quickly, the hero and villain in Mexican-American history reversed roles. Some of the revisionist writers went to the extreme of labeling those who had fought alongside the Anglos in the revolution or who had allied themselves with "them" (such as

21. Among such works appearing were Joseph Dawson, *José Antonio Navarro: Co-creator of Texas* (Waco: Baylor University Press, 1969); Nora Elia Cantú Rios, "José Francisco Ruiz, Signer of the Texas Declaration of Independence," M.A. thesis, Texas Tech University, 1970; George O. Coalson, "Texas Mexicans in the Texas Revolution," in *From Colony to Republic: Readings on American History to 1877*, ed. Terrence J. Barragy and Harry Russell Huebel (Houston: Cayo del Grullo Press, 1983); and several articles by Thomas Lloyd Miller, among them: "José Antonio Navarro, 1795–1871," *Journal of Mexican American History* 2 (spring, 1972): 70–89; "Mexican Texans in the Texas Revolution," *Journal of Mexican American History* 3 (1973): 105–30; "Mexican-Texans at the Alamo," *Journal of Mexican American History* 2 (fall, 1971): 33–44. Malcolm D. Mc-Lean's multivolumed series on *Papers Concerning Robertson's Colony in Texas*, 14 vols. (Ft. Worth: Texas Christian University Press, 1974–76; Arlington: University of Texas–Arlington Press, 1977–present), begin touching upon the Mexican experience in Texas after 1836, although his research portrayed events and personalities at the time of the revolution and after in a drastically different way than did earlier traditional scholarship. See, further, James E. Crisp, "Anglo-Texan Attitudes toward the Mexican, 1821–1845," Ph.D. diss., Yale University, 1976.

22. John Denny Reily, "Santos Benavides: His Influences along the Lower Rio Grande, 1823–1891," Ph.D. diss., Texas Christian University, 1976, pp. 79–80, 98.

31

Benavides) as opportunists looking out for themselves instead of the welfare of their people. Conversely, those who had resisted oppression were now the bona fide heroes in history. Not every writer went to such an extreme, of course, but the new revisionism was certainly more sympathetic to those whom Webb and Richardson had categorized as the enemy of frontiersmen. Emerging as defenders of *la raza* now were Juan Cortina and others, who were now cast in the light of "social bandits." Accounts of some of these personalities as interpreted in *corridos* came in Américo Paredes's *A Texas-Mexican Cancionero*.[23]

A salient feature of the new Chicano writing was its emphasis on the victimization of the Texas Mexicans. This line of analysis portrayed an oppressive white society bent on subordinating Tejanos.[24] Anglo society was exposed as racist, as one bent on inflicting violence, and as one depriving innocent Mexicanos of their landholdings.[25]

23. Pedro Castillo and Albert Camarillo, eds., *Furia y Muerte: Los Bandidos Chicanos* (Los Angeles: Aztlán Publications, Chicano Studies Center, 1973); Rodolfo Acuña, *Occupied America: The Chicanos' Struggle toward Liberation* (San Francisco: Canfield, 1972); Carlos Larralde, *Mexican Americans: Movements and Leaders* (Los Alamitos, Calif.: Hwong, 1976); Robert J. Rosenbaum, *Mexicano Resistance in the Southwest: "The Sacred Right of Self-Preservation"* (Austin: University of Texas Press, 1981); Juan Gómez-Quiñones, "The Plan de San Diego Reviewed," *Aztlán* 1 (spring, 1970): 124–32; Mario D. Longoria, "Revolution, Visionary Plan, and Marketplace: A San Antonio Incident," *Aztlán* 12 (fall, 1981): 211–26; Douglas W. Richmond, "La Guerra en Tejas se Renova: Mexican Insurrection and Carrancista Ambitions, 1900–1920," *Aztlán* 11 (spring, 1980): 1–32; Gilbert M. Cuthbertson, "Catarino E. Garza and the Garza War," *Texana* 12, no. 4: 335–48; Rodolfo Rocha, "The Influence of the Mexican Revolution on the Mexico-Texas Border, 1910–1916," Ph.D. diss., Texas Tech University, 1981; Américo Paredes, *A Texas-Mexican Cancionero: Songs of the Lower Border* (Urbana: University of Illinois Press, 1976).

24. An early work of this sort was S. Dale McLemore, "The Origins of Mexican-American Subordination in Texas," *Social Science Quarterly* 53 (Mar., 1973): 656–70.

25. Arnoldo De León, "White Racial Attitudes toward Mexicanos in Texas, 1821–1900," Ph.D. diss., Texas Christian University, 1974, later published as *They Called Them Greasers* (Austin: University of Texas Press, 1983). De León's 1974 dissertation was countered by another study on racial attitudes, however, as Crisp, in "Anglo-Texan Attitudes toward the Mexican," argued that such attitudes, at least in the years that he studied, were not as fixed as De León thought them to be; instead they were constantly in flux. A recent study touching upon the issue of race as it analyzes the rise and fall of distinct social classes from 1836–1986 is David Montejano, *Anglos and Mexicans in the Making of Texas, 1836–1986* (Austin: University of Texas Press, 1987). Rodolfo Rocha, in "Background to Banditry in the Lower Rio Grande Valley of Texas,

Institutions played their part in the persecution, the new historical writings maintained. School systems practiced "invidious discrimination."[26] Even the Catholic Church came in for denunciation. One study explained that the institutional church in the nineteenth century did not necessarily have the interests of its Tejano parishioners at heart and that Mexican Americans often rejected the clergy as irrelevant. The institutional church was described as another arm of

---

1900–1912," M.A. thesis, Pan American University, 1974, chronicled extensive lynchings and murders in counties along the lower Rio Grande. A case study of land theft in Refugio County is Abel Rubio's *Stolen Heritage: A Mexican American's Rediscovery of His Family's Lost Land Grant* (Austin: Eakin, 1986). See further Gilberto M. Hinojosa, "Texas Mexico Border: A Turbulent History," *Texas Humanist* 6 (Mar.–Apr., 1984): 6–9; Rodolfo Rocha, "The Sting and Power of Rebellion," *Texas Humanist* 6 (Mar.–Apr., 1984): 18–20; Mario T. García, "Porfirian Diplomacy and the Administration of Justice in Texas, 1877–1900," *Aztlán* 16 (1985): 1–25. Miscellaneous studies stressing victimization would be Stanford P. Dyer and Merrell A. Knighten, "Discrimination after Death: Lyndon Johnson and Felix Longoria," *Southern Studies* 17 (winter, 1978): 411–26; Ellen Schneider and Paul H. Carlson, "Gunnysackers, *Carreteros,* and Teamsters: The South Texas Cart War of 1857," *Journal of South Texas* 1 (spring, 1988): 1–9.

26. Jorge C. Rangél and Carlos M. Alcalá, "Project Report: De Jure Segregation of Chicanos in Texas Schools," *Harvard Civil Rights–Civil Liberties Law Review* 7 (Mar., 1972): 307–91. Also see Arnoldo De León, "Blowout 1910 Style: A Chicano School Boycott in West Texas," *Texana* (1974): 124–40; Carl Allsup, "Education Is Our Freedom: The American G.I. Forum and the Mexican-American School Segregation in Texas, 1948–1957," *Aztlán* 8 (spring, summer, fall, 1977): 27–50; Walter E. Smith, "Mexicano Resistance to Schooled Ethnicity: Ethnic Student Power in South Texas, 1930–1970," Ph.D. diss., University of Texas, Austin, 1978; W. Elwood Smith and Douglas E. Foley, "Mexican Resistance to Schooling in a South Texas Colony," *Education and Urban Society* 10 (1978). See also Guadalupe San Miguel, Jr.'s many works: "Endless Pursuits: The Chicano Educational Experience in Corpus Christi, Texas, 1880–1960," Ph.D. diss., Stanford University, 1978; *"Let All of Them Take Heed": Mexican Americans and the Campaign for Educational Equality in Texas, 1910–1981* (Austin: University of Texas Press, 1987); "From a Dual to a Tripartite School System: The Origins and Development of Education Segregation in Corpus Christi, Texas," *Integrated Education* 17 (Sept.–Dec., 1979): 27–38; "Mexican-American Organizations and the Changing Politics of School Desegregation in Texas, 1945–1980," *Social Science Quarterly* 63 (Dec., 1982): 701–15; "The Struggle against Separate and Unequal Schools: Middle-Class Mexican Americans in the Desegregation Campaign in Texas, 1929–1957," *History of Education Quarterly* 23 (fall, 1983): 343–59. Other studies on education are Kenneth L. Stewart and Arnoldo De León, "Education Is the Gateway: Comparative Patterns of School Attendance and Literacy between Anglos and Tejanos in Three Texas Regions, 1850–1900," *Aztlán* 16 (1985): 177–95; Kenneth L. Stewart and Arnoldo De León, "Literacy among Immigrants in Texas," *Latin American Research Review* 20 (fall, 1985): 180–87;

white society playing an ancillary role in subordinating Tejanos. Mexican Catholics resisted by not attending mass or not supporting the church financially.[27]

The Texas Rangers, long regarded by Texas Mexicans as a nemesis, incurred some sporadic assaults, and even admirers of that police body were compelled to reconsider the Rangers' role in South Texas, where the bulk of the Tejano population lived. In the 1960s, it was admonished, law enforcement techniques used by the Rangers to calm the frontier were no longer effective.[28] But the story of the Rangers still remains untold, partly because Ranger records are not easily accessible to researchers.

The Border Patrol, another "enemy" of the Tejano community, escaped attack, although some works briefly touched upon the agency's disruption of Tejano communities at it sought to deport illegal aliens in the 1950s. R. Reynolds McKay's important dissertation on repatriation during the Great Depression discussed how the deportation campaigns in the 1930s violated civil and human rights as authorities sought to rid the country of those allegedly holding jobs that were seen as rightly belonging to "Americans."[29]

Richard Griswold del Castillo, "Literacy in San Antonio," *Latin American Research Review* 15 (1980): 180–85. Books containing chapters on education include Mario T. García, *Desert Immigrants: The Mexicans of El Paso, 1880–1920* (New Haven, Conn.: Yale University Press, 1981); Arnoldo De León, *The Tejano Community, 1836–1900* (Albuquerque: University of New Mexico Press, 1982).

27. José Roberto Juárez, "La Iglesia Católica y el mexicano de sud Tejas," *Aztlán* 4 (fall, 1973): 217–56.

28. Julian Samora et al., *Gunpowder Justice: A Reassessment of the Texas Rangers* (Notre Dame, Ind.: University of Notre Dame Press, 1979); Ben H. Procter, "The Modern Texas Rangers: A Law Enforcement Dilemma in the Rio Grande Valley," in *The Mexican Americans: An Awakening Minority*, ed. Manuel P. Servín (Beverly Hills, Calif.: Glencoe, 1970), 212–27.

29. Juan Ramon García, *Operation Wetback: The Mass Deportation of Mexican Undocumented Workers in 1954* (Westport, Conn.: Greenwood, 1980); R. Reynolds McKay, "Texas Mexican Repatriation during the Great Depression," Ph.D. diss., University of Oklahoma, Norman, 1982. McKay's other studies are "The Impact of the Great Depression on Immigrant Mexican Labor: Repatriation of the Bridgeport, Texas, Coal Miners," *Social Science Quarterly* 65 (June, 1984): 354–63; "The Federal Deportation Campaign in Texas: Mexican Deportation from the Lower Rio Grande Valley during the Great Depression," *Borderlands Journal* 5 (fall, 1981): 95–120; "The Texas Cotton Acreage Control Law of 1931 and Mexican Repatriation," *West Texas Historical Association Year Book* (*WTHAYB*) 59 (1983): 143–55. See also Marilyn Rhinehart and

Accompanying the themes of victimization in the new literature was a corollary that stressed the image of Tejanos struggling against their historical oppression, a notion that sought to debunk the pre-*movimiento* portrayal of Tejanos as passive folks. Labor studies adopted such a point of departure, thereby dissenting with the works of the 1950s and early 1960s that concentrated on exposing the work conditions of Texas Mexicans and explaining the difficulty encountered in union organizing. The many articles published in the 1970s and the early 1980s showed Anglo capitalists relegating Mexicans to the lowest-paid occupations. "Racial dualism in the labor market," "labor controls," "labor segmentation," and "capitalist exploitation" became some of the phrases commonly used to identify the relationship between Anglo employers and Tejano workers. But the new research similarly focused on strike-related episodes, thereby portraying laborers as combating their exploitation and acting on their own behalf despite overwhelming odds. Strikes were found to have historically occurred not only in San Antonio, but also in El Paso, the San Angelo area, and along the lower border. The image of the Mexican as a passive peon faded under the weight of the new studies.[30]

Thomas H. Kreneck, "'In the Shadow of Uncertainty': Texas-Mexican Repatriation in Houston during the Great Depression," *Houston Review* 10, no. 1 (1988): 21–33.

30. The extensive literature on labor includes Richard R. Bailey, "The Starr County Strike," *Red River Valley Historical Review* 4 (winter, 1979): 42–61; Alwyn Barr, "Occupation and Geographic Mobility in San Antonio, 1870–1900," *Social Science Quarterly* 51 (Sept., 1970): 396–403; Josef J. Barton, "Land, Labor, and Community in Nueces: Czech Farmers and Mexican Laborers in South Texas, 1880–1930," in *Ethnicity in the Great Plains,* ed. Frederick C. Luebke (Lincoln: University of Nebraska Press, 1980); Julia Kirk Blackwelder, *Women of the Depression: Caste and Culture in San Antonio, 1929–1939* (College Station: Texas A&M University Press, 1984); Roberto R. Calderón, comp. and ed., *South Texas Coal Mining: A Community History* (Eagle Pass, Tex.: Privately printed, 1984); Victor B. Nelson Cisneros, "La Clase Trabajadora en Tejas, 1920–1940," *Aztlán* 6 (summer, 1975): 239–68; Victor B. Nelson Cisneros, "UCAPAWA Organizing Activities in Texas, 1935–1950," *Aztlán* 9 (spring, summer, 1978): 71–84; Laurie Coyle, Gail Hershatter, and Emily Honig, "Women at Farrah: An Unfinished Story," in *Mexican Women in the United States: Struggles Past and Present,* ed. Magdalena Mora and Adelaida R. del Castillo (Los Angeles: Chicano Studies Research Center, 1980); Arnoldo De León, "*Los Tasinques* and the Sheep Shearers' Union of North America: A Strike in West Texas, 1934," *WTHAYB* 55 (1979): 3–16; Arnoldo De León, "*Rancheros, Comerciantes,* and *Trabajadores* in South Texas, 1848–1900," in *Reflections of the Mexican Experience in Texas,* ed. Margarita B. Melville (Houston: Mexican American Studies Center, University of Houston, 1979), pp. 58–91; Mario T. García, "Ra-

The themes of subjugation and remonstration also found their way into the interpretation of Tejano politics. While early studies had on the one hand seen Tejanos as political pawns, or on the other as middle-class Mexican-Americans struggling for a niche through the clever use of the courts and the drives for poll tax payment, the newer literature embraced a wider range of issues. For one, it sought out antecedents to Tejano political oppression and confrontation. Examples were to be found not only in the middle-class struggles of LULAC and the G.I. Forum, but also among the efforts of common folk seeking to ward off caricaturing, disfranchisement, and disruption of community-owned lands.[31]

But the primary focus of the new literature was on the exciting *movimiento* of the era, with its antiestablishment notions and self-

---

cial Dualism in the El Paso Labor Market, 1880–1920," *Aztlán* 6 (summer, 1975): 197–218; Mario T. García, "The Chicana in American History: The Mexican Women of El Paso, 1880–1920," *Pacific Historical Review* 49 (May, 1980): 315–37; Juan Gómez-Quiñones, "The First Steps: Chicano Labor Conflict and Organizing, 1900–1920," *Aztlán* 3 (spring, 1972): 13–50; George N. Green, "ILGWU in Texas, 1930–1970," *Journal of Mexican American History* 1 (spring, 1971): 144–69; Ray Robert Leal, "The 1966–1967 South Texas Farm Workers Strike," Ph.D. diss., Indiana University, 1983; Camilo Martínez, "The Mexican and Mexican-American Labor Contribution to the Economic Development of the Lower Rio Grande Valley of Texas, 1870–1930," Ph.D. diss., Texas A&M University, 1987; David Montejano, *Race, Labor Repression, and Capitalist Agriculture: Notes from South Texas, 1920–1930* (Berkeley, Calif.: Institute for the Study of Social Change, 1977); Charles Winn, "Mexican Americans in the Texas Labor Movement," Ph.D. diss., Texas Christian University, 1972; Emilio Zamora, Jr., "Chicano Socialist Labor Activity in Texas, 1900–1920," *Aztlán* 6 (summer, 1976): 221–38; Emilio Zamora, Jr., "Mexican Labor Activity in South Texas, 1900–1920," (Ph.D. diss., University of Texas, Austin, 1983; Richard Croxdale, "The 1938 San Antonio Pecan Shellers' Strike," in *Women in the Texas Work Force: Yesterday and Today,* ed. Richard Croxdale and Melissa Hield (Austin: People's History in Texas, 1979), pp. 24–34. Books that include chapters on labor include García, *Desert Immigrants;* De León, *The Tejano Community;* and Montejano, *Anglos and Mexicans in the Making of Texas.*

31. Robert A. Cuellar, "A Social and Political History of the Mexican-American Population of Texas, 1929–1963," M.A. thesis, North Texas State University, 1969; José Limón, "Stereotyping and Chicano Resistance: An Historical Dimension," *Aztlán* 4 (fall, 1973): 257–70; Arnoldo De León, *In Re Ricardo Rodríguez: An Attempt at Chicano Disfranchisement in San Antonio, 1896–1897* (San Antonio: Caravel, 1979); Mary Romero, "The El Paso Salt War: Mob Action or Political Struggle?" *Aztlán* 16 (1985): 119–43. A comprehensive look at the relationship between Tejano constituents and political bosses in the trans-Nueces was done by Evan Anders, *Boss Rule in South Texas: The Progressive Era* (Austin: University of Texas Press, 1982). Books including chapters on politics are García, *Desert Immigrants;* De León, *The Tejano Community.*

determinist slogans. As early as 1965 (before the Chicano movement), one dissertation turned to the Political Association of Spanish-Speaking Organizations (PASO), a new entity growing out of the liberalism of the John F. Kennedy era, and subsequent studies examined Tejano "sleeping giants" in action. The most significant publications during this period, as one would expect, had as their subject two cities in rural South Texas, then the center of exciting political animation. In *Chicano Revolt in a Texas Town*, John S. Shockley skillfully placed the political movement in Crystal City, Texas in its proper historical place, noting how people in that city sought to reorient politics in the 1970s to make it more relevant to the needs of a bicultural people. Three years later Douglas Foley and a group of researchers published an equally competent study, which treated the transformation of Mexican-American political life in a town in Frio County as Tejano inhabitants went from farmhands to adept politicians.[32]

To be sure, the scholars writing from the 1960s through the 1980s were not so prone to tunnel vision that they rejected alternate approaches to the victimization school of interpretation. As noted above, the 1960s and 1970s were in fact years when new trends developed in American historiography; the new social history, for one, prompted scholars to look at history from the bottom up—to heed the role of the little people. Such a cue was taken by many of those initially documenting Chicano oppression; their methodological treatment of their topics included studies of socioeconomic themes, including ingroup institutions, familial arrangements, and social interaction. The result was a movement away from the singular chronicling of injustice. This second wave, therefore, stressed the persistence of a Tejano ethnic culture making an impact on the Texas experience.

32. J. Preston Lepage, "A Study of the Relationship between the Political Association of Spanish-Speaking Organizations and Organized Labor in Texas," M.A. thesis, University of Texas, 1965; Charles R. Chandler, "The Mexican-American Protest Movement in Texas," Ph.D. diss., Tulane University, 1968; Edwin L. Dickens, "The Political Role of the Mexican Americans in San Antonio, Texas," Ph.D. diss., Texas Tech University, 1969; John S. Shockley, *Chicano Revolt in a Texas Town* (Notre Dame, Ind.: University of Notre Dame Press, 1974); Douglas Foley et al., *From Peones to Politicos: Ethnic Relations in a South Texas Town, 1900–1977* (Austin: Center for Mexican American Studies, University of Texas Press, 1977). A second revised issue of this work was published in 1988. See further José Villarreal Martínez, "Internal Colonialism and Decolonization in El Centro: A Sociohistorical Analysis of Chicanos in a Texas City," Ph.D. diss., University of Texas, Austin, 1981.

Two scholars provided a crucial revisionist insight into the activities of the Tejano community during the early years of the American experience in Texas. Fane Downs in her 1970 dissertation focused on the everyday life of Tejanos from 1820–45 and touched on topics that would attract the interest of scholars in subsequent years. Andrew Anthony Tijerina portrayed a Texas Mexican community whose heritage influenced aspects of Texas life after 1836; Texans had borrowed from the Spanish-Mexican experience tenets that affected politics, society, education, and even the formation of the Texas Rangers.[33] Such interpretations hardly jibed with the views of old interpreters of colonial Texas, who either wrote admiringly of Spanish institutions that ended abruptly in 1821 or who dismissed Spain as a "successful failure." Downs and Tijerina stressed continuity, while pre-1970s writers believed that the Tejano role in history dissipated after 1836.

Despite American cultural intrusion, some scholars noted, Mexican culture stood fast among both immigrant and native-born Tejanos in the many ethnic enclaves of the state. Anthropologist-folklorist José E. Limón, for example, argued that some Texas Mexicans in the early years of the twentieth century used folk healer Don Pedrito Jaramillo and the aforementioned Gregorio Cortez as folk symbols to respond to the changing environment of the 1890s and the early twentieth century. Mutual aid societies, previously neglected, became the subject of attention as did other ethnic organizations founded to provide succor within the *barrios*.[34]

But most studies conceded sociocultural change. While the nationalist thrust of the *movimiento* influenced writers to portray Tejanos as resisting complete assimilation because they preferred their ingroup culture, scholars nonetheless recognized that the Mexican-American

---

33. Fane Downs, "The History of Mexicans in Texas, 1820–1845," Ph.D. diss., Texas Tech University, 1970; Andrew Anthony Tijerina, "Tejanos and Texas: The Native Mexicans of Texas, 1820–1850," Ph.D. diss., University of Texas, Austin, 1977.

34. José E. Limón, "Healing the Wounds: Folk Symbols and Historical Crisis," *Texas Humanist* 6 (Mar.–Apr., 1984): 21–23; Julie Leininger Pycior, "La Raza Organizes: Mexican-American Life in San Antonio, 1915–1930, as Reflected in Mutualista Activities," Ph.D. diss., University of Notre Dame, 1979. In a chapter of his book *Mutual Aid for Survival*, José A. Hernández explained how such ethnic institutions in Texas in 1911 sought amalgamation in efforts to provide group security in a hostile world. Also see Yolanda Romero, "Los Socios del Sementerio [sic]: A Mexican-American Burial Society in Early Lubbock, Texas," *WTHAYB* 63 (1987): 123–30.

experience involved the development of a syncretic culture. Despite the concentration of Tejanos in *ranchos* and *barrios,* their experience was tied to the broader political and socioeconomic Texas network, the argument went. For instance, Walter L. Buenger connected the experience of Tejanos with the events in the 1850s, even though Tejanos lived apart from the Anglo community either due to preference or racism. Jerry Don Thompson in several studies arrived at similar conclusions concerning Tejanos and the Civil War.[35] Other scholars presented more forceful explanations of the bicultural way of life that developed in the nineteenth century.[36] Still others explained the Americanizing influence that had engendered a noticeable Mexican-American middle class by the 1940s and 1950s.[37]

Cultural survival, therefore, did not deter Tejanos from playing significant roles in Texas history—a premise reaffirmed by studies of certain rural or urban localities. It was Anglos in nineteenth-century South Texas, one scholar argued, who in many situations had to conform to the cadence of life established by the Tejano majority in the

35. Walter L. Buenger, *Secession and the Union in Texas* (Austin: University of Texas Press, 1984). Jerry Don Thompson's works include "A Stand along the Border: Santos Benavides and the Battle of Laredo," *Civil War Illustrated* (Aug., 1980); *Mexican Texans in the Union Army* (El Paso: Texas Western Press, 1986); "Mutiny and Desertion on the Rio Grande: The Strange Saga of Captain Adrian J. Vidal," *Military History* 12, no. 3:159–69; *Sabers on the Rio Grande* (Austin: Presidial, 1974); *Vaqueros in Blue and Gray* (Austin: Presidial, 1976).

36. De León, *The Tejano Community.* Mario T. García, in *Desert Immigrants,* likewise discussed the evolution of a "border culture" in the El Paso area at the turn of the century. In "El Primer Congreso Mexicanista de 1911: A Precursor to Contemporary Chicanismo," *Aztlán* 5 (spring and fall, 1974): 85–118, José E. Limón even demonstrated a connection between the ideology of a Tejano group in the early twentieth century with that of the Chicano movement (despite its rhetoric of separatism, the latter movement was soundly grounded in the American experience of the 1960s).

37. Manuel Peña, *The Texas Mexican Conjunto: A History of Working Class Music* (Austin: University of Texas Press, 1985). Other articles on Texas Mexican music and its connection to social classes include Manuel Peña, "The Emergence of Conjunto Music, 1935–1955," in *"And Other Neighborly Names": Social Process and Cultural Image in Texas Folklore,* ed. Richard Bauman and Roger Abrahams (Austin: University of Texas Press, 1981); Manuel Peña, "From *Rancho* to *Jaitón*: Ethnicity and Class in Texas Mexican Music," *Ethnomusicology* 29 (winter, 1985): 29–55; José R. Reyna, "Notes on Tejano Music," *Aztlán* 13 (spring, fall, 1982): 81–94; F. Arturo Rosales, "La Música en Houston: Fifty Years of Mexican-American Music," *The Americas Review* 16 (spring, 1988): 12–25.

region. In Laredo, Gilberto M. Hinojosa explained, Mexicans adjusted capably to changing circumstances over the course of three historical eras.[38] Going beyond Downs and Tijerina, Hinojosa illustrated continuity from the pre–Civil War to the postbellum era. Other studies focusing on the twentieth-century bicultural experience at the urban level corroborated the notion of cultural retention and adaptation.[39]

Chicano historical writing in Texas during the period from the later 1960s to the early 1980s had obvious characteristics setting it apart from that which had been written before the mid-1960s. First, the literature claimed the presence of several historians of Mexican descent, whereas no such historian had been present before. That group of scholars, as well as Anglo-American writers who were also doing work on Tejanos, were sympathetic to the nationalistic ardor of the *movimiento,* as they were also to newer perspectives being advanced in the profession in the 1960s and 1970s. Second, Tejanos came to be cast in a light different than that of a previous age. While Tejanos had been portrayed as having almost no history, the new writing pictured Tejanos as victims of oppression who, however, continually resisted attempted subjugation. As "fighters" they claimed a rich history that could easily have been tied to the rebelliousness of the Chicano movement.

But this perspective obviously has some shortcomings. It treated Tejanos as if they were collectively the victims of the same circumstances. In such a scenario, every Mexican American was a victim of labor exploitation, lynchings, and oppression (those who achieved elite status were dismissed as *vendidos,* or sellouts to their community). Troublemakers raising arms against the gringos were transformed into

38. Arnoldo De León, *A Social History of Duval County* (San Diego, Tex.: County Commissioners' Court, 1978); Arnoldo De León, *Benavides: The Town and Its Founder* (Benavides, Tex.: Benavides Centennial Committee, 1980); Gilberto M. Hinojosa, *A Borderlands Town in Transition: Laredo, Texas, 1755–1870* (College Station: Texas A&M University Press, 1983).

39. Arnoldo De León, *Las Fiestas Patrias: Biographic Notes on the Hispanic Presence in San Angelo, Texas* (San Antonio: Caravel, 1978); Arnoldo De León, *San Angeleños: Mexican Americans in San Angelo, Texas* (San Angelo: Fort Concho Museum Press, 1985); Andrés Tijerina, *The History of Mexican Americans in Lubbock County* (Lubbock: Texas Tech University, 1977); Francisco Arturo Rosales, "Mexicans in Houston: The Struggle to Survive, 1908–1975," *Houston Review* 3 (summer, 1981): 224–48; and the aforementioned books by Shockley, Foley et al., and Mario T. García.

heroes fighting for the injustice inflicted on their brethren. Indeed, a marked characteristic of such writings was the neat division made between Anglos and Mexicans, with the Tejano experience described as one of Mexicans resisting their Anglo oppressors.

However, the second scholarly front depicted a more complex community diversified by class and ethnicity and marked a transition away from the unidimensional perspective of the conflict school. It posited the Tejano experience as heterogeneous — there were those who resisted modernization, as Limón noted, and others who functioned on their own bicultural terms in an American setting. Variation, in short, typified the Tejano experience. Also accepted by scholars in the era was the idea that Tejanos were historical insiders whose presence had been misrepresented in the pages of Texas history.

Recent Trends in Tejano Historiography

From the hindsight gained over just a few years, it is difficult to determine with any kind of precision when the recent trends that make up the historiography on Tejanos had their beginnings. I arbitrarily have selected Richard A. Garcia's article, "Class, Consciousness, and Ideology—The Mexican Community in San Antonio, Texas: 1930–1940," as establishing a newer wave. Garcia's article accepted the new Chicano historiography but incorporated a number of insightful and fresher themes: social differentiation, ideological cleavages within the community, and a resurrection of what came to be called the "Mexican-American generation." Garcia's more comprehensive study of the San Antonio community was finished in 1980 as a doctoral dissertation. Other studies followed.[40]

Ideological and cultural change over time, indeed, came to fascinate even those who had been on the cutting edge of documenting

40. Richard A. Garcia, "Class, Consciousness, and Ideology—The Mexican Community in San Antonio, Texas: 1930–1940," *Aztlán* 9 (fall, 1978): 23–70; Richard A. Garcia, "The Making of the Mexican-American Mind, San Antonio, Texas, 1929–1941: A Social and Intellectual History of an Ethnic Community," 2 vols., Ph.D. diss., University of California, Irvine, 1980; Richard Garcia, *Rise of the Mexican American Middle Class: San Antonio, 1929–1941* (College Station: Texas A&M University Press, 1991); Richard A. Garcia, "The Mexican-American Mind: A Product of the 1930s," in *History, Culture, and Society: Chicano Studies in the 1980s,* ed. Mario T. García et al. (Ypsilanti, Mich.: Bilingual Press/Editorial Bilingüe, 1983).

Tejano oppression in the 1970s and 1980s. As early as 1973, Rodolfo Alvarez experimented with a generational approach to the study of Mexican-American history. The Mexican-American experience, Alvarez theorized, could be broken down into at least four different historical epochs: the creation generation, the migrant generation, the Mexican-American generation, and the Chicano generation. According to this thinking, each generation could be distinguished from the others by its collective consciousness in relation to the larger society. By the 1980s, then, scholars commenced testing this line of analysis. Of these several generations, the one to receive the most attention has been the Mexican-American generation, whose experience spanned the years from about 1930 to 1960. Studies that pursue this approach are many, with the foremost advocates being those of Richard A. Garcia, Mario T. García, and Guadalupe San Miguel, Jr.[41]

Specifically, students of the Mexican-American generation argued that sometime around the 1920s, a petit bourgeoisie emerged within the Mexican-American community. Its members believed in the unequivocal acceptance of the American way of life as the proper path to the social betterment of Mexicanos. Previous to this, the immigrant generation (circa 1900–30), made up of newcomers (both rich and poor) who had fled the Mexican Revolution of 1910 and inundated the already settled Tejano community, had looked to Mexico for cultural reinforcement, to the Mexican consul for protection and leadership, to clubs and newspapers for perpetuating Mexican culture and language, and to *mutualistas* for self-protection.[42] But the Mexican-American generation rejected such an ideological orientation. They were products of the nineteenth-century acculturation process in Texas

41. Rodolfo Alvarez, "The Psycho-Historical and Socioeconomic Development of the Chicano Community of the United States," *Social Science Quarterly* 53 (Mar., 1973): 920–42. Selected studies include Garcia, "The Making of the Mexican-American Mind"; Garcia, "The Mexican-American Mind"; Mario Barrera, "The Historical Evolution of Chicano Ethnic Goals: A Bibliographic Essay," *Sage Race Relations Abstracts* 10 (Feb., 1985); Peña, *The Texas Mexican Conjunto;* Montejano, *Anglos and Mexicans in the Making of Texas;* San Miguel, *"Let All of Them Take Heed";* San Miguel, "The Struggle against Separate and Unequal Schools"; Francisco Arturo Rosales, "Shifting Self-Perceptions and Ethnic Consciousness among Mexicans in Houston, 1908–1946," *Aztlán* 16 (1985): 71–94.

42. Mario T. García, *"La Frontera:* The Border as Symbol and Reality in Mexican-American Thought," *Mexican Studies/Estudios Mexicanos* 1 (summer, 1985).

and the impact of World War I: during the war, the federal government, draft boards, and the state took steps to integrate Tejanos into the war efforts; or, Tejanos became voluntarily involved both in Texas and overseas. Veterans and their cohorts became vocal in the 1920s, although their presence became more pronounced late in the decade and after.[43] They believed deeply in the American Constitution and way of life, placed great faith in society to change its racist ways if only Mexican Americans adopted the English language and accepted American ways of doing things, and opposed any form of social protest that would reflect adversely upon Tejanos. To present a united front, the group formed two organizations in the 1920s: La Orden Hijos de América in 1921, which faltered after a few years of existence, and LULAC, organized in 1929. The American G.I. Forum, established in 1948, was an offspring of the same ideological currents. All three organizations placed emphasis on loyalty, on English as the official language of the meetings, and on working through mainstream ways for the amelioration of Mexican-American conditions.

Students of this group came to evaluate it differently than they had in the 1970s. Influenced by the militancy of the Chicano movement in the 1960s and 1970s, writers in that era tended to side with Chicanos, who were then demonstrating and attacking the gringos. The old LULACers and G.I. Forum members seemed pusillanimous in comparison. The new writings (done by some of the same historians who were writing earlier—Mario T. García, for example), however, placed these men in their proper historical context: they were obviously middle-class individuals who could not have been expected to act otherwise. Their approach to doing things was in step with the times—the 1920s, the Great Depression, World War II, and the McCarthy era, when demonstrations and nonconformity met with massive disapproval. They insisted on being called Latin Americans to express their loyalty to flag and country when society thought of the whole of the Tejano community as "Mexicans." Their fight to be classified as white was intended to prevent their grouping with "colored" peoples and thus to thwart segregation on the basis of race. The new heroes emerging from this cadre included Alonso S. Perales, J. T. Ca-

43. Carole E. Christian, "'Joining the American Mainstream': Texas Mexican Americans during World War I," *SHQ* 93 (Apr., 1989): 559–95.

nales, Gus C. García, Hector P. García, George I. Sánchez, Carlos E. Castañeda, John J. Herrera, and many others.[44]

The presence of the above cohorts indicates that Texas Mexican society by the 1930s comprised different social classes. This was no major discovery, for the literature of the 1970s and 1980s had recognized such social differentiation as existing as far back as the colonial era.[45] It was in the years of the Great Depression, however, that a group of middling status asserted itself more forcefully by its ideology, its cultural tastes, and its social bearing. Its presence was discernible in the editorials published in Spanish-language newspapers or in the social pages of those same papers, in its desire to hold separate social functions, in its taste in music (*orquesta* versus *conjunto*), in the types of jobs held by its members, and in its political approach to doing something for fellow Mexicanos. World War II helped to further shape internal divisions. So did a changing American economy which incorporated Tejanos at disparate rates. Poverty, isolation, and immigration separated many from those seduced by the conformity of the 1950s. Ever-increasing diversity resulted.

According to this explanation, the evolution underway in the postwar era led to the presence of "many Mexicanos" by the 1960s,

44. García, "*La Frontera.*" Read also Carl Allsup, *The American G.I. Forum: Origins and Evolution* (Austin: Center for Mexican American Studies, University of Texas Press, 1982); Mario T. García, "Mexican Americans and the Politics of Citizenship: The Case of El Paso, 1936," *New Mexico Historical Review* 59 (Apr., 1984): 187–204; San Miguel, *"Let All of Them Take Heed";* San Miguel, "Mexican-American Organizations and the Changing Politics of School Desegregation in Texas"; San Miguel, "The Struggle against Separate and Unequal Schools"; Arnoldo De León, *Ethnicity in the Sunbelt: Mexican Americans in Houston, Texas* (Houston: Mexican American Studies Center, University of Houston, 1989); Benjamin Márquez, "The Politics of Race and Class: The League of United Latin American Citizens in the Post–World War II Period," *Social Science Quarterly* 68 (Mar., 1987): 84–101; Benjamin Márquez, "The Politics of Race and Assimilation: The League of United Latin American Citizens, 1929–1940," *Western Political Quarterly* 42 (June, 1989): 355–75; Mario T. García, *Mexican Americans: Leadership, Ideology, and Identity* (New Haven, Conn.: Yale University Press, 1989); Adela Sloss-Vento, *Alonso S. Perales: His Struggle for the Rights of Mexican Americans,* ed. and intro. by Arnold C. Vento (San Antonio, Tex.: Artes Gráficas, 1977).

45. See David J. Weber, *The Mexican Frontier, 1821–1846* (Albuquerque: University of New Mexico Press, 1982); Buenger, *Secession and the Union in Texas,* chap. 5; Thompson, *Mexican Texans in the Union Army;* Thompson, *Vaqueros in Blue and Gray;* De León, *The Tejano Community;* Paul D. Lack, "The Texas Revolutionary Experience: A Social and Political History, 1835–1836," monograph in progress.

as Mexican-American communities indeed consisted of various classes. In those divisions could be found the internal conflict that permeated the Chicano movement. Activists had the same goals in mind, but they either pursued them as part of the middle class as members of LULAC, the G.I. Forum, and PASO, or took a more militant stand as advocates for the Mexican-American Youth Organization or organizers for the Raza Unida party. Writings in the 1980s showed the Chicano experience to be one of fragmentation.[46]

If the Tejano experience was in fact heterogeneous, then it was further diversified by regions. This fact was driven home in several articles that explained how circumstances differed for Tejanos depending on their areas of residence in the state. Scholars wondered how the experience in East Texas (Houston, for example) could differ from life in rural South Texas or West Texas, and even from that in the urban areas of Dallas, Fort Worth, and Waco. Mexicans in El Paso could well identify with New Mexico, the speculation went.[47]

Recent trends in historical literature on Tejanos, then, have taken fresh directions and scholars have described the Tejano community as more complex than initially believed. Even the revisionists of the 1970s and early 1980s seem to have distorted their descriptions of the Tejano community. Texas Mexican society since the nineteenth century has been fundamentally diverse in nativity, occupations, family life, education, literacy, and rural/urban residence.[48] Furthermore, recent historiography indicates unquestionably that the presence of clearly defined social classes explains ideological cleavages, especially in the postdepression period. Still more recently, the proposition has been made that the Tejano experience is further diversified by regions where

46. See for example, De León, *Ethnicity in the Sunbelt.*

47. Arnoldo De León and Kenneth L. Stewart, "Tejano Demographic Patterns and Socio-Economic Development," *Borderlands Journal* 7 (fall, 1983): 1–9; Stewart and De León, "Education Is the Gateway"; Stewart and De León, "Literacy among Immigrants in Texas"; Kenneth L. Stewart and Arnoldo De León, "Fertility among Mexican Americans and Anglos in Texas, 1900," *Borderlands Journal* 9 (spring, 1986): 61–67; Kenneth L. Stewart and Arnoldo De León, "Work Force Participation among Mexican Immigrant Women in Texas, 1900," *Borderlands Journal* 9 (spring, 1986): 69–74; Arnoldo De León, "The Tejano Experience in Six Texas Regions," *WTHAYB* 65 (1989): 36–49.

48. Arnoldo De León and Kenneth L. Stewart, *Tejanos and the Numbers Game: A Socio-Historical Interpretation from the Federal Censuses, 1850–1900* (Albuquerque: University of New Mexico Press, 1989).

Tejanos happen to live; in the 1970s, writers sought to portray Tejanos as putting up a united front.

Issues in Need of Study

While twenty years ago there existed practically no literature comparable to the body of works that now make up "Tejano history," the fact of the matter is that the historiography on Tejanos is still in its infancy. The number of works existing on any particular topic, period, or subfield is woefully limited; one does not have the luxury of focusing on one specific event, say repatriation in the 1930s, and evaluating the extensive literature going back for a period of years.[49] Put another way, Tejano history is a wide-open field with numerous gaps and challenges.

There are some approaches and themes in need of special attention. Quantitative methods have made practically no impact on the field, although there are some exceptions.[50] A lack of training in cliometrics might explain the dearth of quantifiers, but students of Mexican-American history need not be too harshly faulted as quantitative approaches have never been popular in Texas history writing in general. Interpretive history has also failed to make inroads, excepting perhaps David Montejano's prize-winning *Anglos and Mexicans in the Making of Texas, 1836–1986*. Instead, writers remain faithful to traditional Texas history writing, which emphasizes facts as true in and of themselves and subordinates ideas to facts. The use of theories and paradigms borrowed from other fields in the social sciences has been shunned thus far. Furthermore, documentary history in its many forms, including the pictorial, lacks chroniclers within the ranks of the scholarly community.[51]

There is also a plethora of topics that beg for notice. Urban cen-

49. See Arnoldo De León, "Tejano History Scholarship: A Review of the Recent Literature," *WTHAYB* 59 (1985): 116–33.

50. See the several works by De León and Stewart listed in these notes. Also see Griswold del Castillo, "Literacy in San Antonio"; Richard Griswold del Castillo, "'Only for My Family': Historical Dimensions of Chicano Family Solidarity—The Case of San Antonio in 1860," *Aztlán* 16 (1985): 145–76.

51. David Montejano, *Anglos and Mexicans in the Making of Texas.* Beginning a trend, hopefully, is Thomas H. Kreneck, *Del Pueblo: A Pictorial History of Houston's Hispanic Community* (Houston: Houston International University, 1989).

ters, for one, remain unexamined — most urban works in Mexican-American history have dealt with southern California. It seems incredible that no one has undertaken comprehensive studies of Mexican Americans in San Antonio, Corpus Christi, Dallas–Fort Worth, and Austin.[52] Political topics make up another field of study. No one has developed a history of the politics of the Tejano masses, nor has there been a detailed study of local politics; the few works on the subject deal mainly with leaders of political factions in the border areas.[53] What has been the historical role of Tejanos vis-à-vis the Democratic party, for example? The role of Tejano elites also demands study. The recent trend toward inspecting the Mexican-American generation has unearthed much about their historical contributions, but beyond that there is much work needed on that small group, which made up the upper crust of Tejano society: newspaper editors, literary figures, and university graduates such as professors, doctors, and attorneys.

Future research needs to touch on biography as well. Personalities such as Juan Seguín, Catarino Garza, George I. Sánchez, or Gus C. García have no biographers, although there are some scholars doing serious research on the life of Juan Cortina.[54]

Women are major subjects for biographies; actually, for any sort of research, as Tejana history is in a lamentable condition. Studies such as those of Julia Kirk Blackwelder's *Women of the Depression* stand almost alone. Now and then a small study finds its way into print,

52. Through the efforts of the Mexican American Studies Center at the University of Houston, much is being done on Houston Hispanics. Among works generated by scholars associated with the center at one time or another are De León, *Ethnicity in the Sunbelt;* the articles of F. Arturo Rosales cited in these notes; and forthcoming works on women in Houston by Emma Pérez. Thomas H. Kreneck's efforts at archival collection at the Houston Metropolitan Research Center, Houston Public Library, have yielded several articles on Mexican Americans in Houston, including his *Del Pueblo.* See notes 38 and 39 for other works on Mexican Americans in other Texas towns.

53. See Anders, *Boss Rule in South Texas;* De León, *The Tejano Community;* Hinojosa, *Borderlands Town in Transition;* García, *Desert Immigrants.* See further, Douglas E. Foley, "The Legacy of the *Partido Raza Unida* in South Texas: A Class Analysis," *Ethnic Affairs* (spring, 1988): 47–73.

54. The recent thesis by James Ridley Douglas, "Juan Cortina: El Caudillo de la Frontera," M.A. thesis, University of Texas, Austin, 1987, fits Cortina into the model used by Latin Americanists to explain *caudillismo* in the Latin American countries. On Catarino Garza, see Cuthbertson, "Catarino Garza and the Garza War."

but even that does not compare to some of the work (itself slight) being carried out on Mexicans in other states.[55] At present, no particular scholar is concentrating on the history of Tejanas, although there are graduate students interested in the topic.

A miscellany of further topics holds possibilities for research. Military history needs to go beyond that done by Professor Jerry Don Thompson on Tejanos in the Civil War. What roles have Texas Mexicans played in every war, especially those of the twentieth century? No studies exist comparable to those done on Afro- and Japanese-American participation in these struggles. There is also a great need for studies that show the "dark" side of Tejano history (students of black history, especially of slavery, have called for a similar corrective). Sometimes it is difficult to accept the fact that all Tejanos have done is be resourceful in finding ways to find a niche in Texas society. Since the late 1960s, we seldom read about men who were indisputably villains, opportunists, or vultures who preyed on their own within the confines of enclaves. Calm and dispassionate studies are needed that avoid both the extreme of melodrama and the stereotypic writings of a past age.

Another topic in need of examination is that of "our gringo *amigos*"

---

55. Blackwelder, *Women of the Depression*. Among recent studies on women are Carolyn Ashbaugh, *Lucy Parsons: American Revolutionary* (Chicago: C. H. Kerr, 1976); Louis Barbash and Frederick P. Close, "Lydia Mendoza: The Voice of a People," *Texas Humanist* 6 (Nov.–Dec., 1983): 18–20; Coyle et al., "Women at Farrah"; Jane Dysart, "Mexican Women in San Antonio: The Acculturation Process," *Western Historical Quarterly* 7 (Oct., 1976): 365–75; García, "The Chicana in American History"; Carlos B. Gil, "Lydia Mendoza: Houstonian and First Lady of Mexican-American Song," *Houston Review* 3 (summer, 1981): 249–60; Carlos Larralde, "Santa Teresa: A Chicana Mystic," *Grito del Sol* 3 (Apr.–June, 1978): 1–114; Ines H. Tovar, "Sara Estela Ramírez: The Early Twentieth-Century Texas Mexican Poet," Ph.D. diss., University of Houston, 1984; Emilio Zamora, Jr., "Sara Estela Ramírez: Una Rosa en el Movimiento," in Mora and Del Castillo, *Mexican Women in the United States*. Studies on other states include Vicki Ruiz, *Cannery Women, Cannery Lives: Mexican Women, Unionization, and the California Food Processing Industry* (Albuquerque: University of New Mexico Press, 1987); Sarah Deutsch, *No Separate Refuge: Culture, Class, and Gender on an Anglo-Hispanic Frontier in the Southwest, 1880–1940* (New York: Oxford University Press, 1987); Patricia Zavella, *Women's Work and Chicano Families: Cannery Workers of the Santa Clara Valley* (Ithaca, N.Y.: Cornell University Press, 1987); Deena Gonzales, "The Spanish Mexican Women of Santa Fe: Patterns of Their Resistance and Accommodation, 1820–1880," Ph.D. diss., University of California, Berkeley, 1986. An older study is Alfredo Mirandé and Evangelina Enríquez, *La Chicana: The Mexican-American Woman* (Chicago: University of Chicago Press, 1979).

in Texas history. Heretofore, the Anglo has been portrayed as the natural enemy of the Tejano. Such a depiction lumps all white people into one category, often that of racists. Society, of course, is not so simple, and the same diversity that historians ascribe to the Tejano community applies to the dominant group. Indeed, Tejanos have had numbers of Anglo *amigos* in Texas history who have sided with them against other Anglo political elements—for example, Henry L. Kinney, John L. Haynes, and Louis Cardis, as well as those like Abraham Kazen, who defended the rights of Tejanos in the 1950s.

A more complex view of Anglos leads to other questions. What relations existed between Mexicanos and specific groups of European immigrants? Did Mexicanos get along with immigrants better than with other native-born Anglos? A comparative ethnic group history would also be revealing. Have interactions between Texas Mexicans and black Americans or American Indians been strained or cordial? Have cotton fields been arenas of conflict or cooperation between blacks and Mexicanos? Places such as Houston or Dallas, which have unique confluences of culture in the twentieth century, seem perfect places to investigate Chicano-black race relations. In a similar vein, what were the relations between Indians and Tejanos on the frontier?

This essay has focused almost strictly on historical writing on Texas Mexicans. To be sure, other fields, especially in the social sciences, have contributed immensely to the understanding we have of the Texas Mexican community over time. Among contributors have been ethnographers and anthropologists such as Américo Paredes and José E. Limón. Additional chroniclers have been cultural geographers, musicologists, and even cinematographers. The filmmaker Jesús S. Treviño, for instance, produced the film *Seguín* (1981), based on the historical figure, while others have reenacted episodes such as Gregorio Cortez's brush with the law in 1901. Still, almost every aspect of Tejano history is in desperate need of further study. What has been done in the last twenty years, however, augurs well for an expanding scholarship.

✒ African Americans in Texas:

From Stereotypes to Diverse Roles

Alwyn Barr

Black history in Texas has been primarily a twentieth-century field of interest. Nineteenth-century white historians mentioned slavery only as an economic, political, or legal issue. In writings on the Reconstruction, white assumptions of inferiority produced descriptions of black Texans as manipulated and unable to act by themselves. These images continued to appear in early twentieth-century general histories of the state.[1] A few black writers described leaders and institutions within their community in more positive terms, but had little impact on popular white views.[2] With the development of graduate education in history came more extensive and careful research by professional historians in the early twentieth century, although they generally remained paternalistic in attitude.[3]

Racial thought in the United States began to shift toward more egalitarian views in the 1920s and 1930s as a result of new studies by scientists and social scientists. Although those attitudes developed slowly in Texas and the South, in the 1930s they helped to stimulate the first efforts among white professional historians to avoid bias in

1. John Henry Brown, *History of Texas from 1685 to 1892*, 2 vols. (St. Louis: L. E. Daniell, 1893); Hubert Howe Bancroft, *History of Texas and the North Mexican States*, 2 vols. (San Francisco: History Co., 1884–89); Louis J. Wortham, *History of Texas from Wilderness to Commonwealth*, 5 vols. (Ft. Worth: Wortham-Molyneaux, 1924).

2. H. T. Kealing, *History of African Methodism in Texas* (Waco, Tex.: C. F. Blanks, 1885); W. A. Redwine, *Brief History of the Negro in Five Counties* (Tyler: n.p., 1901), reprinted in *Chronicles of Smith County* II (fall, 1972): 13–70; Maud Cuney Hare, *Norris Wright Cuney: A Tribune of the Black People* (New York, 1913; reprint, Austin: Steck-Vaughn, 1968).

3. Charles W. Ramsdell, *Reconstruction in Texas* (New York: Columbia University Press, 1910); Abigail Curlee, "The History of a Texas Slave Plantation, 1831–1863," *Southwestern Historical Quarterly (SHQ)* 26 (Oct., 1922): 79–127.

describing black roles. The rise of a black middle class produced more historians who also contributed to the new trend. Despite the existence of several black colleges in Texas, the early historical writing by black scholars remained limited because of heavy teaching loads and problems of access to research materials in a segregated society. Through the 1960s historians focused primarily on the presentation of more balanced studies about various aspects of race relations. As historians made increasing use of new sources such as quantitative data and oral history, as well as psychological and comparative concepts, and placed greater emphasis on social history, studies since 1970 have devoted more attention to internal organizations and activities of black Texans.

Studies of white racial attitudes and their results, the institution of slavery and the unequal status of free blacks, have been more limited for Texas than for some other southern states. A shorter period of Anglo domination in Texas before the Civil War and the twentieth-century stereotype of the state as more western than southern may best explain this limited attention.

Modern studies of racial views on a national scale, from the colonial period to the twentieth century, have raised that topic to a major theme in American history. Opinions vary over the importance that should be placed upon political, economic, psychological, or cultural influences on the development and continuation of whites' belief in ethnic preeminence. But there is general agreement that Europeans brought such attitudes with them to America, where most of their descendants continued to share those views through the nineteenth century, with subtle variations.[4]

In the most extensive essay on the views of white Texans before the Civil War, Billy Don Ledbetter suggests that they developed slavery as "first a labor system." Yet he believes that the institution became "equally important as a means of providing social order and race con-

4. Studies by early black scholars included Monroe N. Work, "Some Negro Members of Reconstruction Legislatures: Texas," *Journal of Negro History* 5 (Jan., 1920): 111–13; and John Mason Brewer, *Negro Legislators of Texas* (Dallas, 1935; reprint, Austin, Tex.: Jenkins, 1970). Among the most important analyses of racial views are: Winthrop Jordan, *White Over Black: American Attitudes Toward the Negro, 1550–1812* (Chapel Hill: University of North Carolina Press, 1968); George M. Frederickson, *The Black Image in the White Mind: The Debate on Afro-American Character and Destiny, 1817–1914* (New York: Harper and Row, 1971).

trol." Jerry B. Cain found that fear of attack by Indians or Mexicans during the time of the Republic of Texas caused whites to allow slave participation in Baptist churches until population growth overcame such concern. Reba W. Palm notes white acceptance of some black congregations in the 1840s and 1850s — possible confirmation of growing separation.[5] The strong, sometimes violent Anglo Texan opposition to any expression of antislavery views is discussed by Madeline B. Stern. Even efforts by Sam Houston to place union above slavery met with disapproval by a majority of white voters in the 1850s, as is noted by Mrs. David Winningham.[6]

These studies provide a sound beginning for the study of Texan racial views, although some questions deserve further scrutiny. Since racial ideas had been present among Anglo-Americans through the seventeenth and eighteenth centuries, it seems probable that the settlers brought such views with them to Texas from the beginning. Thus the interaction of those ideas with slavery and with the attitudes of Mexicans and Native Americans toward blacks is worthy of additional analysis.

The functioning of slavery in Texas continued to be described, within the paternalistic parameters set forth by U. B. Phillips until the 1950s. New views of the institution developed from changing racial views, new research methods, and the use of previously ignored sources. New attention focused on the beginning stage of slavery in Texas has revised views of the Mexican and revolutionary periods. Using traditional sources, Fred Robbins studied the smuggling of slaves through Texas into the United States in the period from 1816 to 1821 and illegal slave trade into Texas itself in 1835-36, noting that prominent figures such as James Bowie and James Fannin were involved. In a thoughtful review of slavery during the Texas Revolution, Paul Lack successfully revived the view that a desire to protect slavery provided one stimulant for Anglo Texan revolt. He notes that war threat-

---

5. Billy Don Ledbetter, "White over Black in Texas: Racial Attitudes in the Antebellum Period," *Phylon* 34 (Dec., 1973): 406-18; Jerry Berlyn Cain, "The Thought and Action of Some Early Texas Baptists concerning the Negro," *East Texas Historical Journal (ETHJ)* 13 (spring, 1975): 3-12; Reba W. Palm, "Protestant Churches and Slavery in Matagorda County," *ETHJ* 14 (spring, 1976): 3-8.

6. Madeline B. Stern, "Stephen Pearl Andrews, Abolitionist, and the Annexation of Texas," *SHQ* 67 (Apr., 1964): 491-523; Mrs. David Winningham, "Sam Houston and Slavery," *Texana* 3 (summer, 1965): 93-104.

ened the institution, but that Texas independence provided a firmer foundation for its postwar growth.[7]

The operation of slavery as a labor institution received attention from George R. Woolfolk, who concluded that slave property had been used in a variety of flexible ways that stimulated economic development rather than retarding economic growth, as some earlier historians had suggested. In a series of articles and in his book on slavery Randolph B. Campbell used county records and quantitative methods to conclude that the peculiar institution usually proved quite profitable for slaveowners in Texas. Thus he agreed with recent analyses of slavery in the South during the nineteenth century. Campbell offers special insights on two aspects of slave labor in Texas that have broader implications. He found that very limited numbers of slaveholders owned slaves occasionally rather than constantly, which suggests a reasonably stable group of slaveowners and an increasing concentration of wealth. Using Texas probate records, however, he noted that 41 percent of those who hired slaves did not themselves own bondsmen, but this hiring out of slaves increased significantly the number of non-slaveholders who benefited from slavery and created greater white commitment to the institution. To those views Cecil Harper, Jr., added proof that slavery could exist beyond the cotton-growing region of Texas. Thus he suggested that the institution did not in 1860 face an immediate natural limitation, as Charles Ramsdell had thought.[8] For blacks the most important implication of these studies is the increased

7. Fred Robbins, "The Origin and Development of the African Slave Trade in Galveston, Texas, and Surrounding Areas from 1816 to 1836," *ETHJ* 9 (Oct., 1971): 153–61; Paul D. Lack, "Slavery and the Texas Revolution," *SHQ* 89 (Oct., 1985): 181–202. See also David Drake, "'Joe,' Alamo Hero," *Negro History Bulletin* 44 (Apr.-June, 1981): 34–35; Margaret Swett Henson, "She's the Real Thing," *Texas Highways* 33 (Apr., 1986): 60–61; Martha Anne Turner, *The Yellow Rose of Texas: The Story of a Song* (El Paso: Texas Western Press, 1971).

8. George R. Woolfolk, "Cotton Capitalism and Slave Labor in Texas," *Southwestern Social Science Quarterly* 37 (June, 1956): 43–52; Randolph B. Campbell, "Local Archives as a Source of Slave Prices: Harrison County, Texas, as a Test Case," *Historian* 36 (Aug., 1974): 660–69; Randolph B. Campbell, "Intermittent Slave Ownership: Texas as a Test Case," *Journal of Southern History (JSH)* 51 (Feb., 1985): 15–23; Randolph B. Campbell, "Slave Hiring in Texas," *American Historical Review (AHR)* 93 (Feb., 1988), 107–14; Cecil Harper, Jr., "Slavery without Cotton: Hunt County, Texas, 1846–1864," *SHQ* 88 (Apr., 1985): 387–405; Randolph B. Campbell, *An Empire for Slavery: The Peculiar Institution in Texas* (Baton Rouge: Louisiana State University Press,

SCCCC - LIBRARY
4601 Mid Rivers Mall Drive
St. Peters, MO 63376
WITHDRAWN

value placed upon their labor contribution to the Texas economy. Quantifiers continue to debate what percentage of the profits slaveholders returned to the slaves in food, clothing, and other necessities. Legal protection for Texas slaves in the state supreme court has been assessed by A. E. Keir Nash as carefully fair, although some of the decisions might have reflected a greater concern for the rights of slaveholders.[9]

A new understanding of slavery from the viewpoint of bondsmen has come from the use of previously ignored interviews with former slaves that were gathered in the 1930s under the direction of the WPA. Ron C. Tyler and Lawrence R. Murphy published selected examples from Texas, while George P. Rawick edited a more elaborate series in which interviews from Texas fill several volumes. Campbell employed these accounts in conjunction with plantation and county records in his history of slavery in Texas to explore living conditions, treatment, religion, and culture among slaves. He generally agreed with the recent studies of Eugene Genovese and John Blassingame which recognize variations among slaveholders while clarifying the economic and social limitations faced by almost all slaves. Campbell also explored the efforts of slaves to exercise control over their own lives by maintaining family relationships, despite a lack of legal support and the breakup of some families by owners. Bondsmen also gathered collective strength through public and private religious services. Slave music, folklore, and folk art are noted as means of expressing emotions and reflecting efforts to survive. Terry G. Jordan has noted the construction of log cabins by slave artisans. John Mason Brewer and others collected slave folklore and music in Texas, but their importance in the lives of slaves is worthy of further study.

1989). See also George R. Woolfolk, "Sources of the History of the Negro in Texas: With Special Reference to Their Implications for Research in Slavery," *Journal of Negro History* 42 (Jan., 1957): 38–47.

9. Robert William Fogel and Stanley L. Engerman, *Time on the Cross: The Economics of American Negro Slavery*, 2 vols. (Boston: Little, Brown, 1974); Paul A. David et al., *Reckoning with Slavery: A Critical Study in the Quantitative History of American Negro Slavery* (New York: Oxford University Press, 1976); A. E. Keir Nash, "The Texas Supreme Court and Trial Rights of Blacks, 1845–1860," *Journal of American History* (*JAH*) 58 (Dec., 1971): 622–42; A. E. Keir Nash, "Texas Justice in the Age of Slavery: Appeals concerning Blacks and the Antebellum State Supreme Court," *Houston Law Review* 8 (Jan., 1971): 438–56.

YRAAELL · JOODS
· · · · · MM · e19viA · biM · hoop
· SW88 OM ,219lo¶ .1S

The role of female slaves has received attention from Ann Malone, who explored their relationships with white males as well as the forced mating and breeding of slaves. In a revision of some earlier studies, she concluded that slave women probably worked harder in Texas than in older, more settled states. The role and raising of slave children should be explored more fully.[10]

Although most slaves lived and labored in rural Texas, a minority populated Texas urban areas. The more relaxed and diverse nature of town slavery in the state has been analyzed by Paul D. Lack and Susan Jackson. They found the institution stronger in growing frontier communities than in older and less dynamic southern cities, which supports the view of Claudia Dale Goldin that slavery could prosper in an urban setting.[11]

Slave resistance usually took the form of escape. The persistent flow of runaways to Mexico and efforts to recapture them are described by Ron Tyler and Rosalie Schwartz. A less understood possibility of escape within the slave system was explored by Lack in his essay on Dave, a slave who ran away from a plantation back to the urban setting from which he had come. Historians continue to debate whether Texas slaves rose in revolt against their masters; Lack notes an uprising during the revolutionary period. Ledbetter believes that too many fires occurred during the slave revolt scare of 1860 to be accepted as

---

10. Campbell, *An Empire for Slavery;* Ron C. Tyler and Lawrence R. Murphy, eds., *The Slave Narratives of Texas* (Austin: Encino, 1974); George P. Rawick, ed., *The American Slave: A Composite Autobiography,* 42 vols. (Westport, Conn.: Greenwood, 1972–79): series 1, vols. 4–5, series 2, vols. 2–10; Terry G. Jordan, *Texas Log Buildings: A Folk Architecture* (Austin: University of Texas Press, 1978); John Mason Brewer, *Dog Ghosts and Other Negro Folk Tales* (Austin: University of Texas Press, 1958); Francis A. Abernethy, ed., *The Folklore of Texas Culture* (Austin: Encino, 1974); Ann Patton Malone, *Women on the Texas Frontier: A Cross-Cultural Perspective* (El Paso: Texas Western Press, 1983); Ruthe Winegarten, "Texas Slave Families," *Texas Humanist* 7 (Mar.–Apr., 1985): 29–30, 33; Randolph B. Campbell, "The Slave Family in Antebellum Texas," *Victoria College Social Science Smyposium* (1988); Leslie H. Owens, "The African in the Garden: Reflections About New World Slavery and Its Lifelines," in *The State of Afro-American History,* ed. Darlene Clark Hine (Baton Rouge: Louisiana State University Press, 1986), pp. 25–36.

11. Paul D. Lack, "Urban Slavery in the Southwest," *Red River Valley Historical Review* 6 (spring, 1981): 8–27; Susan Jackson, "Slavery in Houston: The 1850's," *Houston Review* 2 (summer, 1980): 66–82; Claudia Dale Goldin, *Urban Slavery in the American South, 1820–1860: A Quantitative History* (Chicago: University of Chicago Press, 1976).

coincidence. Yet Don Reynolds suggests that unfounded fears of aboli-
tionists and the spontaneous combustion of faulty matches provide
better explanations for events that occurred that summer.[12]

Free blacks in Texas composed only a limited group, especially
in comparison to the growing slave population after 1836. In the earlier Spanish period, however, persons of full or partial African ancestry accompanied expeditions and probably represented 10 to 15 percent of the settlers. Some achieved social and political prominence,
according to Alicia V. Tjarks.[13] Although free blacks remained less
than four hundred in number even by 1860, they have received the
attention of several historians. Harold Schoen began the effort with
a series of articles on free blacks during the period of Texas nationhood. He found them to be frontiersmen seeking opportunity, in
some cases because of mixed marriages that were not well accepted
in more settled regions. Generally they supported the revolt against
Mexico to protect their status among Anglo Texans. The influence of
Spanish-Mexican culture and the nature of the frontier made "the
Texas borderland . . . a true melting pot" for free blacks, according to
George R. Woolfolk, who may, however, have overestimated the continued impact of those influences after the Texas Revolution. Schoen
noted that Anglo Americans who dominated the new nation opposed
the immigration of more free blacks into Texas. Yet friends of black

12. Rosalie Schwartz, *Across the Rio Grande to Freedom: United States Negroes in Mexico* (El Paso: Texas Western Press, 1975); Ronnie C. Tyler, "The Callahan Expedition
of 1855: Indians or Negroes?" *SHQ* 70 (Apr., 1967): 574–85; Ronnie C. Tyler, "Fugitive
Slaves in Mexico," *Journal of Negro History* 57 (Jan., 1972): 1–12; Paul D. Lack, "Dave:
A Rebellious Slave," in *Black Leaders: Texans for Their Times,* ed. Alwyn Barr and Robert A. Calvert (Austin: Texas State Historical Association, 1981); Billy Don Ledbetter,
"Slave Unrest and White Panic: The Impact of Black Republicanism in Ante-Bellum
Texas," *Texana* 10 (winter, 1972): 335–50; Don E. Reynolds, "Smith County and Its
Neighbors during the Slave Insurrection Panic of 1860," *Chronicles of Smith County* 10
(fall, 1971): 1–8. See also Wendell C. Addington, "Slave Insurrections in Texas," *Journal
of Negro History* 35 (Oct., 1950): 408–34; William W. White, "The Texas Slave Insurrection of 1860," *SHQ* 52 (Jan., 1949): 259–85; Wesley Norton, "The Methodist Episcopal Church and the Civil Disturbances in North Texas in 1859 and 1860," *SHQ* 68
(Jan., 1965): 317–41. See also James Marten, "Slaves and Rebels: The Peculiar Institution in Texas, 1861–1865," *ETHJ* 28 (spring, 1990): 29–36.

13. Alicia V. Tjarks, "Comparative Demographic Analysis of Texas, 1777–1793,"
SHQ 77 (Jan., 1974): 291–338; Jeannette Mirsky, "Zeroing in on a Fugitive Figure:
The First Negro in America," *Midway* 8 (June, 1967): 1–17; John Upton Terrell, *Esta-
vanico the Black* (Los Angeles: Westernlore Press, 1968).

veterans of the revolution, white relatives of free blacks, and former owners who had freed slaves all fought efforts to oust those already present. In the Republic free blacks faced increased discrimination, but retained some basic rights, including property ownership. Victor Treat provided the most careful description of William Goyens, a prominent free black whose career reflected the problems and possibilities of the time.[14]

The decade of the 1850s saw the status of free blacks deteriorate further with new legal restrictions and threats of violence, which have been described by Andrew Forest Muir and Barbara A. N. Ledbetter. Yet sporadic enforcement of the laws allowed free blacks to retain land and a degree of freedom, especially on the frontier.[15] Because the number of free blacks in Texas remained small, free blacks probably could not develop the sense of community and leadership roles that were possible in some older states. These topics deserve further consideration.

Following the abolition of slavery in Texas during the summer of 1865, Afro-Texans sought opportunities to improve their economic and educational status, to stabilize their family life, to develop social institutions and churches, and to achieve equal civil and political rights. Blacks continued to face Anglo reluctance about many of these changes, however, because white Texans retained assumptions of racial superiority. The struggle over the transition has been described most fully by James M. Smallwood in his book and in several articles on Afro-Texans through the Reconstruction period. For blacks in the

---

14. Harold Schoen, "The Free Negro in the Republic of Texas," *SHQ* 39 (Apr., 1936): 292–308, *SHQ* 40 (July–Oct., 1936): 26–34, 83–113, and *SHQ* (Jan.–Apr., 1937): 169–99, 267–89; George R. Woolfolk, *The Free Negro in Texas, 1800–1860: A Study in Cultural Compromise* (Ann Arbor, Mich.: University Microfilms for the *Journal of Mexican American History*, 1976); George R. Woolfolk, "Turner's Safety Valve and Free Negro Westward Migration," *Journal of Negro History* 50 (July, 1965): 185–97; Victor H. Treat, "William Goyens: Free Negro Entrepreneur," in Barr and Calvert, *Black Leaders*.

15. Andrew Forest Muir, "The Free Negro in Harris County, Texas," *SHQ* 46 (Jan., 1943): 214–38; Andrew Forest Muir, "The Free Negro in Fort Bend County, Texas," *Journal of Negro History* 33 (Jan., 1948): 79–85; Andrew Forest Muir, "The Free Negro in Jefferson and Orange Counties, Texas," *Journal of Negro History* 35 (Apr., 1950): 183–206; Andrew Forest Muir, "The Free Negro in Galveston County, Texas," *Negro History Bulletin* 22 (Dec., 1958): 68–70; Barbara A. N. Ledbetter, *Fort Belknap Frontier Saga: Indians, Negroes, and Anglo-Americans on the Texas Frontier* (Burnet, Tex.: Eakin, 1982).

rural Texas of the 1880s and 1890s the basic account is by Lawrence D. Rice.[16]

For the Reconstruction period, Billy Don Ledbetter described whites' resistance to the abolition of slavery in Texas, which evolved into a search for new economic and social controls over black people. While Unionists favored basic civil and political rights for blacks, even they stopped short of desiring equality for all. By the beginning of the twentieth century, Anglo Texans had refined the question of white supremacy into a debate that Bruce A. Glasrud described as being between paternalists who saw blacks as "children" and others who were willing to employ violent means to control a race they viewed as "beasts."[17]

Efforts by blacks to overcome discrimination based upon such attitudes received assistance in the late 1860s from the federal Freedmen's Bureau. Older accounts of the agency have relied on newspapers published by whites, which criticized the bureau's promotion of change in legal and labor relations. New research in bureau records by Smallwood and Barry A. Crouch sees the bureau's limitations because of the few bureau officers scattered across the state, but takes a more positive view of its struggles against white violence and in favor of black education.[18] Those conclusions place these writers among the ranks of recent historians who see neither complete success nor utter failure for the bureau.

16. James M. Smallwood, *Time of Hope, Time of Despair: Black Texans during Reconstruction* (Port Washington, N.Y.: Kennikat, 1981); Lawrence D. Rice, *The Negro in Texas, 1874-1900* (Baton Rouge: Louisiana State University Press, 1971).

17. Billy Don Ledbetter, "White Texans' Attitudes toward the Political Equality of Negroes, 1865-1870," *Phylon* 40 (Sept., 1979): 253-63; Bruce A. Glasrud, "Child or Beast? White Texas' View of Blacks, 1900-1910," *ETHJ* 15 (Apr., 1977): 38-44.

18. James M. Smallwood, "The Freedmen's Bureau Reconsidered: Local Agents and the Black Community," *Texana* 11 (Nov., 1973): 309-20; James M. Smallwood, "Charles A. Culver, a Reconstruction Agent in Texas: The Work of Local Freedmen's Bureau Agents and the Black Community," *Civil War History* 27 (Dec., 1981): 350-61; Barry A. Crouch, "The Freedmen's Bureau and the 30th Sub-District in Texas: Smith County and Its Environs during Reconstruction," *Chronicles of Smith County* 11 (spring, 1971): 15-30; Barry A. Crouch, "Letters of Geoffrey Barrett, Freedmen's Bureau Agent," *Chronicles of Smith County* 12 (winter, 1973): 13-28. See also Barry A. Crouch, "Hidden Sources of Black History: The Texas Freedmen's Bureau Records as a Case Study," *SHQ* 83 (Jan., 1980): 211-26; Diane Neal and Thomas W. Kremm, "'What Shall We Do with the Negro?': The Freedmen's Bureau in Texas," *ETHJ* 27 (fall, 1989): 23-34.

The efforts of freedmen to define a new economic position after the Civil War have also been explored by Smallwood. Using Freedmen's Bureau records and slave narratives, he found that blacks were sharply limited by whites' use of legal and other pressures to retain control of land and labor. Most blacks became sharecroppers, with limited opportunities to save money or acquire land. Although discrimination also existed in these situations, smaller groups of blacks found work as in the lumber industry or moved to towns where they could find more diverse occupations. Smallwood's use of the terms *caste* and *peonage* to describe the new working conditions reflects the view that whites employed both discrimination and economic means to control black labor. Relying on white newspapers and farm records, Lawrence D. Rice described postwar Anglo economic problems and doubts about black workers, views that had dominated older accounts without qualification. Rice placed a greater emphasis on the lack of profits for most tenant farmers, black or white, than on discrimination. The possible impact on blacks of state control over public land in Texas has not been fully explored.

Rice also described the appearance of some African-Texan farm owners and the creation of black agricultural groups, from local protest groups to state organizations. He dismisses the Colored Farmers' Association and the Colored State Grange of the 1870s as failures; further research, however, might be useful. The Colored Farmers' Alliance and the Farmers' Improvement Society, which began in the 1880s, received more attention from Rice because of their greater longevity and success in attracting members. The expansion of the Colored Farmers' Alliance beyond Texas, as well as its cooperation and conflict with the white Farmers' Alliance, have been considered by Floyd J. Miller.[19]

Because Texas remained a frontier state after the Civil War, more black Texans could pursue opportunities available to only small numbers of free blacks on earlier frontiers. Black cowboys numbered about five thousand and formed roughly one-fourth of those who herded

19. Smallwood, *Time of Hope, Time of Despair;* James M. Smallwood, "Perpetuation of Caste: Black Agricultural Workers in Reconstruction Texas," *Mid-America* 61 (Jan., 1979): 5-23; Rice, *The Negro in Texas;* Floyd J. Miller, "Black Protest and White Leadership: A Note on the Colored Farmers' Alliance," *Phylon* 33 (summer, 1972): 169-74.

cattle up the trails to the railroads. Several historians who have explored the roles of blacks in the cattle industry of South and West Texas believe that they probably faced less discrimination than blacks in more settled areas. Yet only a few became ranchers or trail bosses, and those who did have received limited attention. One black cowboy, Bill Pickett, who gained fame for bulldogging and became an international rodeo performer in the early twentieth century, has been the subject of a full-scale biography by Bailey C. Hanes. Hostility toward blacks in West-Central Texas is described by Billy Bob Lightfoot.[20]

Black soldiers joined black cowboys on the post–Civil War frontier. Among the troops who opened the way for ranching were two regiments of black cavalry, the Ninth and Tenth, whose patrol and combat efforts have been recounted by William H. Leckie. The skirmishes and garrison duty of the Twenty-Fourth and Twenty-Fifth infantries have received careful attention from Arlen L. Fowler. African-Seminole scouts who served with black and white regiments have been described by Kenneth Porter.[21] These and other authors have explored specific service from the Trans-Pecos to the Panhandle and agree that the troops maintained low levels of desertion and alcoholism. Former enlisted men generally had positive memories of their service. Yet Henry Flipper, one of the few black officers, believed that his court-martial resulted from discrimination. Bruce J. Dinges presented a good summary of the complex case, which may, however, deserve further study.[22]

20. Phillip Durham and Everett L. Jones, *The Negro Cowboys* (New York: Dodd, Mead, 1965); Kenneth W. Porter, "Negro Labor in the Western Cattle Industry, 1866–1900," *Labor History* 10 (summer, 1969): 346–74; W. S. Savage, "The Negro Cowboys on the Texas Plains," *Negro History Bulletin* 24 (Apr., 1961): 157–58, 163; Hettye Wallace Branch, *The Story of "80 John"* (New York: Greenwich, 1960); R. C. Crane, "D. W. Wallace ('80 John'): A Negro Cattleman on the Texas Frontier," *West Texas Historical Association Year Book* (*WTHAYB*) 28 (1952): 113–18; Bailey C. Hanes, *Bill Pickett: Bulldogger* (Norman: University of Oklahoma Press, 1977); Billy Bob Lightfoot, "The Negro Exodus from Comanche County, Texas," *SHQ* 56 (Jan., 1953): 407–16.

21. William H. Leckie, *The Buffalo Soldiers: A Narrative of the Negro Cavalry in the West* (Norman: University of Oklahoma Press, 1967); Arlen L. Fowler, *The Black Infantry in the West, 1869–1891* (Westport, Conn.: Greenwood, 1971); Kenneth W. Porter, "The Seminole Negro-Indian Scouts, 1870–1881," *SHQ* 55 (Jan., 1952): 358–77.

22. Paul H. Carlson, "William R. Shafter, Black Troops, and the Opening of the Llano Estacado, 1870–1875," *Panhandle-Plains Historical Review* 47 (1974): 1–18; Elvis Eugene Fleming, "Captain Nicholas Nolan: Lost on the Staked Plains," *Texana* 4

For limited numbers of black Texans another opportunity to achieve economic and social independence was the creation of all-black communities, usually villages with surrounding farms, where blacks could exercise more control over their lives. Though less well known than the black towns of Oklahoma, those in Texas probably were more numerous, according to Kirsten Mullen, whose brief survey included the suburbs of larger towns.[23] Factors contributing to the founding of these communities as well as their influence need additional analysis.

While some Afro-Texans moved to the frontier and others gathered in black communities, most lacked the funds for longer migrations. Many who sought to improve their situation shifted from rural to urban areas within the state. Texas cities found that their black population percentage doubled between 1865 and 1870 and remained at the higher level until at least 1900, as explained by Alwyn Barr. Blacks in cities proved as settled as any ethnic group, according to Steven W. Engerrand, but achieved less upward economic advancement than the other groups. A study by Cary D. Wintz suggests that residential segregation increased slowly until 1900 in the Fourth Ward of Houston.[24]

The first migration out of Texas came in the late 1870s as several thousand blacks sought expanded opportunities and joined the exodus from the South to Kansas. As Nell Irvin Painter has shown, the movement had religious overtones and generated debate among black leaders. The migration from Texas also received attention from Rob-

---

(spring, 1966): 1–13; Evin N. Thompson, "The Negro Soldiers on the Frontier: A Fort Davis Case Study," *Journal of the West* 7 (Apr., 1968): 217–35; William A. Dobak, "Black Regulars Speak," *Panhandle-Plains Historical Review* 47 (1974): 19–27; Theodore D. Harris, ed., *Negro Frontiersman: The Western Memoirs of Henry O. Flipper* (El Paso: Texas Western Press, 1963); Bruce J. Dinges, "The Court-Martial of Lieutenant Henry O. Flipper," *American West* 9 (June, 1972): 12–17, 59–61.

23. Kirsten Mullen, "In Search of a Historiography for Black Texas Settlements," *Perspective* 9 (May, 1980): 2–5. See also LaBarbara Wigfall Fly and Everett L. Fly, "Black Vernacular Resources in Texas," *Heritage* 5 (fall, 1987): 24–27.

24. Alwyn Barr, "Black Migration into Southwestern Cities, 1865–1900," in *Essays on Southern History: Written in Honor of Barnes F. Lathrop,* ed. Gary W. Gallagher (Austin: General Libraries, University of Texas at Austin, 1980), pp. 15–38; Steven W. Engerrand, "Black and Mulatto Mobility and Stability in Dallas, Texas, 1880–1910," *Phylon* 39 (Sept., 1978): 203–15; Cary D. Wintz, "The Emergence of a Black Neighborhood: Houston's Fourth Ward, 1865–1915," in *Urban Texas,* ed. Char Miller and Heywood T. Sanders (College Station: Texas A&M University Press, 1990), pp. 96–109.

ert G. Athearn, but is less clearly understood than those from Louisiana and Tennessee.[25]

Studies of the black family represent an important new area of research, which is still limited for Texas. Using census materials, Smallwood showed that two-parent black families formed the large majority of households in 1870, with the percentage little different from that for white households. In the Freedmen's Bureau records, Crouch also found a strong black concern for family. For the period between 1870 and 1900, however, Wintz notes some reduction in the percentage of two-parent families for Houston's Fourth Ward. Afro-Texan women have received limited attention in post–Civil War studies, except for Carolyn Ashbaugh's biography of Lucy Parsons, who became a labor spokesperson after departing the state.[26] Studies of female social and economic roles are also needed to determine the relative impact of race and gender.

The Freedmen's Bureau, white missionary societies, and the black community cooperated to establish the first schools for Afro-Texans after the Civil War, as explained by Smallwood and Alton Hornsby, Jr. The state absorbed those schools into its segregated system, where blacks also faced funding problems, which have been described by Rice. To advance the quality of education and their own professional status, according to Vernon McDaniel, black teachers created their own association. George R. Woolfolk analyzed the struggle to develop Prairie View A&M College within the restraints of white-dominated state supervision. Michael Heintze explored the efforts by black and white religious denominations to found and maintain private colleges for black Texans. He clarified their development of black leaders amid debates over curricula, finances, and the transition from white to black teachers and administrators. Jack Abramowitz explored the

25. Nell Irvin Painter, *Exodusters: Black Migration to Kansas after Reconstruction* (New York: W. W. Norton, 1976); Robert G. Athearn, *In Search of Canaan: Black Migration to Kansas, 1879–1880* (Lawrence: Regents Press of Kansas, 1978).

26. James M. Smallwood, "Emancipation and the Black Family: A Case Study in Texas," *Social Science Quarterly* 57 (Mar., 1977): 849–57; Barry A. Crouch and Larry Madaras, "Reconstructing Black Families: Perspectives from the Texas Freedmen's Bureau Records," *Prologue* 18 (summer, 1986): 109–22; Carolyn Ashbaugh, *Lucy Parsons, American Revolutionary* (Chicago: Charles H. Kerr, 1976); Wintz, "The Emergence of a Black Neighborhood," pp. 96–109. See also Lela Jackson, "Rachel Whitfield (1814–1908)," in *Women in Early Texas*, ed. Evelyn M. Carrington (Austin: Jenkins, 1975).

less successful effort of John B. Rayner to develop white support for a private college in the Booker T. Washington mold of economic education. While the debate over liberal arts versus economic courses at the college level has been analyzed, the nature of black education at the elementary and secondary levels deserves more attention.[27]

Part of the support for black colleges came from black churches. Smallwood has described the complex process by which blacks, seeking control and leadership opportunities, formed their own congregations, while white church members and leaders were divided between their desire for separation from blacks and their effort to retain control over African Texans through churches. The leadership of an Austin minister and the attempt by some Catholics to serve the black community in San Antonio have received some attention. Yet the development of Baptist conventions, Methodist conferences, and other black religious organizations in Texas deserves further analysis because churches formed a central institution within the black community.[28]

Black social life in post–Civil War Texas has received attention from Smallwood and Rice, who have described the development of social events and organizations, including fraternal groups, which represented the small but growing middle class. The important fraternal organizations deserve further study to clarify their roles, which included banking and insurance services.

Segregation became widespread even during the Reconstruction, as Crouch and Smallwood make clear. Yet the continued existence,

27. James M. Smallwood, "Black Education in Reconstruction Texas: The Contributions of the Freedmen's Bureau and Benevolent Societies," *ETHJ* 19 (spring, 1981): 17–40; James M. Smallwood, "Early 'Freedom Schools': Black Self-Help and Education in Reconstruction–Texas, A Case Study," *Negro History Bulletin* 41 (Jan.-Feb., 1978): 790–93; Alton Hornsby, Jr., "The Freedmen's Bureau Schools in Texas, 1864–1870," *SHQ* 76 (Apr., 1973): 397–417; Rice, *The Negro in Texas;* Vernon McDaniel, *History of the Teachers State Association of Texas* (Washington, D.C.: National Education Association, 1977); George Ruble Woolfolk, *Prairie View: A Study in Public Conscience, 1878–1946* (New York: Pageant, 1962); Michael R. Heintze, *Private Black Colleges in Texas, 1865-1954* (College Station: Texas A&M University Press, 1985); Jack Abramowitz, "John B. Rayner—A Grass Roots Leader," *Journal of Negro History* 36 (Apr., 1951): 160–93.

28. James M. Smallwood, "The Black Community in Reconstruction Texas: Readjustments in Religion and the Evolution of the Negro Chruch," *ETHJ* 16 (fall, 1978): 16–28; Jacob Fontaine III and Gene Burd, *Jacob Fontaine: From Slavery to the Greatness of the Pulpit, Press, Public Service* (Austin: Eakin, 1984); Sister Mary Immaculata Turley, *Mother Margaret Mary Healy-Murphy: A Biography* (San Antonio: Naylor, 1969).

until the end of the 1890s, of black militia and unsegregated streetcars, as noted by Barr and by August Meier and Elliott Rudwick, suggests a degree of flexibility that declined in the twentieth century. Thus
both C. Vann Woodward and his critics in the debate over Jim Crow
can find support in the studies of Texas.[29]

The initiation of blacks into politics during the Reconstruction has
been analyzed by Smallwood and Carl Moneyhon, who set aside the
old stereotypes of unprepared and manipulated African Texans. Both
found cooperation and conflict among black and white Republicans,
who faced strong competition and criticism from white Democrats.[30]
Black leaders have received collective and individual attention in several studies. Merline Pitre and Barr portray even Reconstruction legislators as a group with some leadership experience, education, and
property. Yet those leaders exhibited a diversity of styles and interests,
as they represented different constituencies. Moneyhon, Smallwood,
and Randall B. Woods offer subtly different views of George Ruby,
but agree on his political astuteness in representing his district, which
was dominated by Galveston. Ann Patton Malone has presented Matt
Gaines as a fiery preacher representing a rural region in a more outspoken style. Crouch has discussed local leaders, who sometimes faced
dangers as a result of their efforts.[31]

The late nineteenth-century conflict among Republicans over Nor-

29. Smallwood, *Time of Hope, Time of Despair;* Rice, *The Negro in Texas;* Barry A.
Crouch and L. J. Schultz, "Crisis in Color: Racial Separation in Texas during Reconstruction," *Civil War History* 16 (Mar., 1970): 37-49; August Meier and Elliott Rudwick, "The Boycott Movement against Jim Crow Streetcars in the South, 1900-1906,"
JAH 40 (Mar., 1969): 756-75; Alwyn Barr, "The Black Militia of the New South: Texas
as a Case Study," *Journal of Negro History* 63 (July, 1978): 209-19.

30. Smallwood, *Time of Hope, Time of Despair;* Carl H. Moneyhon, *Republicanism
in Reconstruction Texas* (Austin: University of Texas Press, 1980).

31. Merline Pitre, *Through Many Dangers, Toils and Snares: The Black Leadership
of Texas, 1868-1900* (Austin: Eakin, 1985); Alwyn Barr, "Black Legislators of Recon-
struction Texas," *Civil War History* 32 (Dec., 1986): 340-52; Carl H. Moneyhon,
"George T. Ruby and the Politics of Expediency in Texas," in *Southern Black Leaders
of the Reconstruction Era*, ed. Howard N. Rabinowitz (Urbana: University of Illinois
Press, 1982); Randall B. Woods, "George T. Ruby: A Black Militant in the White
Business Community," *Red River Valley Historical Review* 1 (fall, 1974): 269-80; James M.
Smallwood, "G. T. Ruby: Galveston's Black Carpetbagger in Reconstruction Texas,"
Houston Review 5 (winter, 1983): 24-33; Ann Patton Malone, "Matt Gaines: Reconstruc-
tion Politician," in Barr and Calvert, *Black Leaders;* Barry A. Crouch, "Self-Determi-
nation and Local Black Leaders in Texas," *Phylon* 39 (Dec., 1978): 344-55; Greg Can-

ris Wright Cuney, a black leader, is discussed by Rice, Pitre, Barr, and Paul Casdorph. Pitre also described the efforts of black legislators after Reconstruction. Participation in the Greenback and Populist parties is explored by Rice and Pitre, who place more emphasis on fusion by Republican leaders, while Barr and Lawrence Goodwyn see a potential for there having been agreement by black and white voters on issues such as economics, education, and voting rights. By means of the poll tax, violence, and the all-white primary elections, Democrats sharply reduced black voting, according to J. Morgan Kousser. That pattern differed from that of several Deep South states which also employed literacy tests.[32]

Violence played an important role in reducing black political participation and in limiting the exercise of other rights by black Texans beginning in the early days of the Reconstruction. Crouch and Allen Trelease have shattered old myths of a mild and defensive Ku Klux Klan by showing that such organizations, including whites from all classes, intimidated voters and workers (including women) and killed Republican leaders (black and white) and broke up their meetings in the 1860s and 1870s. Even after the Democrats regained control of the state government, whites in areas of concentrated black population in East Texas resorted to violence to seize control of county governments, as recounted by Rice and Barr. White fears of black retaliation in 1883 produced a new wave of Anglo violence which Barr found similar to pre–Civil War slave revolt panics. Federal and black efforts to limit the attacks by use of the Freedmen's Bureau and the army are described by Crouch and William L. Richter, who is critical of

trell, "John B. Rayner: A Study in Black Populist Leadership," *Southern Studies* (winter, 1985): 432–43.

32. Rice, *The Negro in Texas;* Pitre, *Through Many Dangers, Toils and Snares;* Alwyn Barr, *Reconstruction to Reform: Texas Politics, 1876–1906* (Austin: University of Texas Press, 1971); Paul Casdorph, "Norris Wright Cuney and Texas Republican Politics, 1883–1896," *SHQ* 68 (Apr., 1965): 455–64; Lawrence C. Goodwyn, "Populist Dreams and Negro Rights: East Texas as a Case Study," *AHR* 76 (Dec., 1971): 1435–56; J. Morgan Kousser, *The Shaping of Southern Politics: Suffrage Restriction and the Establishment of the One-Party South, 1880–1910* (New Haven, Conn.: Yale University Press, 1974). See also Gilbert Cuthbertson, "The Jaybird Woodpecker War," *Texana* 10 (fall, 1972): 297–309; Robert W. Shook, "The Texas 'Election Outrage' of 1886," *ETHJ* 10 (spring, 1972): 20–30; Frank R. Levstik, "William H. Holland: Black Soldier, Politician and Educator," *Negro History Bulletin* 36 (May, 1973): 110–11; Gregg Cantrell and D. Scott Barton, "Texas Populists and the Failure of Biracial Politics," *JSH* 55 (Nov., 1989): 659–92.

the military. Black efforts to seek more equitable law enforcement through participation in the militia, state police, and local juries are explored by Otis A. Singletary, Ann Patton Baenziger (Malone), and Donald G. Nieman.[33]

Lynching became another frequent form of violence in Texas in the late nineteenth century and did not decline until the 1920s. James M. SoRelle has studied the hanging and burning of Jesse Washington in Waco even after his conviction for murder, with no effort by lawmen to halt the mob or prosecute those involved. A lynching in Longview produced protests by middle-class blacks, which resulted in a riot by whites according to William Tuttle. In 1930, at Sherman, a lynching became a full-scale riot in which the mob defeated the Texas Rangers and the National Guard, as described by Edward Hake Phillips. There is no general history of lynching in Texas that explores the causes, process, and decline of such violent outbursts. A brief survey suggests the white community widely supported lynching as a means of racial control, although victims included some whites and Mexican Americans in Central and South Texas. Reduced public acceptance after 1922 limited such incidents, which ended in the 1940s.[34]

Another form of violence occurred in the 1890s and early 1900s

33. Barry A. Crouch, "A Spirit of Lawlessness: White Violence, Texas Blacks, 1865-1868," *Journal of Social History* 18 (winter, 1984): 217-32; Allen W. Trelease, *White Terror: The Ku Klux Klan Conspiracy and Southern Reconstruction* (New York: Harper and Row, 1971); Rice, *The Negro in Texas;* Barr, *Reconstruction to Reform;* Alwyn Barr, "The Texas 'Black Uprising' Scare of 1883," *Phylon* 41 (June, 1980): 179-86; Barry A. Crouch, "Black Dreams and White Justice," *Prologue* 6 (winter, 1974): 255-65; William L. Richter, "The Army and the Negro during Texas Reconstruction, 1865-1870," *ETHJ* 10 (spring, 1972): 7-19; Otis A. Singletary, "The Texas Militia during Reconstruction," *SHQ* 60 (July, 1956): 21-35; Ann Patton Baenziger, "The Texas State Police during Reconstruction: A Reexamination," *SHQ* 72 (Apr., 1969): 470-91; Donald G. Nieman, "Black Political Power and Criminal Justice: Washington County, Texas, 1868-1884," *JSH* 55 (Aug., 1989): 321-420. See also Gregg Cantrell, "Racial Violence and Reconstruction Politics in Texas, 1867-1868," *SHQ* 93 (Jan., 1990): 333-55.

34. James M. SoRelle, "The 'Waco Horror': The Lynching of Jesse Washington," *SHQ* 86 (Apr., 1983): 517-36; William Tuttle, "Violence in a 'Heathen' Land: The Longview Race Riot of 1919," *Phylon* 33 (winter, 1972): 324-33; Edward Hake Phillips, "The Sherman Courthouse Riot of 1930," *ETHJ* 25 (fall, 1987): 12-19; David L. Chapman, "Lynching in Texas," M.A. thesis, Texas Tech University, 1973. See also George Ohler, "Background Causes of the Longview Race Riot of July 10, 1919," *Journal of the American Studies Association of Texas* 12 (1981): 46-54; Kenneth R. Durham, "The Longview Race Riot of 1919," *ETHJ* 18 (fall, 1980): 13-24.

as black troops found themselves stationed near larger towns, where they met with increased segregation. Garna Christian has explored clashes between blacks and local lawmen at El Paso, Rio Grande City, and Texarkana, which probably led authorities to believe charges of a raid on Brownsville in 1906. John D. Weaver has argued that black troops stationed there had been framed, however, to force their removal from the border. Robert V. Haynes found similar problems of discrimination in Texas towns during World War I, which resulted in a major clash at Houston, where several black soldiers were executed for killing white police and civilians.[35]

Despite the continued violence and discrimination of the early 1900s, black Texans participated in or initiated a variety of changes during the twentieth century. General studies of both the problems and areas of progress have been written by William J. Brophy, Bruce A. Glasrud, and Neil G. Sapper.[36]

The critical influence of changing racial attitudes has received attention from Jacquelyn Dowd Hall in her study of Jessie Daniel Ames, who came to challenge antiblack views because they retarded progressive reforms and women's roles. Through the Commission on Interracial Cooperation in the 1920s Ames opposed prejudice and lynching and promoted advances in black education and housing. The influence of social gospel ideas in moderating racial views among white

35. Garna L. Christian, "The El Paso Racial Crisis of 1900," *Red River Valley Historical Review* 6 (spring, 1981): 28–41; Garna L. Christian, "Rio Grande City: Prelude to the Brownsville Raid," *WTHAYB* 57 (1981): 118–32; Garna L. Christian, "The Violent Possibility: The Tenth Cavalry at Texarkana," *ETHJ* 23 (spring, 1985): 3–15; Garna L. Christian, "The Brownsville Raid's 168th Man: The Court-Martial of Corporal Knowles," *SHQ* 93 (July, 1989): 45–59; John D. Weaver, *The Brownsville Raid* (New York: W. W. Norton, 1970); Robert V. Haynes, *A Night of Violence: The Houston Riot of 1917* (Baton Rouge: Louisiana State University Press, 1976). See also Ann J. Lane, *The Brownsville Affair: National Crisis and Black Reaction* (Port Washington, N.Y.: Kennikat, 1971); James A. Tinsley, "Roosevelt, Foraker, and the Brownsville Affray," *Journal of Negro History* 41 (Jan., 1956): 43–65; Robert V. Haynes, "The Houston Mutiny and Riot of 1917," *SHQ* 76 (Apr., 1973): 418–39; Robert V. Haynes, "Unrest at Home: Racial Conflict between White Civilians and Black Soldiers in 1917," *Journal of the American Studies Association of Texas* 6 (1975): 43–54.

36. William J. Brophy, "The Black Texan, 1900–1950: A Quantitative History," Ph.D. diss., Vanderbilt University, 1974; Bruce A. Glasrud, "Black Texans, 1900–1930: A History," Ph.D. diss., Texas Tech University, 1969; Neil G. Sapper, "A Survey of the History of the Black People of Texas, 1930–1954," Ph.D. diss., Texas Tech University, 1972.

Texas Baptists at midcentury has been analyzed by John W. Storey. Attempts to experience and describe prejudice have resulted in personal accounts by two white Texans, John Howard Griffin and Grace Halsell. A study by Alan Scott of attitudes about race relations based on opinion polls from 1940 to 1965 is also useful. Yet the stages and nature of changing racial views and the lingering existence of racism deserve further study.[37]

Migration from rural to urban areas within the state and out of Texas to the North and West marked the start of major transformations for Afro-Texans. Except for Brophy and Glasrud, however, historians have not studied the beginning of those movements in Texas. While the roles of a few individuals from the Lone Star State have been noted, their collective impact, such as the probable spread of Juneteenth celebrations farther into the Southwest, needs attention.[38]

Urban migration resulted in part from agricultural problems. Most black farmers remained tenants and fell further behind white farmers in economic status. Even the agricultural program of the New Deal, which stabilized farm prices in the depression of the 1930s, offered little aid to black sharecroppers, who found themselves left out as landowners removed land from production.[39]

The greater diversity of urban jobs and their higher wages provided an attraction that promoted migration to cities, although Texas towns did not contain as much industry as northern urban centers during the first half of the twentieth century. An analysis of black laborers in Houston between the world wars by SoRelle has shown that blacks, not surprisingly, faced discrimination in hiring and wages. Randy J. Sparks found that during the depression a higher percentage than the norm of Bayou City blacks lost jobs or received limited

37. Jacquelyn Dowd Hall, *Revolt against Chivalry: Jessie Daniel Ames and the Women's Campaign against Lynching* (New York: Columbia University Press, 1979); John W. Storey, "Texas Baptist Leadership, the Social Gospel, and Race, 1954–1968," *SHQ* 83 (July, 1979): 29–46; John Howard Griffin, *Black Like Me* (New York: Houghton Mifflin, 1960); Grace Halsell, *Soul Sister* (New York: World, 1969); Alan Scott, "Twenty-five Years of Opinion on Integration in Texas," *Southwestern Social Science Quarterly* 48 (Sept., 1967): 155–63.

38. Brophy, "The Black Texan"; Glasrud, "Black Texans."

39. Brophy, "The Black Texan"; Glasrud, "Black Texans"; Sapper, "Black People of Texas"; Frederic O. Sargent, "Economic Adjustment of Negro Farmers in East Texas," *Southwestern Social Science Quarterly* 42 (June, 1961): 32–39.

relief assistance. Brophy has concluded that blacks all across Texas could participate in New Deal programs, but that the aid they were given did not fully meet the problems that existed. Ruth Allen has described the segregation of blacks in the early unions of Texas and the limited cooperation of the State Federation of Labor. White reaction to the developing role of black workers in urban areas burst forth in the Beaumont race riot of 1943. In his study of that crisis James A. Burran found local law enforcement still reluctant to protect blacks, with the state authorities more effective at restoring order. Robert D. Bullard concluded that in the 1970s and 1980s a higher percentage of blacks than whites in Houston remained in blue-collar jobs and had lower pay scales, a higher unemployment rate, and a higher percentage of families below the poverty level.[40]

Despite these limitations, the expanding black urban population represented a concentration of consumers for new businesses owned by black Texans, from newspapers to insurance companies, as described by Brophy, Glasrud, Sapper, and Smallwood. Efforts by blacks to develop small businesses are described by Frances Dressman and Dannehl M. Twomey. A growing black middle class also included more attorneys, doctors, and teachers. Despite financial limitations and the existence of only a few black banks, these groups began to organize early in the twentieth century to promote further progress through black business leagues or chambers of commerce and professional groups such as the Lone Star Medical Association. Nevertheless, the percentage of black businesses in Houston remained well below the black population percentage in the 1970s, according to Bullard. The

40. James M. SoRelle, "'An de po cullud man is in de wuss fix uv awl': Black Occupational Status in Houston, Texas, 1920-1940," *Houston Review* 1 (spring, 1979): 15-26; Randy J. Sparks, "'Heavenly Houston' or 'Hellish Houston'? Black Unemployment and Relief Efforts, 1929-1936," *Southern Studies* 25 (winter, 1986): 353-67; William J. Brophy, "Black Texans and the New Deal," in *The Depression in the Southwest,* ed. Donald W. Whisenhunt (Port Washington, N.Y.: Kennikat, 1980); Ruth Allen, *Chapters in the History of Organized Labor in Texas* (Austin: University of Texas, 1941); James A. Burran, "Violence in an 'Arsenal of Democracy': The Beaumont Race Riot, 1943," *ETHJ* 14 (spring, 1976): 39-51; Robert D. Bullard, *Invisible Houston: The Black Experience in Boom and Bust* (College Station: Texas A&M University Press, 1988). See also James S. Olson and Sharon Phair, "The Anatomy of a Race Riot: Beaumont, Texas, 1943," *Texana* 11 (Jan., 1973): 64-72; Jo Ann P. Stiles, "The Changing Economic and Educational Status of Texas Negroes, 1940-1960," M.A. thesis, University of Texas, Austin, 1966.

ALWYN BARR

membership and activities of business and professional associations are worthy of more analysis.[41]

One major result of black unemployment during the depression of the 1930s seems to have been the beginning of a downward trend in the percentage of two-parent families, based upon national studies. Black female workers in San Antonio found themselves relegated to household and service positions with lower wages, poorer housing, and greater health problems by the 1930s. Furthermore, women already headed a higher percentage of black families than was true for other ethnic groups of the city, according to Julia Kirk Blackwelder. Cary Wintz has noted that women headed one-third of the black families in Houston by 1980. Through the extensive use of oral history, Ruthe Winegarten has described the life of Annie Mae Hunt, who moved from household work into the operation of a small business and political activity. Black family stability and women's roles represent major fields for further study in Texas.[42]

For black men and women, education in Texas offered both problems to be overcome and opportunities to be pursued. Segregation and financial discrimination existed in schools through most of the twentieth century. Yet Afro-Texans in urban areas achieved advances that ranked their public education above that in most southern states.

41. William J. Brophy, "Black Business Development in Texas Cities, 1900–1950," *Red River Valley Historical Review* 6 (spring, 1981): 42–55; Glasrud, "Black Texans"; Sapper, "Black People of Texas"; James M. Smallwood, "Texas," in *The Black Press in the South,* ed. Henry Lewis Suggs (Westport, Conn.: Greenwood, 1983); Frances Dressman, "'Yes We Have No Jitneys!': Transportation Issues in Houston's Black Community, 1914–1924," *Houston Review* 9, no. 2 (1987): 69–81; Dannehl M. Twomey, "Into the Mainstream: Early Black Photography in Houston," *Houston Review,* no. 1 (1987): 39–48; Bullard, *Invisible Houston.* See also Howard Beeth, "Houston and History, Past and Present: A Look at Black Houston in the 1920s," *Southern Studies* 25 (summer, 1986): 172–86; William J. Slaton, "Negro Businesses in Texas," *Texas Business Review* 43 (July, 1969): 194–98; and the essays on Texas in Demitri B. Shimkin et al., *The Extended Family in Black Societies* (The Hague: Mouton, 1978).

42. Herbert G. Gutman, *The Black Family in Slavery and Freedom, 1750–1925* (New York: Pantheon, 1976); Julia Kirk Blackwelder, *Women of the Depression: Caste and Culture in San Antonio, 1929–1939* (College Station: Texas A&M University Press, 1984); Cary D. Wintz, "Blacks," in *Ethnic Groups of Houston,* ed. Fred R. von der Mehden (Houston: Rice University Press, 1985); Ruthe Winegarten, ed., *I Am Annie Mae: The Personal History of a Black Texas Woman* (Austin: Rosegarden, 1983). See also Henry Allen Bullock, "Some Readjustments of the Texas Negro Family to the Emergency of War," *Southwestern Social Science Quarterly* 25 (Sept., 1944): 100–17.

70

Efforts to challenge unequal education began in the 1930s and 1940s, as described by Melvin James Banks and others. Within the system black college presidents struggled for public and private funding. As George R. Woolfolk has shown, W. R. Banks used the threat of de-segregation to strengthen Prairie View A&M in the 1940s. Mary Branch, at Tillotson, worked with the white leaders of Austin while preparing students who eventually would challenge discrimination, according to Olive D. Brown and Michael R. Heintze.[43]

Desegregation in Texas education began with the Sweatt decision in 1950 that opened the University of Texas law school to blacks and proved a forerunner of the Brown decision. Last-minute state efforts to meet the separate-but-equal standard by creating Texas Southern University are described by Alton Hornsby, Jr. The development of the Sweatt case by black Texans and the considerable pressure faced by the plaintiff, Heman Sweatt, have been analyzed by Michael L. Gillette. Major issues in the process of desegregation on the University of Texas main campus — such as housing, programs, admissions, faculty, and sports — have been described by Almetris Marsh Duren and Louise Iscoe. Similar studies of other universities are necessary to clarify larger patterns.

Aspects of integration at the public school level have been described primarily by educators and government studies. William Peters has discussed the early election of a black woman to the Houston School Board, despite considerable opposition. Werner F. Grunbaum has found white opposition to integration to be strongest in areas of larger black population. A U.S. Commission on Civil Rights study, using Houston as the primary example, has described only limited progress in race relations in the fifties and sixties because of white delays in de-

---

43. Melvin James Banks, "The Pursuit of Equality: The Movement for First Class Citizenship among Negroes in Texas, 1920–1950," D.S.S. diss., Syracuse University, 1962; Brophy, "The Black Texan"; Glasrud, "Black Texans"; Sapper, "Black People of Texas"; George Ruble Woolfolk, "W. R. Banks: Public College Educator," in Barr and Calvert, *Black Leaders;* Olive D. Brown and Michael R. Heintze, "Mary Branch: Private College Educator," in Barr and Calvert, *Black Leaders.* See also Henry Allen Bullock, "The Availability of Education in the Texas Negro Separate School," *Journal of Negro Education* 16 (summer, 1947): 425–32; Ira B. Bryant, "Vocational Education in Negro High Schools in Texas," *Journal of Negro Education* 18 (winter, 1949): 9–15; J. Reuben Sheeler, "Negro History Week in the Houston Area," *Negro History Bulletin* 19 (Oct., 1955): 2, 21.

segregating. Dorothy Redus Robinson offers a black teacher's perspective on the changes in black education; a study of teacher tests in the 1980s has suggested that one result may be a reduced percentage of black instructors. Yet the complex events that have occurred since the 1950s in black education need extensive study by historians to clarify the stages of desegregation and variations from one community to another.[44]

Although the role of churches differed in some ways in rural to urban settings and new Pentecostal and Muslim congregations appeared in the twentieth century, those developments have received only limited attention in the general accounts of blacks in Texas. They deserve more study, as does the role of religion in the civil rights movement and the limited racial integration in traditional churches.[45]

Fraternal organizations are also described as important community institutions in the general histories of African Texans, but their role and influence call for further analysis. Wintz has noted that Houston became a stronghold for several groups. The role of William McDonald as a fraternal leader who built his Fort Worth bank upon those connections is clarified by Glasrud. Three scholars have found black membership in a variety of volunteer organizations, from fraternal to church and recreational groups, to be higher than in other ethnic groups. These associations and leaders must be studied to clarify their influence as well as their reflection of class distinctions.[46]

44. Alton Hornsby, Jr., "The 'Colored Branch University' Issue in Texas — Prelude to *Sweatt* v. *Painter*," *Journal of Negro History* 61 (Jan., 1976): 51–60; Michael L. Gillette, "Heman Marion Sweatt: Civil Rights Plaintiff," in Barr and Calvert, *Black Leaders;* Michael L. Gillette, "Blacks Challenge the White University," *SHQ* 86 (Oct., 1982): 321–44; Almetris Marsh Duren and Louise Iscoe, *Overcoming: A History of Black Integration at the University of Texas at Austin* (Austin: University of Texas at Austin, 1979); William Peters, "Houston's Quiet Victory," *Negro History Bulletin* 23 (Jan., 1960): 75–79; Werner F. Grunbaum, "Desegregation in Texas: Voting and Action Patterns," *Public Opinion Quarterly* 23 (winter, 1964): 604–14; U.S. Commission on Civil Rights, *Public Schools: Southern States: Texas* (Washington, D.C., 1963); Dorothy Redus Robinson, *The Bell Rings at Four: A Black Teacher's Chronicle of Change* (Austin: Madrona, 1978); Nelson C. Dometrius and Lee Sigelman, "The Cost of Quality: Teacher Testing and Racial-Ethnic Representativeness in Public Education," *Social Science Quarterly* 69 (Mar., 1988): 70–82.

45. Brophy, "The Black Texan"; Glasrud, "Black Texans."

46. Brophy, "The Black Texan"; Glasrud, "Black Texans"; Sapper, "Black People in Texas"; Wintz, "Blacks"; Bruce A. Glasrud, "William M. McDonald: Business and Fraternal Leader," in Barr and Calvert, *Black Leaders;* J. Allen Williams, Nicho-

Black society also generated a popular culture, including music and sports, which provided entertainment and recreation for large numbers of people as well as economic opportunities for a limited group of individuals. William H. Wiggins, Jr., has offered descriptions of continued celebrations of emancipation and the search for freedom on Juneteenth. Jack Johnson began his career as a heavyweight boxer in his hometown of Galveston, but left the state before he became a controversial and internationally known champion; his life and his impact on society have been described best by Randy Roberts. While Johnson fought white boxers, most sports competition remained segregated until the mid-twentieth century. The desegregation of college football at North Texas State has been analyzed by Ronald E. Marcello, who found the process "relatively smooth" because of good leadership and a "personable black superstar," Abner Haynes. The successes and pressures faced by the first three black football players at Southwest Conference schools, as well as the slower progress of desegregation at the University of Texas, are explored by Richard Pennington. The role of athletes in black schools and colleges and the process of desegregation in other amateur and professional sports in Texas have not yet received full and careful treatment.[47]

Music offered similar possibilities for blacks. Bruce Jackson collected from black convicts work songs of rural East Texas that expressed emotions and influenced the pace of labor. Scott Joplin left Texarkana to play in dance halls and bawdy houses across the Southwest and eventually in St. Louis and New York. There he became the "King of Ragtime" and wrote an opera before his early death. Peter Gammond suggested a further Joplin influence through "Jelly Roll" Morton on the development of jazz. Huddie Ledbetter, or Leadbelly, wrote and played

las Babchuk, and David R. Johnson, "Voluntary Associations and Minority Status: A Comparative Analysis of Anglo, Black, and Mexican Americans," *American Sociological Review* 38 (Oct., 1973): 637–46.

47. William H. Wiggins, *O Freedom! Afro-American Emancipation Celebrations* (Knoxville: University of Tennessee Press, 1987); Randy Roberts, "Galveston's Jack Johnson: Flourishing in the Dark," *SHQ* 87 (July, 1983): 37–56; Randy Roberts, *Papa Jack: Jack Johnson and the Era of White Hopes* (New York: Free Press, 1983); Glasrud, "Black Texans"; Sapper, "Black People of Texas"; Ronald E. Marcello, "The Integration of Intercollegiate Athletics in Texas: North Texas State College as a Test Case, 1956," *Journal of Sport History* 14 (winter, 1987): 286–316; Richard Pennington, *Breaking the Ice: The Racial Integration of Southwest Conference Football* (Jefferson, N.C.: McFarland, 1987).

country blues in Texas and Louisiana towns and prisons before his discovery by John Lomax led to national attention in the 1940s. Post–World War II urban black musicians deserve the attention of scholars for their impact on an increasingly integrated world of music.[48]

The growing black middle class in Texas cities generated a range of more formal cultural expressions in the 1930s and 1940s, from the celebration of Negro History Week to the performance of music by black college choirs. Neil Sapper has noted the published poems of J. Mason Brewer and the drama presentations of the Houston Negro Little Theatre. Black colleges contributed to formal culture through their faculties. Brewer, a graduate of Wiley College and a professor at Huston-Tillotson, became well known as the premier black folklorist in Texas, as James W. Byrd has explained. Melvin Tolson, a professor of English, debate, and drama at Wiley from the 1920s to the 1940s, published poetry, fiction, and plays that won him a national reputation and two literary biographies. The development of an art department at Texas Southern University with nationally known painters and sculptors is described by John Edward Weems in conjunction with the university's leading artists, John Thomas Biggers and Carroll Sims. Untutored folk artists, such as the painter Johnny W. Banks and black women quilters, who use strip and string styles influenced by African concepts, have begun to receive some attention in recent years. Yet the work of other writers and artists also deserves consideration, especially in the period after 1950. The historical geographer Terry G. Jordan has noted the continuation of African-style burial practices such as the use of bare mounds and shell decorations.[49]

48. Bruce Jackson, ed., *Wake-up Dead Man: Afro-American Worksongs from Texas Prisons* (Cambridge, Mass.: Harvard University Press, 1972); Rudi Blesch, "Scott Joplin," *American Heritage* 26 (June, 1975): 26–32, 86–91; Peter Gammond, *Scott Joplin and the Ragtime Era* (London: Angus and Robertson, 1975); James Haskins and Kathleen Benson, *Scott Joplin* (Garden City, N.Y.: Doubleday, 1975); John A. Lomax and Alan Lomax, eds., *Negro Folk Songs as Sung by Leadbelly* (New York: Macmillan, 1936); Richard M. Garvin, *The Midnight Special: The Legend of Leadbelly* (New York: B. Geis, 1971); Alan Govenar, *The Early Years of Rhythm and Blues: Focus on Houston* (Houston: Rice University Press, 1990).

49. Neil Sapper, "Black Culture in Urban Texas: A Lone Star Renaissance," *Red River Valley Historical Review* 6 (spring, 1981): 56–77; James W. Byrd, *J. Mason Brewer, Negro Folklorist* (Austin: Steck-Vaughn, 1967); Robert M. Farnsworth, *Melvin B. Tolson, 1898–1961: Plain Talk and Poetic Prophecy* (Columbia: University of Missouri Press, 1984); Joy Flasch, *Melvin B. Tolson* (New York: Twayne, 1972); John Edward Weems, John

Despite cultural developments, residential segregation and the related problems of housing and health conditions have remained major social issues throughout the twentieth century. Black migrants into Texas cities contributed to the expansion of African-Texan neighborhoods and to the exodus of white residents to the suburbs. Barry J. Kaplan studied the process in Houston and found it to be similar to national patterns. J. Allen Williams has found that some blacks displaced by urban renewal in Austin did not find new housing in the area, which resulted in a lost sense of community. In San Antonio and Houston, Jack Dodson found limitations in the quantity and quality of housing available to blacks, primarily as a result of low income. Although still high, the rate of residential segregation did drop to a limited extent from 1970 to 1980 in Texas cities, according to Sean-Shong Hwang and Steve H. Murdock. A lower percentage of home-ownership and limited public housing, as well as discrimination in home sales and the location of waste dumps, remained part of black life in Houston during the 1970s and 1980s, according to Bullard. Case studies of other cities are needed to confirm the extent of those problems in the late twentieth century.[50]

Crowded living situations interact with low earnings to stimulate higher levels of conflict and criminal activity. Henry Allen Bullock has analyzed Houston murder patterns in the 1950s and found that almost all involved attackers and victims from the same ethnic group.

Thomas Biggers, and Carroll Sims, *Black Art in Houston: The Texas Southern University Experience* (College Station: Texas A&M University Press, 1978); Lynne Adele, *Black History/Black Vision: The Visionary Image in Texas* (Austin: University of Texas Press, 1989); Francis Edward Abernethy, ed., *Folk Art in Texas* (Dallas: Southern Methodist University Press, 1985); Suzanne Yabsley, *Texas Quilts, Texas Women* (College Station: Texas A&M University Press, 1984); Terry G. Jordan, *Texas Graveyards: A Cultural Legacy* (Austin: University of Texas Press, 1982). See also Frank H. Wardlaw, "John Biggers, Artist," in Barr and Calvert, *Black Leaders.*

50. Barry J. Kaplan, "Race, Income, and Ethnicity: Residential Change in a Houston Community, 1920–1970," *Houston Review* 3 (winter, 1981): 178–202; Bullard, *Invisible Houston;* Jack Dodson, "Minority Group Housing in Two Texas Cities," in *Studies in Housing and Minority Groups,* ed. Nathan Glazer and Davis McIntire (Berkeley: University of California Press, 1960); J. Allen Williams, Jr., "The Effects of Urban Renewal upon a Black Community: Evolution and Recommendations," *Social Science Quarterly* 50 (Dec., 1969): 703–12; Sean-Shong Hwang and Steve H. Murdock, "Residential Segregation in Texas in 1980," *Social Science Quarterly* 63 (Dec., 1982): 737–48. See also W. Marvin Dulaney, "The Texas Negro Peace Officers' Association: The Origins of Black Police Unionism," forthcoming in the *Houston Review.*

In a study of the legal response to crimes, Bullock noted that black Texans received shorter periods in prison for murder, usually of other blacks, but more extended penitentiary time for burglary, more often of whites. A personal account by Albert Race Sample spanned his life from childhood; the son of a prostitute, he went to prison for theft and assault in the 1950s. He described the harshness and racism of penitentiary life and his own transition into a counselor for ex-convicts after his release in the 1970s. Blair Justice, William McCord, and other scholars have described different black attitudes in Houston during the 1960s, ranging from apathy to civil rights activity to membership in black power organizations. The causes of the Texas Southern University riot and police overreaction are considered. Bullard described the long-standing tension between white police and blacks in Houston, as well as the changes in the city's law enforcement, with the increase in black police officers from 4 to 8.5 percent of the force between 1960 and 1980 and the appointment of a black chief of police. The causes of crimes within the black community and questions of racial bias in law enforcement represent major topics for study from an historical perspective.[51]

The struggle to overcome various forms of discrimination in Texas has included challenges to disfranchisement. Darlene Clark Hine has analyzed the successful efforts of the urban middle class to eliminate the white voting primary rule through a series of court cases from the 1920s to the 1940s. Brophy notes that some blacks did pay the poll tax to retain the right to vote in the early twentieth century. Charles Bellinger urged black voters to participate in the coalition politics of San Antonio in return for improvements in black neighborhoods. The willingness of some Democrats to include blacks in New Deal programs during the depression of the 1930s caused a majority of blacks to change political parties. Lyndon Johnson's direction of the National

---

51. Henry Allen Bullock, "Urban Homicide in Theory and Fact," *Journal of Criminal Law, Criminology, and Police Science* 45 (Jan.-Feb., 1955): 565-75; Henry Allen Bullock, "Significance of the Racial Factor in the Length of Prison Sentences," *Journal of Criminal Law, Criminology, and Police Science* 52 (Nov.-Dec., 1961): 411-17; Albert Race Sample, *Racehoss: Big Emma's Boy* (Austin: Eakin, 1984); William McCord et al., *Life Styles in the Black Ghetto* (New York: W. W. Norton, 1969); Blair Justice, *Violence in the City* (Ft. Worth: Texas Christian University Press, 1969); Bullard, *Invisible Houston;* W. Marvin Dulaney, "Black Politics in Dallas: The Rise of the Progressive Voters' League," forthcoming in *Legacies.*

Youth Administration in Texas is described as one example of that process by Christie L. Bourgeois.[52]

Voting patterns, participation in party and coalition politics, and the rise of legislative and congressional leadership from the 1950s to the 1980s have received some attention from political scientists. Coalitions of blacks and other ethnic groups produced at least temporary political success and leadership opportunities in both small towns and large cities, according to Chandler Davidson, Herbert H. Werlin, and Harry Holloway. In several studies Holloway found limited voter turnout and little change in Texas towns and cities even after blacks gained voting rights, in part because of economic pressures. A moderate expansion in the number of registered voters followed the abolition of the poll tax in the 1960s, according to Dan Nimmo and Clifton McCleskey. Joyce Williams has explored the development of local political influence by blacks in the Lake Como section of Fort Worth. Jim Schutze has described the black fight in Dallas to overcome a white power structure and gain district representation, which resulted in the rise of new political leaders. The best example of growing black political involvement, the career of Houston legislator and congresswoman Barbara Jordan, has been described in a biography and an autobiography. An analysis of support in Jefferson and Orange counties for presidential candidate Jesse Jackson in 1984 found it to be 90 percent black, despite efforts to broaden his appeal. The development of black voting and officeholding deserves further consideration from an historical perspective to assess changes and limitations as well as the roles of individuals and groups.[53]

52. Darlene Clark Hine, *Black Victory: The Rise and Fall of the White Primary in Texas* (Millwood, N.Y.: KTO Press, 1979); Darlene Clark Hine, "Blacks and the Destruction of the Democratic White Primary, 1935–1944," *Journal of Negro History* 62 (Jan., 1977): 43–59; Darlene Clark Hine, "The Elusive Ballot: The Black Struggle against the Texas Democratic White Primary, 1932–1945," *SHQ* 81 (Apr., 1978): 371–92; Brophy, "The Black Texan"; Banks, "Pursuit of Equality"; Christie L. Bourgeois, "Stepping over Lines: Lyndon Johnson, Black Texans, and the National Youth Administration, 1935–1937," *SHQ* 91 (Oct., 1987): 149–72. See also Conrey Bryson, *Dr. Lawrence A. Nixon and the White Primary* (El Paso: Texas Western Press, 1974); Robert V. Haynes, "Black Houstonians and the White Democratic Primary, 1920–1945," in *Houston: A Twentieth Century Urban Frontier,* ed. Francisco A. Rosales and Barry J. Kaplan (Port Washington, N.Y.: Kennikat, 1983).

53. Herbert H. Werlin, "The Victory in Slaton," *Negro History Bulletin* 25 (Feb., 1962): 112–13; Chandler Davidson, *Biracial Politics: Conflict and Coalition in the Metropoli-

The activities of civil rights organizations seeking an end to discrimination began in the 1920s and continued throughout the century in Texas. The early successes of the National Association for the Advancement of Colored People are analyzed by Gillette, while Sapper explores internal conflicts that reduced the effectiveness of the organization. Barbara Thompson Day explored the problem-solving efforts of sympathetic white religious and political figures through the Houston Council on Human Relations in the 1960s. Accounts of other civil rights groups in the state are necessary for a full picture of the movement, especially during the 1950s and 1960s. Earl Black has found the debate over integration to be a less volatile political issue in Texas, a border South state, compared to states of the Deep South. Robert Goldberg has suggested San Antonio as an example of negotiated change in the border South of the early 1960s. William Brophy drew similar conclusions about Dallas. More local studies will provide useful comparisons to test these judgments and to illuminate other patterns in that period.[54]

tan South (Baton Rouge: Louisiana State University Press, 1972); Harry Holloway, *The Politics of the Southern Negro from Exclusion to Big City Organization* (New York: Random, 1969); Harry Holloway and David M. Olson, "Electorial Participation by White and Negro in a Southern City," *Midwest Journal of Political Science* 10 (Feb., 1966): 99–122; Joyce E. Williams, *Black Community Control: A Study of Transition in a Texas Ghetto* (New York: Praeger, 1973); Jim Schutze, *The Accommodation: The Politics of Race in an American City* (Secaucus, N.J.: Citadel, 1986); Dan Nimmo and Clifton McCleskey, "Impact of the Poll Tax System on Voter Participation: The Houston Metropolitan Area in 1966," *Journal of Politics* 31 (Aug., 1969): 682–99; Ira B. Bryant, *Barbara Charline Jordan: From the Ghetto to the Capitol* (Houston: D. Armstrong, 1977); Barbara Jordan and Shelby Hearon, *Barbara Jordan: A Self Portrait* (Garden City, N.Y.: Doubleday, 1979); Gaither Loewenstein and Lyttleton T. Sanders, "Bloc Voting, Rainbow Coalitions, and the Jackson Presidential Candidacy: A View from Southeast Texas," *Journal of Black Studies* 18 (Sept., 1987): 86–96.

54. Michael L. Gillette, "The Rise of the NAACP in Texas," *SHQ* 81 (Apr., 1978): 393–416; Neil Sapper, "The Fall of the NAACP in Texas," *Houston Review* 7 (summer, 1985): 53–68; Barbara Thompson Day, "The Heart of Houston: The Early History of the Houston Council on Human Relations, 1958–1972," *Houston Review* 8 (spring, 1986): 1–32; Earl Black, *Southern Governors and Civil Rights: Racial Segregation as a Campaign Issue in the Second Reconstruction* (Cambridge, Mass.: Harvard University Press, 1976); Robert A. Goldberg, "Racial Change on the Southern Periphery: The Case of San Antonio, Texas, 1960–1965," *JSH* 49 (Aug., 1983): 349–74; William Brophy, "Active Acceptance—Active Containment: The Dallas Story," in *Southern Businessmen and Desegregation*, ed. Elizabeth Jacoway and David R. Colburn (Baton Rouge: Louisiana

As this essay suggests, the history of blacks in Texas has been the focus of extensive analysis in recent years. One major theme has been the development of a more objective view of race relations, from slavery through the era of segregation to the years of civil rights changes, that eliminated old stereotypes. That effort has been followed by studies that have expanded understanding of the diverse institutions and cultural roles within the black community. Many topics remain unexplored, however, especially since there is no detailed general account of the years following the Brown decision.

Popular history lags behind the latest research because textbooks and general histories assimilate new material only after it appears in articles and monographs. The most recent high school and college texts are clear improvements over earlier editions in their treatment of the black role in state history. Yet the most popular general history, which has not been revised since the 1960s, still omits some topics while retaining dated stereotypes and questionable generalizations.[55] Students and other interested readers may begin to balance those views with the general histories of Afro-Texans that have appeared in recent years.[56] At another level of popular history, county studies vary widely in their treatment of blacks. Some continue to ignore the existence of blacks or to offer only white viewpoints on local events.[57] Others have followed the textbook example of incorporating new topics and revising dated interpretations. To help provide balance, a few

State University Press, 1982). See also Robert Calvert, "The Civil Rights Movement in Texas," in *The Texas Heritage,* ed. Ben Procter and Archie P. McDonald (St. Louis: Forum, 1980); Julius Amin, "Black Lubbock: 1955 to the Present," *WTHAYB* 65 (1989): 24–35.

55. Rupert N. Richardson, Ernest Wallace, and Adrian N. Anderson, *Texas: The Lone Star State* (Englewood Cliffs, N.J.: Prentice-Hall, 1988); Adrian N. Anderson and Ralph A. Wooster, *Texas and Texans* (Austin: Steck-Vaughn, 1986); T. R. Fehrenbach, *Lone Star: A History of Texas and the Texans* (New York: Macmillan, 1968).

56. Alwyn Barr, *Black Texans: A History of Negroes in Texas, 1528–1971* (Austin: Jenkins, 1973); James M. Smallwood, *The Struggle Upward: Blacks in Texas* (Boston: American, 1983). See also the *Texas African American History Journal,* which will publish the papers presented at annual conferences, beginning in 1990, on Afro-American history in Texas, sponsored by the Museum of African-American Life and Culture in Dallas.

57. Matagorda County Historical Commission, *Historic Matagorda County* (Houston: D. Armstrong, 1986); Leon County Historical Book Survey Committee, *History of Leon County, Texas* (Dallas: Curtis Media, 1986).

county histories of blacks have appeared.[58] Yet this realm of historical writing remains in need of what C. Vann Woodward called "an infusion of 'soul.'"[59]

---

58. Waller County Historical Survey Committee, *A History of Waller County, Texas* (Waco: Texian, 1973); James M. Smallwood, *A Century of Achievement: Blacks in Cooke County, Texas* (Gainesville, Tex.: Gainesville American Revolution Bicentennial Committee, 1975); Doris Hollis Pemberton, *Juneteenth at Comanche Crossing* (Austin: Eakin, 1983).

59. C. Vann Woodward, "Clio With Soul," *JAH* 56 (June, 1969): 16.

⫸ Texas Women:
History at the Edges
Fane Downs

Texas women have been integral to the economic, social, cultural, and political history of the state. Yet historians, slow to recognize and incorporate women, have largely relegated women to the edges of historical study. This essay will explore the reasons why Texas women's history remains at the edges, suggest lines of inquiry from southern and western history, and describe recent scholarship and areas for further research and analysis.

The historiography of Texas women suffers from a double burden: it concerns Texas and it concerns women. This absurdly obvious comment is nevertheless serious. The Texas public (and the rest of the world, for that matter) drinks deeply of the image of the masculine, self-reliant, individualistic, larger-than-life hero in cowboy boots making a million dollars (sometimes at the expense of effete easterners), and Texas historians have been affected by the myth. The literary creation of the Texas myth is deeply rooted in Texas popular culture and will never be exterminated. Indeed, Necah Furman entitled her essay in *The Texas Heritage* "Texas Women vs. the Texas Myth."[1] The myth has served to obscure the contributions of all Texans save Anglo males. That women's history as a topic for serious study is a relatively recent phenomenon reflects the power of the myth in shaping what historians think are important topics for study. The myth also encourages an individualistic approach to the history of Texas women. That is, historians treat individual Texas women rather than women in groups, although this tendency has diminished in recent years. Academic history is largely free of the crasser distortions of the

1. Necah S. Furman, "Texas Woman vs. the Texas Myth," in *The Texas Heritage,* ed. Ben Proctor and Archie McDonald (St. Louis: Forum, 1980), pp. 167–84.

myth, but it might have exercised a subtle pressure away from dealing with Texas as a historical entity because scholars do not want to be accused of Texas exceptionalism.

There is another, related difficulty with Texas women's history. Historians are urged not to be provincial; that is, they should cover Texas as a part of a larger arena — the South, the frontier, or twentieth-century urban history. Yet Texas is perhaps sufficiently different from all other states that a distinctive or particular Texas historiography is justified. The perennial intellectual exercise, of which a former president of Texas A&M University has written eloquently, concerns the question of whether Texas is southern or western.[2] These surveys usually conclude that Texas is indeed both southern and western. Texas historiography should reflect that analysis. Anne Firor Scott, in an address to the *Handbook of Texas* conference on women's history, noted, "Texas is not just another southern or western state, but a unique phenomenon: unique because of its size, the complexity and variety of the environment, and the complexity of its history."[3] Lay historians have produced much of Texas women's history and have made little effort to place it in a larger context. Academic historians, on the other hand, approach Texas history either as southern or western history. Can scholars incorporate *both?* Perhaps. This essay will suggest some lines of inquiry from both southern and western women's history that may be productive for Texas women's history.

The difficulty of Texas women's history as *women's* history is that women have been subject to prescriptive and literary interpretations that incorporate the "Cult of True Womanhood" and other literary motifs. Other interpretations apply Turnerian categories and analyze the frontier as a liberating place for women and women as the tamers of the West. While these are legitimate and useful conceptual frameworks, they may have diverted our attention from other promising ones.

Probably one of the most influential works of women's history is Barbara Welter's 1966 article, "The Cult of True Womanhood," in which she analyzed prescriptive literature about women in the first half of

2. Frank Vandiver, *The Southwest: South or West?* (College Station: Texas A&M University Press, 1975). Vandiver's analysis and description are centered on male experiences.

3. Anne Firor Scott, "Address" (paper presented at meeting of Texas State Historical Association conference on women's history for *The Handbook of Texas*, Oct. 25, 1985), p. 1.

the nineteenth century.[4] In countless articles and books historians have
applied her descriptions of the ideal woman to historical women, with
the general result, of course, that actual women did not meet the ex-
acting criteria of piety, submissiveness, domesticity, and purity. The
further one gets from the early nineteenth-century urban middle class,
and the closer one gets to the frontier, where life was more difficult
and precarious, the less likely women were to be "true women." Then
historians asked whether women were affected positively or negatively
by their comparison to the Cult of True Womanhood. Ann Patton
Malone used the Cult of True Womanhood paradigm and concluded
that the experience of the Texas frontier was very difficult for the first
generation of Anglo women who settled there. This useful and seminal work is a pioneering attempt to deal with Texas women's history
in a cross-cultural perspective, and her treatment of Anglo-American
women is rooted in the prescriptive schema. Harriette Andreadis made
a careful study of some forty manuscript diaries of Texas women and
observed: "Taken together, these personal accounts describe women
who often feel themselves isolated and find their lives monotonous,
who live vicariously through husbands and children, who suffer from
feelings of inadequacy, who take comfort in religion and religious activities, and who voice discomfort with the disparity between their public and private selves." Andreadis believes that Texas women were
"deeply affected" by the paradigm of the Cult of True Womanhood.[5]

Other literary images of western women are common. There are
a number of variations, but Sandra Myres's categories are as useful
as any: the tragic, helpless heroine; the exploited drudge; the sturdy
helpmate; and the bad woman. These stereotypical images emerged
from literature about the West and have provided models for women's
experiences in the West. And like the Cult of True Womanhood, the
reality rarely fit the images exactly. Myres argues that both male and
female historians have perpetuated mythic and stereotypical images

4. Barbara Welter, "The Cult of True Womanhood: 1820–1860," *American Quar-
terly* 18 (summer, 1966): 151–74.
5. Ann Patton Malone, *Women on the Texas Frontier: A Cross-Cultural Perspective,*
Southwestern Studies no. 70 (El Paso: Texas Western Press, 1983); Harriette Andreadis,
"True Womanhood Revisited: Women's Private Writing in Nineteenth-Century Texas,"
Journal of the Southwest 31 (summer, 1989): 179–204, quotations from pp. 184, 203. Julie
Roy Jeffrey uses the Cult of True Womanhood prescription as an analytic tool in
Frontier Women: The Trans-Mississippi West, 1840–1880 (New York: Hill and Wang, 1979).

of Texas women, including Walter Prescott Webb, Anna J. H. Penny-
backer, and Annie Doom Pickrell.[6] Evelyn Carrington's *Women in Early
Texas* does not advance women's biography to any great extent. Neither
does Francis Edward Abernethy, editor of *Legendary Ladies of Texas:* "a
book about Texas women whose deeds have so struck the public imagination that they have become archetypes, representing the virtues and
values that people have found interesting and admirable, characteristics that have survival value."[7] One has to admire, though, a book that
covers María de Agreda, the Lady in Blue, and the Dallas Cowboy
Cheerleaders! Myres argues that some historians, in attempting to
banish the old stereotypes, have created new ones, emphasizing women's
oppression on the frontier.[8]

A third common interpretive motif may be classified as Turnerian
in that it tries to determine the extent to which the frontier was a
liberating environment for women. Sandra Myres's *Westering Women,*
intended to be a work of frontier history and not women's history,
is a sophisticated example of this genre. She wrote:

> Whether the frontier provided a liberating experience and economic as
> well as social and political opportunities for women is still a question
> of much debate. Certainly there is some evidence that it did not. . . .
> Some historians have concluded, based on women's reminiscences, dia-
> ries, and letters, that the frontier did not offer as many opportunities
> for women as it did for men and that women often failed to take advan-
> tage of the frontier experience as a means of liberating themselves from
> constricting and sexist patterns of behavior. Yet these same reminiscences,
> diaries, and letters also contain evidence to support the contention that
> women on the frontiers modified existing norms and adopted flexible
> attitudes and experimental behavior patterns. . . . What has perhaps
> confused the various interpretations of woman's place and the westering

6. Sandra L. Myres, *Westering Women and the Frontier Experience, 1800–1915* (Albuquerque: University of New Mexico Press, 1982), pp. 1–11. See also Sandra L.
Myres, "Cowboys and Southern Belles," in *Texas Myths,* ed. Robert F. O'Connor (College Station: Texas A&M University Press, 1986), pp. 122–38.

7. Evelyn Carrington, ed., *Women in Early Texas* (Austin: Jenkins, 1975); Francis
Edward Abernethy, ed., *Legendary Ladies of Texas,* Publications of the Texas Folklore
Society no. 43 (Dallas: E-Heart Press, 1981), quotation from p. xi.

8. See John Mack Faragher, *Women and Men on the Overland Trail* (New Haven,
Conn.: Yale University Press, 1979); Glenda Riley, "Frontier Women," in *American
Frontier and Western Issues: A Historiographical Review,* ed. Roger Nicholds (New York
and London: Greenwood, 1986), p. 180; Myres, *Westering Women,* p. 9.

experience is that the *reality* of women's lives changed dramatically as a result of adaptation to frontier conditions while the public *image* remained relatively static.[9]

Just as the rest of western frontier history has been largely emancipated from Turner, western women's history is moving into new areas in which this question of the frontier as a liberating place is no longer dominant, thus freeing historians to pursue other relevant questions. Another theme in western women's history is that of women as civilizers. Women tamed the rough-and-tumble male world of the West by bringing in culture (pianos and books, for example), founding schools and churches, and generally serving as the builders and shapers of communities. Texas women frequently receive a great deal of credit for civilizing Texas. One of the major themes of a 1981 exhibit entitled "Texas Women: A Celebration of History" is "We build": "Texas women built the community life for hundreds of towns and cities. By creating, enhancing, and preserving institutions, buildings, and traditions, women made life worth living for millions of Texans." In addition to building cities, homes, churches, schools, museums, and so forth along with Texas men, Texas women also "built a 'community life.' . . . They established a civic spirit that promoted the ideal of service. . . . Texas women builders were different from men. They were more concerned with meeting the needs of people than with bricks and mortar." Treating women as community builders allows, even encourages, the inclusion of black and Hispanic women.[10]

The frontier historian John Mack Faragher, in calling for a new interpretive framework for rural women's history, wrote:

> The distinction between "civilizer" and "helpmate" interpretations operates within the polarities of opposing stereotypes. The traditional views

9. Myres, *Westering Women,* p. 269 (italics added).

10. Mary Beth Rogers, *Texas Women: A Celebration of History* (Austin: Texas Foundation for Women's Resources, 1981), p. 14. See for example, Martha Cotera, *Diosa y Hembra: The History and Heritage of Chicanas in the U.S.* (Austin: Information Systems Development, 1976); Olga DeLeon, *Outstanding American Women of Mexican Descent* (Austin: University of Texas, Center for Public School Ethnic Studies, 1973); Ann Fears Crawford and Crystal Sasse Ragsdale, *Women in Texas: Their Lives, Their Experiences, Their Accomplishments* (Burnet, Tex.: Eakin, 1982); Myres, *Westering Women;* Mary Beth Rogers et al., *We Can Fly: Stories of Katherine Stinson and Other Gutsy Texas Women* (Austin: Texas Foundation for Women's Resources, 1983).

do not offer ways of seeing that will help to write a new historical narrative in which men and women are equally subject to the flow of events. We are reduced to arguing the pros and cons of certain stereotypes, rarely penetrating beneath surface generalizations to the substance of relations. Indeed, as sexual ideology, the notion of women as "civilizers" or wives as "helpmates" functions precisely to deflect attention from relationships between real men and women onto the well-thought-out defenses of the established cultural order. The ideologies themselves need to be historically analyzed, and for this we need a way of breaking away from their powerful frame of reference.[11]

Texas women's history, then, reflects the influence of the Texas myth, prescriptive literature bout women, literary images of women, and traditional frontier interpretations. Despite these factors historians of Texas women have made significant contributions.

Yet Texas women's historians—as well as southern women's historians—have produced fewer works than American historians generally. In their article in *Interpreting Southern History,* Jacquelyn Hall and Anne Scott observed, "In little more than a decade, the effort to determine what women were doing has led to important work in American history, inventive in conceptualization and careful in documentation. . . . A comparatively small segment of this growing body of work deals with southern women."[12] Among the dozens of works on the South that Hall and Scott have discussed or cited there are about ten references to Texas, which suggests that Texas women's history is marginal.

Several studies in southern history may serve as promising models for Texas studies. New works in community history offer possibilities. In a pioneering study Suzanne Lebsock, making sophisticated use of local sources, described a women's culture in one community as more complex than had been imagined. A different community study, *Like a Family: The Making of a Southern Cotton Mill World,* grew out of the Southern Oral History Project at the University of North Carolina at Chapel Hill. While this is not exclusively a work of wom-

11. John Mack Faragher, "History from the Inside-Out: Writing the History of Women in Rural America," *American Quarterly* 33 (winter, 1981): 541–42.

12. Jacquelyn Dowd Hall and Anne Scott, "Women in the South," in *Interpreting Southern History: Historiographical Essays in Honor of Sanford W. Higginbotham,* ed. John B. Boles and Evelyn Thomas Nolen (Baton Rouge: Louisiana State University Press, 1987), p. 458.

en's history, it is nevertheless gender conscious. Further, the authors avoided questions of southern distinctiveness, which have dominated regional history (like similar questions that lurk in Texas history), and asked not *whether*, but *how*. Because it is based on oral sources and because the authors let the narrators, not their own presuppositions, drive the story, the history revealed is quite rich and full. In focus and method this work offers a useful model for studies of various Texas phenomena. The collaborative style of authorship likewise has much to commend it. Another recent community study by Robert Kenzer used a wide variety of local sources to describe a southern rural neighborhood over time.[13]

In addition to community studies, other works suggest promising directions for Texas study. Jean Friedman's *Enclosed Garden* tests the thesis in women's history that modernization was the major force in the development of a woman's culture. Friedman argues that this was not the case in the South because of the power of the evangelical community. Using a "multimethodological approach," she examined southern women's identity, investigating both white and black kinship and religious dynamics. While there are no Texas studies quite like this, there are pioneering works in both religion and reform, which are described below. Another exemplary work of southern history deals with the Texas suffragist Jessie Daniel Ames, who became the prime mover in the Association of Southern Women for the Prevention of Lynching. This work is neither strictly biography, social, nor political history, but all three. Hall asked questions of her sources that required that she probe beneath the public records into the lives and motivations of Ames and the other leaders and inquire about the influence on them of southern sexual and racial mythology.[14]

Most Texas women's history is frontier history, if it is anything,

13. Suzanne Lebsock, *The Free Women of Petersburg: Status and Culture in a Southern Town, 1794–1860* (New York and London: W. W. Norton, 1984); Jacquelyn Dowd Hall et al., *Like a Family: The Making of a Southern Cotton Mill World* (Chapel Hill: University of North Carolina Press, 1987); Robert Kenzer, *Kinship and Neighborhood in a Southern Community, Orange County, North Carolina, 1849–1881* (Knoxville: University of Tennessee Press, 1988).

14. Jean E. Friedman, *The Enclosed Garden: Women and Community in the Evangelical South, 1870–1900* (Chapel Hill: University of North Carolina Press, 1985); Jacquelyn Dowd Hall, *Revolt against Chivalry: Jessie Daniel Ames and the Campaign of the Southern Women for the Prevention of Lynching* (New York: Columbia University Press, 1979).

and is therefore more western than southern. Western history is a useful perspective in that it will accommodate Indian and Hispanic women as well as Anglos, although it does not accommodate blacks so well. Historians of western women are moving beyond the traditional questions I mentioned above: Was the frontier a liberating place for women? Were the prescriptive roles of the Cult of True Womanhood applicable in the West? Western women's history should be inclusive, comprehensive, and freed from masculine images, taking into account the variables of ethnicity, class, regional economy, period of settlement, family status, and life cycles. Susan Armitage calls for "a history of waves of settlement beginning, of course, with the first settlers (the American Indians) tied together by a focus on the family experience of adaptation. This would provide a new unifying principle, one in which we could look at all of western history." She believes that by focusing on the daily and ordinary, historians will be freed of the female literary stereotypes and the male myths of adventure, violence, and individualism. Likewise, Elizabeth Jameson suggests that the family is a promising conceptual framework.[15]

Joan Jensen and Darlis Miller call for a multicultural approach to western women's history that will allow for new perspectives on social and political history. They, like southern historians, encourage interdisciplinary efforts—incorporating the use of anthropology and sociology. The same two historians edited *New Mexico Women: Intercultural Perspectives,* an anthology of essays, which could and should be replicated in Texas.[16] Sandra Myres suggests that historians work from a new set of questions, for example: Were the experiences of Spanish-Mexican and French frontier women significantly different from those of women on the predominantly Anglo-American frontiers? Did the frontier provide opportunities for women as well as men? If so, did women take advantage of such opportunities to the fullest possible ex-

15. Susan Armitage and Elizabeth Jameson, eds., *The Women's West* (Norman: University of Oklahoma Press, 1987), pp. 4–5; Susan Armitage, "Through Women's Eyes: A New View of the West," in Armitage and Jameson, *The Women's West,* pp. 15–17; Elizabeth Jameson, "Women as Workers, Women as Civilizers: True Womanhood in the American West," in Armitage and Jameson, *The Women's West,* pp. 159–61.

16. Joan Jensen and Darlis Miller, "The Gentle Tamers Revisited: New Approaches to the History of Women in the American West," *Pacific Historical Review* 2 (May, 1980): 212–13; Joan Jensen and Darlis Miller, eds., *New Mexico Women: Intercultural Perspectives* (Albuquerque: University of New Mexico Press, 1986).

tent? Principally, Myres hopes that research will focus on the reality of women's lives so that the stereotypes will be corrected. Glenda Riley astutely observed, "In not knowing [definitive answers], however, scholars of frontier women have perhaps discovered some larger truths. One of these is certainly that the historical heritage of the women is rich and complex, not to be easily comprehended."[17]

An important recent contribution to southwestern women's history is Sarah Deutsch's *No Separate Refuge*, a study of Hispanic survival strategies in the face of Anglo penetration and domination in northern New Mexico and southern Colorado. Deutsch takes seriously women's functions and responsibilities and analyzes them. She suggests that one can understand the interaction between Anglos and Hispanics only by considering class, culture, and gender in the study of relationships. She demonstrates that Hispanic village economy and cultural autonomy survived as long as women could remain in the villages while men had seasonal migrant jobs. Within the villages the women exercised significant authority. When Hispanics moved to the mining or beet towns of Colorado, women lost authority and became increasingly marginal. "No separate refuge" occurred when the villages could no longer provide it. While Texas does not have congruent community contexts, this work can serve as a paradigm of intercultural and cross-cultural history—community history that takes seriously women's functions in community survival.[18] Certainly one wonders whether this pattern occurred as Mexicans immigrated to Texas.

A final reference to western women's history is *The Women's West Teaching Guide*, which is designed to supplement American public school history texts. There are units on stereotypes and diversity, women's roles, and the influence of women on the West and vice versa; each includes primary material. This work is important because if women's history is ever to move away from the margins, the task must begin in the public schools. Teachers would use a comparable work for seventh-grade Texas history.[19]

17. Sandra Myres, "Women in the West," *Historians and the American West*, ed. Michael Malone (Lincoln and London: University of Nebraska Press, 1983), p. 379; Glenda Riley, "Frontier Women," p. 191.

18. Sarah Deutsch, *No Separate Refuge: Culture, Class, Gender on an Anglo-Hispanic Frontier in the American Southwest, 1880–1940* (New York: Oxford University Press, 1988).

19. Martha Boethel, *The Women's West Teaching Guide: Women's Lives in the Nineteenth-Century American West*, ed. Melissa Hield (Sun Valley, Idaho: Coalition for

The foregoing examples from southern and western women's history suggest lines of research that would move Texas women's history in new directions. In a survey of Texas women's historical writing Ann Patton Malone observed that scholars have become more critical and analytical, moving well beyond early "celebratory" collections that uncritically treated Anglo-American women. An example of this celebratory genre is Annie Doom Pickrell's *Pioneer Women of Texas*. Not surprisingly, the largest volume of Texas women's history consists of biographies and autobiographies of frontier women, reflecting a continuing interest in that Texas experience. With the awakening consciousness of the women's movement, writers produced a wide variety of works that sought to recover women's participation in politics, religion, and community life. In several collections authors described the lives of women who could serve as role models and heroines; e.g., Ann Fears Crawford and Crystal Sasse Ragsdale, *Women in Texas: Their Lives, Their Experiences, Their Accomplishments;* Mary D. Ferrell and Elizabeth Silverthorne, *First Ladies of Texas: The First One Hundred Years, 1836–1936;* and Mary Beth Rogers et al., *We Can Fly: Stories of Katherine Stinson and Other Gutsy Women.* In Malone's opinion, "scholarship since 1981 on women in Texas has been a curious mixture of traditional writings and a few works employing methodologies associated with social history, continuing a trend begun in the 1970s. Thus far in the 1980s writing on the history of Texas women has been relatively sparse compared to that produced in the previous decade."[20]

Recent work in Texas women's history, although "relatively sparse," reveals a variety of topics and approaches. First, one should be aware that bibliographic sources are increasingly available. The pioneering work in this regard is the *Texas Women's History Project Bibliography* edited by Ruthe Winegarten. Another significant work to emerge from the

Western Women's History and the Sun Valley Center for the Arts and Humanities, 1985).

20. Annie Doom Pickrell, *Pioneer Women of Texas* (Austin, Tex.: Steck, 1929); Ann Fears Crawford and Crystal Sasse Ragsdale, *Women in Texas: Their Lives, Their Experiences, Their Accomplishments* (Burnet, Tex.: Eakin, 1982); Mary D. Ferrell and Elizabeth Silverthorne, *First Ladies of Texas: The First One Hundred Years, 1836–1936* (Belton, Tex.: Stillhouse Hollow, 1976); Rogers et al., *We Can Fly;* Ann Patton Malone, "Women in Texas History," *A Guide to the History of Texas,* ed. Light T. Cummins and Alvin R. Bailey, Jr. (New York: Greenwood, 1988), pp. 123–36, quotation from p. 135. Malone's extensive citations make this essay valuable for students of Texas women.

"Texas Women: A Celebration of History" exhibit is the *Finders' Guide to the Texas Women: A Celebration of History Exhibit Archives,* also edited by Winegarten and published by the library at Texas Woman's University, the permanent home of the exhibit.[21] More general bibliographic collections are useful as well; for example, the Center for Research on Women at Memphis State University has published two bibliographies that will be useful as more works on Texas women are published.[22]

A search of the literature and queries of persons working in Texas women's history around the state has revealed few works about black women. Ann Malone's *Women on the Texas Frontier* includes an excellent section on black women. Others include *The Bell Rings at Four: A Black Teacher's Chronicle of Change,* by Dorothy Robinson, and "The Discovery of Being Black: A Recollection," by Ada de Blanc Simond. Ruthe Winegarten's *I Am Annie Mae: The Personal Story of a Black Texas Woman* is an outstanding example of oral history.[23]

Works on Hispanic women are a good bit more common, reflecting an intense interest in the 1970s and perhaps a revival today. Notable works are Martha Cotera, *Diosa y Hembra: The History and Heritage of Chicanas in the United States,* a general history; Jane Dysart, "Mexican Women in San Antonio, 1830–1860: The Assimilation Process," an able study of cross-cultural marriages that suggests other directions for research; Mario T. García, *Desert Immigrants: The Mexicans*

21. Ruthe Winegarten, ed., *Texas Women's History Project Bibliography* (Austin: Texas Foundation for Women's Resources, 1980); Ruthe Winegarten, ed., *Finder's Guide to the Texas Women: A Celebration of History Exhibit Archives* (Denton: Library of Texas Woman's University). Another product of the "Texas Women: A Celebration of History" exhibit is Ruthe Winegarten, *Texas Women: A Pictorial History from Indians to Astronauts* (Austin: Eakin, 1986).

22. Center for Research on Women, Memphis State University, *Bibliography on Southern Women* and *Selected Bibliography of Social Science Readings on Women of Color in the United States* (Memphis, Tenn.: Center for Research on Women, Memphis State University, 1988). Both are frequently updated and available for a reasonable fee. Neither includes more than seven entries on Texas women in recent editions. See also Cynthia E. Harrison, ed., *Women in American History: A Bibliography,* 2 vols. (Santa Barbara, Calif.: Clio Press, 1985).

23. Malone, *Women on the Texas Frontier;* Dorothy Robinson, *The Bell Rings at Four: A Black Teacher's Chronicle of Change* (Austin: Madrono Press, 1978); Ada de Blanc Simond, "The Discovery of Being Black: A Recollection," *Southwestern Historical Quarterly* (*SHQ*) 76 (Apr., 1973): 440–47; Ruthe Winegarten, ed., *I Am Annie Mae: The Personal Story of a Black Texas Woman* (Austin: Rosegarden, 1983).

of El Paso, 1880–1920, which deals with women particularly in the area of work and employment; García's "The Chicana in American History: The Mexican Women of El Paso, 1880–1920," which focuses on women as the guardians of Mexican cultural traditions and speculates about the relatively rarity of married women working outside the home; Richard Griswold del Castillo, *La Familia: Chicano Families in the Urban Southwest, 1848 to the Present,* which includes San Antonio as one of the four cities studied; Vicki L. Ruiz, "By the Day or the Week: Mexicana Domestic Workers in El Paso," which describes through oral history this category of women workers, who suffered from low wages and discrimination; and Cynthia Orozco's forthcoming dissertation on women in the LULAC organization, in which she will analyze organizational strategies, families, and class.[24]

Native American women have yet to be the subject of extensive study, although Ann Malone included them in her *Women on the Texas Frontier.* Sandra Myres's material on women's images of Indians is suggestive for specific Texas study.[25]

There is a critical need for research and writing on black and Native American women's topics, as well as for additional studies of Hispanic women. Relations among groups, perceptions by one group of the others, and political and social activities are only three lines of inquiry. These fields are virtually wide open.

Important cross-cultural and comparative works by Julia Kirk Blackwelder include "Women in the Work Force: Atlanta, New Orleans, and San Antonio, 1930 to 1940," and *Women of the Depression: Caste and*

24. Martha Cotera, *Diosa y Hembra: The History and Heritage of Chicanas in the United States* (Austin: Information Systems Development, 1976); Jane Dysart, "Mexican Women in San Antonio, 1830–1860: The Assimilation Process," *Western Historical Quarterly* 7 (Oct., 1976): 365–75; Mario T. García, *Desert Immigrants: The Mexicans of El Paso, 1880– 1920* (New Haven, Conn.: Yale University Press, 1981); Mario T. García, "The Chicana in American History: The Mexican Women of El Paso, 1880–1920: A Case Study," *Pacific Historical Review* 49 (May, 1980): 315–37; Richard Griswold del Castillo, *La Familia: Chicano Families in the Urban Southwest, 1848 to the Present* (Notre Dame, Ind.: University of Notre Dame Press, 1984); Vicki L. Ruiz, "By the Day or the Week: Mexicana Domestic Workers in El Paso," in *Women on the U.S.-Mexican Border: Responses to Change,* ed. Vicki L. Ruiz and Susan Tiano (Boston: Allen and Unwin, 1987), pp. 61–76; Cynthia Orozco to Fane Downs, Aug. 4, 1988.

25. Malone, *Women on the Texas Frontier;* Myres, "'Land of Savagery/Land of Promise': Women's Views of Indians," in Myres, *Westering Women,* pp. 37–71.

Culture in San Antonio, 1929–1939. Another work concerning San Antonio Hispanic women is Richard Croxdale, "The 1938 San Antonio Pecan Shellers Strike," which is based on oral history sources. Melissa Hield's article in that same publication investigates the ILGWU during 1933–50. I have attempted to describe women's work over time in "Texas Women at Work."[26] I did not set out to write an essay on Texas women's economic history, but used work as an experience common to all women. Topics looking for historians in women's economic history are almost endless: women in the professions, further work on women labor activists and women as union members, women's household work in the nineteenth and twentieth centuries, and rural women's work and their participation in agricultural organizations. The changing functions of women in families as women have entered the paid work force in the last four decades badly need historical analysis.

Recent work on Texas politics reveals an interest in women's suffrage. A. Elizabeth Taylor's pioneering work on the Texas suffrage campaigns, first published in the *Journal of Southern History* in 1951, has been reprinted along with a collection of significant documents in *Citizens at Last: The Woman Suffrage Movement in Texas.* A companion piece is *A Texas Suffragist: Diaries and Writings of Jane Y. McCallum,* edited by Janet G. Humphrey. An exhaustive treatment of the political activities of women in the first years after suffrage is "Petticoat Politics: Political Activism among Texas Women in the 1920s," by Emma Louise Moyer Jackson. Judith McArthur's forthcoming dissertation deals with women and reform during the Progressive era. She is investigating the motives of the white middle-class women reformers and testing Anne Scott's hypothesis that these women became politically active according to a predictable progression that began in church and home

26. Julia Kirk Blackwelder, "Women in the Work Force: Atlanta, New Orleans, and San Antonio, 1930 to 1940," *Journal of Urban History* 4 (May, 1978): 331–58; Julia Kirk Blackwelder, *Women of the Depression: Caste and Culture in San Antonio, 1929–1939* (College Station: Texas A&M University Press, 1984); Richard Croxdale, "The 1938 San Antonio Pecan Shellers Strike," in *Women in the Texas Workforce: Yesterday and Today,* ed. Richard Croxdale and Melissa Hield (Austin: People's History of Texas, 1979), pp. 24–34; Melissa Hield, "'Union-Minded': Women in the Texas ILGWU, 1933–1950," in Croxdale and Hield, *Women in the Texas Workforce,* pp. 1–23; Fane Downs, "Texas Women at Work," in *Texas: A Sesquicentennial Celebration,* ed. Donald Whisenhunt (Austin: Eakin Press, 1984), pp. 309–26.

FANE DOWNS

mission work, moved on to temperance work, and culminated in suffrage agitation.[27]

An article that deals with more recent political events, taking into account both southern and western political cultures in attempting to explain Texas women's political behavior, is Janet K. Boles's "The Texas Woman in Politics: Role Model or Mirage?" in which she concludes that Texas women's relatively low political participation stems from their southern heritage. Martha Swain's useful essay "The Public Role of Southern Women" includes Texas women in a survey of the public role of southern women. One of the most prominent women in Texas politics, Minnie Fisher Cunningham, is the subject of a forthcoming book-length biography by Trish Cunningham. "Minnie Fish" was active in Texas politics for about six decades; therefore, her biography should provide useful new insights and information.[28] Studies of conservative antisuffrage and anti-ERA women need to be expanded and investigations conducted about women's political activism at the local level.[29]

Women's cultural history is gaining increasing attention. A new biography of Elisabet Ney by Emily Cutrer treats that most famous of Texas women artists in the artistic and social environment in which she worked. Ney's career provides a "case study of the interaction between the European intellectual and the American frontier." Cutrer also illuminates the importance of individual women and women's organizations in the cultural history of the state.[30]

27. Ruthe Winegarten and Judith N. McArthur, eds., *Citizens at Last: The Woman Suffrage Movement in Texas* (Austin: Ellen C. Temple, 1987); Janet G. Humphrey, *A Texas Suffragist: Diaries and Writings of Jane Y. McCallum* (Austin: Ellen C. Temple, 1988); Emma Louise Moyer Jackson, "Petticoat Politics: Political Activism among Texas Women in the 1920s," Ph.D. diss., University of Texas, Austin, 1980; Judith McArthur, Abstract, "Women and Reform in Texas During the Progressive Era," diss. in progress.

28. Janet K. Boles, "The Texas Woman in Politics: Role Model or Mirage?" *Social Science Journal* 21 (Jan., 1984); Martha Swain, "The Public Role of Southern Women," in *Sex, Race, and the Role of Women in the South* ed. Jo Anne V. Hawks and Shelia L. Skemp (Jackson: University of Mississippi Press, 1983); Trish Cunningham to Fane Downs, Sept. 11, 1988. See also John Carroll Eudy, "The Vote and Lone Star Women: Minnie Fisher Cunningham and the East Texas Suffrage Association," *East Texas Historical Journal* 14 (fall, 1976).

29. For example, David W. Brady and Kent L. Tudin, "Ladies in Pink: Religion and Ideology in the Anti-ERA Movement," *Social Science Quarterly* 56 (Mar., 1976): 564–75.

30. Emily Cutrer, *The Art of the Woman: The Life and Work of Elisabet Ney* (Lincoln: University of Nebraska Press, 1988), quotation from p. xii.

Two recent publications by SMU Press expand our knowledge of women's cultural history. *Margo: The Life and Theatre of Margo Jones,* by Helen Sheehy, is the first published biography of this theater pioneer. Suzanne Comer has edited *Common Bonds: Stories by and about Modern Texas Women,* which includes selections of both well-known and lesser-known writers. Lou Rodenberger and Sylvia Grider are editing a literary history of Texas women writers. Grider's biography of Dorothy Scarborough will be a helpful addition to our knowledge of that author, who did a great deal to perpetuate the myth of the helpless, despairing woman on the frontier in her 1925 novel of the 1880s, *The Wind.* Fannie Elizabeth Ratchford, longtime rare books librarian at the University of Texas at Austin, is the subject of a forthcoming biography by Margaret A. Cox. Ratchford is a good example of a woman overlooked; most of the published material about her deals with her eccentricities, and none provides a critical assessment of either her publications or her librarianship.[31]

Topics in cultural history that need further investigation are women philanthropists, women in historical preservation, and women teachers of drama, music, and art. Women and Texas folk art and material culture is a rich and timely topic.[32]

Annie Webb Blanton, educator and first statewide-elected female official, is the subject of scholarly scrutiny by Debbie Cottrell. Lay historian Lel Purcell Hawkins is working on a biography of Mrs. R. K. Red, a pioneer teacher. While there have been a number of theses on early day school systems, there has been little critical work done

31. Helen Sheehy, *Margo: The Life and Theatre of Margo Jones* (Dallas: Southern Methodist University Press, 1990); Suzanne Comer, ed., *Common Bonds: Stories by and about Modern Texas Women* (Dallas: Southern Methodist University Press, 1990); Lou Rodenberger and Sylvia Grider to Fane Downs, Apr. 4, 1989; Margaret A. Cox to Fane Downs, Sept. 2, 1988. Other works on librarians include Mary Brown McSwain, "Julia Bedford Ideson, Houston Librarian, 1880–1945," M.A. thesis, University of Texas, Austin, 1966; Claudia Loftiss Pettigrew, "Louise Franklin: The Education of a Texas Librarian," M.A. thesis, University of Texas, 1967; Tom Lea, *Maud Durlin Sullivan, 1872–1944, Pioneer Southwestern Librarian* (El Paso: Carl Hertzog, 1962).

32. Louise Kosches Iscoe, *Ima Hogg: First Lady of Texas, Reminiscences and Recollections of Family and Friends* (Austin: Hogg Foundation for Mental Health, 1976); Jack C. Butterfield, *Clara Driscoll Rescued the Alamo: A Brief Biography* (Austin: Daughters of the Republic of Texas, 1961); Cecilia Steinfeldt, *Early Texas Furniture and Decorative Arts* (San Antonio: Trinity University Press, 1973); Suzanne Yabsley, *Texas Quilts, Texas Women* (College Station: Texas A&M University Press, 1984).

on the history of education in Texas or on most of the state's educators. There do not appear to be works in progress on the Texas State Teachers Association or other statewide teachers' organizations; certainly these organizations would be fruitful areas of inquiry as examples of women's organizational behavior and political action. An interesting and important topic in education is women on college and university faculties. The entire area of the content, form, and purpose of schooling for girls and young women is virtually untouched.[33]

Pioneer women continue to be a source of fascination for historians. My "'Tryels and Trubbles': Women in Early Nineteenth-Century Texas" attempted to survey women's experiences of immigration, home building, education, religion, and the Texas Revolution. Florence Gould and Patricia Pando are currently working on a short book on Texas women homesteaders based on the records of the General Land Office. Sylvia Ann Grider has undertaken a book entitled *Everyday Life on a Frontier Homestead*. A curious recent publication is *This I Can Leave You: A Woman's Days on the Pitchfork Ranch*, by Mamie Sypert Burns, a collection of romanticized autobiographical stories of twentieth-century life on a ranch. Another recent ranch life biography is Ada Morehead Holland, *Brush Country Woman*. Mary Maverick's *Memoirs* have been reprinted with a new introduction by Sandra Myres. In her *Turn Your Eyes Toward Texas*, Paula Marks describes the private life of Mary Maverick and the public life of Samuel Maverick. Ella Elgar Bird Dumont's autobiography illuminates life on the late nineteenth- and early twentieth-century West Texas frontier; Emily Cutrer's brief foreword places Dumont's life in the broader context of frontier women's experiences.[34]

33. Debora Lynn Cottrell, "Annie Webb Blanton: Texas Educator and Feminist," M.A. thesis, University of Texas, Austin, 1989; Lel Purcell Hawkins to Fane Downs, Aug. 31, 1988.

34. Fane Downs, "'Tryels and Trubbles': Women in Early Nineteenth-Century Texas," *SHQ* 90 (July, 1986): 35–56; Florence Gould to Fane Downs, Aug. 7, 1988; Sylvia Ann Grider to Fane Downs, Aug. 26, 1988; Sylvia Ann Grider to Fane Downs, July 28, 1989; Mamie Sypert Burns, *This I Can Leave You: A Woman's Days on the Pitchfork Ranch* (College Station: Texas A&M University Press, 1986); Ada Morehead Holland, *Brush Country Woman* (College Station: Texas A&M University Press, 1989); Mary A. Maverick, *Memoirs*, ed. Rena Maverick Green (San Antonio: Alamo Printing, 1921; reprint, with introduction by Sandra L. Myres, Lincoln: University of Nebraska Press, 1989); Paula Mitchell Marks, *Turn Your Eyes toward Texas: Pioneers Sam and Mary Maverick* (College Station: Texas A&M University Press, 1989); Ella Elgar

One of the few recent works in Texas women's legal history is "Concealed Under Petticoats: Married Women's Property and the Laws of Texas, 1840–1913," by Kathleen Elizabeth Lazarou. In this able study Lazarou argues that the development of Texas law governing married women's property rights reflected a national rather than a local and isolated process. In order to protect the family, Texas laws generally limited married women's control of their property which meant that women's property rights were diminished in relation to those that they were granted under Spanish law. Based on formal legal documents, the study concluded that Texas law reflected the affirmation of the traditional family structure and attempts at public solutions to private misfortunes.[35]

Texas women, like their sisters in the rest of the country, shaped the religious life of the state. One of the few recent critical studies of this phenomenon is Patricia S. Martin's "Hidden Work: Baptist Women in Texas, 1880–1920." She argues that conservative, evangelical women have been ill-treated by scholars. She notes that the church's influence on women both fostered and resisted changing women's roles. "In the Baptist tradition," she writes, "democratic church government and individualistic theology provided avenues for women to act independently, yet the denomination's belief in male dominance in the family and the ministry kept women from exercising all the privileges that men were offered." In missionary societies, however, women found an area of activism, yet these organizations—as effective as they were—avoided all controversy over doctrine and politics in order that the male leaders would leave them alone. This thoughtful and thorough study is a model for other denominational or organizational studies of Texas women's religious life and work.[36]

While there are studies of Roman Catholic women, further critical work is needed to chronicle their work in founding and maintaining schools and hospitals and providing social services. Because the Catholic orders frequently established schools for Hispanic children,

Bird Dumont, *Autobiography,* foreword by Emily Cutrer (Austin: University of Texas Press, 1988); Margaret Henson, *Anglo-American Women in Texas, 1820–1850* (Boston: American Press, 1982).

35. Kathleen Elizabeth Lazarou, *Concealed under Petticoats: Married Women's Property and the Laws of Texas, 1840–1913* (New York: Garland, 1986).

36. Patricia S. Martin, "Hidden Work: Baptist Women in Texas, 1880–1920," Ph.D. diss., Rice University, 1982 (quotation from p. 276).

scholars may profitably conduct cross-cultural studies. One hopes that scholars will study women of all religious traditions in Texas, describing and analyzing their roles in their religious culture and community life. The most unusual Texas women's religious organization was the Women's Commonwealth of Belton, Texas, which functioned successfully as an economically self-sufficient community in the late nineteenth century.[37]

Texas women have long been active in various sorts of organizations; a critical study by Megan Seaholm, "From Self-Culture to Civic Responsibility: Women's Clubs in Texas, 1880–1920," is an important addition. Dorothy DeMoss is conducting research in Texas women's organizations in the period after 1920, focusing on the American Association of University Women, the Texas League of Women Voters, the Texas Federation of Women's Clubs, and the Texas division of the National Federation of Business and Professional Women. A very promising study is underway by Elizabeth Turner entitled "Benevolent Ladies, Clubwomen, and Suffragists: Galveston Women's Organizations, 1880–1920." Turner will test whether Galveston women follow the white southern women's pattern of conservative reform. She will look at women's organizations in the context of the entire community and will analyze the origins and composition of the organizations. In her prospectus Turner writes: "Perhaps most important to this dissertation . . . is to adumbrate the evolvement in Galveston of a women's community, an informal alliance of politically and socially active white women who motivated and sustained women's progressive activism. By focusing on this women's community, on the increasingly democratic nature of the three most important female Progressive-era associations, and the urban environment from which they evolved, patterns will begin to emerge that may shape our understanding of the southern women's Progressive movement." The movement of women from the churches through the Women's Christian Temperance Union to YWCAs to women's clubs to suffrage, as described by Anne Scott,

37. Mary Loyola Hegarty, *Serving with Gladness: The Origin and History of the Congregation of the Sisters of Charity of the Incarnate Word, Houston, Texas* (Houston and Milwaukee: Bruce, 1967); Mother Patricia Gunning, *To Texas with Love: A History of the Sisters of the Incarnate Word and Blessed Sacrament* (Austin: Von Boeckmann–Jones, 1971); Jayme A. Sokolow and Mary Ann Lamanna, "Women and Utopia: The Women's Commonwealth of Belton, Texas," *SHQ* 87 (Apr., 1984): 371–93.

is not apparently the pattern of Galveston women.[38] Turner has found that the evangelical churches did not contribute to the Galveston Progressive women's community, but that the informal alliance of active women evolved out of other organizations. This study will not only be a significant contribution to women's "organizational" history, but to religious and urban history as well, and should cause southern scholars to take another look at urban women's organizations in the South. Perhaps Turner's work will occasion similar work in other Texas, western, and southern cities.

While there are important and significant studies underway and while recent publications have pushed back the frontiers of women's history, Texas women's history remains at the edges. In part these are geographical edges: Texas lies at the western edge of the South and the eastern edge of the West. Texas women's history should be conceptualized and written as both southern and western history, but the difficulties involved are obvious. One of the challenges of scholarship on Texas women is that one must know the main lines of interpretation of southern, western, black, Hispanic, and Anglo history (to say nothing of other ethnic groups). Further, one must master the literature, sources, and methodologies of one's field of inquiry. The geographical edges challenge historians to rethink traditional conceptual frameworks, periods, and interpretations.

Perhaps the more serious problem of history at the edges is the marginalization of women's history. A scholarly commitment in Texas colleges and universities to researching and writing women's history does not appear to exist. Part of the difficulty, of course, lies in what historians consider to be appropriate subjects for historical analysis. Thus, there are no full-scale women's studies programs in the state, although a handful of universities offer an undergraduate minor in women's studies. There are not yet scholars of the stature of Anne Firor Scott or Mary Beth Norton. The archival collection at Texas Woman's University is so little known that it was not mentioned in *A Guide to the History of Texas*. While several historical journals have

38. Megan Seaholm, "From Self-Culture to Civic Responsibility: Women's Clubs in Texas, 1880–1920," Ph.D. diss., Rice University, 1988; Dorothy DeMoss to Fane Downs, Aug. 16, 1988; Elizabeth H. Turner, Prospectus, "Benevolent Ladies, Clubwomen, and Suffragists: Galveston Women's Organizations, 1880–1920"; Hall and Scott, "Women in the South," pp. 488–89.

published issues devoted to women's history, *Southwestern Historical Quarterly* has not.[39]

Texas women's history must be conducted within the context of the suffocating Texas macho myth. Although this myth is very much a part of Texas popular culture, there is evidence that women's history is gaining acceptance with the public. The most significant event in this regard was the exhibit "Texas Women: A Celebration of History," which as mentioned earlier, opened in 1981. Not only did the exhibit sum up the state of women's history at the time, it stimulated new work. Further, since it is now housed at Texas Woman's University, it continues to act as a catalyst for increasing awareness of women's history. For example, Texas Women's History Month annually increases in significance and sparks publications, exhibits, and symposia. Lay and professional historians are beginning to form networks in order to keep one another informed on research progress; moreover, a major Texas women's history conference was held in 1990.

Until Texas women's history is "mainstreamed," it will remain at the edges. Historians are not yet accustomed to asking routinely how women's experiences might have differed (or not) from those of men. Gender (or race and class, for that matter) is not ordinarily used as a category of analysis or description. Textbook writers have not yet presented women's history as integral to the history of the state. Integrating women's history will be more natural with an increase in the scholarly production of monographs and primary sources.[40]

There are signs that the academic exile of women's history is ending. The authoritative *Handbook of Texas* will contain a dramatically increased number of entries on Texas women in its reincarnation, to be published in the 1990s.[41] For several years the Texas State Historical Association has jointly sponsored sessions with the Texas Founda-

39. Journals with theme issues on women's history include *The Pacific Historical Review* (1980); *The Journal of the West* (1982); *Montana, the Magazine of Western History* (1982); *New Mexico Historical Review* (1982); *South Dakota History* (1983); *Frontiers* (1984); and *Great Plains Quarterly* (1985). Glenda Riley, "Frontier Women," p. 193.

40. Ramona L. Ford, "'Why Spend Time on Women Grinding Corn?' Mainstreaming Women's History: A Texas Perspective," *Texas Journal of Ideas, History and Culture* II (spring/summer, 1990): 12–15. This issue of the journal contains other articles dealing with women's absence from the historical and literary record.

41. This will replace Walter P. Webb, H. Bailey Carroll, and Eldon S. Branda, eds., *Handbook of Texas*, 3 vols. (Austin: Texas State Historical Association, 1952, 1976).

tion for Women's Resources and included special sessions on women's history at the annual meetings. That this essay appears in this publication suggests that women's history is gaining acceptance. Most significant, however, is the fine work of historians of Texas women noted in this essay. As these committed, dedicated, and competent scholars continue to produce, women's history will no longer remain at the edges, but will arrive at the center of the discipline — where it belongs.

🙡 Spanish Texas

Donald E. Chipman

"Spanish Texas was a remote and dangerous frontier, huge in area, vague in definition, and, to the end, meager in development." Those words, penned by the distinguished cultural geographer D. W. Meinig, are quotable, but they fail to encapsulate the importance of Spanish Texas in shaping the course of the present Lone Star State.[1] The purpose of this essay is to assess significant historiographical trends, propose avenues for future research and publication, and inform readers of ongoing research projects.

The historiography of the Spanish period in Texas history (1519–1821) bears evidence of cyclical patterns. The first general works of Henderson K. Yoakum and Hubert H. Bancroft in the nineteenth century were clearly inadequate, because the documentation on which sound historical studies must rest lay buried in the archives of Spain and Mexico. That circumstance improved dramatically in the early years and decades of the twentieth century. Herbert E. Bolton and his students led the charge into the dusty *legajos* of regional and national archives. The publication of edited and translated documents and of specialized studies helped lay the groundwork for a second attempt at synthesis, begun by Carlos E. Castañeda in the 1930s. Since the completion of his *Our Catholic Heritage in Texas* (1958), additional publications of documents and monographic works have added to the growing body of literature on Spanish Texas. In light of the approaching five hundredth anniversary of Spain in America, a new synthesis of the Spanish experience is appropriate and now in progress.[2]

1. D. W. Meinig, *Imperial Texas: An Interpretive Essay in Cultural Geography* (Austin: University of Texas Press, 1969), p. 23.
2. The projected publication date for Donald E. Chipman's history of Spanish Texas is 1992.

Most cultures see themselves as the centerpiece of historical importance. Indian tribes, for instance, often referred to themselves as "the people," as though there were no others. Similarly, Texans are famous for their "nationalistic" identification with the state. That phenomenon, however, may well have roots that antedate Anglo settlement of Texas in the early nineteenth century. In the colonial era, missionaries, soldiers, and settlers received almost constant reminders that their world was a relatively unimportant and remote part of a great Spanish empire. That very realization may have encouraged the "provincial elites in Texas," as suggested by Gerald E. Poyo and Gilberto M. Hinojosa, to ignore the "Crown's political desires," thereby making them more independent minded. Poyo and Hinojosa further postulate a regional affinity for Spanish Texas that was more attuned to Louisiana, Coahuila, or even the heartland region of New Spain than was the case with other borderland regions such as Florida, New Mexico, or California. They also speculate that future regional studies emphasizing socioeconomic developments may identify "continuities across sovereignties."[3] Still, it seems vitally important that the historiography of Spanish Texas be placed in imperial context. To do otherwise is to write unbalanced and nearsighted Texas history.

Spanish Texas must first be related to historical developments transpiring in colonial Mexico (New Spain). Second, an understanding of Spain's international rivalries and her internal political, religious, and economic circumstances are essential to comprehending events played out in Texas. Third, many of the central actors in Spanish Texas did not appear full blown on the Texas stage, nor did they vanish into obscurity once they left it. Without knowledge of the Spanish empire as a whole, the earlier and later accomplishments of the first "Texans" cannot be placed in proper historical context.

Henderson K. Yoakum wrote the first scholarly history of Texas after the beginning of statehood in 1846. Volume one of his two-part work covered Texas history to the birth of the Republic, but it is especially weak on the period prior to the founding of Stephen F. Austin's colony. More important to Texas was Hubert H. Bancroft and his bulg-

---

3. Gerald E. Poyo and Gilberto M. Hinojosa, "Spanish Texas and Borderlands Historiography in Transition: Implications for United States History," *Journal of American History* 75 (Sept., 1988): 415–16.

ing staff of ghostwriters and researchers who made up "Bancroft's history-factory." In the first of two volumes devoted to the *History of North Mexican States and Texas,* Bancroft focused on the Spanish Southwest, with emphasis on Texas. The book, like the others in Bancroft's works, contains outdated and often inaccurate information, but the real value of Bancroft's research efforts lay in the collection and preservation of materials pertinent to Texas history.[4] Bancroft and his associates also made sure that Texas and the Spanish Southwest were related to the larger picture of Spain in America.

Aside from Yoakum and Bancroft, interest in Texas history during the nineteenth century was demonstrated in the works of Buckingham Smith and Adolph F. Bandelier. Smith first translated into English the *Relation* of Alvar Núñez Cabeza de Vaca. Cabeza de Vaca, arguably a "First Texan," along with Andrés Dorantes de Carranza, his African-born slave Estevanico, and Alonso Castillo Maldonado, are examples of Spaniards whose significant careers began in Texas, but certainly did not end there.[5]

The forerunners of Texas historiography in the early twentieth century were Herbert E. Bolton and his students, especially William E. Dunn and Charles W. Hackett. Bolton developed a consuming interest in the Spanish Southwest during his tenure at the University of Texas (1901–1909), and he remains as one of the most prolific and influential writers on Spanish Texas. In midsummer of 1902, Bolton launched his first excursion into the Archivo General y Pública de la Nación (AGN) in Mexico City. When he returned to Austin in early September, Bolton had copies of primary documents that would launch

4. H. Yoakum, *History of Texas From Its First Settlement in 1685 to Its Annexation to the United States in 1846,* 2 vols. (New York: Redfield, 1855–56); John H. Jenkins, *Basic Texas Books: An Annotated Bibliography of Selected Works for a Research Library,* rev. ed. (Austin: Texas State Historical Association, 1988), pp. 12–13; Hubert H. Bancroft, *History of the North Mexican States and Texas,* 2 vols. (San Francisco: A. L. Bancroft, 1884–89).

5. Buckingham Smith, trans., *The Narrative of Alvar Núñez Cabeza de Vaca* (Washington, D.C.: [George W. Riggs], 1851); Buckingham Smith, trans., *Relation of Alvar Núñez Cabeza de Vaca* ([Albany, N.Y.: J. Munsell for H. C. Murphy], 1871); A. F. Bandelier, *Hemenway Southwestern Archaeological Expedition: Contributions to the History of the Southwestern Portion of the United States* (Cambridge, Mass.: John Wilson and Son, 1890); for later treatment of the Cabeza de Vaca route see Donald E. Chipman, "In Search of Cabeza de Vaca's Route Across Texas: An Historiographical Survey," *Southwestern Historical Quarterly (SHQ)* 91 (Oct., 1987): 132–35.

"a field of his own."[6] In October of that same year, after an enviable — if not record — interlude between the submission of an article manuscript and its publication, Bolton broke ground in the *Quarterly* of the Texas State Historical Association (TSHA) with the first of a two-part piece entitled "Some Materials for Southwestern History in the Archivo General de México." His second scholarly effort, "Tienda de Cuervo's *Ynspección* of Laredo, 1757," focused attention specifically on Texas, and for the next several years Bolton concentrated his publication efforts on Texas topics.[7]

During his Texas years, Bolton helped secure the foundations of the first scholarly journal in the state. In 1904, he and Eugene C. Barker became associate editors of the *Quarterly*. Bolton also journeyed to Mexico each summer after 1902 with a staff of experienced student helpers who painstakingly hand copied documents on Anglo Texas. He, however, concentrated his personal efforts on finding materials pertinent to Spanish Texas. In the best sense Bolton became an archival "bloodhound." The fruits of his "nose" for research resulted in a spate of articles published in the *Quarterly* — one in 1905, three in 1906, one in 1907, two in 1908, etc. In all, Bolton published eighteen separate titles in the *Quarterly* and its successor, the *Southwestern Historical Quarterly* (*SHQ*).[8] His articles are especially valuable for their treatment of the founding of Missions Rosario, Refugio, and Nuestra Señora de la Luz (Orcoquisac), and those on the San Gabriel River. His archival grubbing also turned up a map which pinpointed the exact location of La Salle's Fort St. Louis.[9]

None of Bolton's books devoted to Spanish Texas is a monograph. They include *With the Makers of Texas: A Source Reader in Texas History* (with Eugene C. Barker, for high school students), *Athanase de Mézières and the Louisiana-Texas Frontier*, and *Texas in the Middle Eighteenth Century*. The latter volume also approximates the format of the Mézières work.

6. John F. Bannon, *Herbert Eugene Bolton: The Historian and the Man, 1870-1953* (Tucson: University of Arizona Press, 1978), p. 35 (as quoted by Bannon).

7. Herbert E. Bolton, "Some Materials for Southwestern History in the Archivo General de México," *Quarterly of the Texas State Historical Association* (*Quarterly*) 6 (Oct., 1902): 103-12, and *Quarterly* 7 (Jan., 1904): 196-213; Herbert E. Bolton, "Tienda de Cuervo's *Ynspección* of Laredo, 1757," *Quarterly* 6 (Jan., 1903): 187-203.

8. Bannon, *Bolton*, pp. 35-37, 275-78.

9. Herbert E. Bolton, "The Location of La Salle's Colony on the Gulf of Mexico," *Mississippi Valley Historical Review* 2 (Sept., 1915): 165-82.

To use Bolton's words, it "is not a history; it is, rather, a collection of special studies [documents in the case of the Mézières volumes], closely related in time and subject-matter, and designed to throw light upon a neglected period in the history of one of the most important of Spain's northern provinces."[10] His *Spanish Exploration in the Southwest*, which has valuable materials on the exploration and settlement of Texas, is likewise a series of letters, diaries, and itineraries presented with translation, notes, and introduction by Bolton.[11]

The capstone of Bolton's brilliant career came with the publication of his prize-winning biography of Francisco Vázquez de Coronado.[12] This volume combined Bolton's powers of synthesis, his love of "trailing" (on-site efforts to match terrain with documentation), and his considerable literary talents. Coronado's crossing of the Texas Panhandle, his discovery of Palo Duro Canyon, his experiences with West Texas weather, and his contacts with prototypical, buffalo-hunting Plains Indians provide exciting and vital details about a region too often neglected in works on Spanish Texas.[13]

Herbert E. Bolton's articles and books are enduring because they are carved from documentary bedrock. Bolton consistently supplied scholarly, contextual settings for his publications, and he knew the history of Spain and of the Spanish experience in America.

Besides studies of Spanish Texas, Bolton also wrote more than one hundred articles on the Indian tribes of Texas and Louisiana for the *Handbook of American Indians North of Mexico* (ed. Frederick Hodge). His *Guide to Materials for the History of the United States in the Principal Archives of Mexico* is still dog-eared by researchers; his "The Mission as a Frontier Institution in the Spanish-American Colonies" is still read and reread. During his long tenure at the University of California, Bolton

10. Herbert E. Bolton and Eugene C. Barker, *With the Makers of Texas: A Source Reader in Texas History* (New York: American, 1904); Herbert E. Bolton, ed. and trans., *Athanase de Mézières and the Louisiana-Texas Frontier, 1768–1780*, 2 vols. (Cleveland, Ohio: Arthur H. Clark, 1914); Herbert E. Bolton, *Texas in the Middle Eighteenth Century: Studies in Spanish Colonial History and Administration* (Austin: University of Texas Press, 1970), p. v.

11. Herbert E. Bolton, ed., *Spanish Exploration in the Southwest, 1542–1706* (reprint, New York: Barnes and Noble, 1963).

12. Herbert E. Bolton, *Coronado, Knight of Pueblos and Plains* (New York: Whittlesey, 1949); also published under title *Coronado on the Turquoise Trail, Knight of Pueblos and Plains* (Albuquerque: University of New Mexico Press, 1949).

13. Bannon, *Bolton*, pp. 238–75.

directed nearly three hundred master's theses and more than one hundred doctoral dissertations. [14]

William E. Dunn, a student of Bolton at the University of Texas, accompanied Bolton on his fourth trip into Mexico. Working in the AGN, Dunn sharpened his skills in Spanish paleography and became a talented and dependable copyist. He followed Bolton to Stanford University and completed his M.A. degree there in 1910. Dunn returned to Austin in 1913, where he became an instructor in history at the University of Texas. [15] In the intervening years he had spent time copying documents for Bolton and himself at the Archivo General de Indias (AGI) in Seville. Dunn was particularly interested in Spanish and French rivalry in the gulf region during the late 1600s and the early 1700s. Aside from the Bexar Archives, his typescript copies of documents housed in the AGI and AGN are probably the largest single collection of Hispanic materials in the Barker Texas History Center at the University of Texas in Austin.

Dunn received his Ph.D. from Columbia University in 1917, but did not remain in academia after the early 1920s. His publications on Spanish Texas are nevertheless highly significant. They center on Spanish-French gulf rivalry and Spanish-Apache relations. His doctoral dissertation became the first number in the "Studies in History" published by the University of Texas. [16] It is a thorough examination of Franco-Spanish competition for control of Pensacola and the lower Mississippi River valley, and it is history placed contextually within international and imperial considerations. Dunn's initial publications, however, appeared earlier as articles in the *Quarterly* of the TSHA. In 1911, the first of three works looked at Spanish-Apache relations in the

14. Herbert E. Bolton, *The Mission as a Frontier Institution in the Spanish-American Colonies* (El Paso: Academic Reprints, 1962); Herbert E. Bolton, *Guide to Materials for the History of the United States in the Principal Archives of Mexico* (New York: Kraus Reprint, 1965).

15. Bannon, *Bolton*, pp. 101, 283; Walter P. Webb, H. Bailey Carroll, and Eldon S. Branda, eds., *Handbook of Texas*, 3 vols. (Austin: Texas State Historical Association, 1952, 1976), 3:256–57.

16. William E. Dunn, "Spanish and French Rivalry in the Gulf Region of the United States, 1678–1702," *Comprehensive Dissertation Index, 1861–1972* (Ann Arbor, Mich.: University Microfilms, 1973), 34:818; Webb, Carroll, and Branda, *Handbook*, 3:256–57; William E. Dunn, *Spanish and French Rivalry in the Gulf Region of the United States, 1678–1702: The Beginnings of Texas and Pensacola*, University of Texas Studies in History no. 1 (Austin: University of Texas Press, 1917).

first half of the eighteenth century, the second examined missionary activities among the eastern Apache tribes, and the third related the founding and failure of Mission Santa Cruz de San Sabá.[17] Dunn's final publications in the *SHQ* appeared in 1916 and 1922. The first addressed the Spanish search for La Salle; the second added to Bolton's prior work on the founding of Mission Nuestra Señora del Refugio.[18] Like his mentor's works, Dunn's publications have stood the test of time.

Charles W. Hackett, a native Texan like Dunn, also followed Bolton to California in 1909. He earned a doctorate at the University of California in 1917, and began his distinguished career at the University of Texas in the following year.[19]

Until his death in 1951, Hackett was the university's surrogate Bolton. Starting as an adjunct professor, he attained the rank of associate professor in 1923, professor in 1926, and distinguished professor in 1944. By 1949 the University of Texas offered "more courses relating to Latin America than any other American university."[20] He and Nettie Lee Benson helped build perhaps the finest Latin American collection in the world. The present Nettie Lee Benson Latin American Collection and the Eugene C. Barker Texas History Center, both in Sid Richardson Hall on the Austin campus, offer an unsurpassed richness of materials on Texas and Latin American history. The collections serve as a fitting legacy of Barker, Benson (still active), Bolton, Castañeda, and Hackett.

Hackett's early publications forecast a near lifelong interest in colonial New Mexico. He was especially interested in the revolt of the Pueblo Indians in 1680, the retreat of the Spaniards down the Rio Grande, and the beginnings of El Paso del Norte.[21] His long-standing interest

17. William E. Dunn, "Apache Relations in Texas, 1718-1750," *Quarterly* 14 (Jan., 1911): 198-274; William E. Dunn, "Missionary Activities Among the Eastern Apaches Previous to the Founding of the San Sabá Mission," *Quarterly* 15 (Jan., 1912): 186-200; William E. Dunn, "The Apache Mission on the San Sabá River: Its Founding and Failure," *SHQ* 17 (Apr., 1914): 379-414.

18. William E. Dunn, "The Spanish Search for La Salle's Colony on the Bay of Espíritu Santo, 1685-1689," *SHQ* 19 (Apr., 1916): 323-69; William E. Dunn, "The Founding of Nuestra Señora del Refugio, the Last Spanish Mission in Texas," *SHQ* 25 (Jan., 1922): 174-84.

19. Bannon, *Bolton,* p. 101.

20. Webb, Carroll, and Branda, *Handbook,* 1:752.

21. Charles W. Hackett, "The Revolt of the Pueblo Indians of New Mexico in 1680," *Quarterly* 15 (Oct., 1911): 93-147; Charles W. Hackett, "The Retreat of the Span-

in New Mexico came to fruition with the publication in 1942 of his two-volume work on the Pueblo Revolt and Governor Antonio de Otermín's attempted reconquest of New Mexico in the early 1680s.[22] Because of the close relationship of New Mexico and Texas in the 1600s, Hackett's work was often germane to the latter. For example, Hackett sought to expose as fraudulent the claims of New Mexico's crafty governor, Diego de Peñalosa, that he had led an expedition in 1662 from Santa Fe to Quivira (Kansas) and thence eastward to the Mississippi River.[23] Peñalosa later appeared at the court of Louis XIV and used his alleged knowledge of lands to the east of New Mexico to try to undermine confidence in René Robert Cavelier, Sieur de la Salle's plan to establish a French colony at the mouth of the Mississippi River.

In the 1920s, Hackett published a massive two-volume collection of documents under the formidable title *Historical Documents Relating to New Mexico, Nueva Vizcaya and Approaches Thereto, to 1773*.[24] The Boltonlike project also contained materials of tangential importance to Spanish Texas. Then, in 1931, Hackett began his magnum opus, a project that would drain his energies for fifteen years, but also one that secured his place in Texas historiography.

Hackett undertook the monumental task of editing and translating *Pichardo's Treatise on the Limits of Louisiana and Texas*. The result was four thick volumes totaling nearly twenty-three hundred printed pages.[25] Father José Antonio Pichardo's original work resulted from an attempt by the Spanish government to counter President Thomas Jefferson's assertion that territory acquired by the United States in the Louisiana Purchase extended to the Rio Grande. The charge of the Pichardo commission was to determine the historic boundary of Texas and Lou-

---

iards from New Mexico in 1680, and the Beginnings of El Paso," part 1, *SHQ* 16 (Oct., 1912): 137–68; part 2, *SHQ* 16 (Jan., 1913): 259–76.

22. Charles W. Hackett, intro. and notes, and Charmion C. Shelby, trans., *Revolt of the Pueblo Indians and Otermín's Attempted Reconquest, 1680–1682*, 2 vols. (Albuquerque: University of New Mexico Press, 1942).

23. Charles W. Hackett, "New Light on Don Diego de Peñalosa: Proof That He Never Made an Expedition from Santa Fe to Quivira and the Mississippi River in 1662," *Mississippi Valley Historical Review* 6 (Dec., 1919): 313–35.

24. Charles W. Hackett, ed., *Historical Documents Relating to New Mexico, Nueva Vizcaya, and Approaches Thereto, to 1773*, 2 vols. (Washington, D.C.: Carnegie Institution of Washington, 1923, 1926).

25. Charles W. Hackett, ed. and trans., *Pichardo's Treatise on the Limits of Louisiana and Texas*, 4 vols. (Austin: University of Texas Press, 1931–46).

isiana. Working night and day for four years, Pichardo copied thousands of documents relating to Spanish Texas. His massive undertaking served to preserve records of original materials that are no longer extant, to prove conclusively that Texas belonged to Spain after 1763, and to establish the borders of Texas and Louisiana at the time of the Transcontinental Treaty. The Hackett edition has been ranked as "one of the most ably edited of all books on Texas." It also provided an enormous storehouse of information on the last years of Spanish Texas.[26] Among Hackett's final works on colonial Texas were his favorable treatment of the Marqués de San Miguel de Aguayo's campaign to recover Texas from the French after the "Chicken War" and his earlier defense of Aguayo against criticisms leveled by Visitador Pedro de Rivera.[27]

At the time Hackett began his teaching career in Austin, a young Mexican-born scholar, Carlos E. Castañeda, enrolled as an undergraduate at the University of Texas. Castañeda earned his B.A. in 1921, his M.A. in 1923, and his Ph.D. in 1932, all from the university. In 1927, Castañeda became librarian of the García Collection, which forms the nucleus of the Latin American Collection. He held that position until he joined the history faculty as an associate professor in 1939.[28] By then he had established sound credentials as a skilled translator and had begun the most exhaustive history of Spanish Texas.

In 1935, Castañeda published an English translation of Father Juan A. Morfi's *History of Texas, 1673–1779*. Father Morfi gained first-hand experience in Texas as chaplain for the inspection tour (1777–78) of Teodoro de Croix, the newly appointed commander general of the *Provincias Internas*. After his return to Mexico, Morfi compiled his scholarly history of Texas, made more useful by Castañeda's excellent translation.[29]

26. Jenkins, *Basic Texas Books*, pp. 428–30 (quotation on p. 429).

27. Charles W. Hackett, "The Marquis of San Miguel de Aguayo and His Recovery of Texas from the French, 1719–1723," *SHQ* 49 (Oct., 1945): 193–214; Charles W. Hackett, "Visitador Rivera's Criticisms of Aguayo's Work in Texas," *Hispanic American Historical Review* 16 (May, 1936): 162–72; for information on the Rivera inspection, see Thomas H. Naylor and Charles W. Polzer, S.J., eds., *Pedro de Rivera and the Military Regulations for Northern New Spain, 1724–1729: A Documentary History of His Frontier Inspection and the Reglamento de 1729* (Tucson: University of Arizona Press, 1988).

28. Webb, Carroll, and Branda, *Handbook*, 3:150.

29. Fray Juan Agustín Morfi, *History of Texas, 1673–1779*, trans. with bibliographic

One year after the publication of Morfi's history, the first and second volumes of Castañeda's massive work, *Our Catholic Heritage in Texas,* were published in Austin under the sponsorship and support of the Texas Knights of Columbus to celebrate Texas's centennial. Those initial volumes, followed by five others, launched Castañeda into a twenty-five-year, lifetime project.[30] His efforts were the first attempt at synthesis since the publications of Yoakum and Bancroft, and they were greatly assisted by the previous works of Bolton, Dunn, and Hackett, as well as by the dozens of articles on Spanish Texas that had appeared in the *Quarterly* and *SHQ*.

It was not originally intended that Castañeda write all the volumes; rather, a general editor was to supervise a cooperative project that called for each volume to be written by a different author. That plan was discarded after the first two volumes were written. Castañeda was asked by the Texas Knights of Columbus's historical commission to complete the series and give it throughout "uniformity of style and presentation."[31]

Castañeda's volumes are the starting point for any serious study of the period. The bibliographies alone point to thousands of previously untapped documents, letters, diaries, and mission records. Castañeda repeatedly discovered evidence of events in Texas history hitherto unrecorded. For example, he uncovered information about shipwrecks on Padre Island in 1554 and the subsequent slaughter of the survivors by coastal tribes, and he proved conclusively that Texas was not totally ignored by the Spanish during the years 1694–1715.[32]

While Castañeda broke new ground in several areas of Texas history, it must be emphasized that his volumes are not the "last word" on Spanish Texas. Anyone conversant with more recent scholarship

---

intro. and annotations by Carlos E. Castañeda (Albuquerque: Quivira Society, 1935); Webb, Carroll, and Branda, *Handbook,* 2:233; the *Provincias Internas* (1776) was an administrative unit created for the northern provinces of Mexico, including Texas.

30. Carlos E. Castañeda, *Our Catholic Heritage in Texas,* 7 vols. (Austin: Von Boeckmann–Jones, 1936–58).

31. Jenkins, *Basic Texas Books,* p. 72; the general editor, Paul J. Foik, died during preparation of the fifth volume.

32. Castañeda, *Our Catholic Heritage,* 1:140–54, 2:21–32; for more recent information on the shipwreck disasters of 1554, see J. Barto Arnold III and Robert S. Weddle, *The Nautical Archeology of Padre Island: The Spanish Shipwrecks of 1554* (New York: Academic, 1978).

on the Spanish period can point to his factual errors. That mistakes were made in a work of this magnitude is hardly surprising.

More troublesome in Castañeda's seven volumes were his analysis, balance, and interpretation. *Our Catholic Heritage in Texas* suffers from an unfortunate choice of general title. Much in the volumes has very little to do with a Catholic heritage or legacy in Texas — for example, the landscape, flora, fauna, and pre-Columbian Indians of Texas. In his treatment of presidios, settlements, and missions, Castañeda seldom presented a balanced view of the civilian and military personnel in Texas. The tenor of the entire work displays an ultra–Roman Catholic bias. Given the sponsorship of his volumes, the makeup of the imprimatur (a "who's who" of Roman Catholic archbishops and bishops in Texas), and the overwhelmingly clerical composition of the executive committee and contributing diocesan historians, all listed in the credits of each volume, *Our Catholic Heritage in Texas* can be adjudged as history with a "mission."[33] Castañeda himself apparently took great pride in his faith and personal satisfaction in being "muy católico romano."

Castañeda, however, should not be taken to task for writing "old-fashioned" history. His emphasis on political, military, and religious topics was very much in the mainstream of historiography during the years that he conceptualized, researched, and wrote his magnum opus on Spanish and Mexican Texas. It can also be said that Castañeda never placed Spanish Texas in an historical vacuum. His understanding encompassed the international scene, the chain of command that flowed from king and Council of the Indies to viceroys and governors, as well as the ecclesiastical hierarchy descending from pope to archbishops and bishops to presidents of the Franciscan missionary colleges to padres in Texas. Without the works of Carlos E. Castañeda, the historiography of Spanish Texas would undoubtedly be much, much poorer.

Vito Alessio Robles, a Mexican-born contemporary of Castañeda, published in 1938 *Coahuila y Texas en la época colonial.* This work addressed Spanish Texas to the year 1821 "from the Mexican viewpoint." Alessio Robles acknowledged two University of Texas professors, J.

---

33. See, for example, Castañeda, *Our Catholic Heritage,* vol. 5, title page and following leaf.

Lloyd Mecham and Carlos E. Castañeda, for their assistance in shaping this volume.[34] His approach was to treat Texas as a province on the frontier of New Spain and to discuss its similarities and dissimilarities with Coahuila. Alessio Robles devoted chapters to agriculture, climate, pre-Spanish Indians, early explorers, economics, Indian revolts, mission history, and the like. For the most part, his treatment of Texas topics, such as the early mission period and La Salle's colony, has been superseded by more recent scholarship. Alessio Robles also relied excessively on the works of Hubert H. Bancroft. The volume, however, is valuable as a reference work. It has an excellent index, especially for a book published in Mexico, and it contains citations to documentary holdings in Spanish and Mexican archives. Among its other strong points are maps, illustrations, and information on the northern Mexican provinces. The careers of Alonso de León and Luis Carvajal y de la Cueva are likewise well portrayed.[35]

Since the passing of Bolton, Hackett, Dunn, Castañeda, and Alessio Robles, the mantle of recent scholarship on Spanish Texas has largely fallen on the capable shoulders of Robert S. Weddle. Weddle, a non-academic historian, is a widely recognized authority on Spanish colonial Texas, especially for the years prior to 1800. A graduate of Texas Technological College, Weddle entered the newspaper business after World War II and moved to Menard, Texas, in 1956. There he became the owner-publisher of the *Menard News*. Shortly after his arrival in Central Texas, Weddle's interest was piqued by the nearby sites of Mission Santa Cruz de San Sabá and Presidio San Luis de las Amarillas. The mission on the San Sabá River (1757–58) represented both a dramatic and disastrous attempt to convert the eastern Apaches to Christianity. Its founding and destruction, problems with the Comanches, and the continued existence of the presidio until 1770 were the subjects of Weddle's first book, *The San Sabá Mission: Spanish Pivot*

34. Jenkins, *Basic Texas Books*, p. 1; Vito Alessio Robles, *Coahuila y Texas en la época colonial* (Mexico City: Editorial Cultura, 1938), p. xi. J. Lloyd Mecham was a professor of Latin American government at the University of Texas, but his publications include many historical works.

35. Jenkins, *Basic Texas Books*, pp. 1–3; Alessio Robles, *Coahuila y Texas*, pp. 675–743. For more recent information on Luis Carvajal y de la Cueva, see Robert S. Weddle, *Spanish Sea: The Gulf of Mexico in North American Discovery, 1500–1685* (College Station: Texas A&M University Press, 1985), pp. 333–49.

in Texas.[36] As evidence of Weddle's enduring scholarship, the University of Texas Press reissued the San Sabá paperback edition in 1988.

More important to the mission period in Texas history is Weddle's excellent study of San Juan Bautista, which he appropriately subtitled "Gateway to Spanish Texas."[37] Founded in 1700 at the site of present-day Guerrero, Coahuila, the mission, two subsequent ones, and Presidio San Juan Bautista del Río Grande anchored the northern passageway of supplies, livestock, settlers, priests, and soldiers into Spanish Texas. Those who passed through the portals of the missions and presidio were a roll call of early Texas personae—fathers Francisco Hidalgo, Isidro Félix de Espinosa, Antonio de San Buenaventura y Olivares, and Antonio Margil de Jesús; soldiers Diego and Domingo Ramón; Governors Martín de Alarcón and the Marqués de San Miguel de Aguayo; and French adventurer Louis Juchereau de St. Denis. One of the satellite missions, the original San Francisco Solano on the Rio Grande, was transferred to San Antonio in 1718 where it was renamed Mission San Antonio de Valero.[38]

Weddle's monograph is based on extensive unpublished materials from the AGN, especially volumes in the section *Provincias Internas,* as well as on a wide range of published articles, books, and documentary collections. Like his other publications, *San Juan Bautista* combines thorough research, considerable detail, solid interpretation, graceful style and, importantly, placement of Spanish Texas within the confines of empire.

Shortly before the publication of the *San Juan Bautista* volume, Weddle joined the staff of the University of Texas Press as production manager. His relocation to Austin gave him access to the rich resources of the Benson Latin American Collection and the University of Texas Archives. Using primarily the typescript copies of AGI documents that William E. Dunn had collected some sixty years earlier, Weddle launched a study of La Salle's ill-fated colony on the Texas coast and of the determined Spanish search for Fort St. Louis.[39] In some re-

36. Robert S. Weddle, *The San Sabá Mission: Spanish Pivot in Texas* (Austin: University of Texas Press, 1964).

37. Robert S. Weddle, *San Juan Bautista: Gateway to Spanish Texas* (Austin: University of Texas Press, 1968).

38. Ibid., p. 173; Castañeda, *Our Catholic Heritage,* 2:93–96.

39. Robert S. Weddle, *Wilderness Manhunt: The Spanish Search for La Salle* (Austin: University of Texas Press, 1973).

spects, this is Weddle's finest book. It is well organized, thoroughly researched, and nicely focused. *Wilderness Manhunt* is also an excellent piece of historical detective work. Weddle examined the intrigues of Diego de Peñalosa at the French court; the strategic importance of planting a French colony on the Gulf Coast; the organization and sailing of La Salle's fleet from La Rochelle; the loss of a vessel in the West Indies; the problems of navigation in the late seventeenth century; the desertion of French sailors at Santo Domingo; and the subsequent capture of the deserters by the Spanish and their interrogation by the Inquisition at Veracruz. Before his execution, information extracted from a young Frenchman, Denis Thomas, alerted the Spanish to the threat posed by La Salle's colony, and that intelligence launched the "wilderness manhunt." Weddle's treatment of the five sea expeditions dispatched from Mexico is particularly valuable. His knowledge of Gulf Coast waters and Spanish sailing vessels is extraordinary.[40]

Weddle concluded that due to La Salle's reading of a faulty astrolabe in 1682 he accidently overshot the mouth of the Mississippi River by some four hundred miles, but Weddle did not elaborate upon the point. That conclusion was expanded and buttressed with the publication of a seminal article by Peter H. Wood of Duke University.[41]

In "La Salle: Discovery of a Lost Explorer," Wood noted that La Salle's unsuccessful search for the mouth of the Mississippi River has generated a host of speculative arguments. They essentially center on whether the French explorer landed on the Texas coast by accident or by design. Wood concluded, however, that "neither of these standard alternatives hits the mark." His article examined La Salle's difficulties in reconciling the location of the mouth of the Mississippi River with existing maps, none of which showed the enormous delta at the mouth of the river; his mistaken belief that the river's mouth was at approximately twenty-seven degrees where it emptied into a series of lagoons; his overcompensation for the eastward tug of gulf currents; and his confusion over a mythical river in the western gulf named the Escondido (with features similar to the actual Rio Grande) and "his river," the Mississippi. Given those circumstances, Wood concluded, "he had no reason to look in the area where we now know

40. Ibid.; Arnold and Weddle, *Nautical Archeology.*
41. Peter H. Wood, "La Salle: Discovery of a Lost Explorer," *American Historical Review* (*AHR*) 89 (Apr., 1984): 294–323.

the base of the river to be."[42] By the time La Salle had discovered his mistake, he was stranded by circumstances and the object of the resolute Spanish manhunt, which Weddle detailed.

In 1987, Weddle, with the assistance of Mary C. Morkovsky and Patricia Galloway, edited a prize-winning volume, *La Salle, the Mississippi, and the Gulf: Three Primary Documents*. In "Part II: The Voyage to the Gulf," the translation of Minet's journal lends support to Wood's "groundbreaking assessment of La Salle as a 'lost explorer.'"[43]

In his otherwise excellent article, Wood contended that "the location of La Salle's outpost in East Texas remains obscure." That matter should be put to rest. La Salle built Fort St. Louis at the precise location identified by Herbert E. Bolton in 1915, and at the exact position of Presidio Nuestra Señora de Loreto (La Bahía) in 1721. The site, on Garcitas Creek near present-day Vanderbilt, Texas, has been confirmed by the archaeological work of Kathleen Gilmore at the University of North Texas.[44]

Robert Weddle's current research centers on the Gulf of Mexico in North American discovery. His *Spanish Sea* (1985) is the first of a projected three-volume work. It is especially well grounded in materials from Spanish archives. Weddle has provided much new information on and approaches to Gulf Coast history, such as his treatment of Alonso Alvarez de Pineda, of the aforementioned naval disasters off Padre Island in 1554, and of Luis Carvajal y de la Cueva's expedition across the Rio Grande in 1572, all important in the early history of Spanish Texas. Weddle's forthcoming volumes are intended to carry Gulf Coast history to 1803. They are eagerly awaited contributions to Texas history.[45]

Another valued contributor to the early history of Spanish Texas is the indefatigable Franciscan historian, Father Lino Gómez Canedo.

42. Ibid., p. 318.

43. Robert S. Weddle, ed., *La Salle, the Mississippi, and the Gulf: Three Primary Documents* (College Station: Texas A&M University Press, 1987), p. x.

44. Wood, "La Salle," p. 294; Bolton, "Location of La Salle's Colony," pp. 165–82; Kathleen Gilmore, "La Salle's Fort St. Louis in Texas," *Bulletin of the Texas Archeological Society* 55 (1984): 61–72.

45. Weddle, *Spanish Sea*, pp. 95–108, 246–50, 335–37. The second volume will be *The French Thorn: Rival Explorers in the Spanish Sea, 1682–1762* (College Station: Texas A&M University Press, forthcoming).

Gómez Canedo possesses perhaps the best working knowledge of Spanish, Latin American, and United States archives and libraries for the history of Spain in America. His two-volume guide is an extremely useful research tool. Likewise, his publication of documents relating to explorers and settlers in Texas during the years 1686–94 is an indispensable collection of primary letters, diaries, and plans.[46] In the latter, the introduction and notes accompanying the documents are especially useful in relating events in Texas to those transpiring in New Spain.

For a slightly later period in Texas history, the standard account of the French adventurer Louis Juchereau de St. Denis is by Ross Phares. His *Cavalier in the Wilderness* is both scholarly and readable. Unfortunately, the text contains not a single footnote reference to the sources listed in the bibliography. The Phares volume, which deals effectively with Franco-Spanish rivalry, should be read in tandem with articles by Lester G. Bugbee and Charmion C. Shelby.[47]

For the early mission period in Spanish Texas, the literature is quite extensive. One should start with the aforementioned *San Juan Bautista* volume by Weddle. Fray Francisco Céliz's diary of the Martín de Alarcón expedition of 1718–19 has been translated by Fritz L. Hoffmann. It complements the Mezquía diary, also translated by Hoffmann, in the *SHQ*. A useful account of the friars of the missionary college of Santa Cruz de Querétaro is the classic volume by Father Juan Domingo Arricivita. A companion work for the friars of the other missionary college, Nuestra Señora de Guadalupe de Zacatecas, is by Father José Antonio Alcocer, O.F.M. Finally, the experiences of Isidro Félix de Espinosa in the Rio Grande missions and those of East

46. Lino Gómez Canedo, *Los archivos de la historia de América: Período colonial español*, 2 vols. (Mexico City: Instituto Panamericano de Geografía e Historia, 1961); Lino Gómez Canedo, *Primeras exploraciones y poblamiento de Texas (1686–1694)* (Monterrey, Mexico: Publicaciones del Instituto Tecnológico y de Estudios Superiores de Monterrey, 1968).

47. Ross Phares, *Cavalier in the Wilderness: The Story of the Explorer and Trader Louis Juchereau de St. Denis* (Baton Rouge: Louisiana State University Press, 1952); Lester G. Bugbee, "The Real Saint-Denis," *Quarterly* 1 (Apr., 1898): 266–81; Charmion C. Shelby, "St. Denis's Declaration Concerning Texas in 1717," *SHQ* 26 (Jan., 1923): 165–83; Charmion C. Shelby, "St. Denis's Second Expedition to the Río Grande, 1716–1719," *SHQ* 27 (Jan., 1924): 190–216.

Texas make him an indispensable source on missionary activity prior to 1740.[48]

Mission San Antonio de Valero in particular and the other missions of San Antonio were the special interest of Marion H. Habig, O.F.M. His *The Alamo Chain of Missions* and *The Alamo Mission* are useful studies. Singly and in cooperation with Habig, Benedict Leutenegger, O.F.M., also published extensively on the San Antonio missions. Leutenegger's articles, translations, and edited works are focused on Mission San José and Father Antonio Margil de Jesús.[49] Likewise of value are works on Margil, the founder of the "Queen of Texas Missions," by Eduardo E. Ríos, and a careful study of the land tenure system at the San Antonio missions by Félix D. Almaráz, Jr. The numerous publications of Frederick C. Chabot also provide some useful information on the early history of San Antonio.[50]

The problems arising in San Antonio with the arrival of fifty-five Canary Islanders in 1731 are dealt with nicely in Jack Jackson's *Los Mesteños*. They are also an important part of a Ph.D. dissertation completed by Jesús F. de la Teja at the University of Texas. A favorable

48. Fray Francisco Céliz, *Diary of the Alarcón Expedition into Texas, 1718–1719*, trans. Fritz L. Hoffman (Los Angeles: Quivira Society, 1935); Fritz L. Hoffman, trans., "The Mezquía Diary of the Alarcón Expedition into Texas, 1718," *SHQ* 41 (Apr., 1938): 312–23; Juan Domingo Arricivita, *Crónica seráfica y apostólica del Colegio de la Santa Cruz de Querétaro en la Nueva España* (Mexico City: Don Felipe de Zúñiga y Ontiveros, 1792); José A. Alcocer, O.F.M., *Bosquejo de la historia del Colegio de Nuestra Señora de Guadalupe y sus misiones, año de 1788* (Mexico City: Editorial Porrúa, 1958); Isidro Félix de Espinosa, *Crónica de los colegios de propaganda fide de la Nueva España* (Washington, D.C.: Academy of American Franciscan History, 1964).

49. Marion A. Habig, *The Alamo Chain of Missions: A History of San Antonio's Five Old Missions* (Chicago: Franciscan Herald, 1968); Marion A. Habig, *The Alamo Mission: San Antonio de Valero, 1718–1793* (Chicago: Franciscan Herald, 1977). Benedict Leutenegger, O.F.M., has more than a dozen publications, many with titles and subtitles too lengthy to list here; the following bibliographical citations are representative of his more important works: *Apostle of America, Fray Antonio Margil* (Chicago: Franciscan Herald, 1956); trans., "Report on the San Antonio Missions in 1792," *SHQ* 77 (Apr., 1974): 478–98.

50. Eduardo E. Ríos, *Life of Fray Antonio Margil, O.F.M.*, trans. and rev. by Benedict Leutenegger, O.F.M. (Washington, D.C.: Academy of American Franciscan History, 1959); Félix D. Almaráz, Jr., *The San Antonio Missions and Their System of Land Tenure* (Austin: University of Texas Press, 1989); Frederick C. Chabot, *The Alamo, Altar of Texas Liberty* (San Antonio: Naylor, 1931); Frederick C. Chabot, *San Antonio and Its Beginnings* (San Antonio: Artes Gráficas, 1936).

and largely fanciful view of the Canary Islanders can be gleaned from Samuel M. Buck's *Yanaguana's Successors.*[51]

Treatment of the missions, towns, and presidios founded beyond San Antonio varies in quality. For example, a book-length study of the Presidio and Mission La Bahía by Kathryn S. O'Connor is sketchy on the period of their founding and removal to the Guadalupe River. For the years after the second transfer (1749) of the mission and presidio to the present-day site at Goliad, the aforementioned works by Bolton and Dunn, as well as William H. Oberste's *History of the Refugio Mission,* should be used in conjunction with O'Connor's work.[52]

A small volume by Gary B. Starnes devoted to the complex story of the San Gabriel missions near present-day Rockdale, Texas, is excellent. Starnes went well beyond the traditional treatment of the missions by Bolton in the *SHQ* and *Texas in the Middle Eighteenth Century.* Here, too, is a sound piece of work, based largely on the typescript manuscripts collected at the AGI by William E. Dunn. Despite its brevity (forty-five pages of text), this work, published in Spain, deserves a more prominent place in the historiography of Spanish Texas.[53]

The founding and collapse of a presidio and mission on the lower Trinity River has likewise depended on the work of Bolton for the better part of a century. The historiography of the region has been enhanced somewhat by the publication of another small book in 1987. John V. Clay's *Spain, Mexico and the Lower Trinity* is of uneven quality, but it adds some new information on Presidio San Agustín de Ahumada and Mission Nuestra Señora de la Luz. An earlier publication in the *SHQ* by Marvin C. Burch has also provided information about the natives of the lower Trinity River.[54]

The most successful enterprise by far in the 1740s and 1750s was

51. Jack Jackson, *Los Mesteños: Spanish Ranching in Texas, 1721–1821* (College Station: Texas A&M University Press, 1986); Jesús F. de la Teja, "Land and Society in Eighteenth-Century San Antonio de Béxar: A Community on New Spain's Northern Frontier," Ph.D. diss., University of Texas, 1988; Samuel M. Buck, *Yanaguana's Successors; the Story of the Canary Islanders' Immigration into Texas in the Eighteenth Century* (San Antonio: Naylor, 1949).

52. Kathryn S. O'Connor, *The Presidio La Bahía del Espíritu Santo de Zúñiga, 1721 to 1846* (Austin: Von Boeckmann–Jones, 1966); see notes 8 and 18; William H. Oberste, *History of the Refugio Mission* (Refugio, Tex.: Refugio Timely Remarks, 1942).

53. Gary B. Starnes, *The San Gabriel Missions, 1746–1756* (Madrid: Ministry of Foreign Affairs, Government of Spain, 1969).

54. John V. Clay, *Spain, Mexico and the Lower Trinity: An Early History of the Gulf*

that carried out by José de Escandón, the governor and military commander of Nuevo Santander. In a burst of energy, Escandón founded twenty-four towns and fifteen missions between 1749 and 1755. The best study to date of his colonization of the Costa del Seno Mexicano is by Lawrence F. Hill, a doctoral student of Bolton. Escandón was also responsible for the removal of Mission and Presidio La Bahía to present Goliad. His founding of Laredo in 1755 and its subsequent development is the subject of Gilberto M. Hinojosa's excellent book, *A Borderlands Town in Transition*. A recent book by Gilbert R. Cruz also examines the municipal origins of Laredo as well as those of El Paso and San Antonio.[55] In Weddle's forthcoming sequel to *Spanish Sea*, he will examine the explorations coordinated and carried out by Escandón, as well as other historical developments along the Gulf of Mexico to 1763.

Shortly before the Treaty of Paris, which ended the French and Indian War in America (1754–63), France had ceded to Spain all French territory west of the Mississippi River. The Spanish soon faced assertive Englishmen rather than tolerant Frenchmen as their neighbors. Twenty years later, Englishmen were supplanted by the even more aggressive citizens of the United States. For Spain, imperial adjustments were necessary to meet the changing circumstances that confronted its North American empire. Elizabeth A. H. John, in *Storms Brewed in Other Men's Worlds*, has dealt effectively with those considerations, especially as they applied to Louisiana and Texas.[56]

In the 1760s the king of Spain ordered a sweeping inspection of the frontier provinces to determine what reforms were needed. The *visitador general* of importance for Texas was the Marqués de Rubí, who arrived in the summer of 1767, accompanied by his engineer, Nicolás

Coast (Baltimore, Md.: Gateway, 1987); Marvin C. Burch, "The Indigenous Indians of the Lower Trinity River of Texas," *SHQ* 60 (July, 1956): 36–52.

55. Lawrence F. Hill, *José de Escandón and the Founding of Nuevo Santander: A Study in Spanish Colonization* (Columbus: Ohio State University Press, [1926]); Gilberto M. Hinojosa, *A Borderlands Town in Transition: Laredo, 1755–1870* (College Station: Texas A&M University Press, 1983); Gilbert R. Cruz, *Let There Be Towns: Spanish Municipal Origins in the American Southwest, 1610–1810* (College Station: Texas A&M University Press, 1988).

56. Elizabeth A. H. John, *Storms Brewed in Other Men's Worlds: The Confrontation of Indians, Spanish, and the French in the Southwest, 1540–1795* (College Station: Texas A&M University Press, 1975).

de Lafora. Rubí's inspection of missions and presidios, old and new, and his subsequent recommendations are nicely summarized in *Texas: The Lone Star State,* by Rupert N. Richardson, Ernest Wallace, and Adrian N. Anderson.[57] In essence, Louisiana would supplant Texas' historic role as a buffer province against foreign penetration, while Texas would serve as a barrier against the Plains Indians, keeping them out of the more vital regions of New Spain. Lafora's descriptive account of the frontiers of New Spain (1766–68), including Texas, has been edited and translated by Lawrence Kinnaird.[58]

Elizabeth John also has an excellent chapter on the Rubí inspection and his radical recommendations: the Spanish empire would henceforth retreat rather than expand; the new frontier, a line running from the Gulf of California to El Paso and thence along the Rio Grande to the Gulf of Mexico, would be defended by fifteen strategically spaced presidios; a war of extermination would be waged against the Apaches; and in Texas only San Antonio would be maintained above the cordon of defense.[59]

Responsibility for selecting the exact sites of the presidios was assigned to Hugo O'Conor in 1772 by the Viceroy Antonio María Bucareli. The administration of this particularly able victory has been studied by Bernard E. Bobb; the O'Conor inspection, by David M. Vigness and by Mary L. Moore with Delmar L. Beene.[60]

The implementation of the new line in 1773 and its consequences for Texas received treatment by Bolton in a piece entitled "The Spanish Abandonment and Reoccupation of East Texas, 1773–1779." Also germane to the period are articles by Isaac J. Cox and Richard Stenberg.[61] Bolton's volumes on Athanase de Mézières examined the

57. Rupert N. Richardson, Ernest Wallace, and Adrian N. Anderson, *Texas: The Lone Star State,* 5th ed. (Englewood Cliffs, N.J.: Prentice-Hall, 1988), p. 45.

58. Lawrence Kinnaird, ed., *The Frontiers of New Spain: Nicolás de Lafora's Description* (Berkeley, Calif.: Quivira Society, 1958).

59. John, *Storms Brewed,* pp. 431–39.

60. Bernard E. Bobb, *The Viceregency of Antonio María Bucareli in New Spain, 1771–1779* (Austin: University of Texas Press, 1962); David M. Vigness, "Don Hugo O'Conor and New Spain's Northeastern Frontier, 1764–1776," *Journal of the West* 6 (Jan., 1967): 27–40; Mary L. Moore and Delmar L. Beene, trans. and eds., "The Interior Provinces of New Spain: The Report of Hugo O'Conor," *Arizona and the West* 13 (Fall, 1971): 265–82.

61. Herbert E. Bolton, "The Spanish Abandonment and Re-Occupation of East Texas, 1773–1779," *Quarterly* 9 (Oct., 1905): 67–137; Isaac J. Cox, "the Louisiana-Texas

Spanish employment of this linguistically talented Frenchman in trying to piece together a general alliance of the northern tribes against
the Apaches. Likewise of value are three volumes of documents on
Spain in the Mississippi Valley, 1765–1794, edited by Kinnaird.[62]

Shortly after the abandonment of East Texas and the relocation
of the capital from Los Adaes to San Antonio, a new political unit,
the *Provincias Internas,* was created for the northern provinces of Mexico, including Texas. The administrative status of the *Provincias Internas* varied considerably from its creation in 1776 to near the end of
the colonial period. Its complex political arrangements within the
Spanish empire are succinctly outlined in the *Handbook of Texas.* Two
studies by the distinguished Spanish historian, Luis Navarro García,
examine the history of the *Provincias Internas* in considerable detail.[63]

The first commander general of the *Provincias Internas* was Teodoro
de Croix. Original documents relating to his service on the northern
frontier of New Spain (1776–83) have been ably edited and translated
by Alfred B. Thomas.[64] As noted above, Father Juan A. Morfi's experiences in Texas as chaplain to the Croix inspection later led to his
classic history of the future Lone Star State.

The best general treatment of Spanish Texas from the creation
of the *Provincias Internas* to independence from Spain in 1821 is Odie B.
Faulk's *The Last Years of Spanish Texas.* This work, originally a Ph.D.
dissertation at Texas Technological College, is solidly grounded in
primary sources from the AGN and the Bexar Archives as well as secondary materials available to the author in 1964.[65] More recent scholar-

Frontier," part 1, *Quarterly* 10 (July, 1906): 1–75, part 2, *Quarterly* 17 (July, 1913): 1–42, part 3, *Quarterly* 17 (Oct., 1913): 140–87; Richard Stenberg, "The Western Boundary of Louisiana, 1762–1803," *SHQ* 35 (Oct., 1931): 95–108.

62. Lawrence Kinnaird, ed., *Spain in the Mississippi Valley, 1765–1794: Translations of Materials from the Spanish Archives in the Bancroft Library,* 3 vols. (Washington, D.C.: U.S. Government Printing Office, 1946–49).

63. Webb, Carroll, and Branda, *Handbook,* 2:416–17; Luis Navarro García, *Don José de Gálvez y la Comandancia General de las Provincias Internas del Norte de Nueva España* (Seville: Escuela de Estudios Hispano-Americanos de Sevilla, 1964); Luis Navarro García, *Las Provincias Internas en el siglo XIX* (Seville: Escuela de Estudios Hispano-Americanos de Sevilla, 1965).

64. Alfred B. Thomas, trans. and ed., *Teodoro de Croix and the Northern Frontier of New Spain, 1776–1783* (Norman: University of Oklahoma Press, 1941).

65. Odie B. Faulk, *The Last Years of Spanish Texas, 1778–1821* (The Hague: Mouton, 1964).

ship and specialized studies of the late Spanish period should be read in conjunction with the Faulk volume.

Soon after the creation of the *Provincias Internas,* Juan de Ugalde began his six-year tenure as governor of Coahuila (1777–83). During his governorship, Ugalde led a series of successful campaigns against the Indians, and he was later called to Texas (1786) to deal specifically with the Apaches. Ugalde's career in Coahuila and Texas has been the subject of two unpublished Ph.D. dissertations by Al B. Nelson and Gary B. Starnes.[66]

Early Anglo-American influences in Spanish Texas have been the subject of several works. In particular, early filibusters have attracted the attention of Maurine T. Wilson with Jack Jackson, Mattie A. Hatcher, J. Villasana Haggard, and Faulk. A recent prize-winning book by Dan L. Flores draws attention to the important but neglected role played by Anglo-American traders of the southern Plains.[67]

The decades of revolution in Mexico and Texas have been examined in considerable detail. Perhaps the best overview of these turbulent years, entitled *The Revolutionary Decades,* is by David Vigness. For studies of the Mexican revolution of 1810 and its impact on Texas, Hugh M. Hamill, Jr.'s book on the Hidalgo revolt remains valuable. Also useful is a brief article on Tadeo Ortiz and Texas by Wilbert H. Timmons. More recent scholarship on the Mexican independence movement by Timothy E. Anna is exceptionally sound.[68] These works should be

66. Light T. Cummins, "Texas under Spain and Mexico," in *A Guide to the History of Texas,* ed. Light T. Cummins and Alvin R. Bailey, Jr. (New York: Greenwood Press, 1988), p. 11; Al B. Nelson, "Juan de Ugalde and the Río Grande Frontier, 1779–1790," Ph.D. diss., University of California, 1937; Gary B. Starnes, "Juan de Ugalde (1729–1816) and the *Provincias Internas* of Coahuila and Texas," Ph.D. diss., Texas Christian University, 1971.

67. Maurine T. Wilson and Jack Jackson, *Philip Nolan and Texas: Expeditions to the Unknown Land, 1791–1801* (Waco: Texian Press, 1987); Mattie A. Hatcher, "Conditions in Texas Affecting the Colonization Problem, 1795–1801," *SHQ* 25 (Oct., 1921): 81–97; J. Villasana Haggard, "The Houses of Barr and Davenport," *SHQ* 44 (July, 1945): 66–88; J. Villasana Haggard, "The Neutral Ground between Louisiana and Texas, 1806–1821," *Louisiana Historical Quarterly* 28 (Oct., 1945): 1001–28; Odie B. Faulk, trans. and ed., "A Description of Texas in 1803," *SHQ* 66 (Apr., 1963): 513–15; Dan L. Flores, ed., *Journal of an Indian Trader: Anthony Glass and the Texas Trading Frontier, 1790–1810* (College Station: Texas A&M University Press, 1985).

68. David M. Vigness, *The Revolutionary Decades* (Austin: Steck-Vaughn, 1965); Hugh M. Hamill, Jr., *The Hidalgo Revolt: Prelude to Mexican Independence* (Gainesville:

DONALD E. CHIPMAN

supplemented by Félix D. Almaráz, Jr.'s prize-winning work on Governor Manuel Salcedo of Texas, by Haggard on the counterrevolution of Bexar, by Chabot on the Las Casas and Zambrano revolutions, and by Benson on the period of the Hidalgo revolt in Texas.[69] The Bernardo Gutiérrez de Lara and Augustus W. Magee filibustering expedition of 1812–13 has been the subject of several works by Walter F. McCaleb, Elizabeth H. West, Harry M. Henderson, Henry P. Walker, Richard W. Gronet, and Ted Schwarz.[70] General Javier Mina's invasion of Mexico has likewise drawn the attention of Harris G. Warren, Lota M. Spell, and Martín L. Guzmán. The Napoleonic exiles at Champ d'Asile have been studied in works by Jesse S. Reeves, Fannie E. Ratchford, and J. Autrey Dabbs.[71] Two book-length

University of Florida Press, 1970); W. H. Timmons, "Tadeo Ortiz and Texas," *SHQ* 72 (July, 1968): 21–33; Timothy E. Anna, *The Fall of the Royal Government in Mexico City* (Lincoln: University of Nebraska Press, 1978).

69. Félix D. Almaráz, Jr., *Tragic Cavalier: Governor Manuel Salcedo of Texas, 1808–1813* (Austin: University of Texas Press, 1971); J. Villasana Haggard, "The Counter-Revolution of Béxar, 1811," *SHQ* 43 (Oct., 1939): 222–35; Frederick C. Chabot, ed., *Texas in 1811: The Las Casas and Sambrano Revolutions* (N.p.: Yanaguana Society, 1941); Nettie L. Benson, "Bishop Marin de Porras and Texas," *SHQ* 51 (July, 1947): 16–40; Nettie L. Benson, "Texas's Failure To Send a Deputy to the Spanish Cortes, 1810–1812," *SHQ* 64 (July, 1960): 144–35; Nettie L. Benson, ed. and trans., "A Governor's Report on Texas in 1809," *SHQ* 71 (Apr., 1968): 603–15.

70. Walter F. M'Caleb, "The First Period of the Gutiérrez-Magee Expedition," *Quarterly* 4 (Jan., 1901): 218–29; Elizabeth H. West, ed. and trans., "Diary of José Bernardo Gutiérrez de Lara, 1811–1812," *AHR* 34 (Oct., 1928): 55–77. and *AHR* (Jan., 1929): 281–94; Harry M. Henderson, "The Magee-Gutiérrez Expedition," *SHQ* 55 (July, 1951): 43–61; Henry P. Walker, ed., "William McLane's Narrative of the Magee-Gutiérrez Expedition, 1812–1813," *SHQ* 66 (Oct., 1962): 234–51, *SHQ* (Jan., 1963): 457–79, and *SHQ* (Apr., 1963): 569–88; Richard W. Gronet, "The United States and the Invasion of Texas," *Americas* 25 (Jan., 1969): 281–306; Ted Schwarz, *Forgotten Battlefield of the First Texas Revolution: The Battle of Medina, August 18, 1813,* ed. and annotated by Robert H. Thonhoff (Austin: Eakin, 1985).

71. Harris G. Warren, "The Origins of General Mina's Invasion of Mexico," *SHQ* 42 (July, 1938): 1–20; Lota M. Spell, *Pioneer Printer: Samuel Bangs in Mexico and Texas* (Austin: University of Texas Press, 1963); Martín L. Guzmán, *Javier Mina, héroe de España y de México* (Mexico City: Compañía General de Ediciones, 1966); Jesse S. Reeves, *The Napoleonic Exiles in America: A Study in American Diplomatic History, 1815–1819* (Baltimore, Md.: Johns Hopkins University Press, 1905); Fannie E. Ratchford, ed., *The Story of Champ d'Asile as Told by Two of the Colonists,* trans. Donald Joseph (Dallas: Book Club of Texas, 1937); Jack A. Dabbs, trans. and ed., "Additional Notes on the Champ-d'Asile," *SHQ* 54 (Jan., 1951): 347–58.

studies of the later Anglo-American adventurers, who spilled over into the Mexican period, are those of Julia K. Garrett and Warren.[72] James Long's abortive expeditions into Mexico have not been adequately studied. More attention has centered on his wife, Jane Long, as evidenced by Anne A. Brindley's piece in the *SHQ*. The early Anglo settlers in northeastern Texas have been the subject of an excellent unpublished Ph.D. dissertation by Rex Strickland. In a published article Strickland has examined the impact of Miller County, Arkansas Territory, residents on the northeastern Red River frontier.[73]

The capstone for the last years of Spanish Texas and Mexican Texas has been provided by David J. Weber's "masterful blend of archival research with a timely synthesis." Weber's volume, *The Mexican Frontier, 1821–1846,* approaches the former Spanish Borderlands as a whole, but it achieves the goal of placing Spanish Texas in its proper historical context.[74]

From Bancroft, Bolton, Castañeda, Hackett, and Yoakum to Almaráz, Faulk, Poyo and Hinojosa, Vigness, Weber, and Weddle, Spanish Texas has been the subject of both general and specialized studies that have spanned a century of scholarly effort. The literature varies in quality, but the best of it places Spanish Texas in its imperial setting. Again, notably lacking is a satisfactory one-volume synthesis of the Hispanic experience in Texas. Faulk's *Successful Failure* misses the mark. Its strength is readability; its weakness is a lack of detail, analysis, and interpretation. Gerald Ashford's *Spanish Texas: Yesterday and Today* is often anecdotal and of such uneven quality that one has difficulty coming away from its pages with a coherent view of the Spanish period. Like the Faulk volume, T. R. Fehrenbach's *Lone Star* reads

72. Julia K. Garrett, *Green Flag over Texas: A Story of the Last Years of Spain in Texas* (New York: Cordova Press, 1939); Harris G. Warren, *The Sword Was Their Passport: A History of American Filibustering in the Mexican Revolution* (Baton Rouge: Louisiana State University Press, 1943).

73. Anne A. Brindley, "Jane Long," *SHQ* 56 (Oct., 1952): 211–38; Rex W. Strickland, "Anglo-American Activities in Northeastern Texas, 1803–1845," Ph.D. diss., University of Texas, 1937; Rex W. Strickland, "Miller County, Arkansas Territory, the Frontier that Men Forgot," *Chronicles of Oklahoma* 18 (1940): 12–34, and *Chronicles of Oklahoma* 19 (1941): 37–54.

74. Cummins, "Texas under Spain and Mexico," pp. 12; David J. Weber, *The Mexican Frontier, 1821–1846: The American Southwest under Mexico* (Albuquerque: University of New Mexico Press, 1982).

nicely, but Fehrenbach devoted only seventy-eight pages exclusively to Indian and Spanish Texas. While it is obviously limited in coverage, one can turn with confidence to the various editions of *Texas: The Lone Star State*. With rare exception, this text is remarkably accurate. Seymour V. Connor's *Texas: A History*, another basic text, is especially valuable for its summary of the missionary era in Texas history.[75]

Lacking an adequate one-volume history, even the most basic outlines of the geography and history of Spanish Texas are not readily available. Geographically, for example, the province of Texas was but a tiny portion of the present Lone Star State. It lay above the Nueces River, to the east of the Medina River headwaters, and extended into Louisiana. A recent book by Terry G. Jordan, John L. Bean, Jr., and William M. Holmes does provide a much-needed synthesis of Texas geography.

Historically, present Texas was a part of four provinces of New Spain: the El Paso area was under the jurisdiction of New Mexico; the missions founded near La Junta de los Ríos were under Nueva Vizcaya; the coastal region from the Nueces River to the Rio Grande and thence upstream to Laredo fell under Nuevo Santander after 1749; and, of course, Texas was initially under joint jurisdiction with the province of Coahuila. An atlas of Texas by A. Ray Stephens and Holmes supplements the earlier work by Stanley A. Arbingast and provides another valuable tool for teaching and researching the history of Spanish Texas.[76]

Weddle, in an unpublished paper, has added valuable perspective on the historical framework of Spanish Texas by dividing it into three logical and useful stages: the era of *early exploration*, in which there was a preliminary evaluation of the land and its resources; the period of

75. Odie B. Faulk, *A Successful Failure* (Austin: Steck-Vaughn, 1965); Gerald Ashford, *Spanish Texas: Yesterday and Today* (Austin: Jenkins, 1971); T. R. Fehrenbach, *Lone Star: A History of Texas and the Texans* (New York: Collier, 1980); Richardson, Wallace, and Anderson, *Texas;* Seymour V. Connor, *Texas: A History* (Arlington Heights, Ill.: AHM Publishing, 1971).

76. Terry G. Jordan, John L. Bean, Jr., and William M. Holmes, *Texas: A Geography* (Boulder, Colo.: Westview, 1984); Robert S. Weddle, "Edge of Empire: Texas as a Spanish Frontier, 1519–1821," unpublished paper prepared for Spanish Symposium, Texas A&M University, College Station, Oct. 11, 1986; A. Ray Stephens and William M. Holmes, *Historical Atlas of Texas* (Norman: University of Oklahoma Press, 1989); Stanley A. Arbingast et al., *Atlas of Texas* (Austin: Bureau of Business Research, 1976).

cultural absorption, in which the natives began to acquire Spanish cultural elements, at first indirectly from Indian intermediaries and then directly from the Spanish themselves; and the time of *defensive occupation,* in which Spanish presence in Texas was much more the result of reflexive actions dictated by international considerations, rather than due to the momentum of an expanding empire.[77]

The ethnology of Texas Indians likewise deserves increased attention. W. W. Newcomb, Jr.'s *The Indians of Texas* stands unchallenged as the best single book, but it is outdated by twenty-five years of specialized research and publication. An excellent annotated research bibliography on the Indians of Texas by Michael L. Tate may facilitate a new effort.[78] Also, the contributions of anthropologists Newcomb, Thomas N. Campbell, and others to the massive revised *Handbook of Texas* project, now in progress, will provide updated information on specialized Indian topics.

Another aspect of Spanish Texas that deserves further attention is a study of documents relating to the era of exploration and discovery. The various projects associated with the approaching Columbian quincentenary may yield more information on Alonso Alvarez de Pineda, Alvar Núñez Cabeza de Vaca, Francisco Vázquez de Coronado, Hernando de Soto, and Luis de Moscoso. The Panhandle-Plains Historical Museum in Canyon, Texas, for example, has copies of documents from the AGI that relate to the Coronado expedition but were not used by Bolton.[79] A systematic search of Spanish and Mexican archives might well produce maps of Spanish Texas that have heretofore eluded scholars. In particular, maps are needed that are more than mere objects of art. An analysis of maps that were available to La Salle in the 1680s, for instance, does much to explain the state of cartographic knowledge about the northern Gulf Coast and to account for his unintentional landing at Matagorda Bay.

As suggested by Weddle, the topic of cultural absorption by the native peoples of Spanish Texas merits greater consideration in forthcoming studies. The Spanish occupation of the American Southwest

77. Weddle, "Edge of Empire."

78. W. W. Newcomb, Jr., *The Indians of Texas: From Prehistoric to Modern Times* (Austin: University of Texas Press, 1961); Michael L. Tate, ed., *The Indians of Texas: An Annotated Research Bibliography* (Metuchen, N.J.: Scare Crow, 1986).

79. Dianna Everett, "The Research Center, Panhandle-Plains Historical Museum," in Cummins and Bailey, *Guide,* pp. 185–91.

spawned a technological and material revolution that permanently changed the lives of Indians—the introduction of the horse being the most dramatic example. As early as the mid-1680s, La Salle found horses that had strayed northward from Chihuahua among the Indians of East Texas. Natives who had trudged on foot for centuries found their modes of hunting and warfare irreversibly transformed by this animal.[80] Mounted warriors preyed on other Indians who remained afoot, and they contested Spanairds who invaded their ancestral lands.

From New Mexico, contacts with Jumano Indians, beginning in the late 1620s, introduced Spanish products into Texas in exchange for buffalo hides. The Jumanos, who have remained something of a mystery to historians and anthropologists, were apparently a transitional people. Some of them probably lived in fixed houses at La Junta de los Ríos. On other occasions they hunted buffalo far to the north of their homes; and, as Weddle has noted, they were the early agents of commerce in Texas, carrying European goods as far as the eastern Gulf Coast and the Tejas villages in East Texas.[81]

It is worth noting, too, that after the founding of missions in Texas, neophytes who deserted and returned to their old haunts inevitably carried with them a veneer of Spanish culture. Unfortunately, another aspect of European contact—the introduction of diseases, notably measles and smallpox—devastated Indian populations both within and outside the missions.

Texas Indians also acquired European cultural accouterments from shipwrecks on the Gulf Coast. For example, Weddle found evidence that the Karankawas so valued iron that they burned wrecked vessels to recover nails. They and other Indians learned to use iron instead of flint for their knives and arrow tips, and they soon appreciated the advantages of muskets and lead over bows and arrows.[82] Too little attention has been directed to the impact of European technology on the native population prior to the founding of the first Texas missions in the early 1690s.

In recent years more attention has been directed to the cattle in-

80. Weddle, "Edge of Empire."

81. Ibid.; Herbert E. Bolton, "The Jumano Indians in Texas, 1650–1771," *Quarterly* 15 (July, 1911): 66–84; France V. Scholes and H. P. Mera, "Some Aspects of the Jumano Problem," in *Contributions to American Anthropology and History*, vol. 6 (Washington, D.C.: Carnegie Institution of Washington, 1940).

82. Weddle, "Edge of Empire."

dustry in Texas, a subject of controversy between Terry G. Jordan and Jack Jackson. Their differences, set forth, respectively, in *Trails to Texas* and *Los Mesteños*, over Anglo versus Spanish influences in ranching seem far from resolved and will likely be the subject of future discourse.[83] The first cattle herds to enter Texas were of course due to the outgrowth of ranching that had begun in northern Mexico near the midpoint of the sixteenth century. Treatment of the early history of the range cattle industry in northern Mexico and the expansion of that industry toward Texas may be found in two articles in *Agricultural History* by Richard J. Morrisey and Donald D. Brand. Also useful is the somewhat dated work, *Land and Society in Colonial Mexico,* by François Chevalier; articles by Faulk and Dan Kilgore; and a short monograph on the ranch in Spanish Texas by Sandra M. Myres.[84]

An area of recent focus in the historiography of Spanish Texas is the impact of Spanish culture on the ecology and natural history of Texas. The pioneers in this area of research and publication are Dan L. Flores and Jack M. Inglis. Flores has written a prize-winning article on the ecology of the Red River region in the early 1800s. Inglis has studied the brush country in extreme South Texas along the Rio Grande plain.[85]

Hispanic society in colonial Texas has been examined in the works of Oakah L. Jones, Jr., Jesús F. de la Teja, and Alicia Tjarks. Jones in *Los Paisanos* found that class rivalry, so commonplace in the heartland of New Spain, scarcely existed in Texas, "except in San Fernando de Béxar between the Canary Islanders and the original inhabitants."

83. Terry G. Jordan, *Trails to Texas: Southern Roots of Western Cattle Ranching* (Lincoln: University of Nebraska Press, 1981); Jackson, *Los Mesteños.*

84. Richard J. Morrisey, "The Northward Expansion of the Range Cattle Industry in Northern Mexico," *Agricultural History (AH)* 35 (July, 1961): 115–21; Donald D. Brand, "The Early History of the Range Cattle Industry in Northern Mexico," *AH* 35 (July, 1961): 132–39; François Chevalier, *Land and Society in Colonial Mexico: The Great Hacienda,* trans. Alvin Eustis and ed. Lesley B. Simpson (Berkeley: University of California Press, 1970); Odie B. Faulk, "Ranching in Spanish Texas," *Hispanic American Historical Review* 45 (May, 1965): 257–66; Dan Kilgore, "Texas Cattle Origins," *Cattleman* 69 (Jan., 1983): 110–20; Sandra L. Myres, *The Ranch in Spanish Texas* (El Paso: Texas Western Press, 1969).

85. Dan L. Flores, "The Ecology of the Red River in 1806: Peter Custis and Early Southwestern Natural History," *SHQ* 88 (July, 1984): 1–42; Jack M. Inglis, *A History of Vegetation of the Rio Grande Plain,* Texas Parks and Wildlife Department Bulletin no. 45 (Austin, [1964]).

129

That trouble existed between the *isleños* and the older *bexareños* in the 1730s is well documented. De la Teja, however, has demonstrated in an unpublished paper that even in San Antonio the passage of time, shared dangers and isolation, limited economic opportunity, and the forging of strong kinship ties eventually produced a "dynamic community." Tjarks's comparative demographic analysis of Texas in the late eighteenth century has provided valuable data and statistical information on the Hispanic population.[86] Her study should be supplemented with census data available for January to December, 1804. The figures for civil settlements, presidial companies, and missions in Texas total 3,605. To this number should be added the population of Laredo, which stood at 636 in 1795. The data for 1804 have not been a part of any overall analysis of Texas' population on the eve of Anglo incursions. The figures do not include unsettled Indians or Negro slaves. In the latter category, however, Randolph B. Campbell has demonstrated that there were virtually no black bondsmen in Spanish Texas on the eve of Mexican Independence.[87]

In the last years of Spanish Texas, evidence suggests that the majority of the population was mestizo, a mixture of Indian and Spanish ancestry. Despite the comparative absence of class rivalry in Texas, there were caste distinctions in what would soon become the Mexican population. Jack Jackson has identified names such as *español, indio, mulato, coyote, lobo,* and *zambo.* He noted that Anglos ignored these finer caste distinctions and lumped all Mexicans into one "despicable" race.[88] It is to be hoped that Jackson's work will prompt further studies of race relations in the late colonial period.

The contribution of women in Spanish Texas has been another

86. Oakah L. Jones, Jr., *Los Paisanos: Spanish Settlers on the Northern Frontier of New Spain* (Norman: University of Oklahoma Press, 1979); Jesús F. de la Teja, "Indians, Soldiers, and Canary Islanders: The Making of a Texas Frontier Community," paper presented at the Texas State Historical Association meeting, Galveston, Tex., Mar. 3–5, 1987); Alicia V. Tjarks, "Comparative Demographic Analysis of Texas, 1777–1793," *SHQ* 77 (Jan., 1974): 291–338.

87. Carmela Leal, comp. and trans., *Transactions of Statistical and Census Reports of Texas, 1782–1836, and Sources Relating to the Black in Texas, 1603–1803* (San Antonio: University of Texas Institute of Texan Cultures, 1979, microfilm), 3rd roll; Hinojosa, *Borderlands Town in Transition;* Randolph B. Campbell, *An Empire for Slavery: The Peculiar Institution in Texas, 1821–1865* (Baton Rouge: Louisiana State University Press, 1989), pp. 10–11.

88. Jackson, *Los Mesteños,* p. 604.

neglected topic until the recent past. Pioneering work in this field began with a project of the Texas Foundation for Women's Resources
of Austin, Texas. From those efforts have come the permanent exhibit
"Texas Women: A Celebration of History," now housed in the main
library at Texas Woman's University; biographical and topical files to
support the exhibit; and publications by Mary B. Rogers and Ruthe
Winegarten. Featured women from the Hispanic period include: María
Jesús de Agreda, the legendary "Woman in Blue"; María Betancourt,
one of the original Canary Island settlers at San Antonio; and María
del Carmen Cavillo, an early rancher of present Floresville, Texas.[89]
    The influence of Spanish law on the contemporary legal system
in Texas has been the subject of recent research and publication by
two law professors, Joseph W. McKnight of Southern Methodist University and Hans W. Baade of the University of Texas at Austin. As
McKnight has pointed out in *The Spanish Element in Modern Texas Laws,*
persistent aspects of Hispanic, or Castilian, law in contemporary Texas
fell into three groupings: rules of judicial procedure, land and water
law, and the law of family relations. The latter category is particularly important in matters of community property for married couples
and the protection of the family against creditors. Seminal articles
by Baade have focused on real estate transactions and marriage contracts in Spanish North America.[90]

    The cyclical pattern for the historiography of Spanish Texas dis-
plays early attempts at synthesis by Yoakum and Bancroft in the second half of the nineteenth century, followed by the publication of
dozens of documents, articles, and monographs throughout the first

89. Mary B. Rogers, *Texas Women: A Celebration of History* (Austin: Texas Foundation for Women's Resources, 1981); Ruthe Winegarten, ed., *Finder's Guide to the Texas
Women: A Celebration of History Exhibit Archives* (Denton: Texas Woman's University
Library, 1984); Ruthe Winegarten, *Texas Women, a Pictorial History: From Indians to Astronauts* (Austin: Eakin, [1986]).
    90. Joseph W. McKnight, "The Spanish Elements in Modern Texas Law," paper
delivered to the Texas State Historical Association meeting, Austin, Mar. 4, 1978;
Hans W. Baade, "The Form of Marriage in Spanish North America," *Cornell Law
Review* 61 (Nov., 1975): 1–89; Hans W. Baade, "Marriage Contracts in French and Spanish Louisiana: A Study in 'Notarial' Jurisprudence," *Tulane Law Review* 53 (Dec., 1979):
3–92; Hans W. Baade, "The Formalities of Private Real Estate Transactions in Spanish North America: A Report on Some Recent Discoveries," *Louisiana Law Review*
38 (1978): 655–745.

third of the twentieth century. In the mid-1930s Castañeda began a twenty-five-year effort toward a new synthesis that greatly enriched the literature on Spanish colonial Texas. Since Castañeda's death, however, the publication of additional articles and monographs on Spanish topics, the increased accessibility of documents housed in Mexican and Spanish archives, the microfilming of the Bexar Archives and the continuing translation of those materials into English by John Wheat, the researching and writing of hundreds of articles on Spanish Texas that will make up an important part of the new *Handbook of Texas*, and the increased emphasis on Spanish contributions to the Americas resulting from the approaching Columbian quincentenary all point to the need for a new one-volume survey of Spanish Texas, now in progress by Donald E. Chipman.

Through the emphasis placed on the history of Spanish Texas by individual scholars, Hispanic writers for the *Handbook of Texas* and outside contributors, and the various funding agencies that seek to commemorate the opening of America to European settlement by Christopher Columbus, the Spanish colonial period continues to stimulate research and publication. Several ongoing projects are exciting and potentially rewarding to the broad topic of Spain in Texas.

The second volume of Weddle's proposed trilogy on the Spanish Caribbean and Gulf Coast has been accepted for publication at Texas A&M University Press; the National Park Service will commission a new history of the San Antonio missions in observation of the Columbian quincentenary; Poyo and Hinojosa are editing a book that will examine the eighteenth-century origins of the Tejano community of San Antonio; Elizabeth A. H. John is at work on a sequel volume to *Storms Brewed in Other Men's Worlds;* Jesús F. de la Teja's article manuscript, "Indians, Soldiers, and Canary Islanders: The Making of a Texas Frontier Community," has been accepted for publication; Gary Anderson at Texas A&M University is at work on a cultural and ethnographic study of Texas Indians of the late Spanish period and beyond; Almaráz's forthcoming biography of Castañeda is near completion; the De Soto Trail Commission in cooperation with the National Park Service is dedicated to a new study of the route traveled by De Soto across ten southern states, including Texas; Jack Jackson, Robert Weddle, and Winston DeVille have a manuscript on mapping the Gulf Coast accepted for publication by Texas A&M University Press; and a demographic analysis of Spanish missions and presidios at Nacogdoches, La Bahía, and San Antonio is the subject of graduate research by Tina Meacham at the University of Texas at Austin.[91]

Future publications on Spanish Texas will likely place more emphasis on ethnic, social, and economic topics. At the forefront of that trend in historiography are Poyo and Hinojosa, F. de la Teja, Oakah Jones, and Jack Jackson. The efforts of these scholars and others will continue to emphasize the multifaceted contributions of Spaniards, Indians, and Tejanos to Texas history.

91. In Nov., 1989, Adán Benavides, Jr., published *Béxar Archives, 1717–1836: A Name Guide* (Austin: University of Texas Press, 1989). This guide will greatly aid researchers who use the largest collection of documentation in the United States relating to Spanish and Mexican Texas.

ᘓ In the Long Shadow of Eugene C. Barker: The Revolution and the Republic

Paul D. Lack

In the last sixty years scholars of the period 1821–45 in Texas history have performed their research and formulated their hypotheses in the long shadow of one of the giants of southwestern historiography, Eugene C. Barker. His pioneering research and thorough studies centered on the most significant figure of the era, Stephen F. Austin, in a biography that remains today not just the standard account but the only major treatment of the "Father of Texas." Barker's work shaped interpretations of the era, placing Austin and his views at its center. The colonizer became the rational statesman in a heroic age, and the history of Texas became the story of his colonies. In an understated style Barker described the subject as wise, moderate, prudent, self-sacrificing, patient, and dedicated. His achievements in repeatedly gaining, confirming, and defending empresario grants, in soothing political disputes that threatened to erupt into rebellion or repression, and in responding to the manifold needs of the people are chronicled in a sympathetic but restrained fashion appropriate to the personality of the subject. Barker's contribution — gathering and editing the vast majority of the Austin papers and constructing a readable, accurate narrative of the central figure in Texas history — was undeniable.[1]

---

1. Eugene C. Barker, ed., *The Austin Papers,* 3 vols. (Austin: University of Texas Press, 1926); Eugene C. Barker, *The Life of Stephen F. Austin: Founder of Texas* (Nashville and Dallas: Cokesbury Press, 1925). Recently some specific aspects of Austin's life and thought have been treated in brief but useful studies; however, these do not fundamentally alter Barker's essential concepts. Joseph W. McKnight, "Stephen Austin's Legalistic Concerns," *Southwestern Historical Quarterly (SHQ)* 89 (Jan., 1986): 239–68; Howard Miller, "Stephen F. Austin and the Anglo-Texan Response to the Religious Establishment in Mexico, 1821-1836," *SHQ* 91 (Jan., 1988): 283–316.

The study of Austin alone made Barker's work fundamental to the understanding of this period, but he also wrote about other issues: relations between Texas and Mexico, the influence of slavery and the slave trade in colonization, the political and military affairs of the Texas Revolution, biographical sketches of other leaders, and U.S.-Mexican relations regarding Texas; he even wrote a brief essay on the "Latin American contribution" to Texas independence. What Barker did not undertake himself was often accomplished by his students. His productivity and influence were so great and his work gained such general acceptance that many assumed that he left little to do in the way of either research or reformulation.[2] Indeed, the widespread assumption that the history of Texas was essentially Austin's story appears to have contributed to the neglect of East Texas, West Texas, Tejanos, other colonizers, and the colonists themselves during this period. In the sense that Barker's triumph seems to have discouraged fresh scholarship in the field, he may have succeeded too well.

Barker gained general respect as a skilled professional, more thorough and dispassionate by far than those who had come before; nevertheless, he shared the fundamental view that Texas history in the period from 1821 to 1836 represented the march of Anglo-American democracy westward in triumph over inferior races. Because he advocated scientific or objective history, few have acknowledged that Barker's work rested essentially on an ideological foundation similar

2. The most significant examples of Barker's works are *Mexico and Texas, 1825–1835* (Dallas: P. L. Turner, 1928); "The San Jacinto Campaign," *Quarterly of the Texas State Historical Association (Quarterly)* 4 (Apr., 1901): 236–345; "The African Slave Trade in Texas," *Quarterly* 6 (Oct., 1902): 145–58; "James H. C. Miller and Edward Gritten," *Quarterly* 13 (Oct., 1909): 145–52; "Stephen F. Austin and the Independence of Texas," *Quarterly* 13 (Apr., 1910): 257–84; "President Jackson and the Texas Revolution," *American Historical Review* 12 (July, 1907): 788–809; "The United States and Mexico, 1835–1837," *Mississippi Valley Historical Review* 1 (June, 1914): 3–15; "Don Carlos Barrett," *SHQ* 20 (Oct., 1916): 139–45; "The Influence of Slavery in the Colonization of Texas," *SHQ* 28 (July, 1924): 1–33; "Native Latin American Contribution to the Colonization and Independence of Texas," *SHQ* 46 (Jan., 1943): 317–35; "The Annexation of Texas," *SHQ* 50 (July, 1946): 49–74. For a list and more complete summary of these works see William C. Pool, *Eugene C. Barker: Historian* (Austin: Texas State Historical Association, 1971), pp. 139–72. Barker's students who published in the 1821–45 period included Walter Prescott Webb, Rudolph L. Biesele, Raymond Estep, William R. Hogan, Herbert P. Gambrell, Llerena Friend, Ohland Morton, and Amelia Williams, whose works are all cited below. Pool, *Barker,* p. 167.

PAUL D. LACK

to that of the Texas chauvinists and romanticists who came before him.[3]

Until the 1980s no substantial revision occurred on many subjects, and others still await adequate treatment. Nevertheless, important foundations for revisionism of this kind have been laid. Perhaps reflecting the general awe of Barker, much of the important scholarship on the period of Anglo colonization and the revolution has been editorial, as if this provided a means of contributing without intruding on the master's domain. Improved access to materials began years ago with the publication of some landmark works: diaries, journals, and memoirs, and, under William C. Binkley, two volumes of documents on the revolution.[4]

One example of editorial advancement for the colonization and revolution period is the massive *Papers Concerning Robertson's Colony in Texas,* by Malcolm McLean, which is also exceptional in being critical of Barker's interpretations on almost every front. Currently in its fourteenth folio-sized volume, the series reproduced virtually every conceivable document of importance on this region of the upper Brazos. The publication focused on the struggle to colonize a remote area amid Indian attacks and an equally debilitating empresario rivalry involving colonizers Robert Leftwich, the Nashville Company, and Sterling C. Robertson against the team of Samuel May Williams and Stephen F. Austin. The *Papers* document matters from local to international and everything in between. McLean also provided in-

3. Stephen Stagner, "Epics, Science, and the Lost Frontier: Texas Historical Writing, 1836–1936," *Western Historical Quarterly* 12 (Apr., 1981): 177–79. A less critical appraisal of Barker is presented in Pool, *Barker,* pp. 139–72, which sees Barker as implicitly Turnerian but reasonably fair-minded in his treatment of Mexico and an opponent of "the typical provincial Texas point of view" (p. 159).

4. Among the most important of the published primary sources are Jean Louis Berlandier, *Journey to Mexico during the Years 1826 to 1834,* ed. and trans. Sheila M. Ohlendorf et al., 2 vols. (Austin: Texas State Historical Association, 1980); William Campbell Binkley, ed., *Official Correspondence of the Texan Revolution, 1835–1836,* 2 vols. (New York: D. Appleton–Century, 1936); Mary Austin Holley, *Texas* (Austin: Texas State Historical Association, 1985); and J. P. Bryan, ed., *The Texas Diary, 1835–1838* (Austin: University of Texas Press, 1956); David J. Weber, ed., *Troubles in Texas, 1832: A Tejano Viewpoint from San Antonio* (Dallas: DeGolyer Library at Southern Methodist University, 1984); Carlos E. Castañeda, ed. and trans., "Statistical Report of Texas by Juan N. Almonte," *SHQ* 28 (Jan., 1925): 177–222; José María Sánchez, "A Trip to Texas in 1828," trans. Carlos E. Castañeda, *SHQ* 29 (1926): 249–95.

troductions that serve as vehicles for his largely unconventional hypotheses. While these challenges to the Barker consensus might be otherwise applauded, McLean's unbalanced pro-Robertson views reflect a partisan perspective. Further, the indiscriminate inclusion of so many documents of such varying degrees of importance has led to an excessively lengthy series that now needs a single-volume summary on the history of the Robertson colony.[5]

No Texas colony of the Mexican period—not even Austin's—has received adequate treatment, although some useful research has been done. Hobart Huson has written a thorough chronicle of the Refugio area. The De Witt colony has been described in a dissertation, and other graduate students are projecting studies of long-neglected subjects. Nevertheless, much needed work remains undone and unproposed.[6] Even biography, generally the strongest field of scholarship for the period 1821–45, is deficient for the era of Mexican Texas. Margaret Henson has written a useful account of Samuel May Williams, a land speculator and political broker who came under criticism for machinations that hurt the popularity of his partner Stephen F. Austin. Henson provided a useful antidote to McLean, whose views threatened to triumph by sheer weight of volume. Duncan W. Robinson's biography of Robert M. Williamson is also sound, but the several works on Tejano leaders are far less ably done.[7]

5. The publication begins with a few works from the Spanish period, and a recent volume (IA) reproduces in manuscript and typescript the diary and letter book kept by Robert Leftwich in Mexico between 1822 and 1824. Malcolm McLean, ed., *Papers Concerning Robertson's Colony in Texas*, 14 vols. (Arlington: University of Texas at Arlington Press, 1974–87).

6. Hobart Huson, *Refugio: A Comprehensive History of Refugio County from Aboriginal Times to 1953*, 2 vols. (Woodsboro, Tex.: Rooke Foundation, 1953). The two volumes are repetitive in places and short on interpretation; however, they are richly detailed and useful to other historians exploring social, military, or political subjects. Edward B. Lukes, "The De Witt Colony of Texas," Ph.D. diss., Loyola University, 1971. Two other less exhaustive accounts provide introductions to but not the last words on the Irish colonies of Southwest Texas during the 1830s. Rachel B. Hébert, *The Forgotten Colony: San Patricio de Hibernia* (Burnet, Tex.: Eakin, 1981); William Herman Oberste, *Texas Irish Empresarios and Their Colonies* (Austin: n.p., 1953). Carolina Castillo is working on the de León colony as a dissertation at the University of Texas at Austin and Jodella Kite is doing a social history of the Austin colonies at Texas Tech University.

7. Margaret Swett Henson, *Samuel May Williams: Early Texas Entrepreneur* (College Station: Texas A&M University Press, 1976); Duncan W. Robinson, *Judge Robert*

A fair amount of decent research also lies buried in that scholarly graveyard reserved for theses or remains not hidden but scattered in scholarly journals, most notably the *Southwestern Historical Quarterly*. Wide reading in these monographs plus the author's own research in primary materials helped make possible an incisive new perspective on the entire period, David J. Weber's *The Mexican Frontier, 1821–1846: The American Southwest Under Mexico*.[8] This volume placed Texas in the context of Mexico in general and its northern provinces in particular. Weber emphasized several themes. The protracted Mexican movement for independence caused economic devastation, population loss, military and religious weaknesses, and political disorder that limited Mexico's ability to respond to serious problems in its distant provinces. During this era the entire northern frontier region began to experience a vitality, traced in part to the growth of Anglo-American influences, that challenged the resources of the new nation. The institutional church went into decline, most clearly illustrated by the secularization of the missions. Likewise the presidios, weakened by the drain of years of war, no longer provided adequate defense against hostile *indios*. Mexico generally failed to integrate the frontier areas into its economy by developing the coastal trade or otherwise responding to the dynamic threat represented by the expanding United States.

Frequent political change in the interior also undermined the chances to implement clear and forceful policies in the northern states. The major effort to develop the frontier—the liberal immigration policies in the 1820s—stimulated discontent along with population growth and thus hastened Mexico's decline in other northern provinces as well as Texas. The trend toward centralization and militarization in the mid-1830s brought on separatism and revolt throughout the frontier

---

McAlpin Williamson: Texas' Three-Legged Willie (Austin: Texas State Historical Association, 1948). None of the brief biographies of Tejanos of this period are definitive. See Joseph Martin Dawson, *José Antonio Navarro: Co-Creator of Texas* (Waco: Baylor University Press, 1969); A. B. J. Hammett, *The Empresario Don Martin de León* (Waco: Texian, 1973); Raymond Estep, "The Life of Lorenzo de Zavala," Ph.D. diss., University of Texas, 1942; and Raymond Estep, "Lorenzo de Zavala and the Texas Revolution," *SHQ* 57 (Jan., 1954): 322–35. Amazingly, in light of the blossoming of scholarship on Mexican Texans, no full study of Juan Seguín has been completed. Even his classic autobiography is rare, though available in David J. Weber, ed., *Northern Mexico on the Eve of the American Invasion* (New York: Arno Press, 1976).

8. David J. Weber, *The Mexican Frontier, 1821–46: The American Southwest Under Mexico* (Albuquerque: University of New Mexico Press, 1982).

rather than restoring the region to the orbit of the interior as intended. Weber's perceptive synthesis succeeded in placing Texas in a meaningful broader perspective different from the march-of-democracy emphasis legitimatized by Barker. Weber's study may also stimulate renewed scholarship by disproving another common judgment, that the study of Texas is necessarily narrow or parochial and therefore to be shunned.

Easily the most stimulating study dealing with Mexican Texas since the last of Barker's publications, Weber's *The Mexican Frontier* was not intended to be exhaustive or to preclude additional work on Mexican Texas. Many subjects still need to be addressed more definitively, and Weber's shifting focus to earlier time periods means that scholars cannot anticipate his impending resolution of these issues. The largest such topic is the nature of Mexico's relations with Texas in the 1821–35 period as background to the Texas Revolution.

To some extent the historiographical debate on that subject has reflected the views of the participants. Many historians continue to defend the Texas position in its rebellion against Mexico by restating the explanation of the rebels at the outset of the fighting: they were conservatively defending freedom and the status quo against military tyranny in the form of centralist military dictatorship. Mexican scholars have somewhat shied away from this period, but they seem generally to reject the Texas position out of hand as mere propaganda. As Josephina Vázquez has written recently, "centralism formed the pretext for the Texas Revolution."[9]

Despite contributions by recent scholars, Barker's *Mexico and Texas, 1821–1835* has not been supplanted as a study of the background of the Texas Revolution. He considered that event to be "the inevitable result of the racial inheritances of the two peoples" who had been joined in an unwieldy political union. This emphasis on race, described more benignly as cultural conflict by most other scholars, became the most widely emphasized factor in explaining the tensions between Texas and Mexico. Although in places Barker attempted to mute his critique of the Mexican character with praise for well-intentioned officials, he generally held that Mexico was unfit for self-government, especially under the federalistic 1824 constitution.

9. Josefina Zoraida Vázquez, "The Texas Question in Mexican Politics, 1836–1845," *SHQ* 89 (Jan., 1986): 310.

PAUL D. LACK

The emphasis on an inevitable clash of cultures arose in part because Barker discounted other long-range factors over which there had been disagreement. Certain "dull, organic aches" of discontent had arisen among Anglo settlers but were largely resolved by the eve of conflict. The state church posed an irritant but in theory only, since Mexico engaged in no active persecution. Slavery had been successfully maintained by the Texans as they fended off abolitionist measures and established the institution by subterfuge; however, Barker perceived no clash over bondage among the immediate factors that led to revolt. Immigration restrictions provided a more basic irritant, but these had been abandoned by 1834. Similarly, Mexico had conceded to Anglo demands for judicial reforms and improved local government by that date. The concessions forestalled a clash but also signaled the inability of Mexico to establish a revitalized system of rule in Texas. What emerged instead, in Barker's interpretation, was a cycle that led to conflict. Genuine reforms failed, creating defensive measures by Mexico, causing resentment in Texas, and forcing more reforms on the government, which in turn feared the aggressive designs of the United States and the disloyalty of the Anglo settlers. Austin staved off full-scale rebellion, but he and other moderates became increasingly dissatisfied with Mexican politics. In the end, Barker asserted, Mexican instability precipitated revolt in Texas. The triumph of centralism under Santa Anna in 1834 exhausted Texas patience and threatened it with military despotism. Rebellion in the name of the constitution of 1824, affection for which was not emphasized by Barker, grew out of more basic sources of conflict: mutual distrust and conflicting "racial and political inheritances of the two peoples."[10]

Samuel Lowrie's *Culture Conflict in Texas* gained some notoriety, but it contributed little to the interpretations that Barker had already molded and was decidedly inferior in craftsmanship. Even its title is deceptive: Lowrie concluded that the "opposing habits and traditions" of Anglos and Mexicans caused the Texas Revolution but then asserted that the two groups had little contact and that their leaders frequently cooperated on issues of mutual benefit, raising questions about the nature and significance of culture conflict in Texas. Similarly, he gave credence to the theory that alleged religious bigotry by Mexico con-

10. Barker, *Mexico and Texas*, p. v (first quotation), p. 86 (second quotation), p. 146 (third quotation).

tributed mightily to the rebellion but also acknowledged the shortage of priests and nonenforcement of anti-Protestant laws. Lowrie's understanding of Mexican history rested on *la leyenda negra.* His harsh descriptions of the inherent intolerance and illiberalism of Mexico were contradicted by such evidence as liberal land inducements. Further, rather than describing the issue of racial slavery, where Mexico's position was decidedly more liberal than that of the Anglo migrants, Lowrie more or less dismissed it out of hand. In essence, then, he argued that the Texas Revolution resulted from "differences in folkways" that led to mutual misunderstandings, but these cultural differences were not systematically defined and the way in which they actually led to the rebellion was unclear because the author failed to describe the events of 1835. The focus on culture conflict has remained a starting point for all explanations of the background of the Texas Revolution and has been emphasized by recent scholars who do not suffer from Lowrie's scholarly deficiencies; however, Anglo-Tejano relations in this period have not yet been fully studied.[11]

The most clearly focused work on the Texas Revolution, William C. Binkley's lectures at Louisiana State University in 1952, shifted attention somewhat to political matters, namely the struggle to maintain the 1824 constitution. However, he differed little from Barker and other earlier scholars in emphasizing cultural conflict as well. Thus Binkley also depicted the Texans as conservative defenders of the existing arrangement of government and Santa Anna's centralists as the aggressors. Similarly, his analysis concurred with Barker in placing Austin at center stage.[12]

Emerging interest in the Mexican Texans became an important historiographical factor in the 1970s, but it recast the emphasis on cultural clash rather than originating a new view of the background to the Texas rebellion. Arnoldo De León and David Weber empha-

11. Samuel Harman Lowrie, *Culture Conflict in Texas, 1821–1835* (New York: Columbia University Press, 1932), p. 7 (first quotation), p. 74 (second quotation). For a recent and far more sophisticated study of the religious issue see Miller, "Stephen F. Austin and the Anglo-Texan Response to the Religious Establishment." This article concludes that active religious conflict did not occur but that Austin harbored strong Enlightenment attitudes and that "repressed resentment" (p. 316) against the state church was a factor in the Texas Revolution.

12. William C. Binkley, *The Texas Revolution* (Baton Rouge: Louisiana State University Press, 1952).

sized Anglo racism as the predominant factor in leading to the 1835–36 revolt.[13] Though some have read his recent work as an alteration of this view, Weber has recently reiterated his emphasis on Anglo-Mexican cultural differences, pointing out that the two groups largely lived apart, that Anglos who had the least contact with Tejanos became leaders of the revolt while only those settlers who lived as a minority amid the Mexican Texans made substantial efforts to adjust their prejudices, and that Anglo inhabitants generally disliked the potential of living permanently under the rule of a people whom they considered inferior. He also suggests that comparative analysis with other borderland revolts reveals that these lacked the virulence of the Texas version, further emphasizing the significance of ethnic factors.[14]

The major challenge to the "clash of cultures" theory came in the unpublished dissertation of James Crisp, which held that racial conflict bore little responsibility for the origins of the Texas Revolution. He asserted that people in the United States expressed sympathy for Mexicans as victims of Spanish tyranny and that analogies between English-American and Spanish-American independence movements tended to mitigate ethnic animosity. Thus, Crisp argued, emigrants to Texas in the 1820s and 1830s came without a full-blown set of negative preconceptions to serve as a taproot for rebellion and learned to get along reasonably well with the Tejano elite. He concluded that the ugliest expression of racism triumphed with and after the Texas Revolution, its ironic consequence rather than its cause.[15]

Without accepting the view that Anglo racism toward Mexicans

13. David J. Weber, ed., *Foreigners in Their Native Land* (Albuquerque: University of New Mexico Press, 1973), pp. 89–90; Arnoldo De León, *They Called Them Greasers* (Austin: University of Texas Press, 1983), pp. 11–13.

14. Weber's restatement came as the commentator at the session "Social Backgrounds of the Texas Revolution" of the Texas State Historical Association meeting in Austin in Mar., 1986. All students of Anglo racial attitudes seem to agree that they became more intolerant over time. Weber also concludes that differences in political culture played an important role in the emergence of the conflict.

15. Crisp's paper presented at the 1986 meeting of the Texas State Historical Association, "Race, Revolution, and the Republic: Toward a Reinterpretation," restated the position of his dissertation, "Anglo-Texan Attitudes toward the Mexican, 1821–1845," Ph.D. diss., Yale University, 1976, pp. 7–194. Another paper presented at this meeting, by Rondel V. Davidson, emphasized the significance of European intellectual origins of the Texas Revolution and thus implicitly supported the position taken by Crisp.

was initially mild, at least one historian of the Tejanos of this period has also deemphasized cultural conflict. Gilberto M. Hinojosa has suggested that economic matters—frustrations over land titles and the bonds of trade that had been growing and promoting prosperity in the Tejano community—persuaded many of Mexican descent to revolt alongside the Anglo settlers. The conclusion that Texans rebelled in response to "real" as well as ideological stimuli is similar to my own emphasis, that the federalist political system was the vehicle by which the Texans defended their economic interests and overall hegemony against repeated centralist threats to the institution of racial bondage in Texas.[16]

No full-scale treatment of the Texas issue has been produced by Mexican scholars, but gradually some reappraisal of the causes of the Texas Revolution has emerged from the new perspectives and sources of Mexico. A fine pioneering monograph by Barker student Ohland Morton, *Terán and Texas,* remains still the best researched and most balanced study of Mexican policy toward Texas in the years before the Texas Revolution. This work carefully detailed the struggles of a key official (shown as liberal, humane, and able) who sought to devise and implement farsighted reforms between 1827 and 1832, in particular efforts to control Anglo-American immigration and to promote settlement from Europe and Mexico. Morton showed how well-intentioned policies came apart as a result of political instability and inadequate resources, with tragic results for Terán. The author investigated source material in both Texas and Mexico and arrived at judicious conclusions, even without providing a complete reformulation of the relationship between the Mexican government and its troubling northern province. Margaret S. Henson's thoroughly researched and clearly written biography of Juan Davis Bradburn serves as a kind of companion study in that it details the story of one official responsible for implementing Terán's plans. She has provided a corrective on this Anglo-Mexican commander at Anahuac, whose actions convulsed the southeastern area into a conflict that very nearly brought on full-scale rebellion in Texas in 1832, and also a defense of the cen-

16. Gilberto M. Hinojosa, "Mexican-Texans in the Revolution," paper presented at the Texas State Historical Association meeting, Mar., 1986. This study remains unpublished but is being complemented by work underway by the author's students. Paul D. Lack, "Slavery and the Texas Revolution," *SHQ* 89 (Oct., 1985): 181–202.

tralist position. Malcolm McLean, in emphasizing the conspiratorial role of land speculators in the Coahuila legislature, has also defended centralist policy, asserting that its primary and genuine goal in militarizing Texas in 1835 was the righteous arrest of evildoers.[17]

A well-balanced, readable, and brief account of the origins and coming of the Texas rebellion is contained in Weber's *The Mexican Frontier*, which emphasized a variety of factors. In addition to describing the institutional decline that occurred in the northern region during and after independence, Weber demonstrated that the loose federalist system had provided but little in the way of governmental restraints. Changes in the 1830s, including attempts to reverse the liberal immigration policies, led to growing tension. Other political factors included widespread dissatisfaction (even among Tejanos) with a marriage in statehood with Coahuila and the blunder of the centralists in attempting to restore military strength in 1835. Weber's account also provided the Texas rebellion with a kind of legitimacy in demonstrating that separatism grew throughout Mexico's northern provinces in the years 1835-46. In a sense the Texas Revolution acquires a sense of inevitability in his description of various ways in which independence left Mexico weakened at the very time that the dynamic influences of the United States surged into this frontier region.

A consensus of recent works seems to confirm the view that internal disorders in Mexico undermined construction of a coherent policy toward Texas; however, historians have not satisfactorily analyzed

17. Ohland Morton, *Terán and Texas: A Chapter in Texas-Mexican Relations* (Austin: Texas State Historical Association, 1948). Morton's generally able study was of course limited in scope and research, reflective of the absence of much other scholarship on related subjects. Strangely, the Bexar Archives were not cited by Morton and have not yet been mined exhaustively by a comprehensive study of Mexico-Texas relations. Margaret Swett Henson, *Juan Davis Bradburn: A Reappraisal of the Mexican Commander of Anahuac* (College Station: Texas A&M University Press, 1983). Henson's defense is somewhat overdone. Admitting the difficulties of Bradburn's task, he still appears to have been quarrelsome, unrealistic, and possessed of a poor combination of rigidity and indecisiveness. For McLean's views on the role of land speculators see *Papers Concerning Robertson's Colony*, 10:55-70. Barker's conclusion, that those who sought personal advantage by making large purchases of land from the Coahuila state government retarded rather than advanced the course of rebellion in Texas, still seems more valid. Eugene C. Barker, "Land Speculation as a Cause of the Texas Revolution," *Quarterly* 10 (July, 1906): 76-95. Pool, *Barker*, p. 159, concludes that the absence of important documents on this issue is likely to prevent a final resolution.

the origins or the workings of those policies in practice. Few new studies have been done employing the Bexar and Nacogdoches archives much less the abundant resources of Mexican depositories. An exception is Nettie Lee Benson's lengthy article on "Texas as Viewed from Mexico, 1820–1834," based on exhaustive research in books, newspapers, and government documents produced in Mexico City during that period. She demonstrated that Mexico's leaders believed Texas to be a valuable territory and acted out of an abiding concern over the likelihood of U.S. aggression. A great need remains for a comprehensive study of Mexico in the period 1821–35 that develops imperial or provincial matters in the context of its politics and analyzes the coming of the Texas rebellion from Mexican sources.[18]

Uncertainties resulting from the absence of definitive work on the background of the Texas rebellion has allowed conspiracy theories to continue to find some support. The most lasting of these centers on scheming between Andrew Jackson and Sam Houston. Fifty years ago Richard Stenberg attempted to unravel the duplicity of these leaders' efforts to detach Texas from Mexico. His arguments have continued to attract attention and support, but they rest on unsolid ground — inference from indirect evidence and excessive reliance on rumors or memoirs that emanated from a later animosity toward Houston.[19] De-

18. Nettie Lee Benson, "Texas as Viewed from Mexico, 1820–1834," *SHQ* 90 (Jan., 1987): 219–91. The best survey of Mexican politics in this period, Michael P. Costeloe's *La primera república de México, 1824–1835,* is not available in English translation. Weber has identified numerous documents related to Texas in the Archivo General de la Nación in Mexico that historians have not exploited. Letter to the author, Oct. 24, 1988.

19. Richard R. Stenberg, "The Texas Schemes of Jackson and Houston, 1829–1836," *Southwestern Social Science Quarterly* 15 (Dec., 1934): 229–50. His account points out that the U.S. president had encouraged several such projects and suggests that Houston came to Mexico's northern province as Jackson's filibusterer, a possibility that is documented mostly on the basis of speculation about what might have occurred at meetings between the two. Given the nature of the subject it was perhaps inevitable that Stenberg's case would rest on contemporary rumors, elaborate descriptions of bogus letters designed to cover the tracks of the alleged conspirators, and random bragging done by Houston. The author admits the existence of evidence that weakens his case: Houston did not maintain a consistent course of agitation for rebellion in his first years in Texas and did not emerge in a position of leadership until the conflict was well on its way. In fact, Stenberg writes, the Texas Revolution "would have taken place, and just as successfully, had Houston never set foot on Texas soil" (p. 245). He also presents a case for conspiracy involving the Texas general's

spite the recent contribution of Weber, treatment of the background of the Texas rebellion remains incomplete and segmented, abundant archival materials have never been systematically examined, and recent methodological approaches and historiographical assumptions have not been applied to the issue.

Much more also remains to be done on the Texas Revolution. The years 1835–36 have not been fully explored from the Mexican perspective. The most significant publications are primary sources. Carlos E. Castañeda's translation of the memoirs of several leading military figures in *The Mexican Side of the Texas Revolution* and Carmen Perry's edition of the remarkable diary of José Enrique de la Peña provide insight on divisions within the military leadership. No thorough treatment of developments in the interior has been published. Recently, though, Michael P. Costeloe analyzed Mexico's understanding of the Texas Revolution as shown in the press, and his brief work provided several important conclusions. The revolt was perceived as an unsubstantial threat at first, a view challenged only by those who feared that success might further the kingly or Napoleonic ambitions of Santa Anna. The early centralist triumphs thus contributed to anti-Yankee xenophobia and to overconfidence which in the end made the Mexican defeat a serious blow to national pride. The failure of the Texas rebellion to take advantage of divisions in Mexican politics had been partially explained in C. Alan Hutchinson's study of federalist José Antonio Mexia, which documents the subject's disillusionment at the virulent anti-Mexican prejudice among Anglo Texans.[20]

The matter of the impact of the Texas Revolution on the United

possible goal of retreating to the area of the Sabine in order to involve U.S. troops in the defeat of Santa Anna in the spring of 1836. Ultimately this is a theory that cannot be proven (or disproven in some minds, given the nature of conspiracy theories in general and of the evidence in this case) but clearly rests on unsatisfactory evidence.

20. Carlos E. Castañeda, trans., *The Mexican Side of the Texas Revolution* (Dallas: P. L. Turner, 1928); José Enrique de la Peña, *With Santa Anna in Texas: A Personal Narrative of the Revolution,* trans. Carmen Perry (College Station: Texas A&M University Press, 1975); Vicente Filisola, *Evacuation of Texas* (Waco: Texian, 1965); Michael P. Costeloe, "The Mexican Press of 1836 and the Battle of the Alamo," *SHQ* 91 (Apr., 1988): 533–44; C. Alan Hutchinson, "General José Antonio Mexia and His Texas Interests," *SHQ* 82 (Oct., 1978): 117–42; and C. Alan Hutchinson, "Mexican Federalists in New Orleans and the Texas Revolution," *Louisiana Historical Quarterly* 29 (Jan., 1956): 1–47.

States and vice versa has been rather fully detailed; several articles traced the origins and development of the Texas enthusiasm in various parts of the United States. Barker's work included an analysis of U.S. aid to Texas in the context of neutrality violations, concluding that lukewarm efforts by the Jackson administration contributed to Mexico's defeat and resulting resentment. Several scholars have emphasized the Texas issue in U.S. politics. Merton Dillon is the principal student of Benjamin Lundy, the earliest critic of the Texas rebellion as slaveocracy conspiracy. Frederick Merk analyzed the annexation issue in terms of politics rather than diplomacy, with emphasis on the impact of antislavery forces in retarding the movement to acquire Texas; his conclusions have been reinforced by other recent works.[21]

Many Texas topics for this same period have been inadequately examined, although Binkley's *The Texas Revolution* provided a much-needed overview. Half of his essays covered the war period. No single leader proved able to organize, much less dominate, the revolution, Binkley concluded. A malcontented and poorly provisioned army, respecting no outside authority and thus divided into hopelessly independent units, lurched from one strategic vision to another with the result that no concerted policy prevailed. Political disunity contributed to the overall malaise, as Texas leaders established and destroyed no fewer than five governments during the year after hostilities commenced. Binkley's essays provided a fine summary of the leading events, but their purpose was to serve as an introductory rather than a definitive

---

21. During Barker's era, J. E. Winston wrote a series of articles detailing state by state reactions to the Texas Revolution, independence, and campaign for annexation. These covered Kentucky, Virginia, Mississippi, New York, and Pennsylvania. See *SHQ* 16 (July, 1912): 27–62; *SHQ* (Jan., 1913): 277–83; *SHQ* 17 (Jan., [1914]): 262–82; *SHQ* 18 (Apr., 1915): 368–85; and *SHQ* 21 (July, 1917): 35–60. Claude Elliott extended the coverage in "Alabama and the Texas Revolution," *SHQ* 50 (Jan., 1947): 315–28, and "Georgia and the Texas Revolution," *Georgia Historical Quarterly* 28 (Dec., 1944): 233–50. For Barker's work see "The United States and Mexico, 1835–1837," *Mississippi Valley Historical Review* 1 (1914): 1–30. Merton L. Dillon, "Benjamin Lundy in Texas," *SHQ* 63 (July, 1950): 46–62; John H. Schroeder, "Annexation or Independence: The Texas Issue in American Politics, 1836–1845," *SHQ* 89 (Oct., 1985): 137–64; Frederick Merk, *Slavery and the Annexation of Texas* (New York: A. A. Knopf, 1972). This is the one area on which the interpretations of Barker's era, which tended to be highly defensive of the conduct of Tyler, Polk, and the United States, have been thoroughly revised; however, Barker's principal writings did not focus on these topics. Pool, *Barker*, pp. 170–72.

PAUL D. LACK

work. Naturally, many intriguing questions remained: What were the sources of Texas disunity? Was there serious opposition to the Texas cause from within? Should the term "Texas Revolution" be taken seriously? Further, Binkley made no pretense at providing a social history, thus leaving to other scholars questions regarding the responses by the people of different regions and the impact of the war on their lives. In fact, he ended his work with an open invitation for historians to fill the gaps left by his study: "The one thing which can be suggested with assurance is that the last word concerning the meaning or significance of the Texas Revolution has not yet been said." Yet, just as few had written of the Texas Revolution in the quarter-century after Barker's major works came out, so only scattered accounts of some specific subjects would appear in a similar period after the publication of Binkley's lectures.[22]

For detailed analysis of most topics in the period of the Texas Revolution attention must be given to the scholarly journals. The best accounts of internal political dynamics come from articles on the General Council and the Texas Constitution of 1836. Two efforts have been made to analyze opposition to the revolution within Texas; regrettably, they arrived at different conclusions and failed to analyze the actual center of pro-Mexican behavior, western Texas. Brief community histories of Bexar and Harrisburg, although they covered different eras, demonstrated the existence of variables and attitudes not necessarily present in the Austin colonies. Fane Downs's study of women in this era made one of the few contributions to much-neglected social history.[23] However excellent these pieces of history are, collectively they

22. Binkley, *Texas Revolution*, p. 132 (quotation). On the issue of its revolutionary qualities, Binkley hedged by stating that the Texas cause should be seen as a continuation of the pattern established by the American and Spanish American revolutions but that the term *revolution* is subject to such vague interpretations that serious exploration of revolutionary qualities could not be undertaken (see p. 1). Andreas Reichstein addresses the issue of whether the Texas Revolution had revolutionary qualities and concludes that it did not (see below for a fuller discussion of his work).
23. Ralph W. Steen, "Analysis of the Work of the General Council, Provisional Government of Texas, 1835-1836," *SHQ* 40 (Apr., 1937): 309-33, *SHQ* 41 (Jan., 1938): 225-40, *SHQ* (Apr., 1938): 324-48, and *SHQ* 42 (July, 1938): 23-54, provides useful detail on the conflict against Governor Henry Smith and other topics. Rupert Richardson, "Framing the Constitution of the Republic of Texas," *SHQ* 31 (Jan., 1927): 191-220, is especially valuable for its analysis of the antecedents of this document in various state constitutions. Andrew F. Muir, "Tories in Texas, 1836," *Texas Military*

do not reflect many common themes and cannot substitute for the kind of general interpretations that arise from single-volume, single-author studies. A contemporary European scholar, Andreas Reichstein, has recently published in German a book on the Texas independence movement, which attempts to broaden the scope and to improve the depth of Binkley's study and to break from the predominant views established by Barker.[24]

One barrier to scholarship for this period—the suffocating power of its heroes—appears in some ways ready to be overcome. The pathbreaking work in that respect, *How Did Davy Die?* by Dan Kilgore, explored a narrow portion of the folklore-Hollywood version of the Alamo story. It dispassionately reviewed the evidence, discarding those sources made unreliable by distance in time and place, and presented findings that rankled those who placed Texas chauvinism above historical veracity. Kilgore demonstrated that all the firsthand accounts, written independently of each other and thus not easily discarded, indicate that Crockett was captured toward the end of the fighting along with five or six other defenders who were then promptly executed by Santa Anna's orders. The fact that the author was a Certified Public Accountant and past president of the Texas State Historical Association rather than a professional debunker (or left-wing academician)

History 4 (summer, 1964): 81–94, turned his usual skeptical eye on the tradition that substantial Tory behavior occurred in Southeast Texas, pointing out that the Mexicans received little if any actual aid and comfort from the citizenry and explaining these allegations in terms of the tradition of familial feuding. Margaret S. Henson, although also known for a revisionist mentality, constructed a longer list of Tory suspects and gave credence to the charges against them. "Tory Sentiment in Anglo-Texan Public Opinion, 1832–1836," *SHQ* 90 (July, 1986): 1–34. Frank de la Teja and John Wheat, "Bexar: Profile of a Tejano Community, 1820–1832," *SHQ* 89 (July, 1985): 7–34, show the conflict of 1835 ending and disrupting the growth of Bexar. Muir described a divided region of Southeast Texas which behaved on the whole quite unheroically during the rebellion and war in "The Municipality of Harrisburg, 1835–1836," *SHQ* 56 (July, 1952): 36–50. Also see Fane Downs, "'Tryels and Trubbles': Women in Early Nineteenth-Century Texas," *SHQ* 90 (July, 1986): 35–56.

24. Andreas Reichstein, *Der texanische Unabhangigdeitskrieg, 1835/6: Ursachen und Wirkungen* (Berlin, West Germany: Dietrich Reimer Verlag, 1984). An English translation under the title *Rise of the Lone Star* was published by Texas A&M University Press in 1989. According to one review, this study deals mostly with questions regarding causation, emphasizing the role of land speculators and of U.S. expansionism, but underplays internal ethnic and regional influences. See the review by Theodore Gish, *SHQ* 89 (Jan., 1986): 361–62.

made his conclusion no less galling to those emotionally committed to the more heroic mythical tradition. Kilgore aroused a storm of protest; nevertheless, his conclusions have gained growing acceptance, and he seems to have paved the way for a milder reception of the large body of recent revisionist work on related topics.[25]

For years the Alamo has attracted by far the greatest amount of attention of any aspect of the Texas Revolution, whether by historians or in the varied expressions of popular culture. As Don Graham observes, insofar as writers and filmmakers are concerned, "in the final analysis the story of the Revolution is the story of the Alamo." Historically it has served as the springboard for indoctrinating the public with a variety of ideological principles, from anti-Catholicism to racism to the elevation of the Texas experience to classical stature. However, as overt bigotry has come to seem increasingly impolite over the last thirty years, one paradigm—the heroic democratic struggle for freedom against tyranny—has remained as the central theme. The Alamo has become so closely identified with the revolution (and indeed the story of Texas) that even media-centered revisionists turn to it as the focus of their productions.[26]

This continual retelling of the Alamo tale may be viewed with mild amusement by scholars because it seems somehow characteristic of that lowbrow expression known as popular culture. Yet, if the number of publications is used as a gauge, historians have also surrendered to the Alamo mystique. They have covered the subject from a variety of angles and depths, pitched toward both popular and professional audiences. The resulting works defy easy categorization. Perhaps the most widely read, *A Time To Stand,* by Walter Lord, has considerable research merit behind its stirring narrative.[27] The sesqui-

25. Dan Kilgore, *How Did Davy Die?* (College Station: Texas A&M University Press, 1978).

26. Don Graham, "Remembering the Alamo: The Story of the Texas Revolution in Popular Culture," *SHQ* 90 (July, 1985): 35–66.

27. Walter Lord, *A Time to Stand* (New York: Harper, 1961). Much of the research on which the various studies rely came out of the pioneering work done by Amelia Williams. See "A Critical Study of the Siege of the Alamo and of the Personnel of Its Defenders," *SHQ* 37 (July, 1933): 1–44, *SHQ* (Oct., 1933): 79–115, *SHQ* (Jan., 1934): 157–84, and *SHQ* (Apr., 1934): 237–312. Another popular account, Lon Tinkle, *13 Days to Glory* (New York: McGraw-Hill, 1958), relied on fictional conventions of style and contributed no new insights.

centennial of the Texas Revolution sparked renewed depictions of the Alamo. The state historical association published a pamphlet in response to the anticipated thirst for a reliable, readable, and short narrative. Some fresh and original scholarship also occurred, especially reconceptualizing the Alamo experience as cultural phenomenon. Paul A. Hutton, along with Graham and Weber, explored the origins of the Alamo myth in history, film, and literature; a book-length work on *Alamo Images* extended this coverage to include prints and other artistic expressions. Edward Tabor Linenthal detailed the uses of the structure as a source of patriotic inspiration. His symbolic interpretation employed techniques of religious linguistic analysis to dissect ways in which the Alamo story has been used to teach inspirational lessons and, more recently, ways in which the shrine has stimulated both intercultural debate and reconciliation. Michael R. Green traced the origins and travels of the famous Travis letter. All of these help not only to set the record straight but to account for the grip that this event has had on the American imagination.[28]

Even if these efforts were largely revisionist, they did not correct the narrowness of focus of scholarship on the Texas Revolution. Research materials became easily accessible after 1973 with the publication of John H. Jenkins's edition of nine five-hundred-page volumes of *Papers* on the subject.[29] However, even the military phases have not been fully treated, although recent and pending publications promise

28. Ben Procter, *The Battle of the Alamo* (Austin: Texas State Historical Association, 1986). Paul Andrew Hutton provided excellent summaries of the various Alamo legends in the introduction to Susan Prendergast Schoelwer, *Alamo Images: Changing Perceptions of a Texas Experience* (Dallas: DeGolyer Library and Southern Methodist University Press, 1985), and in *American History Illustrated* (Mar., 1986). *Alamo Images* contains a good overall summary of the event as both history and myth. See also Schoelwer, "The Artist's Alamo: A Reappraisal of Pictorial Evidence, 1836–1850," *SHQ* 91 (Apr., 1988): 403–56; Michael R. Green, "'To the People of Texas & All Americans in the World,'" *SHQ* 91 (Apr., 1988): 483–508; Edward Tabor Linenthal, "'A Reservoir of Spiritual Power': Patriotic Faith at the Alamo in the Twentieth Century," *SHQ* 91 (Apr., 1988): 509–32; Frederick S. Voss, "Portraying an American Original: The Likenesses of Davy Crockett," *SHQ* 91 (Apr., 1988): 457–82; David J. Weber, "Refighting the Alamo: Mythmaking and the Texas Revolution," in *Myth and the History of the Hispanic Southwest: Essays by David J. Weber* (Albuquerque: University of New Mexico Press, 1988).

29. John Holmes Jenkins, ed., *The Papers of the Texas Revolution, 1835–1836*, 10 vols. (Austin: Presidial, 1973).

correctives. James Pohl and Stephen Hardin have contributed a fine article that served as a military overview of the revolution. Recognizing that wars reflect society, they suggested that each side used a strategy that grew out of its heritage and resources. Although its scope prevented this work from answering many of the controversies that still surround the military history of the revolution (why did Houston retreat so far? why was Fannin so dumbfounded? . . .), the article raised the military history of the Texas Revolution to a higher level and created great expectations of Pohl's and Hardin's impending books on the subject. If sufficiently thorough, they may lessen the need for reassessment of the campaigns that resulted in the Battle of San Jacinto and the Goliad massacre.[30]

The other major engagement, the siege and storming of Bexar in 1835, is the subject of a fine new study by Alwyn Barr. He demonstrates convincingly the significance of this episode and shows how the substantial body of Texas troops (comparable in numbers to those who served with Houston at San Jacinto) managed to dig out a hard-fought victory in the house-to-house encounter in San Antonio. This study includes descriptions of the structure, composition, and size of both the Texas and Mexican armies as well as the problems of strategy and command on both sides. Barr concludes that the Tex-

---

30. James W. Pohl and Stephen L. Hardin, "The Military History of the Texas Revolution: An Overview," *SHQ* 89 (Oct., 1985): 137–64. Illustrating their thesis, the authors point out that Mexico, with superior cavalry and artillery, a more disciplined army, and a commander dedicated to Napoleonic visions, generally attempted a conventional war of open-field maneuvers. Most Texans recognized their disadvantage in such engagements and preferred "woods" tactics, which produced their only victories. Similarly, Urrea's success against Fannin's army demonstrated that the Texans fared poorly in stand-up fights against Mexican cavalry. Pohl and Hardin viewed the contest for the Alamo as an aberration in the sense that both sides placed exaggerated importance on the place. For studies of individual campaigns see Frank X. Tolbert, *The Day of San Jacinto* (New York: McGraw-Hill, 1959); and Jakie L. Pruett and Everett B. Cole, Sr., *Goliad Massacre: A Tragedy of the Texas Revolution* (Austin: Eakin, 1985). These are useful summaries but based on fragmentary research and provide neither adequate depth nor solutions to the controversies that surround these engagements. The best account of Goliad is still the unpublished work by Harbert Davenport in the Archives Division of the Texas State Library. Also useful because they are based on original research in primary materials are Richard G. Santos, *Santa Anna's Campaign against Texas, 1835–1836* (Salisbury, N.C.: Documentary, 1982); and Hobart Huson, *Captain Phillip Dimmitt's Commandancy* (Austin: Von Boeckmann-Jones, 1974), on Goliad before Mar., 1836.

ans won because of advantages in position and arms rather than superior valor.[31]

These welcome advances in the field of military history do not resolve all the needs for additional scholarship. In my view, as set forth in my book, forthcoming from Texas A&M Press, the proper way to advance understanding of this period is to treat the Texas Revolution as political and social history. Such an analysis reveals certain revolutionary dimensions of internal conflict. Texans entered into their quarrel with Mexico as a fragmented people, individualistic, divided from one community to another by rivalries for land and other jealousies, bothered by ethnic and racial tensions, and lacking a consensus about the meaning of political changes in Mexico. Their pursuit of unity and a government possessed of the necessary force proved elusive. A sizable body of Texans rallied to the side of the Mexican centralists, and the war stimulated other divisions: panic over slave rebellion, tensions between army volunteers and the majority who refused military service, conflicts between soldiers and civilians over the impressment of supplies, and suspicions on issues such as land policy. For the masses of Texans the revolution was a time of dislocation and grief which even the eventual outcome of battle did not heal. The experiences of the years 1835–36 left a new nation burdened by political upheaval, social disorder, and ethnic bitterness that helped to define the Texas identity for the future.

The Lone Star Republic, a topic addressed more by his students than by Barker, has attracted some able scholarship. Stanley Siegel's *Political History of the Texas Republic, 1836–1845* provided a more detailed account than has been written for Mexican Texas or the revolution. However, this work was essentially a chronological narrative based primarily on published sources and without a discernible thesis. Several points nevertheless emerge clearly: Texas achieved a degree of political stability under Sam Houston, who brought the popularity of a military hero to office but retained a powerful commitment to civilian rule and policies of restraint in terms of the army and defense. Despite factional disputation and talk of "party" influences, Texas did not develop a regular party system, and politics remained largely a matter of personality. Siegel emphasized diplomatic history, with the

31. Alwyn Barr, *Texans in Revolt: The Battle for San Antonio, 1835* (Austin: University of Texas Press, 1990).

result that vital issues of domestic politics received little if any attention. He provided no overall discussion of the complicated machinations of land policies, efforts to promote settlement, local government, or such issues as education and economic development. Some characteristics of Texas political life become clear anyway: regional conflict was pervasive, and intraregional disharmonies also prevailed in such instances as the Regulator-Moderator war of Shelby County; nationalism did not develop sufficiently to present even a modest obstacle to the movement for annexation to the United States. So, while Siegel did not ask some basic questions (Was Texas acquiring the characteristics of nationhood despite its early struggles? Was Texas making progress or merely surviving?), his work can be used to formulate some initial answers. His book presented a solid foundation on which the political history of the Republic could be constructed.[32]

Some of the important topics that Siegel neglected, including colonization in the Republic, have attracted good historians. Seymour V. Connor on the Peters colony and Bobby Weaver on Castro's colony were both thorough. Several scholars have traced the origins of German colonization that dated from the Republic period. Compared to the sparse treatment of colonization during Mexican Texas, these accounts provide reasonably complete coverage. Just as military topics have attracted the bulk of scholarship on the Texas Revolution, many studies have been done on the problem of defense in the nation. Joseph Milton Nance produced two massive volumes on the problems of the Texas-Mexican frontier, and others have detailed the history of the navy. Likewise, the diplomacy of the Republic has been admirably described, including a fine study of the French Legation by Nancy Barker.[33]

32. Stanley Siegel, *A Political History of the Texas Republic* (Austin: University of Texas Press, 1956). Two other useful narrative accounts are Seymour V. Connor, *Adventure in Glory* (Austin: Steck-Vaughn, 1965); and John Edward Weems, *Dream of Empire: A Human History of the Republic of Texas, 1836–1846* (New York: Simon and Schuster, 1971). Connor's "The Evolution of County Government in the Republic of Texas," *SHQ* 55 (Oct., 1951): 163–200, is a fine monograph on a complicated subject.

33. Seymour V. Connor, *The Peters Colony of Texas* (Austin: Texas State Historical Association, 1959). Bobby D. Weaver, *Castro's Colony: Empresario Development in Texas, 1842–1865* (College Station: Texas A&M University Press, 1985), is exhaustively researched and contains comparative analyses of other Texas colonial enterprises. The standard history of German colonization is R. L. Biesele, *The History of the German*

The kind of questions that Siegel and other narrative accounts failed to address have been explored by Mark Nackman, who in *A Nation Within a Nation* presents a bold and spirited attempt to explain the origins of Texas distinctiveness. He asserts that, despite its brief and troubled experience as an independent country, Texas acquired a nationalism that lingered on after annexation. Common experiences of frontier living and conflicts with Mexico separated Texans from other peoples and gave them a sense of nationalism. They were by definition "all expatriates," often fleeing from the law, creditors, or failed family relationships. In the vastness of their new land the emigrants dreamed of even greater future glories while defending themselves from the hardships imposed by the natural and human environment. Nackman recognized the connection between political and social topics. For example, defenses remained so weak that the sturdy yeomanry shied away from the lures of free land, meaning that the new nation attracted instead a class of adventurers who gave Texas a deserved reputation for social instability. This factor in turn developed a peculiar national "character." Nackman asserted that Texas' origin as a haven for malcontents gave birth to distinctive qualities—an expansiveness made barely tolerable by a self-derogating brand of humor, a "hunger for distinction" moderated by the democratic flavor of politics and society, a knights-errant mystique and penchant for suicidal behavior, and a willingness to embrace a newcomer despite the individual's pre-Texas past. Nackman maintained that pride in nationhood became a powerful force despite the failures of the young Republic in defense, diplomacy, war, and finance. Nationalism grew on fertile ground in that the Republic had a set of revolutionary heroes, a modicum of progress, and emotional symbols (the Lone Star flag, a battleground

Settlements in Texas, 1831–1861 (Austin: Privately printed, 1930). A good biography of one of the leaders is Irene M. King, *John O. Meusebach, German Colonizer in Texas* (Austin: University of Texas Press, 1967). Terry G. Jordan, *German Seed on Texas Soil: Immigrant Farmers in the Nineteenth Century* (Austin: University of Texas Press, 1966), makes fine use of the census records to demonstrate the process of adaptation. Joseph Milton Nance, *After San Jacinto: The Texas-Mexican Frontier, 1836–1841* and *Attack and Counterattack: The Texas-Mexican Frontier, 1842* (Austin: University of Texas Press, 1963, 1964). On the navy see Tom Henderson Wells, *Commodore Moore and the Texas Navy* (Austin: University of Texas Press, 1960), which is overly defensive of its subject; and Jim Dan Hill, *The Texas Navy* (Chicago: University of Chicago Press, 1937); Nancy Barker, ed. and trans., *The French Legation in Texas,* 2 vols. (Austin: Texas State Historical Association, 1971, 1973).

of heroic remembrance, a sacred tomb in the Alamo) all celebrated on Independence Day. Texas, like the United States, had found a usable past. Further, the continuing failure to make peace with Mexico provided the people with a neighboring scapegoat to hate. Even though emotions gave way to reality in the instance of annexation, Nackman concluded that "allegiance to the Lone Star" lived on and "Texas would remain a country within a country."[34]

His valuable insights notwithstanding, Nackman's modest research base, combined with a tendency toward speculative fancies, led to some poorly conceived theories. For example, his assertion that Texas' distinctiveness from the South grew out of an unusually large northern or foreign-born percentage of the population may have some validity. Yet his conclusion that this factor, combined with the dominance of upland southern migration to Texas, retarded the development of slavery is clearly exaggerated, especially in light of Randolph B. Campbell's conclusion to the contrary in his study *Empire for Slavery*. The thesis of this work, as suggested by the title, places Texas squarely within the southern tradition.[35] Nackman's hypothesis also suffered from some deficiencies. His insistence on the genuineness of Texas nationalism cannot explain away one incontrovertible factor: the overwhelming desire of both people and leaders to abandon independence for statehood, a prevailing attitude from the beginning to the end of the young Republic. Nevertheless, Nackman provided a bold and imaginative study that took seriously the matter of distinctiveness, an issue fundamental to Texas studies.

Readers who have the patience to blend the narratives of historians like Siegel and the analytical account of Nackman can gain an informed perspective on the political history of the Texas Republic, although a more complete and integrated work would be welcome. One possible approach would be to view the entire period from 1835 to 1846 through the leadership provided by Sam Houston. Even though

34. Mark E. Nackman, *A Nation within a Nation: The Rise of Texas Nationalism* (Port Washington, N.Y.: Kennikat Press, 1975), p. 6 (first quotation), p. 55 (second quotation), p. 108 (third quotation). Nackman's article, "Anglo-American Migrants to the West: Men of Broken Fortunes? The Case of Texas, 1821–1846," *Western Historical Quarterly* 5 (Oct., 1974): 441–55, presented a theory similar to that of Hogan on an important topic of social history, the background of immigrants to Texas.

35. Randolph B. Campbell, *An Empire for Slavery: The Peculiar Institution in Texas, 1821–1865* (Baton Rouge: Louisiana State University Press, 1989).

biography is the field of scholarship most fully developed for this period and Houston has been the subject of many works, no full study
has been done of his leadership of the Republic. The one of most use
to professional historians is *The Great Designer,* by Llerena Friend. Yet
this volume, although balanced in respect to the varied and lengthy
career of the subject, devoted but little space to the Republic, with
coverage further diluted by the need to include both private and public concerns. Thus Friend's work placed Houston at the center of events
but neither detailed the nature of his leadership nor provided much
in the way of interpretation or definitive analysis of the most crucial
questions that surrounded him. Of his two-term presidency the author
concluded, "Houston had received an undue measure of both criticism and praise," a lukewarm view that almost cries out for bold reappraisal.[36]
Other biographies focus on careers more exclusively identified with
the Republic period. The best of these is Herbert Gambrell's study
of Anson Jones, which gave useful coverage to political, diplomatic,
and other topics. This author's work on Lamar was less satisfactory,
and some important figures have not yet attracted able modern biographers. Mary Whatley Clarke's studies of David G. Burnet and
Thomas J. Rusk provided a beginning point, but they were short on
interpretation and based on only fragmentary research. Rusk in particular should be given full-scale treatment because his prominence
in the Texas Revolution, Republic, and early statehood has not been
fully appreciated.[37]
The social history of this period, as revealed in several landmark
studies, has been treated extensively but not exhaustively. William R.

36. Llerena Friend, *Sam Houston, the Great Designer* (Austin: University of Texas
Press, 1954), p. 114. Henry W. Barton, "The Problem of Command in the Army of
the Republic of Texas," *SHQ* 62 (Jan., 1959): 299–311, is a fine analytical study of an
important episode in Houston's leadership; it complements William C. Binkley, "The
Activities of the Texan Revolutionary Army after San Jacinto," *Journal of Southern His-
tory* 6 (Aug., 1940): 331–46.
37. Herbert Gambrell, *Anson Jones, the Last President of Texas* (Garden City, N.Y.:
Doubleday, 1948); and *Mirabeau Buonaparte Lamar, Troubadour and Crusader* (Dallas: South-
west, 1934). A more recent but still not definitive study of Lamar is Jack C. Ramsay,
Jr., *Thunder beyond the Brazos* (Austin: Eakin, 1985). Mary Whatley Clarke, *David G.
Burnet* (Austin: Pemberton, 1969); and Mary Whatley Clarke, *Thomas J. Rusk: Soldier,
Statesman, Jurist* (Austin: Pemberton, 1971). See also Ernest C. Shearer, *Robert Potter,
Remarkable North Carolinian and Texan* (Houston: University of Houston Press, 1951).

Hogan's *The Texas Republic: A Social and Economic History* remains the most significant single volume ever written on the decade that followed the revolution. This work offered a clear thesis: Texas gained and maintained "a virile independence" which set it apart from other areas. "Special qualities," namely "certain brash characteristics commonly attributed to inhabitants of the Lone Star state," derived from the experiences of everyday life in the frontier republic.[38] The population and economy grew and culture experienced a degree of maturation between 1836 and 1845, most notably in the beginnings of an education system and religious organizations. Yet the quality that set Texans apart, their rampant individualism, continued to dominate their character. Acknowledging that this attribute flourished elsewhere on the frontier, Hogan nevertheless insisted that it marked Texas in a more pronounced fashion. Specifically, religion demonstrated variety, vitality, and resistance to uniformity; medicine an opposition to standardization; the law a pattern of vigilantism, personalism, and violence; literature a penchant for the tall tale; speech a tradition of word-mongering; and society as a whole a celebration of the gusto of fighting.

The average person did not profit greatly during the period of the Republic; speculation, simultaneous financial depression and inflation, and backwardness of transportation combined to limit genuine prosperity to the mercantile and planter classes. Hope for the future and the broad distribution of landownership helped to calm potential discontent. Based on the belief that in Texas "all start fair" with their pasts left behind, society developed other forms of cohesion. "Cooperative action freely taken by individuals" moderated the potential of unfettered individualism. In other words, volunteering for military service provided for national defense, house raisings built a sense of neighborliness, conventions expressed the collective political opinions of free men, and camp meetings promoted sociability. Texas patriotism grew from a common consciousness that the generation was making history. Pride characterized the remembrance of the Alamo and San Jacinto. The "fighting spirit" became both an "individual necessity" and a "national compulsion." Patriotic toasting made drinking to excess an ingredient of nationalism as well as a threat to order and mo-

38. William R. Hogan, *The Texas Republic: A Social and Economic History* (Norman: University of Oklahoma Press, 1976), p. vii.

rality, historical consciousness helped to provide further grist for developing a distinctive literature, and a belief in a peculiar spirit of "stamina, individualism, 'go ahead' initiative," and Texas pride existed to "set its own ineffable stamp" on succeeding generations of emigrants to the land.[39]

Hogan consciously described the experience of the majority only; blacks, Mexicans, and the foreign-born received scant passing references. He justified these omissions by insisting that culture conflict rather than assimilation had characterized minority relations with the Anglo-Americans in Texas. Even so, his decision to exclude these groups must be seen as a serious weakness, if only because he failed to note the impact of the culture conflict in molding the character of the majority. Hogan's shortcoming left it to succeeding scholars to write the histories of ethnic and racial minorities for this period. Arnoldo De León's *Tejano Community* summarizes recent scholarship on the period 1821–45, emphasizing the increasingly minority status of Mexican Texans who lived either in isolation from Anglos or, when in contact with the ever-growing majority population, suffered from racism in general and attacks against property interests in particular. David Montejano arrives at similar conclusions using a sociological model.[40] Until recently the free black experience in this period has been more fully described than the history of slavery. Among the many works on this subject the most useful are Harold Schoen's "The Free Negro in the Republic of Texas," which reflected an unusual amount of sensitivity to the matter of racial injustice for the time it was written and an impressive amount of documentation. Campbell's *Empire for Slavery*, mentioned earlier, is especially strong in its use of local records and quantification.[41]

39. Ibid., pp. 295–98 (quotations).

40. Arnoldo De León, *The Tejano Community, 1836–1900* (Albuquerque: University of New Mexico Press, 1982); David Montejano, *Anglos and Mexicans in the Making of Texas, 1836–1986* (Austin: University of Texas Press, 1987). De León's study reflected the findings of unpublished theses by other scholars, most notably the pioneering work of Fane Downs, "The History of Mexicans in Texas," Ph.D. diss., Texas Tech University, 1970, which remains the most detailed account of the 1821–45 period; and Andrés Tijerina, "Tejanos and Texas: The Native Mexicans of Texas, 1820–1850," Ph.D. diss., University of Texas, Austin, 1977, which especially emphasized the decline of Tejanos as landowners after the Revolution. A full monographic treatment of Tejanos in the Republic is in order to detail the history of the period and to test the ideas presented by De León and Montejano.

41. Harold Schoen, "The Free Negro in the Republic of Texas," *SHQ* 39 (Apr.,

Sophisticated use of statistical sources for the study of Texas social history began forty years ago. In a striking innovation of methodology Barnes Lathrop in 1949 published *Migration Into East Texas,* notable not only for its findings on the origins of the Texas people but also for its pioneering use of manuscript census records. He established a child ladder technique of measuring date and origin of immigration (identifying dates of immigration by birthplaces and ages of children) and applied the method to half of the counties east of the Trinity River for the 1850 and 1860 censuses. Lathrop provided a basic profile of the emigrants to East Texas and produced numerous tables to allow others with somewhat varying interests to make use of the findings. He depicted a more ordinary set of circumstances in the background of Texas emigrants than the wildly individualistic profile set forth by Hogan (or more recently Nackman). Lathrop showed a certain restlessness of background in the prevailing pattern of geographical mobility, usually from one part of the southern backcountry to another. Most of the emigrants were young but already married; many failed to prosper either before or after resettlement. The longer their residence in Texas the greater the value of their property, but between 18 and 30 percent failed to acquire real estate at all in spite of the early abundance and continued cheapness of land.

Lathrop did not intend his work to be definitive. The volume focused on East Texas, although it contained one table and a slight narrative comparing origins of arrivals east and west of the Trinity. He suggested specific topics for future researchers, including the addition of slaveownership as a variable. His methodology did not attempt to account for or analyze the origins of single men. Lathrop's role as a pioneer in employing quantitative methods is widely recognized; however, his work has not been immune from criticism. Recently Richard Griswold del Castillo noted that although Lathrop "organized and interpreted a wealth of new social data on frontier families, he did not make the leap to larger conclusions and integrate his findings into a body of historical work on Texas."[42] Unfortunately, neither these kinds

---

1936): 292–308, *SHQ* 40 (Oct., 1936): 85–113, *SHQ* 40 (Jan., 1937): 169–99, *SHQ* 40 (Apr., 1937): 267–89, *SHQ* 41 (July, 1937): 83–108.

42. Barnes F. Lathrop, *Migration into East Texas, 1835–1860* (Austin: Texas State Historical Association, 1949); Richard Griswold del Castillo, "Quantitative History in the American Southwest: A Survey and Critique," *Western Historical Quarterly* 15 (Oct., 1984): 409.

of observations nor Lathrop's own suggestions for further research have prompted substantial quantitative studies of this formative era. As a result the conflicting profiles of early Texas society posed by Hogan and Lathrop remain unresolved: was Texas distinctive or merely an example of the southern frontier experience?

The failure to apply the quantitative methods of the new social history has resulted more from ignoring the period 1821-45 than from any general unwillingness to employ the approach in studying Texas. In fact, the recent survey of quantitative history in the Southwest by del Castillo asserted that from the earliest of the statistically oriented works, "Texas was the most thoroughly studied area . . . in terms of quantitative demographic histories," so prominent that he identified a "Texas school of demographic history." Virtually all the major articles, books, and dissertations he cited covered Spanish Texas or periods after the Republic, whether they concerned family history, ethnic groups, immigration, mobility studies, or politics. As for the most recent scholarship, del Castillo found that "Texas continued to be the locale for the most thorough community and demographic studies based on quantitative sources," but none of these works redressed the gaps in coverage of the period from 1821 to 1845. This shortcoming is not a result of inadequacy of materials; in fact, abundant resources exist for studies of migration and community development during the period of Mexican Texas and the Republic. Several factors may explain the inattentiveness to this era: the new social history has tended to focus on urban topics, many of which appear inapplicable to this time of rude town beginnings. Perhaps the most serious historiographic problem that has retarded interest in the revolution and the Republic is conceptual. Despite the recent reconceptualization by David Weber that analyzes Texas in the context of the Mexican frontier, the emphasis on exceptionalism by scholars like Hogan tinges the period with an aura of provincialism. Therefore, those who undertake to correct the gaps in scholarship must address del Castillo's warning of the need to make use of the latest methodologies but "to avoid the associated problems of parochialism and inadequate conceptualization."[43]

43. Del Castillo, "Quantitative History in the American Southwest," p. 413 (first quotation), p. 420 (second quotation), p. 419 (third quotation), p. 426 (fourth quotation). One interesting attempt at community history using new methodologies is James Michael McReynolds, "Family Life in a Borderland Community: Nacogdoches, Texas, 1779-1861," Ph.D. diss., Texas Tech University, 1978.

Research on vital subjects of social history has not been retarded by the absence or inaccessibility of primary sources. An abundance of diaries, memoirs, and travel accounts are available for the Republic period. Among the most useful of these was prepared for publication by the diligent researcher Andrew F. Muir under the title *Texas in 1837*.[44] The most essential primary materials for the study of this period of Texas history may well be land records, for the social history of nineteenth-century Texas was inextricably tied to the land. This great (and sometimes almost only) resource was fundamental to the development of Texas, to the politics of all its early governments, and indeed to the very nature of the Texas identity. Much of the historiographical groundwork for using these materials has been done. Land policy has attracted scholars with widely varying perspectives. Elgin Williams, whose *Animating Pursuits of Speculation* appeared in 1949, attempted unsuccessfully to demonstrate that nefarious schemers were responsible for much of public policy, including the character of annexation. Most basic is Thomas Miller's survey of public land policy, which provides a convenient and reliable account of constitutional and congressional enactments for the disposing of the domain of Texas in order to promote settlement and provide for defense. Miller also collected the bounty and donation grants from the period of the Texas Revolution and Republic by individual grantee.[45] Other published

44. The anonymous author walked and rode through much of the new nation and possessed the keen eye and broad interests common to all the classic travel accounts. Andrew Forest Muir, ed., *Texas in 1837: An Anonymous, Contemporary Narrative* (Austin: University of Texas Press, 1958). Among the other good accounts, some of which date back to the beginnings of the revolution, are *Dr. J. H. Barnard's Journal*, ed. Hobart Huson, ([Refugio, Tex.]: n.p., 1950); William Fairfax Gray, *From Virginia to Texas, 1835* (Houston: Fletcher Young, 1965); and W. Eugene Hollan, ed., *William Bollaert's Texas* (Norman: University of Oklahoma Press, 1956).

45. Williams's work reflected considerable digging in primary materials, but it meandered through a wide array of topics in such a disjointed way as to create confusion even on its basic thesis. It attracted criticism from the time of its publication. Pool, *Barker*, p. 159n. This and similar studies fail to acknowledge that in Texas speculation in lands touched virtually everyone. Elgin Williams, *The Animating Pursuits of Speculation: Land Traffic in the Annexation of Texas* (New York: Columbia University Press, 1949). A more understandable if narrowly focused study by Muir unravels the machinations of one of the companies that grew out of the land speculation mania of the late Mexican period. Andrew Forest Muir, "The Union Company in Anahuac, 1831–1833," *SHQ* 70 (Oct., 1966): 256–68. Thomas Lloyd Miller, *Bounty and Donation Land*

enumerations and ever-improving finding aids at the archives of the General Land Office have eased the difficulty of researching these materials and documents such as certificates of character and claims records that touched the lives of the masses of early Texans.[46] Historians should also investigate probate, court, and tax records in county courthouses, and materials emanating from military and other claims against the government located in the archives of the Texas State Library.

Any list of topics for future research is of necessity long and at the same time incomplete, but several such subjects stand out. A basic demographic analysis of Mexican Texas is needed as a foundation for other work. One useful way to explore the social history of Texas for the years 1821–45 might be a series of community studies.[47] The experiences of the citizen soldier have long been seen as central to the Texas identity and as such have attracted considerable scholarship. However, the fundamental work of this subject, *The Texas Rangers*, by Walter Prescott Webb, is a classic in need of substantial revision. The study was organized in a loosely chronological, almost episodic manner, with pithy summary analysis and interpretive sections interspersed irregularly on such matters as the character of the Rangers and their contribution to the evolution of plains warfare and weaponry. Webb expressed an unabashed racial and ethnic bias, less toward Indians than Mexicans, whom he characterized as "volatile and mercurial," "cruel," ignorant, dishonest, superstitious, and "wholly unequal" to the Texans as fighters. The historian Mark Nackman added to Webb's

---

Grants of Texas, 1835–1888 (Austin: University of Texas Press, 1967); Thomas Lloyd Miller, *The Public Lands of Texas, 1519–1970* (Norman: University of Oklahoma Press, 1972).

46. Published compilations based on early census, tax, and land records include Marian Day Mullins, *The First Census of Texas, 1829–1836* (Washington, D.C.: National Genealogical Society Publication, 1959); and several works compiled by Gifford White, *Character Certificates in the General Land Office of Texas* (St. Louis: Ingmire, 1985); *1830 Citizens of Texas* (Austin: Eakin, 1983); and *The 1840 Census of the Republic of Texas* (Austin: Pemberton, 1966).

47. In addition to the works cited as being in progress in note 6, above, many other community histories are potentially interesting. Some stout-hearted scholar needs to unravel the complicated web of East Texas history during this era, because it has been largely ignored on the false assumption that the history of Texas rested entirely with Austin and his colonists. More specifically, the fate of the Nacogdoches Tejanos in general and the Córdova rebellion of 1839 in particular is an intriguing subject.

PAUL D. LACK

group characterization in a fine article on the "citizen soldiers"; this study should be extended.[48]

With scarcely any exceptions, the experiences of the people in the 1821–45 period have been told without the insights or methodology of the "new" social history, in striking and unfortunate contrast to a previous generation of historians like Hogan and Lathrop who explored Texas subjects on the cutting edge of the historiographical frontier. Models for the kind of work that needs to be done have existed for longer than a full generation of scholars. The sources are scattered but increasingly accessible in various Texas depositories, and other materials in Mexico are still being discovered. The issues are vital and the research is challenging but manageable as historians continue to explore the impact of Mexican Texas, the revolution, and the Republic.

Since the years 1821–45 represent in so many ways the formative period, it is difficult to conceive of a successful reworking of Texas history that does not include substantial work in this era. In 1980, Stephen Stagner, reviewing the first century of Texas historiography, noted that the views of past historians still held the field in a death grip, "that their assumptions are still recognizable," and that "in the 1980s Texas history has not gone far beyond them." Insofar as the 1821–45 period is concerned the prevailing image remained one of "sure-shooting, morally upright frontiersmen" against "bloodthirsty and tyrannous Mexicans." The fact that this stereotype has not been fully dispelled as we enter the 1990s means that Texas history still suffers from intolerable immaturity. Stagner concludes: "Historians often build on the foundations of others' work, layer upon layer. In the case of Texas history, the bottom layers have not been subjected to the cleansing acids of skepticism that they deserve."[49]

48. Walter Prescott Webb, *The Texas Rangers: A Century of Frontier Defense* (Austin: University of Texas Press, 1935); Mark Nackman, "The Making of the Texan Citizen Soldier, 1835–1860," *SHQ* 78 (Jan., 1975): 231–53.
49. Stagner, "Epics, Science, and the Lost Frontier," pp. 180–81.

⁊ꝏ Statehood, Civil War, and Reconstruction, 1846-76

Randolph B. Campbell

Customarily, as the title of this essay indicates, the years from 1846 to 1876 comprise three distinct periods in Texas historiography. Most studies deal exclusively with either the antebellum years ending in 1861, the Civil War, or the era of Reconstruction from 1865 into the mid-1870s. Few historians have crossed the lines separating these periods, and only one has attempted a broad, interpretive synthesis of events and developments during the entire thirty years.[1] Existing historiographical essays reflect this periodization. Ralph A. Wooster and Randolph B. Campbell have dealt exclusively with writings on the years prior to secession. Edgar P. Sneed, Merline Pitre, and Barry A. Crouch began their examinations of Reconstruction historiography with developments in 1865. Only Wooster, in a recent essay entitled "The Civil War and Reconstruction in Texas," crossed one of these lines in the historiographical dirt of the Lone Star State.[2]

---

1. Ernest Wallace, *Texas in Turmoil, 1849-1875* (Austin: Steck-Vaughn, 1965), covers almost the entire period but is semipopular in format and offers little depth in research or interpretation. Two more specialized studies dealing with most of the era are Rupert N. Richardson, *The Frontier of Northwest Texas, 1846 to 1876: Advance and Defense by the Pioneer Settlers of the Cross Timbers and Prairies* (Glendale, Calif.: Arthur H. Clarke, 1963), and Randolph B. Campbell, *A Southern Community in Crisis: Harrison County, Texas, 1850-1880* (Austin: Texas State Historical Association, 1983).

2. Ralph A. Wooster, "Early Texas Statehood: A Survey of Historical Writings," *Southwestern Historical Quarterly* (*SHQ*) 76 (Oct., 1972): 121-41; Randolph B. Campbell, "Antebellum Texas: From Union to Disunion, 1846-1861," in *A Guide to the History of Texas*, ed. Light T. Cummins and Alvin R. Bailey, Jr. (Westport, Conn.: Greenwood Press, 1988), pp. 21-35; Edgar P. Sneed, "A Historiography of Reconstruction in Texas: Some Myths and Problems," *SHQ* 72 (Apr., 1969): 435-48; Merline Pitre, "A Note on the Historiography of Blacks in the Reconstruction of Texas," *Journal of Negro History* 66 (winter, 1981): 340-48; Barry A. Crouch, "'Unmanacling' Texas Re-

Reasons for dividing the years from 1846 to 1876 into three histori-cal periods in Texas are obvious — secession in 1861 and the end of the war in 1865 marked sharply defined endings and beginnings for dis-tinctively different eras. Such periodization, however, is unfortunate in that it tends to obscure the extent of change brought on by several of the most dramatic events and developments in Texas history. Surely every aspect of life in Texas felt the impact of sectional extremism, disunion, war, emancipation, and Reconstruction between 1846 and 1876. But how great were the discontinuities, and how extensive were the continuities during these thirty tumultuous years in the Lone Star State?

This essay seeks to determine how well historians have dealt with the basic question of change over time in Texas from the inception of statehood to the end of Reconstruction by examining existing his-torical literature topically. The topics examined include the state's population, the frontier, the economy (although that subject is dealt with primarily in another essay in this collection), social life and social structure, and politics. This topical approach reveals how the existing literature is periodized, indicates the gaps in that literature, and sug-gests that, both in terms of specific studies and broad syntheses, the history of Texas in the era of Civil War and Reconstruction offers proj-ects enough to occupy a generation of students.

Mid-nineteenth-century Texas was populated primarily by immi-grants, so, as the population grew from 212,592 in 1850 to 1,591,749 in 1880, it is important to know the origins of these people and what cultural "baggage" they were likely to have brought with them. Barnes F. Lathrop and William W. White have described the influx of settlers, the great majority of whom were southerners, during the statehood period. Natives of the lower South constituted an increasing percent-age of migrants into East Texas during the 1850s, whereas the gener-ally more lightly populated counties west of the Trinity River attracted more settlers from the border states. An article by Richard G. Lowe and Randolph B. Campbell characterizing the heads of Texas families in 1850 and 1860 reinforced these conclusions concerning antebellum immigration by demonstrating that natives of the South headed three-

---

construction: A Twenty-Year Perspective," *SHQ* 93 (Jan., 1990): 275–302. Ralph A. Wooster, "The Civil War and Reconstruction," in Cummins and Bailey, *Guide to His-tory of Texas*, pp. 37–50.

quarters of all households in both census years and that individuals born in the lower South constituted a rising proportion of the whole during the decade.[3]

Lowe and Campbell's study also demonstrated, as had three previous articles by cultural geographer Terry G. Jordan, that immigrants from the lower South settled primarily in eastern and southeastern Texas, while those from the upper South concentrated in the northern and north-central parts of the state. Indeed, according to Jordan, settlement patterns were so distinctive that by 1860 Texas was divided into upper and lower South regions as clearly as the southern states from which the immigrants had come. The people of eastern and southeastern Texas, he wrote, depended on cotton planting and slavery and, like lower southerners in general, overwhelmingly favored secession, while northern areas and some portions of the interior concentrated on self-sufficient agriculture, had fewer slaves and, like upper southerners, were less unanimous on disunion. Seymour Connor's study of the Peters colony, the huge empresario enterprise that brought many settlers to North Texas during the early statehood period, also emphasized the upper South origins and Unionist sentiment of immigrants to that area.[4]

The Civil War brought numerous refugees to Texas from Confederate states overrun by federal forces. Most of these people may have stayed only temporarily, but their story is a fascinating one that has never been fully told. Kate Stone's diary and the general study of refugees in the Confederacy by Mary Elizabeth Massey provide interesting glimpses into the situation in Texas. However, a full in-

3. Terry G. Jordan, "A Century and a Half of Ethnic Change in Texas, 1836–1986," *SHQ* 89 (Apr., 1986): 385–422, provides a good introduction to the peopling of Texas. Barnes F. Lathrop, *Migration into East Texas, 1850–1860: A Study from the United States Census* (Austin: Texas State Historical Association, 1949); William W. White, "Migration into West Texas, 1845–1860," M.A. thesis, University of Texas, 1948; Richard G. Lowe and Randolph B. Campbell, "Heads of Families in Antebellum Texas: A Profile," *Red River Valley Historical Review* 5 (spring, 1980): 68–80.

4. Terry G. Jordan, "The Imprint of the Upper and Lower South on Mid-Nineteenth Century Texas," *Association of American Geographers, Annals* 57 (Dec., 1967): 667–90; Terry G. Jordan, "Population Origins in Texas, 1850," *Geographical Review* 59 (Jan., 1969): 83–103; Terry G. Jordan, "The Texas Appalachia," *Association of American Geographers, Annals* 60 (Sept., 1970): 409–27; Seymour V. Connor, *The Peters Colony of Texas: A History and Biographical Sketches of the Early Settlers* (Austin: Texas State Historical Association, 1959).

vestigation of where refugees came from, their reactions to Texas, and their impact on the state has not been written.[5]

A 1966 article by Homer Lee Kerr pointed out that the rate of immigration from the older southern states actually increased in the postwar years, especially between 1866 and 1871 and 1875 and 1878. Unfortunately, this article is the only important publication drawn from Kerr's massive 1953 dissertation on migration into Texas from 1865 to 1880. His study points out, for example, that the rate of migration from the lower South slowed after the war, that northern Texas received a proportionately larger share of the state's immigrants, and that the Lone Star State was not very attractive to freedmen after 1865. The data in Kerr's dissertation should be "mined," combined with other materials on migration, and analyzed—not only for what can be learned about population movements, but for social and economic implications as well.[6]

Blacks constituted a second major component group in the population of mid-nineteenth-century Texas. Randolph B. Campbell's general study of slavery in the Lone Star State, which builds on a wide variety of earlier, more specialized studies, has pointed out that the majority of blacks arrived as bondsmen with their owners from the older southern states, although many came through the interstate slave trade and a relatively small number from the illegal African trade. By 1860, they constituted approximately one-third of the population. Free blacks, who were concentrated in southeastern Texas, constituted only a tiny fraction of the population before 1860 (fewer than four hundred appear in the census of that year), but they have received considerable attention, especially from George R. Woolfolk and Andrew Forest Muir. It is suggested, however, by bits and pieces of miscellaneous evidence that the census undercounted the state's free black population and that the number could have been twice as large at that reported. Documenting this possibility will be extremely difficult if not impossible, of course, but the matter is significant, especially in

5. John Q. Anderson, ed., *Brokenburn: The Journal of Kate Stone, 1861–1868* (Baton Rouge: Louisiana State University Press, 1955); Mary Elizabeth Massey, *Refugee Life in the Confederacy* (Baton Rouge: Louisiana State University Press, 1964).

6. Homer Lee Kerr, "Migration into Texas, 1860–1880," *SHQ* 70 (Oct., 1966): 184–216; Homer Lee Kerr, "Migration into Texas, 1865–1880," Ph.D. diss., University of Texas, 1953.

light of the importance of free black populations in providing leadership to former slaves during Reconstruction.[7]

Campbell's study of slavery has shown that the black population of Texas increased notably during the Civil War years as thousands of bondsmen were "refugeed" into the state to escape advancing federal forces. Many returned home after the war, however, and in 1870 blacks still constituted, as they had in 1860, slightly less than one-third of all Texans. Blacks then began to decline, not in absolute numbers but as a proportion of the population, until they amounted to only 20 percent of the total by 1900. This, as Lawrence D. Rice pointed out in 1971, lessened their political power and "seemingly retarded their general advancement." Did this period of relative decline set in during Reconstruction, particularly during the 1870s? Kerr's dissertation shows that blacks did not migrate to Texas in large numbers after 1865. This fact should be described and explained in published work, and we should also ask if other factors such as declining family size or outmigration appeared during the 1870s to help explain the relatively slow growth of Texas' black population. Greater knowledge of black demographics seems essential to a better understanding of what happened to this important part of the Texas population at a critical time in its history.[8]

German immigrants were numerous enough to play a major role in mid-nineteenth-century Texas, and they have received a great deal of careful study. Terry Jordan's *German Seed in Texas Soil* is the best general work on this group, and he has elsewhere called particular atten-

7. Randolph B. Campbell, *An Empire for Slavery: The Peculiar Institution in Texas, 1821–1865* (Baton Rouge: Louisiana State University Press, 1989). The most detailed recent account of the African trade is Fred H. Robbins, "The Origins and Development of the African Slave Trade into Texas, 1816–1860," M.A. thesis, University of Houston, 1972. George R. Woolfolk, *The Free Negro in Texas, 1800–1860: A Study in Cultural Compromise* (Ann Arbor, Mich.: University Microfilms, 1976); Andrew Forest Muir, "The Free Negro in Harris County, Texas," *SHQ* 46 (Jan., 1943): 214–38; Andrew Forest Muir, "The Free Negro in Jefferson and Orange Counties, Texas," *Journal of Negro History* 35 (Apr., 1950): 183–206.

8. Campbell, *An Empire for Slavery;* Lawrence D. Rice, *The Negro in Texas, 1874–1900* (Baton Rouge: Louisiana State University Press, 1974). Alwyn Barr, *Black Texans: A History of Negroes in Texas, 1528–1971* (Austin: Jenkins, 1973), surveys black population movements in the postbellum era but does not go into the sort of depth suggested here.

tion to the fact that, although historians have paid most attention to immigrants arriving during the antebellum years, more Germans came to the state between 1865 and 1890 than in the thirty years before the Civil War. The Germans' reputation for opposition to slavery and secession, due in large measure to the writings of Frederick Law Olmsted, has been significantly modified by the work of Jordan and Walter Buenger. Nevertheless, most Germans worked relatively small farms without the aid of slaves, and they did contribute significantly to Unionism and Republicanism in the area centering on Austin and San Antonio.[9]

Nineteenth-century Texas also attracted smaller groups of immigrants from many other European nations, and each has received attention from historians. There are studies of Texans of English, Polish, Czech, Wendish, Irish, and French descent. Generally, emphasis is placed on how these peoples tended to settle in their own tight-knit communities and mind their own affairs. This is no doubt appropriate, but, as Ralph Wooster has pointed out, the foreign born (including, of course, many Germans as well as individuals from the other groups) constituted one-third of the population in five of the six largest towns in Texas during the 1850s and provided much of the leadership of those fledgling cities.[10] Did European immigrants continue to play such a large role in Texas' towns during the years of Civil War and Reconstruction?

9. Terry G. Jordan, *German Seed in Texas Soil: Immigrant Farmers in Nineteenth Century Texas* (Austin: University of Texas Press, 1966); Terry G. Jordan, "The German Settlement of Texas After 1865," *SHQ* 73 (Oct., 1969): 193–212; Walter L. Buenger, "Secession and the Texas German Community: Editor Lindheimer v. Editor Flake," *SHQ* 82 (Apr., 1979): 379–402. For reiterations of the claim made by Olmsted during the 1850s that Germans generally opposed slavery, see Rudolph L. Biesele, *The History of the German Settlements in Texas, 1831–1861* (Austin: Privately printed, 1930), and Glen E. Lich, *The German Texans* (San Antonio: Institute of Texan Cultures, 1981). On the matter of German attitudes toward all sectional questions in this era, see Robert W. Shook, "German Unionism in Texas during the Civil War and Reconstruction," M.A. thesis, North Texas State College, 1957; and Egan Richard Tausch, "Southern Sentiment among the Texas Germans during the Civil War and Reconstruction," M.A. thesis, University of Texas, 1965. Irene Marschall King, *John O. Meusebach: German Colonizer in Texas* (Austin: University of Texas Press, 1967), offers a biographical perspective on German settlement.

10. Thomas W. Cutrer, *The English Texans* (San Antonio: Institute of Texan Cultures, 1985); T. Lindsay Baker, *The First Polish Americans: Silesian Settlements in Texas*

Texas' Mexican, or Tejano, population during the mid-nineteenth century has been thoroughly described by Arnoldo De León. Living primarily in the area south of San Antonio, Tejanos concentrated on developing a bicultural identity and maintaining autonomy within a prejudiced Anglo society. Their proportion of the population of the state remained relatively stable throughout the period. Much like the Germans, Tejanos have received notice for opposition to slavery and for Unionism, whereas, in fact, many supported the Confederacy and the conservative approach to Reconstruction.[11]

Most of these mid-nineteenth-century Texans—Anglos, blacks, and the foreign-born alike—lived in the eastern portion of the state well removed from the border with Mexico. Nevertheless, all were affected to some extent by the boundary disputes and troubles along the Rio Grande that plagued Texas between 1846 and 1876. Historians have recognized the importance of the Mexican border during this era and given it extensive study.

The Mexican War, which began partly from American insistence on the Rio Grande boundary almost immediately after statehood in 1846, has been discussed in detail by K. Jack Bauer, Seymour V. Connor and Odie Faulk, and Otis Singletary. Walter Prescott Webb and Henry W. Barton have focused more narrowly on the role of Texans in the conflict.[12] Victory in the war guaranteed the Rio Grande bor-

---

(College Station: Texas A&M University Press, 1979); Jacek Przygoda, *Texas Pioneers from Poland: A Study in Ethnic History* (Waco: Texian, 1971); Clinton Machann and James W. Mendl, *Krasna Amerika: A Study of Texas Czechs, 1851–1939* (Austin: Eakin, 1983); Sylvia A. Grider, *The Wendish Texans* (San Antonio: Institute of Texas Cultures, 1982); John Brendan Flannery, *The Irish Texans* (San Antonio: Institute of Texan Cultures, 1980); William J. and Margaret F. Hammond, *La Reunion: A French Settlement in Dallas* (Dallas: Royal, 1958); Randel V. Davidson, "Victor Considerant and the Failure of La Reunion," *SHQ* 76 (Jan., 1973): 275–96; Bobby D. Weaver, *Castro's Colony: Empresario Development in Texas, 1842–1865* (College Station: Texas A&M University Press, 1985); Ralph A. Wooster, "Foreigners in the Principal Towns of Ante-Bellum Texas," *SHQ* 66 (Oct., 1962): 208–20.

11. Arnoldo De León, *The Tejano Community, 1836–1900* (Albuquerque: University of New Mexico Press, 1982): Arnoldo De León, *They Called Them Greasers: Anglo Attitudes toward Mexicans in Texas, 1821–1900* (Austin: University of Texas Press, 1983); John Denny Riley, "Santos Benavides: His Influence on the Lower Rio Grande, 1823–1891," Ph.D. diss., Texas Christian University, 1976.

12. K. Jack Bauer, *The Mexican War, 1846–1848* (New York: Macmillan, 1974); Seymour V. Connor and Odie B. Faulk, *North America Divided: The Mexican War,*

der but hardly ended problems in that area. Instead, one border incident after another kept affairs unsettled throughout the era. J. Fred Rippy's account of border troubles, which deals only with the antebellum years, is badly dated, and the subject probably deserves a general study extending through the era of Reconstruction. Coincidentally, the career of Juan N. Cortina, the most troublesome (from the Texan point of view) border adventurer during his period, ended with his arrest in 1875. There are several accounts of his life, but a definitive biography is needed. The story of José María Jesús Carvajal's role in border conflict during the fifties has been told by Ernest Shearer. Also, Shearer and Ron Tyler have both written about the expedition of Texas Rangers led by James H. Callahan that crossed into Mexico near Piedras Negras in 1855, ostensibly in search of marauding Indians. Tyler argued that Callahan may well have been seeking to capture some of the numerous runaway slaves residing in Mexico, while Shearer accepted the official explanation of the expedition.[13]

Regardless of the intent of Callahan's expedition, the suggestion that fugitive slaves may have been involved points out another way in which the Mexican border was significant during the antebellum years. A secondary, and often overlooked, part of Charles W. Ramsdell's famed "natural limits of slavery" argument was that the "peculiar institution" could not move into Southwest Texas because Mexico offered an easily reached haven for runaway bondsmen. Ron Tyler and Rosalie Schwartz have pointed out that thousands of fugitive slaves did cross the Rio Grande, and Campbell's general study of slavery concludes that, in this respect at least, Ramsdell was probably cor-

---

1846-1848 (New York: Oxford University Press, 1971); Otis A. Singletary, The Mexican War (Chicago: University of Chicago Press, 1960); Walter Prescott Webb, The Texas Rangers: A Century of Frontier Defense (Boston: Houghton Mifflin, 1935); Henry W. Barton, Texas Volunteers in the Mexican War (Wichita Falls: Texian, 1970); Henry W. Barton, "Five Texas Frontier Companies during the Mexican War," SHQ 66 (July, 1962): 17–30.

13. J. Fred Rippy, "Border Troubles along the Rio Grande, 1848–1860," SHQ 23 (Oct., 1919): 91–111; Lyman L. Woodman, Cortina: Rogue of the Rio Grande (San Antonio: Naylor, 1950); Charles W. Goldfinch, "Juan Cortina, 1824–1892: A Reappraisal," in Juan N. Cortina: Two Interpretations (New York: Arno, 1974); Ernest C. Shearer, "The Carvajal Disturbances," SHQ 55 (Oct., 1951): 201–30; Ernest C. Shearer, "The Callahan Expedition, 1855," SHQ 54 (Apr., 1951): 430–51; Ronnie C. Tyler, "The Callahan Expedition of 1855: Indians or Negroes?" SHQ 70 (Apr., 1967): 574–85.

rect. Slavery would have had serious difficulties once it expanded to within one hundred and fifty miles of the Mexican border.[14]

Even as they struggled with a variety of problems along the border following victory in the Mexican War, state and federal authorities faced the task of exploring and "pacifying" a huge expanse of forbidding West Texas terrain populated primarily by ever-dangerous Comanche Indians. Two articles by A. B. Bender and biographical works on Robert S. Neighbors and Earl Van Dorn provide good descriptions of explorations during the antebellum period. W. Eugene Hollon's biography of Randolph B. Marcy tells the story of one important explorer whose career spanned the era of Civil War and Reconstruction. Frank Bishop Lammons and Thomas L. Connelly have described and explained the failure of the army's attempt to use camels in West Texas, an experiment that, although exotic and imaginative, seems to have received attention somewhat beyond its historical significance.[15]

Explorations and the westward movement of settlers led to a bitter conflict between Texas and the Indians of West Texas, especially the Comanches, that spanned the years from statehood to the end of Reconstruction. Rupert N. Richardson's studies of the struggle with the Comanches, Robert Wooster's description of garrison life on the Texas frontier, and W. C. Holden's three articles on frontier defense

14. Charles W. Ramsdell, "The Natural Limits of Slavery Expansion," *Mississippi Valley Historical Review* 16 (Sept., 1929): 151–71; Ronnie C. Tyler, "Slave Owners and Runaway Slaves in Texas," M.A. thesis, Texas Christian University, 1966; Ronnie C. Tyler, "Fugitive Slaves in Mexico," *Journal of Negro History* 57 (Jan., 1972): 1–12; Rosalie Schwartz, "Runaway Negroes: Mexico as an Alternative for United States Blacks, 1825–1860," M.A. thesis, San Diego State University, 1974; Schwartz, *Across the Rio to Freedom: U.S. Negroes in Mexico* (El Paso: Texas Western Press, 1975).

15. A. B. Bender, "Opening Routes across West Texas, 1848–1850," *SHQ* 37 (Oct., 1933): 116–35; and A. B. Bender, "The Texas Frontier, 1848–1861," *SHQ* 38 (Oct., 1934): 135–48; Kenneth Franklin Neighbours, "The Marcy-Neighbors Exploration of the Headwaters of the Brazos and Wichita Rivers in 1854," *Panhandle-Plains Historical Review (PPHR)* 27 (1954): 27–46; Kenneth Franklin Neighbours, "The Expedition of Major Robert S. Neighbors to El Paso in 1849," *SHQ* 58 (July, 1954): 36–59; Thomas Robert Havins, *Beyond the Cimarron: Major Earl Van Dorn in Comanche Land* (Brownwood, Tex.: Brown, 1968); W. Eugene Hollon, *Beyond the Cross Timbers: The Travels of Randolph B. Marcy, 1812–1887* (Norman: University of Oklahoma Press, 1955); Frank Bishop Lammons, "Operation Camel: An Experiment in Animal Transportation in Texas, 1857–1860," *SHQ* 61 (July, 1957): 20–50; Thomas L. Connelly, "The American Camel Experiment: A Reappraisal," *SHQ* 69 (Apr., 1966): 442–62.

deal with the entire period. Most other works on Indian affairs and frontier defense, however, examine fewer years. For example, Kenneth F. Neighbours's account of Indian affairs in Texas and his life of Robert Simpson Neighbors, the state's best-known Indian agent, close in 1859 with Neighbors's death. Lena Clara Koch's detailed account of federal Indian policy in Texas covered only the statehood years, as did Arrie Barrett's description of the state's western forts. William J. Hughes's life of "Rip" Ford describes the career of the most famed explorer/frontier fighter during the antebellum years and war, and Ernest Wallace's biography of Ranald Slidell Mackenzie picks up a major figure in the story during the 1870s and provides information on the final successes that opened West Texas to settlement.[16] The frontier experience of Texas in the mid-nineteenth century deserves a synthesis that will build upon these works and present that struggle from the perspective of both settlers and Indians and integrate information on federal and state policies and military actions.

The fact that Texas had a line of frontier settlement and saw Indian warfare throughout the era of Civil War and Reconstruction doubtless contributed heavily to the state's image as part of the West. So, too, did the rapid expansion of cattle ranching during this era, a subject that has received a tremendous amount of attention from historians.[17] Regardless of the frontier experience and the rise of cattle ranching, however, economic life in Texas between 1846 and 1876

16. Rupert N. Richardson, *The Comanche Barrier to South Plains Settlement: A Century and a Half of Savage Resistance to the Advancing White Frontier* (Glendale, Calif.: Arthur H. Clarke, 1933); Richardson, *Frontier of Northwest Texas, 1846 to 1876;* Robert Wooster, *Soldiers, Sutlers, and Settlers: Garrison Life on the Texas Frontier* (College Station: Texas A&M University Press, 1987); W. C. Holden, "Frontier Defense, 1846–1860," *West Texas Historical Association Year Book (WTHAYB)* 6 (1930): 35–64; W. C. Holden, "Defense in Texas during the Civil War," *WTHAYB* 4 (1928): 16–31; W. C. Holden, "Frontier Defense, 1865–1889," *PPHR* 2 (1929); Kenneth F. Neighbours, *Indian Exodus: Texas Indian Affairs, 1835–1859* (Quanah, Tex.: Nortex, 1973); Kenneth F. Neighbours, *Robert Simpson Neighbors and the Texas Frontier, 1835–1859* (Waco: Texian, 1975); Lena Clara Koch, "The Federal Indian Policy in Texas, 1845–1860," *SHQ* 28 (Jan., 1925): 223–34, *SHQ* 28 (Apr., 1925): 259–68, *SHQ* 29 (July, 1925): 19–35, and *SHQ* 29 (Oct., 1925): 98–127; Arrie Barrett, "Western Frontier Forts of Texas, 1845–1861," *WTHAYB* 7 (1931): 115–39; William J. Hughes, *Rebellious Ranger: Rip Ford and the Old Southwest* (Norman: University of Oklahoma Press, 1964); Ernest Wallace, *Ranald Slidell Mackenzie on the Texas Frontier* (Lubbock: West Texas Museum Association, 1965).

17. For bibliographic information on cattle ranching, see B. Byron Price, "The Texas Frontier," in Cummins and Bailey, *Guide to the History of Texas,* pp. 51–63.

identified the majority of its people with the Deep South rather than with the West. Most of the planters and plain folk who settled antebellum Texas were southerners, and they built an overwhelmingly agricultural economy highly similar to that found in the older southern states.[18] Farming provided the livelihood for the vast majority of Texans from 1846 to 1876, and we still need to know more about it, particularly as it evolved during Reconstruction. A detailed discussion of the historiography of agriculture in Texas and all other aspects of the economy, including commerce, finance, industry, and transportation, is found in Walter Buenger's essay elsewhere in this volume.

Not surprisingly for an overwhelmingly agricultural state with limited commercial, financial, and industrial development and poor transportation facilities, Texas had no large cities during the era of Civil War and Reconstruction. This fact has by no means, however, discouraged historical study of its towns and fledgling urban centers. Earl W. Fornell's *Galveston Era* is tremendously informative on life in the Crescent City before 1861, and Kenneth W. Wheeler has provided a good introduction to the study of Houston, Austin, and San Antonio as well as Galveston from 1836 to 1865. Four unpublished studies tell the story of San Antonio's rise to the status of a major city by 1880. Two articles and a thesis describe life and events in Austin during the war and Reconstruction. And there are studies of smaller towns such as El Paso, Indianola, Marshall, Nacogdoches, and Jefferson as well. Paul D. Lack's dissertation, "Urban Slavery in the Southwest," deals effectively with this important subject in Galveston and Austin, and Susan Jackson published an article on the "peculiar institution" in Houston.[19]

18. Richard G. Lowe and Randolph B. Campbell, *Planters and Plain Folk: Agriculture in Antebellum Texas* (Dallas: Southern Methodist University Press, 1987).

19. Earl W. Fornell, *The Galveston Era: The Texas Crescent on the Eve of Secession* (Austin: University of Texas Press, 1961); Kenneth W. Wheeler, *To Wear a City's Crown: The Beginnings of Urban Growth in Texas, 1836–1865* (Cambridge, Mass.: Harvard University Press, 1968); Paeder Joel Hoovestel, "Galveston in the Civil War," M.A. thesis, University of Houston, 1950; Ronald B. Jager, "Houston, Texas, Fights the Civil War," *Texana* II (spring, 1973): 30–51; Carland Elaine Crooke, "San Antonio, Texas, 1846–1861," M.A. thesis, Rice University, 1964; Marjorie Paulus, "Fifteen Years in Old San Antonio, 1850–1865," M.A. thesis, St. Mary's University, 1939; Thomas A. Jennings, "San Antonio in the Confederacy," M.A. thesis, Trinity University, 1957; William Foster Fleming, "San Antonio: The History of a Military City, 1865–1880," Ph.D. diss., University of Pennsylvania, 1963; Larry Jay Gage, "The City of Austin on the Eve

These works are all useful, but none deal with the era from 1846 to 1876 as a whole with the intention of analyzing a particular city's growth and the relationship of that city to broader economic development. David McComb's general histories of Houston and Galveston transcend these years, of course, but they cannot offer the sort of detail possible in a more focused study. Urban histories covering 1846 to 1876 could also deal with significant social questions. What, for example, did cities mean to Texas blacks? Lack and Fornell indicated that slaves preferred city life, and Smallwood showed that many freedmen went to the cities for employment. Alwyn Barr has demonstrated that black migrants, driven by factors such as economic aspirations and the desire for education, poured into Houston and San Antonio during the years after 1865. We need to know the magnitude of this movement statewide and to attempt measurements of the impact of urban life on those who took up residence in cities from 1846 to 1876. It would be interesting, for example, to compare the economic status of urban and rural blacks, especially in 1870 and 1880, to see if those who moved really found a better life in the cities.[20]

Texas' young cities thus offer opportunities for work on social as well as economic history from 1846 to 1876. Most Texans, however, did not live in cities, and social history, like examinations of basic

---

of the Civil War," *SHQ* 63 (Jan., 1960): 428–38; A. C. Greene, "The Durable Society: Austin in the Reconstruction," *SHQ* 72 (Apr., 1969): 492–506; James A. Irby, "Confederate Austin," M.A. thesis, University of Texas, 1953; W. H. Timmons, "American El Paso: The Formative Years, 1848–1854," *SHQ* 88 (July, 1983): 1–36; J. L. Waller, "The Civil War in the El Paso Area," *WTHAYB* 22 (1946): 3–14; Brownson Malsch, *Indianola: The Mother of Western Texas* (Austin: Shoal Creek Publishers, 1977); Roney Johnson III, "Marshall, Texas, 1860–1865," M.A. thesis, Baylor University, 1967; Virgie W. Scurlock, "Ante-Bellum Nacogdoches, 1846–1861," M.A. thesis, Stephen F. Austin State College, 1954; Judy Watson, "Jefferson, Texas: The Rise and Decline of the Cypress Port, 1842–1873," M.A. thesis, Texas Christian University, 1967; Paul Dean Lack, "Urban Slavery in the Southwest," Ph.D. diss., Texas Tech University, 1973; Susan Jackson, "Slavery in Houston: The 1850s," *Houston Review* 2 (summer, 1980): 66–82.

20. David G. McComb, *Houston: The Bayou City* (Austin: University of Texas Press, 1969; rev. ed., 1981); David G. McComb, *Galveston: A History* (Austin: University of Texas Press, 1986); Lack, "Urban Slavery in Southwest"; Fornell, *Galveston Era;* James M. Smallwood, *Time of Hope, Time of Despair: Black Texans during Reconstruction* (Port Washington, N.Y.: Kennikat Press, 1981); Alwyn Barr, "Black Migration into Southwestern Cities, 1865–1900," in *Essays on Southern History Written in Honor of Barnes F. Lathrop,* ed. Gary W. Gallagher (Austin: General Libraries, University of Texas, 1980), pp. 17–38.

economic activities, must focus primarily on rural areas. There are important studies that at least touch on most major aspects of social and cultural life in Texas from statehood through Reconstruction — the family, race relations, religion, education, and communication — but a great deal remains to be done.[21]

Thanks to the recent upsurge in interest in women's history, we have several accounts of female settlers in antebellum Texas, their reactions to the state, and their changing legal status. Interest in the black family has led to examinations of it in slavery and in freedom. There are, however, no studies of the white family in all its ramifications and no comparisons of white and black families after 1865. Were there any signs during this era of the much-discussed "disintegration" of the black family, either in rural areas or the cities? Were there notable differences in the structures of white and black families by 1880? Answers to questions such as these would help us to understand the impact of the Civil War and emancipation on all Texans.[22]

Race relations constituted an omnipresent part of social life in mid-nineteenth-century Texas. During the antebellum years, most white Texans lived to some extent with a fear of black rebellion. Descriptions of the laws of slavery and the extreme reactions of whites to any hint of a slave uprising prove this point. Also, free blacks faced severe restrictions on their very presence in Texas. Following emancipation, the Freedmen's Bureau, the one federal agency that seem-

21. For general accounts of social life during this era, see Llerena B. Friend, "The Texan of 1860," *SHQ* 62 (July, 1958): 1–17; John A. Edwards, "Social and Cultural Activities of Texans During Civil War and Reconstruction, 1861–1873," Ph.D. diss., Texas Tech University, 1985; Ralph A. Wooster, "Life in Civil War East Texas," *East Texas Historical Journal (ETHJ)* 3 (fall, 1965): 93–102; S. S. McKay, "Social Conditions in Texas in the Eighteen Seventies," *WTHAYB* 14 (1938): 32–51.

22. Bessie Malvina Pearce, "Texas through Women's Eyes, 1823–1860," Ph.D. diss., University of Texas, 1965; Kathleen Elizabeth Lazarou, "Concealed under Petticoats: Married Women's Property and the Law in Texas, 1840–1913," Ph.D. diss., Rice University, 1980; Ann Patton Malone, *Women on the Texas Frontier: A Cross-Cultural Perspective* (El Paso: Texas Western Press, 1983); Crystal Sasse Ragsdale, ed., *The Golden Free Land: The Reminiscences and Letters of Women on the American Frontier* (Austin: Landmark, 1976); Barry A. Crouch and Larry Madaras, "Reconstructing Black Families: Perspectives from the Texas Freedmen's Bureau Records," *Prologue* 18 (summer, 1986): 109–22; James M. Smallwood, "Emancipation and the Black Family: A Case Study in Texas," *Social Science Quarterly* 57 (Mar., 1977): 849–57; Smallwood, *Time of Hope, Time of Despair.*

ingly threatened to aid blacks in becoming equal citizens in a white society, became probably the most hated part of Reconstruction. Reconstruction was marked by a great deal of white violence aimed at blacks and, according to several accounts, Texas was well on the way by 1876 to a system of racial segregation.[23]

Religion may not have been as important to all Texans as the family and race relations, but it also played a vital role for many, not only because it provided spiritual inspiration and moral guidance, but also because it was a primary way of bringing people together socially. General histories of all the major denominations describe the growth and activities of each during this period and give at least some idea of what churches meant to the people. Studies of slavery show that religion was a vital part of bondsmen's social and cultural life, too. Worship for them did not necessarily mean attending a church to which they belonged, but some denominations, especially the Baptists and the Methodists, actively sought black members. After emancipation, as Paul W. Stripling's dissertation showed so well in the case of the Baptists, blacks left the white denominations and formed their own churches, which, according to Smallwood, became the "central institution of the Negro community." The outlines of the story of blacks' religion and churches are clear, but the whole should be detailed in one publication.[24]

23. Campbell, *Empire for Slavery;* Bill Ledbetter, "White over Black in Texas: Racial Attitudes in the Ante-Bellum Period," *Phylon* 34 (Dec., 1973): 406–18; Wendell C. Addington, "Slave Insurrections in Texas," *Journal of Negro History* 35 (Oct., 1950): 408–24; William W. White, "The Texas Slave Insurrection in 1860," *SHQ* 52 (Jan., 1949): 259–85; Claude Elliott, "The Freedmen's Bureau in Texas," *SHQ* 56 (July, 1952): 1–24; Smallwood, *Time of Hope, Time of Despair;* Barry A. Crouch and L. J. Schultz, "Crisis in Color: Racial Separation in Texas during Reconstruction," *Civil War History* 16 (Mar., 1970): 37–49; Bruce A. Glasrud, "Jim Crow's Emergence in Texas," *American Studies* 15 (spring, 1974): 47–60. Thomas W. Kremm, "Race Relations in Texas, 1865–1870," M.A. thesis, University of Houston, 1970, argues that segregation did not develop this early.

24. Robert E. Ledbetter, Jr., "The Planting and Growth of Protestant Denominations in Texas Prior to 1850," Ph.D. diss., University of Chicago, 1951; Carter E. Boren, *Religion on the Texas Frontier* (San Antonio: Naylor, 1968); R. Douglas Brackenridge, *Voice in the Wilderness: A History of the Cumberland Presbyterian Church in Texas* (San Antonio: Trinity University Press, 1968); Lawrence L. Brown, *The Episcopal Church in Texas, 1838–1874* (Austin: Church History Society, 1963); James Milton Carroll, *A History of Texas Baptists: Comprising a Detailed Account of Their . . . Achievements,* ed. J. B. Cranfill (Dallas: Baptist Standard Publishing, 1923); Walter N. Vernon et al., *The*

The development of public education in Texas after 1846 has received attention from both historians and educators. Their work, most of which has not been published, shows that powerful opposition from private schools, inadequate funding, and extreme localism virtually defeated all efforts to create an effective public school system in the years before 1876.[25] Progress was virtually nil before the Civil War, and then emancipation made public education an even more difficult matter after 1865. The Freedmen's Bureau first took up the job of providing schools for blacks and, by even the most critical accounts, accomplished a great deal during its relatively brief period of operation in Texas. The bureau's efforts, however, and those of the blacks themselves, could not perform the immense task at hand. The most ambitious efforts came during the administration of Governor E. J. Davis, but they faced the additional obstacle of having been established by a hated "Radical Republican." Once the "Redeemers" dismantled the system established in 1870–71, Texas was as far from providing adequate public education as it had been during the antebellum years.[26]

Methodist Excitement in Texas: A History (Dallas: Texas United Methodist Historical Society, 1984); William Stuart Red, *A History of the Presbyterian Church in Texas* (Austin: Steck, 1936); Paul Wayne Stripling, "The Negro Excision from Baptist Churches in Texas (1861–1870)," Ph.D. diss., Southwestern Baptist Theological Seminary, 1967; Smallwood, *Time of Hope, Time of Despair,* p. 97.

25. William Franklin Ledlow, "History of Protestant Education: A Study of the Origin, Growth, and Development of Educational Endeavors in Texas," Ph.D. diss., University of Texas, 1926; Jay Littman Todes, "The Constitutional and Statutory Development of Public Education in Texas, 1845–1860," Ed.D. diss., University of Houston, 1967; Michael Allen White, "History of Education in Texas, 1860–1864," Ed.D. diss., Baylor University, 1969.

26. James M. Smallwood, "Black Education in Reconstruction Texas: The Contributions of the Freedmen's Bureau and Benevolent Societies," *ETHJ* 19 (spring, 1981): 17–40; James M. Smallwood, "Early 'Freedom Schools': Black Self-Help and Education in Reconstruction Texas: A Case Study," *Negro History Bulletin* 41 (Jan.–Feb., 1978): 790–93; Alton Hornsby, Jr., "The Freedmen's Bureau Schools in Texas, 1865–1870," *SHQ* 76 (Apr., 1973): 397–417; Robert W. Warren, "Public Elementary and Secondary Education in Texas During the Administration of Governor E. J. Davis, 1870–1874," Ph.D. diss., East Texas State University, 1969; Betty Jane Slaughter Briscoe, "Governor Richard Coke's Influence on Texas School Systems," M.Ed. thesis, University of Texas, 1946; Stewart Dean Smith, "Schools and Schoolmen: Chapters in Texas Education, 1870–1900," Ph.D. diss., North Texas State University, 1974; Alton Hornsby, Jr., "Negro Education in Texas, 1865–1917," M.A. thesis, University of Texas, 1962; Michael R. Heintze, *Private Black Colleges in Texas, 1865–1954* (College Station: Texas

Newspapers, which were generally intensely personal and highly political, played an important part in the social and cultural lives of Texans between 1846 and 1876. They provided news, literary material, gossip, and editorial opinions. Marilyn McAdams Sibley's *Lone Stars and State Gazettes* provides an excellent description of antebellum newspapers in general, and Wesley Norton has emphasized the importance of religious newspapers during the years before 1861. Donald Reynolds's account of the "Texas Troubles" of 1860 in *Editors Make War* is a good example of the role played by newspapers during the secession crisis. Newspapers were no less important during Reconstruction, but unfortunately, there is no general work such as Sibley's for the years after 1865. At least there are several accounts of the black press at this time.[27]

Nearly all aspects of social and cultural life in Texas from statehood through Reconstruction have received more attention than the basic structure of society itself and the important matter of social mobility. There is a study of the distribution of wealth among economic classes during the antebellum years, an article on geographical mobility among the population of Houston during the 1850s, and an examination of occupational and geographical mobility in San Antonio from 1870 to 1900, but generally the kind of quantitative research necessary to deal with such matters has not been done.[28] Work on Texas' class structure and questions of social mobility will likely prove highly

A&M University Press, 1984); Carl H. Moneyhon, "Public Education and Texas Reconstruction Politics, 1871–1874," *SHQ* (Jan., 1989): 393–416.

27. Marilyn McAdams Sibley, *Lone Stars and State Gazettes: Texas Newspapers before the Civil War* (College Station: Texas A&M University Press, 1983); William Jesse Stone, Jr., "A Historical Survey of Leading Texas Denominational Newspapers, 1846–1861," Ph.D. diss., University of Texas, 1974; Wesley Norton, "Religious Newspapers in Antebellum Texas," *SHQ* 79 (Oct., 1975): 145–65; Donald E. Reynolds, *Editors Make War: Southern Newspapers in the Secession Crisis* (Nashville: Vanderbilt University Press, 1966); Charles William Grose, "Black Newspapers in Texas, 1868–1970," Ph.D. diss., University of Texas, 1972; James M. Smallwood, "Texas," in *The Black Press in the South, 1865–1979*, ed. Henry L. Suggs (Westport, Conn.: Greenwood, 1983).

28. Randolph B. Campbell and Richard G. Lowe, *Wealth and Power in Antebellum Texas* (College Station: Texas A&M University Press, 1977); Susan Jackson, "Movin' On: Mobility through Houston in the 1850s," *SHQ* 81 (Jan., 1978): 251–82; Alwyn Barr, "Occupational and Geographic Mobility in San Antonio, 1870–1900," *Social Science Quarterly* 51 (Sept., 1970): 393–403. See also Ralph A. Wooster, "Wealthy Texans, 1870," *SHQ* 74 (July, 1970): 24–35; and Randolph B. Campbell, "Population Persistence and Social Change in Nineteenth-Century Texas: Harrison County, 1850–1880," *Journal of Southern History (JSH)* 48 (May, 1982): 185–204.

controversial as well as very revealing. How will classes be defined — by wealth alone, or by some combination of wealth and other considerations such as the elusive "family standing" in the community? How will changes in the class structure and social mobility or the lack of it be interpreted? The economist Gavin Wright, for example, has argued that the continued membership of individuals and families in the wealthiest class from 1850 to 1880 has no significance for measuring their attitudes and policies because their economic interests had changed dramatically with the end of slavery.[29] Will historians agree that a change in economic interests will totally remake a man's ideas and attitudes? And what of class conflict? Does the demonstration of the existence of social classes prove the presence of conflict between those classes? Do intrastate differences in economic interests that led to political conflict between the representatives of different regions signal the presence of class conflict? The potential for significant and controversial research on social structure, social mobility, and class conflict is tremendous.

Historians have given more attention to political life in Texas from statehood through Reconstruction than to the state's economy, social and cultural life, and social structure combined. This is with good reason, too, in that probably more political excitement occurred during this thirty-year period than during the entire following century. Consider, for example, the fact that Texas has had four constitutions (not counting the revisions made in 1861 when the state joined the Confederacy) since entering the Union in 1845 and that all four came during the first thirty years of statehood. The drafting of each of these fundamental laws has been studied in detail, and the authors all had a tendency to praise the final result. John C. McGraw's dissertation calls the Presidential Reconstruction Constitution of 1866 the "best" organic law in Texas history—a judgment that Unionists and blacks might well dispute. Betty J. Sandlin overcame her obvious dislike of Radicals such as E. J. Davis to conclude that the strengths of the Radical Constitution of 1869 overmatched its weaknesses. J. E. Erickson emphasized the educational attainments and experience of those who drafted the "Redeemer" Constitution of 1876. Perhaps if all the political emotionalism of participants and observers could be removed the

29. Gavin Wright, *Old South, New South: Revolutions in the Southern Economy Since the Civil War* (New York: Basic Books, 1986).

case might be, as John P. Carrier's thesis suggests, that all three Reconstruction constitutions were essentially "moderate" documents written by longtime Texas residents who were concerned above all with economic interests and expansion. In any case, an examination of the similarities as well as differences in these constitutions would be useful.[30]

The historiography of political parties during this era is curiously unbalanced in that the Democratic party, which dominated state and local government for all but a brief period during Reconstruction, has received virtually no attention, whereas the opposition—Whigs, Know-Nothings, Constitutional Unionists, and Republicans—has been the subject of numerous studies. Richard L. Briggs's thesis deals with the Democrats from 1846 to 1857, as they became fully organized statewide, but, although there are biographies of major leaders and accounts of secession, no one has focused on the party as such during the critical years from 1857 to 1861. An even more glaring historiographical omission is the lack of a history detailing the Democrats' role in Reconstruction and "Redemption."[31]

By contrast, there are more than a dozen works analyzing the opposition and its role during this era. The Whigs, Know-Nothings, and Constitutional Unionists who followed each other in turn from the late 1840s to 1860 could never take statewide control from the Democrats. They appealed to the voters on a variety of issues—the Know-Nothings played on nativism, for example—but Unionism always ran through their platforms. Although not every Whig or Know-Nothing opposed secession and not every Democrat was a disunionist, there was a strong correlation between opposition leadership and support for the Union. Many supported Sam Houston in 1859 when he won

30. Annie Middleton, "The Texas Convention of 1845," *SHQ* 25 (July, 1921): 26–62; Frederic L. Paxson, "The Constitution of 1845," *SHQ* 17 (Apr., 1915): 386–98; John C. McGraw, "The Texas Constitution of 1866," Ph.D. diss., Texas Tech University, 1959; Betty J. Sandlin, "The Texas Reconstruction Convention of 1868–1869," Ph.D. diss., Texas Tech University, 1970; S. S. McKay, *Seven Decades of the Texas Constitution of 1876* (Lubbock: Texas Technological College Press, 1942); J. E. Ericson, "The Delegates to the Convention of 1875: A Reappraisal," *SHQ* 67 (July, 1963): 22–27; J. E. Ericson, "Origins of the Texas Bill of Rights," *SHQ* 62 (Apr., 1959): 457–66; Leila Clark Wynn, "A History of the Civil Courts in Texas," *SHQ* 60 (July, 1956): 1–22; John Pressley Carrier, "Constitutional Changes in Texas during the Reconstruction," M.A. thesis, North Texas State University, 1967.

31. Richard Lee Briggs, "The Democratic Party in Early Texas," M.A. thesis, Lamar State University, 1970.

the governorship as a Unionist Democrat.[32] Following the Civil War, as Carl Moneyhon and James Alex Baggett have ably demonstrated, antebellum Unionists formed the basis for the Republican party in Texas. Not all Unionists became Republicans, but the new party drew most of its leadership from those who had opposed secession. In general, Unionist-Republicans wanted an end to violence against themselves and freedmen, protection of political and civil rights (but not social equality) for blacks, a public school system, and promotion of economic expansion. The party, however, suffered from its dependence on black votes and from internal dissension that came with the attainment of power. According to Moneyhon, as opposing factions with conflicting goals bid for black support, they initiated more programs benefiting blacks than white Texans were willing to tolerate or pay for. "Given the numerical dominance of whites in Texas," he wrote, "race and taxes proved an insurmountable barrier to Republican success." Baggett saw the internal factions as the result more of differences in racial attitudes between moderate and radical Republicans than of disputes over policy. In any case, both agree that the Republicans, not having found a way to gain enough white votes to build a majority, were left dependent on federal support. When that was withdrawn in 1873–74, they became essentially a party of blacks and federal officeholders that would not win a governor's race in Texas for more than a century.[33]

32. Ronald C. Ellison, "The Whig Party of Texas," M.A. thesis, Lamar State University, 1971; Ronald C. Ellison, "Texas Whigs and the Gubernatorial Election of 1853," *ETHJ* 22 (spring, 1984): 33–41; Randolph B. Campbell, "The Whig Party of Texas in the Elections of 1848 and 1852," *SHQ* 73 (July, 1969): 17–34; Sister Paul of the Cross McGrath, *Political Nativism in Texas, 1825–1860* (Washington, D.C.: Catholic University of America, 1930); Waymon L. McClellan, "1855: The Know-Nothing Challenge in East Texas," *ETHJ* 12 (fall, 1974): 32–44; Waymon L. McClellan, "The Know-Nothing Party and the Growth of Sectionalism in East Texas," *ETHJ* 14 (fall, 1976): 26–36; Ralph A. Wooster, "An Analysis of the Texas Know-Nothings," *SHQ* 70 (Jan., 1967): 414–23; James Alex Baggett, "The Constitutional Union Party in Texas," *SHQ* 82 (Jan., 1979): 233–64.

33. James Alex Baggett, "Birth of the Texas Republican Party," *SHQ* 78 (July, 1974): 1–20; James Alex Baggett, "Origins of Early Texas Republican Party Leadership," *JSH* 40 (Aug., 1974): 441–54; James Alex Baggett: "The Rise and Fall of the Texas Radicals, 1867–1883," Ph.D. diss., North Texas State University, 1972; Carl H. Moneyhon, *Republicanism in Reconstruction Texas* (Austin: University of Texas Press, 1980); Philip J. Avilo, Jr., "Phantom Radicals: Texas Republicans in Congress,

Political life from 1846 to 1876 has been examined through several variations on the biographical approach; that is, attempting to improve understanding of politics by examining the lives of officeholders and party leaders. First, there are collective biographies, based largely on census data, of state and local officials during the antebellum period, of the members of the Secession Convention, of the constitutional conventions of 1866 and 1868–69, and of local officeholders during Reconstruction. Although these compilations were not created with the same goals in mind or presented with the same types of analysis, they make some very worthwhile points. Those on the antebellum period, for example, indicate that political leaders tended to be southern-born slaveholders who were far wealthier than members of the population in general. Those on Reconstruction indicate that, although officeholders and leaders from 1867 to 1873 were somewhat different in background than those who usually led Texas, claims about carpetbagger and black dominance amount to wild exaggerations.[34]

Second, there are collections of brief biographies, some lengthy enough to be called biographical essays, dealing with leaders of this era. Ralph Wooster and Fredericka Meiners each gave high marks to Texas' three Civil War governors, Edward Clark, Frank Lubbock, and Pendleton Murrah. William C. Nunn's graduate students at Texas Christian University dealt with twenty of the best-known Confederate Texans in two collections of biographical sketches. Important black leaders during Reconstruction such as George T. Ruby and Matt Gaines received attention first in a biographical collection from J.

1870–1873," *SHQ* 77 (Apr., 1974): 431–44; Paul Casdorph, *A History of the Republican Party in Texas, 1865–1965* (Austin: Pemberton, 1965).

34. Ralph A. Wooster, "Democracy on the Frontier: Statehouse and Courthouse in Ante-Bellum Texas," *ETHJ* 10 (fall, 1972): 83–97; Ralph A. Wooster, "Membership in Early Texas Legislatures, 1850–1860," *SHQ* 69 (Oct., 1965): 163–73; Ralph A. Wooster, "An Analysis of the Membership of the Texas Secession Convention," *SHQ* 62 (Jan., 1959): 322–34; Richard G. Lowe and Randolph B. Campbell, "Wealthholding and Political Power in Antebellum Texas," *SHQ* 79 (July, 1975): 21–30; Randolph B. Campbell, "Political Conflict within the Southern Consensus: Harrison County, Texas, 1850–1880," *Civil War History* 26 (Sept., 1980): 218–39; Randolph B. Campbell, "Grassroots Reconstruction: The Personnel of County Government in Texas, 1865–1876," unpublished paper presented at annual meeting of Southern Historical Association, Nov., 1988; Charles Hale, "Political Leadership in Texas during Reconstruction," M.A. thesis, Lamar University, 1965.

Mason Brewer and more recently from Alwyn Barr, Ann Patton Malone, Carl Moneyhon, and Merline Pitre.[35] Third, there are scholarly articles surveying the lives of men who, while they certainly deserve historical attention, may not have been significant enough or left adequate materials to merit full-scale biographies. Examples of these very useful studies include Ralph Wooster on Ben H. Epperson, Claude Hall on Tom Ochiltree, Randy Sparks on John P. Osterhout, Max S. Lale on Robert W. Loughery, and both Randall B. Woods and James M. Smallwood on George T. Ruby.[36] Possible subjects for similar articles are numerous. Certainly, for example, the early statehood governors, George T. Wood and Peter Hans-

35. Ralph A. Wooster, "Texas," in *The Confederate Governors*, ed. W. Buck Yearns (Athens: University of Georgia Press, 1985), pp. 195–215; Fredericka Ann Meiners, "The Texas Governorship, 1861–1865: Biography of an Office," Ph.D. diss., Rice University, 1975; William C. Nunn, ed., *Ten Texans in Gray* (Hillsboro, Tex.: Hill Junior College Press, 1968); William C. Nunn, ed., *Ten More Texans in Gray* (Hillsboro, Tex.: Hill Junior College Press, 1980); J. Mason Brewer, *Negro Legislators of Texas and Their Descendants* (Dallas: Mathis, 1935); Alwyn Barr, "Black Legislators of Reconstruction Texas," *Civil War History* 32 (Dec., 1986): 340–52; Carl H. Moneyhon, "George T. Ruby and the Politics of Expediency in Texas," in *Southern Black Leaders in the Reconstruction Era*, ed. Howard N. Rabinowitz (Urbana: University of Illinois Press, 1982), pp. 363–92; Ann Patton Malone, "Matt Gaines: Reconstruction Politician," in Barr and Calvert, *Black Leaders*, pp. 49–81; Merline Pitre, *Through Many Dangers, Toils and Snares: The Black Leadership of Texas, 1868–1900* (Austin: Eakin, 1985); Merline Pitre, "The Evolution of Black Political Participation in Reconstruction Texas," *ETHJ* 26 (spring, 1988): 36–45.
36. Ralph A. Wooster, "Ben H. Epperson: East Texas Lawyer, Legislator, and Civic Leader," *ETHJ* 5 (spring, 1967): 29–42; Claude H. Hall, "The Fabulous Tom Ochiltree: Promoter, Politician, and Raconteur," *SHQ* 71 (Jan., 1968): 347–76; Randy J. Sparks, "John P. Osterhout: Yankee, Rebel, Republican," *SHQ* 90 (Oct., 1986): 111–38; Alma Dexta King, "The Political Career of Williamson Simpson Oldham," *SHQ* 33 (Oct., 1929): 112–33; Robert L. Jones and Pauline Jones, "Edward H. Tarrant," *SHQ* 69 (Jan., 1966): 300–23; Matthew Ellenberger, "Illuminating the Lesser Lights: Notes on the Life of Albert Clinton Horton," *SHQ* 88 (Apr., 1985): 363–86; Alwyn Barr, "The Making of a Secessionist: The Antebellum Career of Roger Q. Mills," *SHQ* 79 (Oct., 1975): 129–44; Randall B. Woods, "George T. Ruby: A Black Militant in the White Business Community," *Red River Valley Historical Review* 1 (fall, 1974): 269–80; James M. Smallwood, "G. T. Ruby: Galveston's Black Carpetbagger in Reconstruction Texas," *Houston Review* (winter, 1983): 24–33; Max S. Lale, "Robert W. Loughery: Rebel Editor," *ETHJ* 21 (fall, 1983): 3–15; Randolph B. Campbell, "George W. Whitmore: East Texas Unionist," *ETHJ* 28 (spring, 1990): 17–28.

borough Bell, deserve brief biographies as do Unionist-Republicans such as Congressman Edward Degener. Without adding to the list, the point should be clear—students of any aspect of the period from 1846 to 1876 should be alert to the stories of men who, although not generally well known, played significant roles in shaping the history of these years.[37]

Finally, some political leaders of this era have been the subjects of full-scale biographies. There are good, or at least adequate, published accounts of the lives of Sam Houston, John H. Reagan, Louis T. Wigfall, James W. Throckmorton, and James P. Newcomb.[38] Unfortunately, published biographies of other leaders such as James Pinckney Henderson, Thomas Jefferson Rusk, John Hemphill, David G. Burnet, Ashbel Smith, Sul Ross, and A. J. Hamilton generally were based on thin research and do little more than sketch major portions of the careers of these men without exhibiting awareness of the interpretive questions involved.[39] Even worse, a good many major figures

37. C. Luther Coyner, "Peter Hansborough Bell," *Quarterly of the Texas State Historical Association* 3 (July, 1899): 49–53; S. H. Sherman, "Governor George Thomas Wood," *SHQ* 20 (Jan., 1917): 260–68.

38. Llerena Friend, *Sam Houston: The Great Designer* (Austin: University of Texas Press, 1954); Marquis James, *The Raven: A Biography of Sam Houston* (Indianapolis: Bobbs, Merrill, 1929); Ben H. Proctor, *Not without Honor: The Life of John H. Reagan* (Austin: University of Texas Press, 1962); Alvy L. King, *Louis T. Wigfall: Southern Fire-Eater* (Baton Rouge: Louisiana State University Press, 1970); Claude Elliott, *Leathercoat: The Life of a Texas Patriot* (San Antonio: Privately printed, 1938); John Fowler, *James P. Newcomb: Texas Journalist and Political Leader* (Austin: Department of Journalism, University of Texas, 1976). Articles contributing further to understanding of the careers of these men include Philip J. Avilo, Jr., "John H. Reagan: Unionist or Secessionist?" *ETHJ* 13 (spring, 1975): 23–33; Billy D. Ledbetter, "The Election of Louis T. Wigfall to the United States Senate, 1859: A Reevaluation," *SHQ* 77 (Oct., 1973): 241–54; Dale A. Somers, "James P. Newcomb: The Making of a Radical," *SHQ* 72 (Apr., 1969): 449–69.

39. Robert G. Winchester, *James Pinckney Henderson: Texas' First Governor* (San Antonio: Naylor, 1971); Mary W. Clarke, *Thomas J. Rusk: Soldier, Statesman, Jurist* (Austin: Jenkins, 1971); Cleburne Huston, *Towering Texan: A Biography of Thomas J. Rusk* (Waco: Texian, 1971); Rosalee M. Curtis, *John Hemphill: First Chief Justice of the State of Texas* (Austin: Pemberton, 1971); Mary W. Clarke, *David G. Burnet* (Austin: Pemberton, 1969); Elizabeth Silverthorne, *Ashbel Smith of Texas: Pioneer, Patriot, Statesman, 1805–1886* (College Station: Texas A&M University Press, 1982); Judith Ann Benner, *Sul Ross: Soldier, Statesman, Educator* (College Station: Texas A&M University Press, 1983); John L. Waller, *Colossal Hamilton of Texas: A Biography of Andrew Jackson Hamilton, Militant Unionist and Reconstruction Governor* (El Paso: Texas Western Press, 1968).

including, for example, Hardin R. Runnels, Oran M. Roberts, Richard Coke, E. M. Pease, and Edmund J. Davis, although serving as subjects for theses and dissertations, have never had their biographies published. Given the importance of the last four of these men during Reconstruction, it is easy to conclude that the biographical dimension of that era has been badly neglected.[40]

No historian has attempted to write a general account of political issues and developments during the thirty tumultuous years following statehood. Robert K. Peters's unpublished dissertation, "Texas: Annexation to Secession," offers a synthesis of politics from 1846 to 1861, but no one has dared to publish such a work extending to 1876. Perhaps the task is too daunting, although there are certainly many excellent studies with which to work.[41]

Developments during the years immediately following the launching of the new government in 1846 have been described by Lucien Elliot Peevy and Ralph Wooster. Leila Clark Wynn has provided a sketch of the state's court system, and a dissertation by Edward B. Weisel at Rice University explores intergovernmental relations from 1835 to 1860, emphasizing how insistence on local autonomy hindered effective government during the antebellum years.[42]

As the 1850s unfolded, Texas politics, slowly at first and then more rapidly, took on an ultra-southern cast. The decade opened with a dispute over the Texas–New Mexico boundary that had important sec-

40. Leila Bailey, "The Life and Public Career of O. M. Roberts," Ph.D. diss., University of Texas, 1932; Roger Allen Griffin, "Connecticut Yankee in Texas: A Biography of Elisha Marshall Pease," Ph.D. diss., University of Texas, 1973; Ronald Norman Gray, "Edmund J. Davis: Radical Republican and Reconstruction Governor of Texas," Ph.D. diss., Texas Tech University, 1976; William T. Hooper, Jr., "Governor Edmund J. Davis, Ezra Cornell, and the A&M College of Texas," *SHQ* 78 (Jan., 1975): 307–12; Jane Lynn Scarborough, "George W. Paschal: Texas Unionist and Scalawag Jurisprudent," Ph.D. diss., Rice University, 1972; John A. Moretta, "William Pitt Ballinger: Public Servant, Private Pragmatist," Ph.D. diss., Rice University, 1986; Virginia Neal Heinze, "Norris Wright Cuney," M.A. thesis, Rice University, 1965.

41. Robert K. Peters, "Texas: Annexation to Secession," Ph.D. diss., University of Texas, 1977.

42. Lucien Elliot Peevy, "The First Two Years of Texas Statehood, 1846–1847," Ph.D. diss., University of Texas, 1948; Ralph A. Wooster, "Early Texas Politics: The Henderson Administration," *SHQ* 73 (Oct., 1969): 176–92; Ralph A. Wooster, "Early Texas Politics: The Wood Administration," *Texana* 8 (summer, 1970): 183–99; Wynn, "History of the Civil Courts in Texas"; Edward Berry Weisel, "City, County, State: Intergovernmental Relations in Texas, 1835–1860," Ph.D. diss., Rice University, 1975.

tional implications. Works by William C. Binkley, Morris F. Taylor, and Kenneth F. Neighbours explain the basis of this dispute and the unsuccessful efforts of Texas to make good its claim to all of New Mexico east of the Rio Grande. Holman Hamilton's *Prologue to Conflict* describes how the boundary question became part of the larger Crisis of 1850 and how Texas bondholders played a major role in developing a compromise whereby the Lone Star State gave up its claims to eastern New Mexico in return for $10 million to pay its debts. There is no recent study of the overall impact on Texas of this great crisis of the Union, although Randolph B. Campbell has shown in an article on the Nashville convention that, in 1850 at least, moderate sentiment prevailed there as elsewhere across the South.[43]

Moderation began to wane in 1854, however, when northern opposition to the Kansas-Nebraska Act so excited the southern sensibilities of Texans that many even attacked Sam Houston for his vote against the act. By the late fifties, as Earl W. Fornell showed, a vocal minority agitated for reopening the African slave trade, one of the most ultra-southern demands of the day, and some Texans even supported the Knights of the Golden Circle, a group promoting the fantasy of a gigantic slaveholding empire centered on Havana, Cuba. Nancy Ann Head's thesis shows that the southern states' rights ideology grew steadily through the decade, too.[44] Most important, the slavery issue, with its emotion-laden complex of racism, fear of servile insurrection, and hatred of Yankee Republicans, increasingly threatened to still "the

43. William C. Binkley, "The Question of Texas Jurisdiction in New Mexico under the United States, 1848–1850," *SHQ* 24 (July, 1920): 1–38; Morris F. Taylor, "Spruce McCoy Baird: From Texas Agent to New Mexico Official, 1848–1860," *New Mexico Historical Review* 53 (Jan., 1978): 39–58; Neighbours, *Robert Simpson Neighbors;* Randolph B. Campbell, "Texas and the Nashville Convention of 1850," *SHQ* 76 (July, 1972): 1–14; Holman Hamilton, *Prologue to Conflict: The Crisis and Compromise of 1850* (Lexington: University of Kentucky Press, 1964); Clarence A. Bridges, "Texas and the Crisis of 1850," M.A. thesis, University of Texas, 1925.

44. Charles L. Moore, "Texas and the Kansas-Nebraska Act of 1854," M.A. thesis, North Texas State University, 1974; Earl W. Fornell, "Agitation in Texas for Reopening the Slave Trade," *SHQ* 60 (Oct., 1956): 245–59; Roy Sylvan Dunn, "The KGC in Texas, 1860–1861," *SHQ* 70 (Apr., 1967): 543–73; C. A. Bridges, "The Knights of the Golden Circle: A Filibustering Fantasy," *SHQ* 44 (Jan., 1941): 287–302; Ollinger Crenshaw, "The Knights of the Golden Circle," *American Historical Review* 47 (Oct., 1941): 23–50; Nancy Ann Head, "States' Rights in Texas: The Growth of an Idea, 1850–1860," M.A. thesis, Rice Institute, 1960.

voice of reason," as Sam Houston called it. By 1860-61, as several studies have demonstrated, Texans might disagree over the value of the Union, but their entire society had no place for anyone who questioned slavery or saw the Republican party as anything except a serious threat to the "peculiar institution." These works, most of which are unpublished, do not explain the events and the reasons involved in the actual decision on secession, but obviously they are essential to understanding disunion. A synthesis, focusing only on attitudes and developments before 1860 and at the same time placing these Texas studies in the context of recent interpretations of rising extremism across the South during the 1850s, would be welcome.[45]

Walter Buenger's *Secession and the Union in Texas* does an excellent job of pulling together the various factors behind disunion and at the same time explaining the complexity of the situation in the Lone Star State. Texans were influenced, he has explained, by their ethnocultural backgrounds, their traditions of support for the Union or for the Democratic party, their views of what the Union meant to them (especially if they lived on the frontier and needed protection from the Indians), and their reactions to emotionally disturbing events in 1859-61. Buenger's work may be supplemented by more specialized studies such as Ralph Wooster's description of the delegates to the Secession Convention, Allen Ashcraft's discussion of East Texas' overwhelming support for disunion, and Joe T. Timmons's careful review of the actual vote across Texas, but it is doubtful that his explanation will be challenged for many years.[46]

Unionism, which obviously was far less prevalent than secession-

45. Billy Don Ledbetter, "Slavery, Fear, and Disunion in the Lone Star State: Texans' Attitude Toward Secession and the Union, 1846-1861," Ph.D. diss., North Texas State University, 1972; Billy Don Ledbetter, "Slave Unrest and White Panic: The Impact of Black Republicanism in Ante-Bellum Texas," *Texana* 10 (1972): 335-50; Oran Lonnie Sinclair, "Crossroads of Conviction: A Study of the Texas Political Mind, 1856-1861," Ph.D. diss., Rice University, 1975; Joe T. Timmons, "Texas on the Road to Secession," Ph.D. diss., University of Chicago, 1973; Wesley Norton, "The Methodist Episcopal Church and the Civil Disturbances in North Texas in 1859 and 1860," *SHQ* 68 (Jan., 1965): 317-41.

46. Walter L. Buenger, *Secession and the Union in Texas* (Austin: University of Texas Press, 1984); Walter L. Buenger, "Texas and the Riddle of Secession," *SHQ* 87 (Oct., 1983): 151-82; Ralph A. Wooster, *The Secession Conventions of the South* (Princeton: Princeton University Press, 1962); Allan C. Ashcraft, "East Texas in the Election of 1860 and the Secession Crisis," *ETHJ* 1 (July, 1963): 7-16; Joe T. Timmons, "The Referen-

ist sentiment, may be more difficult to identify and explain. Opposition political parties tended to emphasize support for the Union but, at the same time, attracted non-Unionist voters with appeals to all sorts of other issues. For example, as Frank Smyrl has pointed out, most Unionists might be Know-Nothings, but many Know-Nothings were not necessarily Unionists. By the same token, Unionist-Democrats in North Texas might well have voted for Breckinridge in 1860 because their partisanship would not permit them to support the old Whig, John Bell. Moreover, we can only guess at which voters actually participated in particular elections. Thus, the only true test of Unionism was the referendum on secession in 1861. Several studies have pointed out that strongholds of support for the Union were in the North Texas area settled primarily by nonslaveholding natives of the North, in the heavily German Hill Country west of Austin, and in the relatively secure southwestern frontier counties. Even then, however, as Buenger has demonstrated, it is an exaggeration to say that a majority of Germans opposed secession, and a recent article by Robin E. Baker and Dale Baum contends that, although the usual explanations of Unionism have validity, the best statistical indicator of antisecession sentiment is "knowledge of religious preferences." Lutherans and Disciples of Christ, they say, supported the Union.[47]

Political differences did not simply go away during the Civil War. Instead, as unpublished dissertations by Robert P. Felgar, Allan C. Ashcraft, and Nancy Head Bowen remind us, the state's leaders grappled with problems of supporting the war effort, defending the state, regulating the cotton trade, and controlling internal divisions. Bowen in particular has suggested the need for a deeper understanding of how antebellum alignments and issues carried over into the years from

dum in Texas on the Ordinance of Secession, February 23, 1861: The Vote," *ETHJ* 11 (fall, 1973): 12–28.

47. Frank H. Smyrl, "Unionism, Abolitionism, and Vigilantism in Texas, 1856–1865," M.A. thesis, University of Texas, 1961; Smyrl, "Unionism in Texas, 1861–1865," *SHQ* 68 (Oct., 1964): 172–95; Claude Elliott, "Union Sentiment in Texas, 1861–1865," *SHQ* 50 (July, 1947): 449–77; Walter L. Buenger, "Unionism on the Texas Frontier, 1859–1861," *Arizona and the West* 22 (fall, 1980): 237–54; Floyd F. Ewing, Jr., "Origins of Unionist Sentiment on the West Texas Frontier," *WTHAYB* 32 (1956): 21–29; Ewing, "Unionist Sentiment on the Northwest Texas Frontier," *WTHAYB* 33 (1957): 58–70; Robin E. Baker and Dale Baum, "The Texas Voter and the Crisis of the Union, 1859–1861," *JSH* (Aug., 1987): 395–420.

1861 to 1865 and how state politics were affected by Confederate policies. A book on this subject could also detail and evaluate the importance of Unionism during the war years. Several historians have suggested that those who opposed secession created significant problems for Texas and hindered its support of the Confederacy, and they generally point to events in 1862 on the Nueces River and in Gainesville to support their case. Bowen has shown, however, that when Texans had to elect a new chief justice of the supreme court in 1864, Oran M. Roberts, a leading secessionist, easily defeated Unionist James H. Bell. Texans may have grown weary of the war by 1864–65, but studies to this point have not proven that the majority had turned against the Confederacy or their old leaders.[48]

The general political history of Reconstruction in Texas has been dominated for three-quarters of a century by the Dunning interpretation, applied to the Lone Star State first by Charles W. Ramsdell in 1910 and continued in relatively recent years by W. C. Nunn's *Texas Under the Carpetbaggers.* Their story of oppression by federal troops, the Freedmen's Bureau, rapacious carpetbaggers and scalawags, and ignorant freedmen is too familiar to require repeating here. In short, from the beginning of Congressional Reconstruction in 1867 until the end of the Republican party's "reign" in 1874, white Texans suffered a loss of constitutional liberties under a government that was both extravagant and corrupt. It was, in the words of one student of disfranchisement under the Reconstruction Acts, an "ordeal." Only with "redemption" under the Democratic party was there a return to decency and good government in the Lone Star State.[49]

48. Robert P. Felgar, "Texas in the War for Southern Independence, 1861–1865," Ph.D. diss., University of Texas, 1935; Allan C. Ashcraft, "Texas: 1860–1866, the Lone Star State in the Civil War," Ph.D. diss., Columbia University, 1960; Nancy Head Bowen, "A Political Labyrinth: Texas in the Civil War—Questions in Continuity," Ph.D. diss., Rice University, 1974; Nancy Head Bowen, "A Political Labyrinth: Texas in the Civil War," *ETHJ* 11 (fall, 1973): 3–11; James A. Marten, "Drawing the Line: Dissent and Disloyalty in Texas, 1856 to 1874," Ph.D. diss., University of Texas, 1986 (published as *Texas Divided: Loyalty and Dissent in the Lone Star State* [Lexington: University of Kentucky Press, 1990]); James M. Smallwood, "Disaffection in Confederate Texas: The Great Hanging at Gainesville," *Civil War History* 22 (Dec., 1976): 349–60; Richard B. McCaslin, "Tainted Breeze: The Great Hanging at Gainesville, Texas, October 1862," Ph.D. diss., University of Texas, 1988.

49. Charles William Ramsdell, *Reconstruction in Texas* (New York: Columbia University Press, 1910; William C. Nunn, *Texas under the Carpetbaggers* (Austin: University

Revision of this Dunning interpretation began in Texas during the 1960s, but the process has been slow and remains incomplete. John P. Carrier's 1971 dissertation at Vanderbilt, for example, attacked the myth of carpetbagger rule, pointed out that Republicans were no more corrupt than Democrats, and stressed the similarities between the parties in economic policy. Carrier's study, however, has not been published, and the only general revisionist account in print is Richard R. Moore's brief sketch in *The Texas Heritage*.[50] Revisionism is found in James M. Smallwood's general study of black Texans during Reconstruction, which devoted a chapter to explaining the political role of freedmen and defending their contributions. Barry A. Crouch and Donald G. Nieman also have added significantly to revising the image of the ignorant and helpless freedman by pointing out that former slaves effectively used courts to protect their interests and thus demonstrated considerable ability to function in a free society. Smallwood, Crouch, and Cecil Harper, Jr. have each contributed to a reinterpretation of the Freedmen's Bureau that emphasizes its necessity in protecting the former slaves and the good intentions of many of its agents.[51]

of Texas Press, 1962); William R. Russ, Jr., "Radical Disfranchisement in Texas, 1867–1870," *SHQ* 38 (July, 1934): 40–52; Ernest Wallace, *The Howling of the Coyotes: Reconstruction Efforts to Divide Texas* (College Station: Texas A&M University Press, 1979).

50. John Pressley Carrier, "A Political History of Texas during the Reconstruction, 1865–1874," Ph.D. diss., Vanderbilt University, 1971; Richard R. Moore, "Reconstruction," in Procter and McDonald, *Texas Heritage*, pp. 95–107.

51. Smallwood, *Time of Hope, Time of Despair;* Barry A. Crouch, "Black Dreams and White Justice [Texas, 1865–1868]," *Prologue* 6 (winter, 1974): 255–65; Donald G. Nieman, "Black Political Power and Criminal Justice: Washington County, Texas, as a Case Study, 1868–1884," *JSH* 55 (Aug., 1989): 391–420; James M. Smallwood, "The Freedmen's Bureau Reconsidered: Local Agents and the Black Community," *Texana* 11 (spring, 1973): 309–20; James S. Smallwood, "Charles E. Culver, A Reconstruction Agent in Texas: The Work of Local Freedmen's Bureau Agents and the Black Community," *Civil War History* 27 (Dec., 1981): 350–61; Barry A. Crouch, "The Freedmen's Bureau and the 30th Sub-District in Texas: Smith County and Its Environs during Reconstruction," *Chronicles of Smith County* 11 (spring, 1972): 15–30; Cecil Harper, Jr., "Freedmen's Bureau Agents in Texas: A Profile," paper presented at annual meeting of Texas State Historical Association, 1987. See also Diane Neal and Thomas W. Kremm, "'What Shall We Do with the Negro?': The Freedmen's Bureau in Texas," *ETHJ* 27 (fall, 1989): 23–34; and Merline Pitre, "The Evolution of Black Political Participation in Reconstruction Texas," *ETHJ* 26 (spring, 1988): 36–45.

New examinations of the role of the United States Army in Reconstruction Texas, while challenging to some extent the traditional view, have, in turn, provided interesting historiographical problems themselves. Robert W. Shook's 1970 dissertation on federal occupation of Texas from 1865–70 was frankly revisionist and insisted that the army's role in general, and its oppressive acts in particular, had been exaggerated by both contemporaries and historians. The military, he said, did not have the manpower to enforce the law adequately, let alone push a radical program on the state. By contrast, William L. Richter in his dissertation, also completed in 1970, in numerous articles, and in a book published in 1987 has contended that the army was probably the key factor in Reconstruction. It was strong enough to guarantee Radical Republican success in 1869, and its interference with society in general provided a focus for white opposition. The role of the military, he concludes, "went a long way toward compromising the promises of Union victory" by serving as a "convenient excuse for the denial of justice and equality to blacks." Richter's work tends to defy Reconstruction historiography typology in that his emphasis on the failure of Reconstruction places him with the so-called postrevisionists, but his support for the conservative government elected in 1866 with Throckmorton as governor, his criticism of the whole idea of military occupation, and his view that the army somehow provoked violence against Unionists and blacks seem perfectly in line with the positions taken by Ramsdell in 1910.[52]

Revisionists have also taken a new look at racial violence in Reconstruction Texas and found that it was at least as common as Unionists and blacks claimed. Barry A. Crouch, for example, has argued that whites used violence to control both the political and economic aspirations of the freedmen, and James Smallwood has urged historians to recognize that Klansmen and their ilk were "vicious murderers." Any general study of this era will have to come to grips with just

52. Robert W. Shook, "Federal Occupation and Administration of Texas, 1865–1870," Ph.D. diss., North Texas State University, 1970; Robert W. Shook, "The Federal Military in Texas, 1865–1870," *Texana* 6 (spring, 1967): 3–53; William Lee Richter, *The Army in Texas during Reconstruction, 1865–1870* (College Station: Texas A&M University Press, 1987). Richter has also published at least ten articles relating to the army during Reconstruction. Otis A. Singletary, "The Texas Militia during Reconstruction," *SHQ* 60 (July, 1956): 23–35, also emphasizes the political role of military forces.

how cheap life was in Reconstruction Texas, who was to "blame" for such conditions, and the impact of violence on politics from 1865 to 1876.[53]

A variety of works on limited periods or specific topics also contributed to a revised view of Reconstruction politics. Allen C. Ashcraft, for example, has looked at the first nine months of A. J. Hamilton's tenure as provisional governor in 1865–66 and praised him for sagacity and leadership. Nora Estelle Owens's dissertation concludes that Presidential Reconstruction was doomed from the outset, since it assumed that Texans wanted only to prove their loyalty to the United States. She also was highly critical of the obstructionist nature of Governor Throckmorton's relations with federal authorities. Texas's versions of the infamous Black Codes of 1865–66 have been defended as models of discretion compared to those adopted in other states, but the very existence of such legislation indicates that Texans did not mean to accord blacks equality before the law. Richard R. Moore has aptly summed up events and developments before 1867 by calling Radical Reconstruction "the Texas choice." The majority had no intention of recognizing any changes except the end of slavery, and their attitude and actions contributed directly to the congressional takeover in 1867. No new directions could be taken in state politics during 1868–69 as the government operated essentially under military control. Once Texas returned to the Union, the administration of E. J. Davis from 1870 to 1873 pursued policies that, according to Ann Patton Baenziger, constituted bold and progressive beginnings. Free public schools, for example, were badly needed and the state police, rather than an agency of Republican oppression, supported law and order for all.[54]

53. Barry A. Crouch, "A Spirit of Lawlessness: White Violence; Texas Blacks, 1865–1868," *Journal of Social History* 18 (winter, 1984): 217–32; Charles V. Keener, "Racial Turmoil in Texas, 1865–1874," M.A. thesis, North Texas State University, 1971; James M. Smallwood, "When the Klan Rode: White Terror in Reconstruction Texas," *Journal of the West* 25 (Oct., 1986): 4–13; Billy D. Ledbetter, "White Texans' Attitudes toward the Political Equality of Negroes, 1865–1870," *Phylon* 40 (Sept., 1979): 253–63.

54. Allan C. Ashcraft, "Texas in Defeat: The Early Phase of A. J. Hamilton's Provisional Governorship of Texas, June 17, 1865 to February 7, 1866," *Texas Military History* 7 (1970): 199–219; Nora Estelle Owens, "Presidential Reconstruction in Texas: A Case Study," Ph.D. diss., Auburn University, 1983; Winnell Albrecht, "The Black Codes of Texas," M.A. thesis, Southwest Texas State University, 1969; Theodore Branter Wilson, *The Black Codes of the South* (University: University of Alabama Press, 1965); Richard R. Moore, "Radical Reconstruction: The Texas Choice," *ETHJ* 16 (spring,

Several aspects of the political history of Reconstruction remain in need of examination or careful reexamination. First, little has been written on the politics involved in achieving "redemption" by conservative whites during the mid-1870s. Work on that subject should contribute helpful background to the story already told by Alwyn Barr's study of conservative political leadership from 1876 to 1906. Second, there is a need to know more about how Reconstruction came home to Texans at the local level. County government was far more important than is generally recognized, and local studies grounded in modern historiography would add an essential dimension to understanding developments from 1865 to 1876. What, for example, was the impact of the army and Freedmen's Bureau agents on local officials, on the budding Republican party, and on the local judicial system? Third, there must be a general history to replace Ramsdell and Nunn. It need not stand Ramsdell on his head and find only good intentions and sound policies in federal officials, Unionists, and freedmen and only bad in the white conservatives. It should, however, recognize how far Reconstruction historiography has come since Dunning and try to appreciate the perspectives of Texas Unionists, freedmen, Freedmen's Bureau agents, and federal officers and troops as well as those of the white majority and former Confederates.[55]

In summary, the era of statehood, Civil War, and Reconstruction, although it has received a great deal of attention from capable historians, offers many opportunities for future scholarship. Subjects for monographs and biographies, suggested throughout this essay, are too numerous to list here. Scholars who undertake these topics, with the

---

1978): 15–23; Ann Patton Baenziger, "Bold Beginnings: The Radical Program in Texas, 1870–1873," M.A. thesis, Southwest Texas State University, 1970; Ann Patton Baenziger, "The Texas State Police during Reconstruction: A Reexamination," *SHQ* 72 (Apr., 1969): 470–91; William T. Field, Jr., "The Texas State Police, 1870–1873," *Texas Military History* 5 (fall, 1965): 131–41.

55. Alwyn Barr, *Reconstruction to Reform: Texas Politics, 1876–1906* (Austin: University of Texas Press, 1971). Examples of works on Reconstruction at the local level include Robert W. Shook, "Military Activities in Victoria, 1865–1866," *Texana* 3 (winter, 1965): 347–52; Robert W. Shook, "Toward a List of Reconstruction Loyalists," *SHQ* 76 (Jan., 1973): 315–20; David Ryan Smith, "Reconstruction and Republicanism in Grayson, Fannin, and Lamar Counties, Texas, 1865–1873," M.A. thesis, University of Texas, 1979; John Robert Crews, "Reconstruction in Brownsville, Texas," M.A. thesis, Texas Tech University, 1969; and Barry A. Crouch, "Self-Determination and Local Black Leaders in Texas," *Phylon* 39 (Dec., 1978): 344–55.

exception of those working in the era of Reconstruction, generally will not find much in the way of conflicting interpretations or historiographical debate. This circumstance results from how thin the literature is—most subjects have only one study—and from the fact that some of the potentially more controversial topics such as social structure and class conflict have been studied so little.

The general lack of historiographical debate may also result from the shortage of works of synthesis. There is a serious need for histories that will combine new research with existing studies to take broad, interpretive looks at what happened to particular facets of life in Texas from 1846 to 1876. This will mean addressing more carefully the basic questions of change over time during those thirty years. In a way Texas saw two attempted revolutions during that period—one aimed at attaining independence from the United States, and then one aimed at changing social and political structures across the state. But the first revolution failed, and the second one was, at the very most, incomplete. They brought changes, of course, but exactly how new—economically, socially, and politically—was the Texas that emerged from the era of secession, Civil War, emancipation, and Reconstruction? This is a crucial question and, due largely to the periodization of existing studies, it has not been answered.

Finally, historians must ask, regardless of the extent of change and continuity through the era, how many of the traditions of modern Texas had taken root by 1876? The state still operates under the constitution adopted that year. Does it still live with the attitudes toward political life and good government held by the majorities who wrote and approved that document? In short, more and better writing on the most tumultuous era in Texas history is important, not only for the sake of the historical record but also, as is true of all studies of the past but more obviously so in this case, for a better understanding of the present.

Agrarian Texas

Robert A. Calvert

In 1989 less than 2 percent of Texans farmed or ranched. Those 174,000 who operated farms tilled the second largest in individual size in the nation. The move from a rural, agrarian state in the late nineteenth century to one now 80.5 percent urban (this figure is higher than the national average), and one with a more heterogeneous citizenry than any of the others except California and New York, has not been adequately described. Yet farms and farmers dominated Texas political debate and social development until World War II, and agriculture and agribusiness long supported much of the state's economic development.[1]

Several reasons explained the reluctance of historians to work on Texas agricultural topics. Most historians of the state have favored the period prior to the Civil War and usually focused on the alleged glories of independence, the Republic, secession, and battles, while their counterparts who write on postbellum Texas must consider sharecropping, poverty, and the state's colonial economy. Self-congratulatory history was difficult to write for those interested in farming. Those who did choose a postbellum agricultural topic usually picked the cattle industry. Scholars have never decided if the Lone Star State should fly southern or western colors, and the romance of ranches appealed to Texas historians, who have tended to be sentimental about the history of the state. Cattle gave to the state cowboys and western glamour; cotton made it southern, hence Confederate, defeated, poor, and prosaic.[2]

1. *Texas Almanac and Industrial Guide, 1988–1989* (Dallas: *Dallas Morning News,* 1989): 574–75.
2. For the purpose of this essay, the author will concentrate on farms rather

197

Almost regardless of choice of topics, scholars of the late nineteenth-century Texas have more and better secondary literature available to them than do those who work in twentieth-century state history. The nineteenth-century bias of Texas historians made the age of industrialism more attractive for research than the later decades. Moreover scholars traditionally have been interested in the politics of third parties and disfranchisement. Nevertheless the attention paid to the cattle frontier and not the cotton frontier, and the ambivalence concerning Texas as either southern or western has let the state fall between the historical cracks of some of the current national and regional scholarship on agriculture.

For those interested in late nineteenth- and early twentieth-century Texas much work remains to be done. This essay introduces readers to the historiography of late nineteenth-century agricultural history and pursues some subjects on rural Texas into the twentieth century. The state economy of 1930 had much more in common with 1890 than it did with the postwar 1945 economic development. Cotton still dominated trade. Sharecropping characterized much of agricultural life. Prior to World War II, then, the economy responded to agricultural rhythms and problems of cotton. To break southern history at 1900 creates artificial boundaries for many topics.

The best general survey of late nineteenth-century Texas remains Billy Mac Jones's *The Search for Maturity*.[3] This volume was the fifth book in the *Saga of Texas* series, designed to be short, well-written historical period studies for students and the general public. As with most general surveys, the description of political and economic events dominated the books, with scanty coverage allotted to social and intellectual history. The general theme of *The Search for Maturity* was the economic transformation of the period from a frontier, subsistence existence to a more mature economy. Jones fulfilled the editors' charge by mining secondary literature to produce a readable overview based on the then historical consensus of the period. The era needs a new monograph drawn from secondary sources that revises Jones and that allots more space to social developments.

----

than ranchers. See Walter Buenger's essay, "Flight from Modernity," this volume, for comments on ranching.

3. Billy Mac Jones, *The Search for Maturity, 1875–1900* (Austin: Steck-Vaughn, 1965).

The historical bias that until very recently directed scholars toward political history has generated much of the better scholarship on late nineteenth-century Texas. Scholars have been well served, for example, by Alwyn Barr's political history of the state from 1877 to 1906.[4] His book, like a number of monographs on the postbellum political history of southern states published about the same time, was heavily influenced by C. Vann Woodward's body of work.[5] This genre of scholarship analyzed political tensions and conflicts as the states of the New South went from Reconstruction to the disfranchisement of Afro-Americans. They depicted the New South as a period of political turmoil where farmers refused to readily submit to Democratic party control. Woodward and his adherents saw the New South as a clean break from the old, with redeemers replacing planters in the state establishment.

The break does not seem as sharp in Texas. Barr rejects the concept of the New South creed as dominating the Texas consciousness as it did in other former Confederate states.[6] Rather, he saw agrarian progressives as influencing Texas politics not only through the administration of James S. Hogg but into the early twentieth century, a point concurred with by Worth Robert Miller.[7] One of the major strengths of *From Reconstruction to Reform* was the author's careful evaluation of political interest groups from the Greenbackers through the conservative gubernatorial administrations that replaced Hogg after 1895. Agrarian insurgency and the emergence of the Hogg coalition

4. Alwyn Barr, *Reconstruction to Reform: Texas Politics, 1876–1906* (Austin: University of Texas Press, 1971). A shorter book, Cary D. Wintz, *Texas Politics in the Gilded Age, 1873–1890* (Boston: American Press, 1971), is a first-rate introduction to politics in the period.

5. See, for example, William Ivy Hair, *Bourbonism and Agrarian Protest: Louisiana Politics, 1877–1900* (Baton Rouge: Louisiana State University Press, 1969); and William Warren Rogers, *The One-Gallused Rebellion: Agrarianism in Alabama, 1865–1896* (Baton Rouge: Louisiana State University Press, 1970). C. Vann Woodward's survey of the New South is *Origins of the New South, 1877–1913* (Baton Rouge: Louisiana State University Press, 1951).

6. Paul M. Gaston, *The New South Creed: A Study in Southern Mythmaking* (New York: Alfred A. Knopf, 1970). Gaston described the intellectual journey from the glorification of agriculture to the celebration of industrialism.

7. Worth Robert Miller, "Building a Progressive Coalition in Texas: The Populist-Reform Democrat Rapprochement, 1900–1907," *Journal of Southern History (JSH)* 52 (May, 1986): 163–82.

may well be the most often described political phenomena in all of Texas history. In a conservative state, progressive academicians have uncovered little to validate their liberalism outside agrarian insurgency. Third-party revolts, furthermore, have been very popular as national historical research topics, and nineteenth-century Texans led and participated in such movements. A number of able scholars, thereby convinced that research based on Texas sources was not provincial, examined Populism and its antecedents.

The frontier thesis of Frederick Jackson Turner influenced many of the first of the national historians of the 1930s, who saw the agrarian insurgency as fueled by small farmers, schooled in frontier democracy, and embittered by the rise of monopolies as well as the depression of the 1890s.[8] The People's party endorsed free silver and William Jennings Bryan in 1896 to combat the depression. Populism died when prosperity returned briefly to the farming community after 1897. Many of the party's reforms were adopted in the Woodrow Wilson and Franklin Roosevelt administrations. These historians drew a rather straight line from the early Greenback movements through Populism and by implication on into the New Deal.

A spate of studies along this interpretive line cataloged the development of agrarian movements in individual states. One of the earliest works on state Populism, *The People's Party in Texas*, by geographer Roscoe Martin, was a classic of that genre and has not been replaced by a later history of Populism in Texas. Martin wrote as well about the politics of the Greenback party and the Patrons of Husbandry. A contemporary of his, the historian Ralph A. Smith, investigated the business activities of the Farmers' Alliance and the Grange.[9] These au-

8. See, for example, John D. Hicks, *The Populist Revolt: A History of the Farmers' Alliance* (Minneapolis: University of Minnesota Press, 1931). Hicks's general description of agrarian insurgency dominated approaches to Populism until the 1950s.

9. Roscoe C. Martin, *The People's Party in Texas: A Study in Third-Party Politics*, University of Texas Bulletin no. 3308 (Austin: University of Texas, 1933); Roscoe C. Martin, "The Greenback Party in Texas," *Southwestern Historical Quarterly (SHQ)* 30 (Jan., 1927): 161–77; Roscoe C. Martin, "The Grange as a Political Factor in Texas," *Southwestern Political and Social Science Quarterly* 6 (Mar., 1926): 363–84; Ralph A. Smith, "A. J. Rose, Agrarian Crusader of Texas," Ph.D. diss., University of Texas, 1938; Ralph A. Smith, "The Cooperative Movement in Texas, 1870–1900," *SHQ* 44 (July, 1940): 33–54; Ralph A. Smith, "Farmers' Alliance in Texas, 1875–1900," *SHQ* 48 (Jan., 1945): 346–69; Ralph A. Smith, "The Grange Movement in Texas, 1873–1900," *SHQ*

thors were sympathetic to agrarian reform and used a wealth of secondary and primary sources to document their views. This interpretation of Texas agrarian movements culminated with Robert L. Hunt, himself a farmer who earned a Ph.D. in agricultural economics and taught at Texas A&M University, who carried the story down through the Farmers' Union. The strength of these works lay in the descriptions of the chronological development of the organizations and their stated goals. This general body of information and similar studies completed in the 1930s continue as necessary reading for those interested in agrarian Texas.[10]

The concept of frontier democracy and agrarian reform dominated writing on third parties until the seminal work of Richard Hofstadter. An intellectual historian and a practitioner of consensus history, he saw status anxiety as the stimulus for farmers' revolts as the businessmen became heroes of the Gilded Age and the image of the farmer turned from Thomas Jefferson's noble yeoman into that of the rural hick. The demands of Populists and their supporters, as he described them, were not the progressive platforms attributed to them by the historians of the 1930s, but retrogressive, backward-looking goals that

---

42 (Apr., 1939): 297–315; Ralph A. Smith, "'Macuneism' of the Farmers of Texas in Business," *JSH* 13 (May, 1947): 220–44; Ralph A. Smith, "The Contribution of Grangers to Education in Texas," *Southwestern Social Science Quarterly* 21 (Mar., 1941): 312–24. Those scholars interested in the latter article should also see Curtis E. McDaniel, "Education and Social History of the Grange in Texas, 1873–1905," M.A. thesis, University of Texas, 1938.

10. Robert L. Hunt, *A History of Farmer Movements in the Southwest, 1873–1925* (College Station: Texas A. and M., 1935). A helpful overview of the agrarian crusade is also found in Stanley Howard Scott, "Angry Agrarian: The Texas Farmer, 1865–1914," Ph.D. diss., Texas Christian University, 1973; James A. Tinsley, "The Progressive Movement in Texas," Ph.D. diss., University of Wisconsin, 1955, discusses the activities of the union in promoting legislation in the state legislature. Students of the agrarian movement have access to two fine bibliographies that will guide them to the abundance of articles and books written during this period: Dennis S. Nordin, comp., *A Preliminary List of References for the History of the Granger Movement* (Davis, Calif.: Cooperative Project by the Agricultural History Branch, Economic Research Service, U.S. Department of Agriculture and the Agricultural History Center, 1967); and Henry Dethloff and Worth Robert Miller, comps., *A List of References for the History of the Farmers' Alliance and the Populist Party* (Davis, Calif.: Cooperative Project by the Agricultural History Branch, Economic Research Service, U.S. Department of Agriculture and the Agricultural History Center, 1989).

ROBERT A. CALVERT

aimed to protect the farmers' image and livelihood. For Hofstadter the New Deal was rooted in urban areas and not agricultural or Progressive revolts.[11]

The revisionist direction of Hofstadter quickly got out of hand, and others, frequently not historians, joined the clamor and soon Populists were not reformers at all but intolerant neofascists. The hinterlands produced nineteenth-century fanatics, who spawned twentieth-century ones such as Joseph McCarthy. The defenders of the farmers strode forward, reclaiming for Populism part of the Progressive tradition and in some cases identifying the People's party with socialism. The ensuing historiographical debate served Texas history well. Those national scholars, looking for the roots of Populist reform, returned to the early organization of the Southern Farmers' Alliance on the Texas frontier and reevaluated agrarian revolts. The impact of new social history, whose disciples asked that history be written from the bottom up, and the vicissitudes of the Vietnam War, which led young, radical intellectuals to attack the conservative thrust of consensus writers, added impetus to those who wished to correct the image of Populists as rural mastodons.[12]

One of those New Left historians was Lawrence Goodwyn. He argued that Populism grew out of the experiences of southern alliancemen, who joined the cooperative movement, and the lecturers who organized the Farmers' Alliance on the Texas frontier. He saw an educational process in the cooperative crusade that brought to alliancemen a movement culture, which identified and explained the methods and the need to reform late nineteenth-century America.[13] The Populist critique of capitalism was a real one, one that fell within

11. Richard Hofstadter, *The Age of Reform* (New York: Alfred A. Knopf, 1955). The implications of Hofstadter's approach, not a subject of this essay, can best be seen by reading C. Vann Woodward, "The Populist Heritage and the Intellectual," in Woodward, *The Burden of Southern History*, enlarged ed. (Baton Rouge: Louisiana State University Press, 1968), pp. 141–66.

12. A perceptive guide to the debate following Hofstadter's book can be found in the bibliographical essay in Worth Robert Miller, *Oklahoma Populism: A History of the People's Party in the Oklahoma Territory* (Norman: University of Oklahoma Press, 1988), pp. 256–65.

13. Lawrence Goodwyn, *Democratic Promise: The Populist Moment in America* (New York: Oxford University Press, 1976).

the American tradition and one whose failure limited the boundaries of the debate over capitalism and thus limited democracy itself. In this first full-scale study of the People's party since the work of Hicks, Goodwyn maintained that the Northern Farmers' Alliance and free-silver forces were "a shadow movement," not Populism. When those elements and their supporters within the People's party won the debate in 1896, fused with the Bryan forces within the Democratic party, and won for him the nomination on both party tickets, they destroyed Populism and any chance for meaningful reform. Progressivism became a celebration of capitalism, a conservative movement, which rejected rather than absorbed Populist goals.[14]

Goodwyn's influential book took agrarian revolts out of the hands of the consensus historians, but did not settle the issue of the causes of agrarian discontent. By the mid-1970s the issue of the nature of Populism spurred historians on to describe its origins and to analyze its philosophy and antecedents. These historians gravitated to Texas sources for the origins and results of the movement. Some of them had been working concurrently to Goodwyn, and were also responding to changes in American society and disputing the work of consensus historians. James R. Green, for example, pushed the study of radicalism forward.[15] His work seemed to some critics, as had that of Goodwyn, as too romantic and too much influenced by the work of E. P. Thompson, who wrote on the British laboring class and what it took to develop a movement culture.[16] Nevertheless Green's work did deal with the rise of the Farmers' Union, founded by Texan Newt Gresham,

14. Theodore Mitchell, *Public Education in the Southern Farmers' Alliance, 1887–1900* (Madison: University of Wisconsin Press, 1987), describes in excellent fashion how the Farmers' Alliance critiqued American society. This book is a first-rate addition to the literature on Populism.

15. James R. Green, *Grass Roots Socialism: Radical Movements in the Southwest, 1865–1943* (Baton Rouge: Louisiana State University Press, 1978); and James R. Green, "Tenant Farmer Discontent and Socialist Protest in Texas, 1901–1917," *SHQ* 81 (Oct., 1977): 133–54. See also James R. Green, "Populists, Socialism and the Promise of Democracy," *Radical History Review* 24 (1980): 7–24.

16. E. P. Thompson, *The Making of the English Working Class* (London: V. Gollanz, 1963). For critics of Goodwyn, see in particular the work of Stanley Parsons, Karen Toombs Parsons, Walter Killilae, and Beverly Bogers, "The Role of the Cooperative in the Development of the Movement Culture of Populism," *Journal of American History* (*JAH*) 69 (Mar., 1983): 866–85.

an old Populist with socialist proclivities. The Farmers' Union awaits a full-scale study that places the organization in the proper intellectual perspective of southern and Texas agrarianism.

Other historians working about the same time as Goodwyn turned to southern farm organizations that preceded the People's party to explain its origin and agrarianism. Robert McMath traced the Southern Farmers' Alliance from the Texas frontier until the organization spun off Populism. Although he saw the cooperative movement as instrumental to the creation of the Southern Farmers' Alliance, McMath viewed the early lecturers as people who drew upon the religious fundamentalism and the community network of southern culture to create a movement.[17] Robert Calvert, influenced too much by Hofstadter, looked to the southern frontier for its impact on the national Patrons of Husbandry. He saw the cooperative movement and the lecturers as the key to the growth of the southern Patrons of Husbandry, but identified the movement as a conservative one that warred with middlemen. By implication mainstream Populism was a continuation of Patron goals made more radical by the drop in cotton prices and the increase in farm tenancy.[18]

By the late 1970s the debate over the nature of the People's party and its origins had rejected Hofstadter but looked askance at any other single explanation. With the increasing popularity of the new social history, some had turned to county-level studies. James Turner iden-

---

17. Robert C. McMath, Jr., *Populist Vanguard: A History of the Southern Farmers' Alliance* (Chapel Hill: University of North Carolina Press: 1975); Robert C. McMath, Jr., "Sandy Land and Hogs in the Timber: (Agri)cultural Origins of the Farmers' Alliance in Texas," in *The Countryside in the Age of Capitalist Transformation: Essays in the Social History of Rural America,* ed. Steven Hahn and Jonathan Prude (Chapel Hill: University of North Carolina Press, 1985), pp. 205–29; Robert C. McMath, Jr., "The Godly Populists: Protestantism in the Farmers' Alliance and People's Party of Texas," M.A. thesis, North Texas State University, 1968; Robert C. McMath, Jr., "Populist Base Communities: The Evangelical Roots of Farm Protest in Texas," in *Locus: An Historical Journal of Regional Perspectives* 1 (fall, 1988): 53–61. See also Keith L. King, "Religious Dimensions of the Agricultural Protests in Texas, 1870–1908," Ph.D. diss., University of Illinois, Urbana-Champaign, 1985.

18. Robert A. Calvert, "The Southern Grange: Farmers Search For Identity in the Gilded Age," Ph.D. diss., University of Texas, 1969; Robert A. Calvert, "Nineteenth-Century Farmers, Cotton and Prosperity," *SHQ* 73 (Apr., 1970): 509–21; Robert A. Calvert, "A. J. Rose and the Agrarian Concept of Reform," *Agricultural History (AH)* 51 (Jan., 1977): 181–96.

tified a group of Texas counties as core Populist ones; fifteen of which voted for the People's party in 1892, 1894, and 1896. He compared these with nearby Democratic counties and concluded that Texas Populists were more isolated than their counterparts. Third-party Texans, according to Turner, were more suspicious of the market forces they could not control and fell outside the psychological mainstream.[19]

Those conditions made the Populists more susceptible to lecturers' exhortations. When the isolation of the farm population ended, the attraction of Populism did too. Turner posited an interesting but not convincing explanation for Texas Populism. Calvert and William Witherspoon, for example, used census and precinct voting returns in Jack County, a Populist stronghold, and argued that in that county members of the People's party identified and understood economic realities. They broke with the more conservative alliancemen, who, residing in villages or farming the better lands, were more financially secure, and thus stayed with the Democratic party. When the national People's party fused with the Democrats, the local Populists lost a clear definition of their goals, quarreled among themselves, and abandoned the third party.[20]

Other scholars have aimed at broad syntheses based upon analyses of national or statewide agrarian movements. Michael Schwartz and Donna Barnes, two sociologists, built models to explain both national and state agrarian movements. Schwartz used Marxist social theory to posit that after the initial successes of the agrarian movement the local leadership, who understood radical demands, lost control to more conservative politicians, who joined the Farmers' Alliance late and were willing to sacrifice principles for political offices. The switch to politics diverted economic and political resources needed for the cooperative movement and radical reform. Schwartz assumed that the rank and file cannot radicalize the leadership, which has not been altogether true in southern history. Barnes used a theoretical construct that portrayed the Texas agrarian experience as one of organizational adjustment to changing economic patterns. The leaders of the organization reacted to business interests and economic deprivation by moving first to cooperatives and then to politics. The failure of the

19. James Turner, "Understanding the Populists," *JAH* 66 (Sept., 1980): 354–73.
20. Robert A. Calvert and William A. Witherspoon, "Populism in Jack County, Texas," *Southern Studies* 25 (spring, 1986): 181–96.

leaders of the Texas Farmers' Alliance to mobilize its membership into a class-oriented political party meant that the organization died without accomplishing its end goal of protecting the small farmer.[21]

Both Schwartz and Barnes were captured by their methodology. Schwartz does not discuss the subtreasury, which all historians have agreed was an instrumental issue in separating third-party men from their Alliance counterparts. In neither book did race play much of a role. And both scholars assumed that tenant farming developed at an equal rate in all parts of the South. In Texas farm tenancy was only beginning in those cross-timbers areas that gave birth to third-party movements in the 1880s. Barnes and Schwartz have created models that almost function without human direction. As such their studies were good examples of sociological theory, interesting additions to the debate over the origins and goals of Populism, valuable to historians who need to find a new method to evaluate the movement, but not the answer to Texas agrarianism.

In the 1980s, historians have described Populism as a humanist response to the development of laissez-faire capitalism and the competitiveness of a society influenced by social Darwinism. Some historians have placed Populism in the older tradition of republicanism that dated back to the founding fathers. Historians writing on the early republic asserted that the founding fathers held a common ideology that came from the English Whig historical tradition. This belief embraced a fear that concentration of power would corrupt politics and morality by undermining communal values. This philosophy contradicted Lockean liberalism, which endorsed individual rights and laissez-faire economics. Historians have traced the philosophy past the early republic and applied it to later historical developments.[22]

The neorepublicanism of Populism endorsed a market economy that operated through services and trade but not one that accepted

21. Michael H. Schwartz, *Radical Protest and Social Structure: The Southern Farmers' Alliance and Cotton Tenancy, 1880–1890* (New York: Academic Press, 1976); Donna A. Barnes, *Farmers in Rebellion: The Rise and Fall of the Southern Farmers' Alliance and the People's Party in Texas* (Austin: University of Texas Press, 1984).

22. Bernard Bailyn, *The Ideological Origins of the American Revolution* (Cambridge, Mass.: Harvard University Press, 1967); and Gordon S. Wood, *The Creation of the American Republic, 1776–1787* (Chapel Hill: University of North Carolina Press, 1969). The *American Quarterly* 37 (fall, 1985), gave a complete issue over to what neorepublicanism was and how the philosophy influenced politics and culture.

206

the use of labor as a commodity. Populists believed that profiting off the labor of others was wrong. Their vision of America was one of producers, cooperative enterprises, and the public regulation of trade and services that created a communal society. Populism thus rejected liberalism and its endorsement of competitiveness. The betrayal of neo-republicanism through fusion, not the prosperity after 1896, destroyed the movement.[23]

No author has applied the overall framework of neorepublicanism to Texas Populism. Worth Robert Miller has used such an interpretation in Oklahoma, where early on Texans and Southern Farmers' Alliance organizers influenced Populist development, and David Gregg Cantrell placed the philosophy of J. B. Rayner, the black Texas Populist, in the neorepublican tradition. According to these scholars, the fear of concentrated power and not just the impact of the economic system stimulated the growth of the Southern Farmers' Alliance and the People's party.[24] It remained unclear if the new parameters of neorepublicanism were the guidelines needed to rewrite the history of Populism in the state. The subject deserves a new comprehensive look, however.

Regardless of the framework, the scholars who revise Roscoe Martin's perspective should consider several points raised by those who wrote on national topics and incompletely explored by those interested in Texas history. The relationship of black Texans to agrarian goals needs addressing. Alwyn Barr wrote a good general survey of black Texans in 1973, and Lawrence Rice produced a monograph on Afro-Texans from the "Redeemer" Constitution convention to 1900. Both of these scholars argued convincingly that most of the support for the Republican party came from the black community. Yet the most important book on the Republican party sheds little light on the role

---

23. Bruce Palmer, *"Man over Money": The Southern Populist Critique of American Capitalism* (Chapel Hill: University of North Carolina Press, 1980); Steven Hahn, *The Roots of Southern Populism: Yeoman Farmers and the Transformation of the Georgia Upcountry, 1850–1890* (New York: Oxford University Press, 1983); Barton C. Shaw, *The Wool-Hat Boys: Georgia's Populist Party* (Baton Rouge: Louisiana State University Press, 1984).

24. Worth Robert Miller, *Oklahoma Populism: A History of the People's Party in the Oklahoma Territory* (Norman: University of Oklahoma Press, 1987); David Gregg Cantrell, "The Limits of Southern Dissent: The Lives of Kenneth and John B. Rayner," Ph.D. diss., Texas A&M University, 1988.

of blacks in the party, and another survey that includes recent research is in order.[25] Several historians have written on black political leaders in the period, including some active in the Populist party.[26]

These historians have produced a body of information for scholars to build upon and from which to speculate on the relationship of blacks and whites within the agrarian movements in Texas. The Southern Farmers' Alliance was segregated, and the blacks joined the Colored Farmers' Alliance. Not much is known about the Texan Richard M. Humphrey, the white minister whom blacks asked for aid in the organization of the Colored Farmers' Alliance. Nor is a great deal known about the activities of the organization. No proceedings or papers survived. It is unlikely that historians can put together a fuller account of the Colored Farmers' Alliance than the sketchy one that now exists without some fortuitous discovery of documents.[27]

There was nevertheless a connection between the two alliances that led to the possibility of interracial cooperation in agrarian Texas. Goodwyn found a strong Populist intent to recruit blacks into the move-

25. Alwyn Barr, *Black Texans: A History of Negroes in Texas, 1528-1971* (Austin: Pemberton, 1973); Lawrence D. Rice, *The Negro in Texas, 1874-1900* (Baton Rouge: Louisiana State University Press, 1971); Paul Casdorph, *A History of the Republican Party in Texas, 1865-1965* (Austin: University of Texas Press, 1965).

26. Merline Pitre, *Through Many Dangers, Toils and Snares: The Black Leadership of Texas, 1868-1900* (Austin: Eakin, 1985); Carl H. Moneyhon, "George T. Ruby and the Politics of Expediency in Texas," in *Southern Black Leaders of the Reconstruction Era,* ed. Howard N. Rabinowintz (Urbana: University of Illinois Press, 1982); Maud Cuney Hare, *Norris Wright Cuney: A Tribute to the Black People* (New York: Crisis, 1913); Jack Abramowitz, "John B. Rayner—A Grass Roots Leader," *Journal of Negro History* 36 (Apr., 1951): 160-93; Jack Abramowitz, "The Negro in the Agrarian Revolt," *AH* (Apr., 1951): 89-95; Jack Abramowitz, "The Negro in the Populist Movement," *Journal of Negro History* 38 (July, 1953): 257-59; Robert M. Saunders, "Southern Populists and the Negro, 1893-1895," *Journal of Negro History* 40 (July, 1969): 140-61; and the previously mentioned Cantrell, "The Limits of Southern Dissent."

27. R. M. Humphrey, "History of the Colored Farmers' National Alliance and Cooperative Union," in *The Farmers' Alliance History and Agricultural Digest,* ed. Nelson A. Dunning (Washington, D.C.: Alliance Publishing, 1891), p. 288; Martin Dann, "Black Populism, A Study of the Colored Farmers' Alliance Through 1891," *Journal of Ethnic Studies* (fall, 1974): 58-71; William F. Holmes, "The Demise of the Colored Farmers' Alliance," *JSH* 41 (May, 1975): 187-200; Floyd J. Miller, "Black Protest and White Leadership: A Note on the Colored Farmers' Alliance," *Phylon* 33 (summer, 1972): 169-74.

ment in Texas. Other historians have disputed that goal. McMath argued that within the limits of racism that dominated southern society, the Southern Farmers' Alliance and the People's party were at least a moderate alternative to the bleak rise of segregation. Both views represent a rather middle-of-the-road position between historians who have seen a biracial coalition as a distinct possibility and those who have suggested that the racial animosity was so great that both races looked upon any cooperation as a Hobson's choice.[28] For blacks, Populism perhaps represented an alternative to the white violence and intimidation that was increasing during the period. For politicians in the People's party, black votes offered some possibility of economic reform.

Unlike the Democratic party, black people did serve the People's party as lecturers and on executive councils on both local and state levels. John B. Rayner, for example, was held in esteem by other leaders for his oratory and writing skills. Yet in Texas counties where the racial mix contained a high percentage of black people, the racism of whites evidently prohibited much biracial politics. Recent work has indicated, also, that former Texas Populists cooperated with the conservative Democrats in disfranchising blacks and passing Jim Crow legislation after the failed strategy of the 1896 election. Two young scholars using ecological regression techniques have estimated the extent to which the fusion of Republicans and Populists worked in the 1894 and 1896 Texas elections. They have concluded that when the choice

28. A good survey of the literature on this issue can be found in Richard L. Watson, Jr., "From Populism through the New Deal," in *Interpreting Southern History: Histriographical Essays in Honor of Stanford W. Higginbotham*, ed. John B. Boles and Evelyn Thomas Nolen (Baton Rouge: Louisiana State University Press, 1987), pp. 318–20; and Cantrell, "The Limits of Southern Dissent," p. 255. Those who have endorsed the Populist coalition have been most notably Lawrence Goodwyn, "Populist Dreams and Negro Rights: East Texas as a Case Study," *American Historical Review* (*AHR*) 76 (Dec., 1971): 1436–56; C. Vann Woodward, *The Strange Career of Jim Crow* (New York: Oxford University Press, 1957); and C. Vann Woodward, *Tom Watson: Agrarian Rebel* (New York: Macmillan, 1938). Those dissenters include William F. Holmes, "Lawrence Goodwyn's *Democratic Promise:* An Essay-Review," *Georgia Historical Quarterly* 61 (summer, 1977): 169–76; Robert M. Saunders, "Southern Populists and the Negro, 1893–1895," *Journal of Negro History* 54 (July, 1969): 240–61; Gerald H. Gaither, *Blacks and the Populist Revolt: Ballots and Bigotry in the "New South"* (Tuscaloosa: University of Alabama Press, 1977).

came between white supremacy and Populist goals, members of the People's party chose racism.[29] That seemed a southern and not just a Texas phenomenon.

Probably the best method of rewriting the history of Texas Populism and of considering biracial coalitions will be through some variety of statistical analysis. In many Texas counties precinct election returns remain from this period. Possibly the best technique would be through the use of multiple regression to determine who voted for which candidate and what the characteristics of these voters were. Statistical methodology would, for example, give certain social characteristics such as the religion, race, and economic status of the voters. Multiple regression can be applied to find out possible characteristics of members of farm organizations. Dale Baum and Robert Calvert have used such a technique to evaluate the Grangers in Texas. They discovered that members of the Texas Patrons of Husbandry tended to be native-born Protestants, most of whom belonged to the Methodist church, who farmed relatively small farms that produced cotton and corn. They tended to be more active on all political levels than their neighbors, and after the death of the Grange, drifted toward the Populist party.[30]

A like analysis of the Texas Farmers' Alliance would be more difficult, because no long runs of either proceedings of the state alliance meetings or local membership roles exist. Despite calls from historians for narrow studies of the alliance that would reveal more about

29. Gregg Cantrell, "John B. Rayner: A Study in Black Populist Leadership," *Southern Studies* 24 (winter, 1985): 432–43; J. Morgan Kousser, *The Shaping of Southern Politics: Suffrage Restrictions and the Establishment of the One-Party South, 1880–1910* (New Haven, Conn.: Yale University Press, 1974); Gregg Cantrell and D. Scott Barton, "Texas Populists and the Failure of Biracial Politics," *JSH* 55 (Nov., 1989): 659–92. See also Worth Robert Miller, "Building a Progressive Coalition in Texas: The Populist-Progressive Rapprochement, 1900–1907," *JSH* 52 (May, 1986): 163–82. An interesting use of Texas sources that disputed Woodward and concentrates on prejudice in the Populist party is Bernice Rash Fine, "Agrarian Reform and the Negro Farmer in Texas, 1886–1896," M.A. thesis, North Texas State University, 1971; see also Harrell Budd, "The Negro in Politics in Texas, 1877–1898," M.A. thesis, University of Texas, 1928. For a discussion of regression techniques see J. Morgan Kousser, "Ecological Regression and the Analysis of Past Politics," *Journal of Interdiscipline History* 4 (fall, 1973): 238–40.

30. E. Dale Baum and Robert A. Calvert, "The Texas Grangers: A Statistical Analysis," *AH* 63 (fall, 1989): 36–55.

the broader nature of the organization, the historian who heeds the clarion call must be prepared to spend long hours in archives collecting partial lists of those who joined the agricultural organization.

The lack of primary sources has limited the investigation of other aspects of agrarian Texas. Major biographies of agrarian leaders are lacking. Charles Macune, Jr., the grandson of the founder of the Texas alliance exchange and the popularizer of the subtreasury plan, is presently working on a biography of his grandfather. Cantrell did an admirable job in using the few available sources to describe and evaluate the career of Rayner. Ralph Smith wrote about the public life of A. J. Rose, the most important Texas Grange leader, but he might be worthy of a more complete study as an example of the more conservative wing of the agrarian movement.[31]

Good biographies of political figures other than Populists during the period are also in short supply. That should be less surprising, since Populism attracted national scholars, and the interest has led to a more careful mining of the sources. The two best studies of political leaders during the period, for example, were of those Democratic politicians who had major national reputations. Ben Procter wrote a gracefully styled and sympathetic portrait of John H. Reagan.

---

31. Cantrell, "The Limits of Southern Dissent"; Charles W. Macune, Jr., "The Wellspring of a Populist: Dr. C. W. Macune before 1886," *SHQ* 90 (Oct., 1986): 139–58; Smith, "A. J. Rose, Agrarian Crusader of Texas." These biographies can be filled out with such specialized studies as Howard L. Meredith, "Charles W. Macune's 'Farmers' Alliance,'" *Library Chronicle of the University of Texas* 8 (spring, 1966): 42–45; Fred A. Shannon, "C. W. Macune and the Farmers' Alliance," *Current History* 28 (June, 1955): 330–35. Other important studies of agrarian radicals include Alwyn Barr, "Ben Terrell: Agrarian Spokesman," *West Texas Historical Association Year Book* 45 (1969): 58–71; Alwyn Barr, "B. J. Chambers and the Greenback Party Split," *Mid-America* 49 (1967): 276–84; Wayne T. Alford, "T. L. Nugent, Texas Populist," *SHQ* 57 (July, 1953): 65–81; Keith L. Bryant, Jr., "'Alfalfa' Bill Murray: The Formative Years," *East Texas Historical Journal* 3 (Oct., 1965): 103–18; Catherine Nugent, ed., *Life Work of Thomas L. Nugent* (Stephenville, Tex.: Privately published, 1896); Gary Ward Schmidt, "The Populist Character of Thomas L. Nugent," M.A. thesis, University of Texas, 1974; Genevieve Pyle Demme, "Owen Pinkney Pyle: Champion of the Farmer," M.A. thesis, Rice Institute, 1958; Gwin C. Morris, "James Harvey 'Cyclone' Davis: Texas Populist," *Journal of the Student Association of Texas* (June, 1971): 49–54; James L. Ranchino, "The Work and Thought of a Jeffersonian in the Populist Movement: James Henry 'Cyclone' Davis," M.A. thesis, Texas Christian University, 1964; Marshall L. Williams, "The Political Career of Cyclone Davis," M.A. thesis, East Texas State University, 1937.

The better part of the book traced his career through the Civil War years.[32] The account of the creation of the Interstate Commerce Commission needs revision in light of later historical research concerning regulatory commissions. The biography needs updating also in its account of Reagan's return to Texas after he accepted Hogg's offer to head the Texas Railroad Commission. The issue of an elected versus appointed commission, and conservative reaction to the creation of the regulatory body, helped shape both the politics of Populism and of George Clark's gubernatorial campaign of 1893. Barr did well with the election, but a detailed account of Reagan's relationship with the more conservative wing of agrarian reform and with Hogg is in order.

The account given by Procter concerning the appointment of Reagan to the commission supported the version offered by Robert Cotner's massive biography of Hogg. This copious portrait of him became one of the reasons that most Texas historians considered Hogg the best governor since Sam Houston. That uncritical opinion of his career has been challenged by both Lewis Gould and Goodwyn. Gould asserted that the governor's regulatory measures were anticolonial in origin and were designed to protect Texas investments. Goodwyn saw Hogg as an example of those moderate, free-silver Democrats who by moving slightly to the left were able to attract enough alliancemen, who wished to vote for the party of their fathers, to emasculate Populist reform. Both of the authors, in effect, described the governor's political actions as cynical: a portrait far removed from the perceptions of Cotner.[33]

The historical controversy over Hogg's motives emphasized the need for not only a new biography of the governor but a full study of the Texas Railroad Commission that would replace the earlier works of Robert L. Peterson and David F. Prindle.[34] Peterson's study was

32. Ben H. Procter, *Not without Honor: The Life of John H. Reagan* (Austin: University of Texas Press, 1962).

33. Robert Cotner, *James Stephen Hogg: A Biography* (Austin: University of Texas Press, 1959); Goodwyn, *Democratic Promise;* Lewis L. Gould, *Progressives and Prohibitionists: Texas Democrats in the Wilson Era* (Austin: University of Texas Press, 1971).

34. David F. Prindle, *Petroleum Politics and the Texas Railroad Commission* (Austin: University of Texas Press, 1981); Robert L. Peterson, "Jay Gould and the Railroad Commission of Texas," *SHQ* 58 (Jan., 1955): 422–32; Robert L. Peterson, "State Regulation and the Railroad Commission in Texas," Ph.D. diss., University of Texas, 1960.

written prior to the voluminous work done by historians on the progressives' concept of the purpose of regulation. Prindle, of course, was concerned with oil and not railroads, which were much more politically important to agrarians.

Less intellectually satisfying than the Hogg and Reagan biographies were the more recent portraits of Samuel Bell Maxey, the Confederate general, who served in the United States Senate from 1875 to 1887, and Lawrence Sullivan Ross, the frontiersman and commander of Ross's Brigade, who was governor from 1887 to 1891, and then president of Texas A. and M. College. Although based on original research, these uncritical biographies were short on historical analysis. In style and tone they harked back to early decades of writings on Texas where biographical subjects emerged as heroic figures with few flaws.[35] Both of these men should have been evaluated in light of southern Redeemer policies as they applied to Texas politics.

Other major figures in the period worthy of a biography include Governor and later Senator Richard Coke and Joseph Weldon Bailey, a colorful transitional figure of the wars beginning with Populism and going through progressivism. He served both in the United States House of Representatives and the Senate. The charismatic Bailey won a reputation for opposition to imperialism and to the nation's entry into World War I. He allied himself from time to time with both corrupt businessmen and reformers. His appeal to rural voters could shed some light on the historical controversy on the collapse of Populism after 1896. Sam Hanna Atcheson, a journalist, wrote a biography of the controversial senator, but failed to explain the attraction of Bailey to farmers.[36] Coke, a favorite of the Grangers, managed to keep both moderate conservatives and agrarians in his political camp. A study

---

See also J. R. Norvell, "The Railroad Commission of Texas: Its Origin and History," *SHQ* 68 (Apr., 1965): 465–80; Gerald Nash, "The Reformer Reformed: John H. Reagan and Railroad Regulation," *Business History Review* 29 (June, 1955): 189–96; Gerald Nash, "A Chapter from an Active Life, John H. Reagan and Railroad Regulation," M.A. thesis, Columbia University, 1952.

35. Louise Horton, *Samuel Bell Maxey: A Biography* (Austin: University of Texas Press, 1974); Judith Ann Brenner, *Sul Ross: Soldier, Statesman, Educator* (College Station: Texas A&M University Press, 1983).

36. Sam Hanna Atcheson, *Joe Bailey: The Last Democrat* (New York: Macmillan, 1932). A more up-to-date work is Bob Charles Holcomb, "Senator Joe Bailey, the Decades of Controversy," Ph.D. diss., Texas Tech University, 1967.

ROBERT A. CALVERT

of his career would add detail to the admirable work Barr has done in explaining political coalitions in agrarian Texas.

Another yawning gap in studies of agrarian movements and of agriculture lies in the history of women. Estimates of the number of women who joined the Patrons of Husbandry and the Farmers' Alliance usually fall in the 25 percent range.[37] They played major roles in the functioning of the agricultural organizations, where they held offices (most of which were reserved for women), led discussions, served as lecturers, and participated in all of the meetings and social events. Melissa G. Wiedenfield has written on women in the Texas Farmers' Alliance, and a very good dissertation by Mary Jo Wagner looked at women in the southern and northern alliances and in the Populist movement. The value of both of these works lay in their description of the movement, and they should be judged as excellent starting points.[38]

For example, Julie Roy Jeffrie has described women's role in the North Carolina Farmers' Alliance as one proscribed by upper-class men, who assigned to them obligations of moral rectitude in the conducting of alliance affairs. Others have pointed out that such a description ignored the widely held concept of Victorian womanhood. Rather than stereotypical relations within an organization, Farmers' Alliance women saw their job of extolling cooperation to soften the harshness of competitive capitalism as woman's traditional responsibility of nurturing the family.[39]

The investigation of women in the Farmers' Alliance and Grange movements should also be compared to their activities in more radical causes. Historians should ask, what happened to Farmers' Alliance women once the organization moved to Populism? Did rural women differ from their more urban sisters in approaches to reform

37. See Baum and Calvert, "The Texas Grangers," who drew their statistics from manuscript charters in the national Grange offices, which list all the original charter members, and also Julie Roy Jeffrie's study of the North Carolina Alliance: "Women in the Southern Farmers' Alliance: A Reconsideration of the Role and Status of Women in the Late Nineteenth-Century South," *Feminist Studies* 3 (fall, 1975): 72–91.

38. Melissa G. Wiedenfield, "Women in the Texas Farmers' Alliance," M.A. thesis, Texas Tech University, 1983; Mary Jo Wagner, "Farms, Families, and Reform: Women in the Farmers' Alliance and the Populist Party," Ph.D. diss., University of Oregon, 1986.

39. Jacquelyn Dowd Hall and Anne Firor Scott, "Women in the South," in Boles and Nolan, *Interpreting Southern History*, pp. 479–80.

214

causes? Could the work of women in agricultural movements have stimulated the roles they played in temperance and women's suffrage? Indeed, the existing studies of women's suffrage and the temperance movement in Texas are outdated and need revising.[40]

Similarly general descriptions of women in Texas agriculture would be welcome additions to the historical literature. Here too possible problems for historians of rural life lay in the ambivalence of descriptions of Texas women: southern or western? The literature on women in the ranching industry far exceeds any on farming, even though the number of women engaged in farm work far exceeded that of their ranching counterparts. Once more the romance of the West was more attractive than the drudgery of the cotton field.[41] Perhaps all rural women had more in common than they had differences created by what these farms and ranches produced, and a study of women in rural Texas could describe much about the value system that united them. Nevertheless, women and the cotton culture in the South and in Texas deserves a specialized study, because of the particular demands sharecropping made on women. This study might focus on the transition of the role of women from subsistence agriculture to sharecropping. Scholars of women's history have said that tenant farming and the demand for staple crops devaluated the role farm women fulfilled as mothers, helpmates, and planners on self-sufficient farms.

The historians who undertake such a task will not have much on which to model their efforts. Margaret Jarman Hagood's *Mothers of the South: Portraiture of White Tenant Farmers* was cited recently as the

40. A. Elizabeth Taylor, "The Woman Suffrage Movement in Texas," *JSH* 17 (May, 1951): 195–215; Sean Collins Murray, "Texas Prohibition Politics, 1877–1914," M.A. thesis, University of Houston, 1968; and Gould, *Progressives and Prohibitionists,* described suffrage and prohibition campaigns. Gould dealt with cultural politics in his excellent book. Works on the origins of the movements in nineteenth-century Texas are inadequate.

41. See as examples of this sort of work, in particular, Sandra L. Myres, *Westering Women and the Frontier Experience* (Albuquerque: University of New Mexico Press, 1982); and Jo Ella Powell Exley, *Texas Tears, Texas Sunshine: Voices of Frontier Women* (College Station: Texas A&M University Press, 1985); and Bettye Ann Showers Key, "Women of Texas Cattle Ranches, 1870–1915," M.A. thesis, University of Texas, Arlington, 1971. A further listing of this genre of historical literature can be found in Anne Patton Malone, "Women in Texas History," in *A Guide to the History of Texas,* ed. Light T. Cummins and Alvin R. Bailey (Westport, Conn.: Greenwood, 1988), pp. 123–38.

best book on women and farm tenancy. Published in the 1930s, when sharecropping was considered the major economic national disaster, this book fell into the same category as the work by Rupert Vance and others who wrote to stimulate reform. The authors attempted to construct a combination documentary and description of sharecropping. They used on-site observations, statistics, and oral interviews to portray the plight of those who sharecropped. Ruth Allen did a like study on women in the Texas cotton culture during the same period. As with most of Allen's work, the book was based on solid research and should be appreciated as a clasic study. She included black, Hispanic, and white women in her investigation. Those who write on women in the cotton culture should follow her example, and do comparative multicultural and multiethnic evaluations, because it may well be that the cotton culture made women, regardless of color or language, more alike than different.[42]

The investigation of tenant farming in this period and beyond should not be limited to women. Historians of agrarian Texas have no real concept of the impact of tenancy upon the state. No specific history of postbellum agriculture compares to the work of Randolph Campbell and Richard Lowe for the 1850s. The unpublished research of Samuel Lee Evans gave the best description of postbellum agriculture in Texas.[43] Although he ended his dissertation before the impact of Roosevelt's reforms, he looked at Texas agriculture from the perspective of the New Deal. Evans did a prodigious amount of research in census and newspaper sources, but tended, as did many agricultural historians, to let the accumulated numbers speak for themselves. He concluded by implication that mechanization and agribusiness solved

42. Margaret Jarman Hagood, *Mothers of the South; Portraiture of the White Tenant Farm Woman* (Chapel Hill: University of North Carolina Press, 1939). The comment on women in tenant farming was made by Hall and Scott, "Women in the South," p. 480; Rupert Bayless Vance, *Cotton Tenancy* (Chapel Hill: University of North Carolina Press, 1935); Rupert Bayless Vance, *Human Factors in the Cotton Culture: A Study in the Social Geography of the American South* (Chapel Hill: University of North Carolina Press, 1929); Ruth Alice Allen, *The Labor of Women in the Production of Cotton,* University of Texas Bulletin no. 3134 (Austin: University of Texas, 1931).

43. Richard Lowe and Randolph B. Campbell, *Planters and Plain Folk: Agriculture in Antebellum Texas* (Dallas: Southern Methodist University Press, 1987); Samuel Lee Evans, "Texas Agriculture, 1865–1880," M.A. thesis, University of Texas, 1955; and Samuel Lee Evans, "Texas Agriculture, 1880–1930," Ph.D. diss., University of Texas, 1960.

the problems of cotton farmers. Historians such as Evans insisted that efficiency and growth were the engines of prosperity that ended Populist complaints. The family farm died not from governmental neglect, as suggested by Goodwyn, but from the inevitable forces of progress.

John Spratt wrote a similar book that serves so far as the best economic survey of the period. As with Evans, the quality of the research was impressive, but Spratt molded the story to fit the theme of industrial expansion. The move from a Texas that existed on a barter, subsistence economy to one linked together by railroads and poised for expansion explained for him the history of the state in the Gilded Age. In this context, farmers joined the Grange and the Farmers' Alliance for business purposes, and they were incipient capitalists themselves. Their solutions looked to past experiences and not to the changing economy. Spratt commended Texas farmers for their determination to plant cotton despite the advice of agricultural reformers. He described the crop as the best possibility for farm profits, given its little demand on the soil and its resistance to heat and drought. The cause of farm poverty, according to Spratt, was the increased cost of moving to commercial agriculture, which demanded larger farms serviced by machines. Progress, not cotton, produced tenant farming.[44]

Surveys of national agriculture have not always supported Spratt's thesis. The most recent book of this sort was Gilbert C. Fite's *Cotton Fields No More: Southern Agriculture, 1865–1980*. The author disagreed with Spratt in that Fite saw crop liens as defeating southern farmers' need to diversify their crops if they intended to escape poverty, and argued that landlords and furnishing merchants refused to loan money for tenants to buy livestock or to invest in crops other than cotton. Agricultural diversification demanded capital investments, and that pointed toward extensive agriculture. To accept the charge of agricultural experts, sharecroppers needed enough land to experiment with various crops. Diversification then promised an end to tenant farming that did not come until government measures forced farmers to diversify and to till larger farms.[45]

Although Fite was very sympathetic to family farmers, he felt that

44. John S. Spratt, *Road to Spindletop: Economic Change in Texas, 1875–1901* (Dallas: Southern Methodist University Press, 1955).

45. Gilbert C. Fite, *Cotton Fields No More: Southern Agriculture, 1865–1980* (Lexington: University of Kentucky Press, 1984).

scientific agriculture made larger farms necessary. Similar to Spratt, Fite saw as deterministic, even if regrettable, the progression from family farms to agribusiness. *Cotton Fields No More* deserved the high praise that it received from agricultural historians as an excellent description of postbellum southern farming. Yet Texas, which produced about 33 percent of the nation's yearly cotton crop from 1885 to the present, was almost omitted from the book's narrative flow. Fite found himself in a position not unusual for southern historians: how do you fit the growth of Panhandle agriculture into your historical paradigm?

Farmers moved to the High Plains in the 1880s. The real growth in cotton production and settlement occurred after 1900, and that crop became a major part of the economy after 1927 when Texas A&M University perfected varieties suitable for the West Texas climate. By 1930, High Plains farmers worked about 450,000 improved acres. The story of cotton farming in West Texas did not fit the southern mode, and its story has been left out of most regional surveys. Some good articles have chronicled the growth of High Plains agriculture, however. Gary Nall published two articles on the subject which serve as a good outline of the area's agricultural development.[46]

One major factor that separated the Panhandle from the cotton culture of the rest of Texas was aridity. Donald Green has told scholars about the development of the impeller pump which allowed the tapping of the Ogallala aquifer.[47] The development of irrigation techniques in the early twentieth century stimulated the growth of mechanization and the diversification of crops. The story of crop diversification and the development of commercial farming has not been adequately told.

Robert L. Martin sketched some of the history of agricultural marketing and urban development on the High Plains in *The City Moves West.* Studies of the rise of agricultural marketing centers are in short supply in all of Texas history. The High Plains would be an excellent

46. Gary L. Nall, "The Farmer's Frontier in the Texas Panhandle," *Panhandle-Plains Historical Review* (*PPHR*) 45 (1972): 1–20; and Gary L. Nall, "Panhandle Farming in the 'Golden Age' of American Agriculture," *PPHR* 46 (1973): 94–112. He has also written some interesting insights on Panhandle farming in "The Texas Panhandle Farmer as a New Minority," in *Agricultural Legacies,* ed. R. Alton Lee (Vermillion: University of South Dakota Press, 1986).

47. Donald E. Green, *Land of the Underground Rain: Irrigation on the Texas High Plains, 1910–1970* (Austin: University of Texas Press, 1973).

218

starting point for comparing the development of its regional marketing areas with those that developed more to the South and were rooted in the cotton culture. In a like fashion, immigration to the High Plains certainly deserves more study. The large cattle companies recruited settlers soon after the drought of the mid-1880s devastated the livestock market. Where did these recruits come from, and what cultivating tradition did they bring with them? Some of those recruited came from European stock. Was their agricultural heritage such that their communities developed different methods of agricultural production? Or did southerners simply transfer their plantation farming techniques to the extensive agriculture of the High Plains?[48]

The impact of ethnics in agrarian Texas raises a number of important issues about agricultural development in all of the state. Terry Jordan has contributed much in describing migration into Texas. The thesis of much of his work on immigration was that culturally Texas constituted a "balkanized" zone that produced no such human as a typical Texan. Using that as a thesis, historians need to look at rural Texas and decide if different cultures had different values, and if some cultures embraced diversification or other novel farming techniques more readily than did the majority culture.[49]

Agricultural organizations certainly had a difficult time recruiting in immigrant communities. The Grange, for example, printed

48. Robert L. Martin, *The City Moves West: Economic and Industrial Growth on the High Plains* (Austin: University of Texas Press, 1969); as an example of recruiting by land companies see David B. Gracy II, *Littlefield Land: Colonization on the High Plains* (Austin: University of Texas Press, 1968): *PPHR* 50 (1977) gave that issue over to foreign immigration to the High Plains. For a discussion of bibliographies that would aid studies of the region's agriculture, see B. Byron Price, "The Texas Frontier," in Cummins and Bailey, *A Guide to the History of Texas*, pp. 60–63.

49. Terry G. Jordan, "A Century and a Half of Ethnic Change in Texas, 1836–1986," *SHQ* 89 (Apr., 1986): 318–419, quotation from p. 385. That article gives a good overview of ethnic migrations and in the notes some guide to important works by Jordan. Interested scholars should also see Terry G. Jordan, John L. Bean, and William M. Holmes, *Texas: A Geography* (Boulder, Colo.: Westview Press, 1984); Terry G. Jordan, *Immigration to Texas* (Boston: American Press, 1980); Terry G. Jordan, "The Imprint of the Upper and Lower South on Mid-Nineteenth-Century Texas," *Annals of the Association of American Geographers* 57 (Dec., 1967): 667–90; and Homer L. Kerr, "Migrations to Texas, 1865–1880," Ph.D. diss., University of Texas, 1965. W. Phil Hewitt, *Land and Community: European Migration to Rural Texas in the 19th Century* (Boston: American Press, 1981); the Institute of Texan Cultures at San Antonio has published pamphlets describing the history of most of the ethnic groups in the state.

ROBERT A. CALVERT

propaganda leaflets in German, sent lecturers to ethnic areas, and noted
in its annual state Grange meetings its lack of success in regions other
than those settled by Anglo farmers. Several reasons may have explained
this phenomena. Both the Farmers' Alliance and the Grange used the
techniques of rural Protestantism to recruit members. That lecture
method may have discouraged those who did not belong to Evangelical churches. Furthermore, the Grange and the Farmers' Alliance frequently celebrated the Confederate past. That might have limited their
recruiting in areas such as the Hill Country, where ethnics denied
the validity of secession. It could also have been that in ethnic folk
islands the tradition of community living supported the less fortunate
in such a way that more broadly conceived organizations had trouble
attracting the dispossessed. In a similar fashion, the lodges of ethnic
groups may have created a sense of community that excluded those
who urged the joining of national organizations led by southern Anglo-
Americans. Historians who look at these questions should draw their
methodology from the work done by the new social history in tracing
immigration and describing communities. Someone should also write
for the late nineteenth and early twentieth century a book similar to
Jordan's study of Germans in the mid-nineteenth century. More Germans entered the state after the Civil War than before, and a history
of their rural communities and farming methods through the 1920s
would be a valuable point of comparison to other agrarians.[50]

Scholars who write on any aspect of Texas agriculture and rural
ethnicity must consider the impact of sharecropping. Several questions need to be determined about tenancy. The work of southern historians and interdisciplinary studies will serve as examples of how to
explain and describe tenancy. Historians traditionally have considered

50. Ander O. Fritiof, "The Immigrant Church and the Patrons of Husbandry,"
AH 8 (Oct., 1934): 155–68, described one experience of the difficulty in recruiting
immigrants, who for religious reasons distrusted the ritual of the Patrons of Husbandry. A like scenario probably existed in Texas. Charles Reagan Wilson, *Baptized
in the Blood: The Religion of the Lost Cause* (Athens: University of Georgia Press, 1980),
discussed the enduring hold of the Confederacy on Anglo-Americans. For an example of new social history and community culture, see Robert C. Kenzer, *Kinship and
Neighborhood in a Southern Community, 1849–1881* (Knoxville: University of Tennessee
Press, 1987); Terry G. Jordan, *German Seed in Texas Soil: Immigrant Farmers in Nineteenth
Century Texas* (Austin: University of Texas Press, 1966). On German inmmigrants in
postbellum Texas see Terry G. Jordan, "The German Settlement After 1865," *SHQ*
73 (Oct., 1969): 193–212.

220

the rise of sharecropping as a Reconstruction development that merged available land with labor in a war-ravaged society short of capital. This inefficient system allegedly destroyed fertile soils through lack of care and encouraged sloppy agricultural techniques and lazy farmers. Implicit in the accounts of those who wrote contemporaneously with sharecropping and agrarian revolts was that black people contributed to the problem of sharecropping because of their supposed lack of responsibility.[51]

The 1970s witnessed the start of a sharp revision of the above conclusions. Some historians linked sharecropping with racial control rather than the harnessing of labor for efficient agriculture. Others used Marxist analyses to explain sharecropping and racism. Some of these historians assumed that planters, unwilling to surrender economic control in the New South, instituted sharecropping to continue hegemony over lower classes. Their control went past economic intimidation to include willfully underfunding schools and leasing convicts in order to control the poor. As a result of their manipulations, planters controlled society in such a way that the progressives' reforms, unlike those of Populists, did not threaten the dominance of the elite class. Other Marxists, while not rejecting the above description, included violence and Jim Crow laws, along with sharecropping, as methods that kept a docile work force. The impact of the agricultural measures of the New Deal and the industrialization of World War II disrupted planter hegemony and allowed an emerging middle class to gain power.[52]

51. William L. Laird and James R. Rhinehart, "Deflation, Agriculture, and Southern Development," *AH* 42 (Apr., 1968): 115–24; Eugene M. Lerner, "Southern Output and Agricultural Income, 1860–1880," *AH* 33 (July, 1959): 117–45; Theodore Saloutos, "Southern Agriculture and the Problem of Readjustment," *AH* 30 (Apr., 1956): 58–76; Theodore Saloutos, *Farmer Movements in the South, 1865–1933* (Berkeley: University of California Press, 1960). On those who argued that black people needed management control see Calvert, "The Grange in the South," chap. 1.

52. See, for example, Jonathan W. Wiener, *Social Origins of the New South: Alabama—1865–1885* (Baton Rouge: Louisiana State University Press, 1978); and Jay R. Mandel, *The Roots of Black Poverty: The Southern Plantation Economy after the Civil War* (Durham, N.C.: Duke University Press, 1978). Mandel's discussion of sharecropping owes a debt to Harold D. Woodman, "Sequel to Slavery: The New History Views the Postbellum South," *JSH* 43 (Nov., 1977): 523–54; and his "Economic Reconstruction and the New South," in Boles and Nolen, *Interpreting Southern History*, pp. 254–307.

The New Marxists used census and other records to analyze and describe the social landscape of the South. Cliometricians, who dominated new economic history, used data in more detail but much like that chosen by Marxists. They came to absolutely opposite conclusions. The beginning point of their ideology shaped their final product. Robert Higgs assumed that free market competition, for him a desirable commodity, configured southern economics. Southerners chose sharecropping because the system was the most efficient means to begin farming in the New South. Poverty came from the economic starting point of the South as compared to the North after the Civil War. The cost of war and the freeing of slaves left southern capital and income far behind that of the northern states. Both sections grew at the same rate, but the South could not attract enough free market capital to an economy based on raw materials to overcome the northern industrial edge. Higgs did not disallow the lowly economic and social condition of Afro-Americans. Rather, he denied that sharecropping caused or played a role in their misfortune. Mutual self-interest meant that the landlord would not use race to destroy economic gains.[53]

One of Higgs's fellow cliometricians, Joseph D. Reid, Jr., agreed that the marketplace determined southern methods of farming. Moreover, he argued that sharecropping was an efficient system of farming, because the free market dictated management supervision on the landlord's part and good farming habits on the tenant's end if profits were to be maximized. Stephen DeCanio buttressed his free-market compatriots by asserting that sharecropping and crop liens were efficient ways to arrive at needed farm credit. Afro-American and white poverty derived from landlessness.[54]

A middle ground between Marxists and free-enterprise advocates

53. Robert Higgs, *Competition and Coercion: Blacks in the American Economy* (Cambridge, England: Cambridge University Press, 1977). See, too, Robert Higgs, "Did Southern Farmers Discriminate?" *AH* 56 (Apr., 1972): 325–28; and Robert Higgs, "Did Southern Farmers Discriminate?—Interpretive Problems and Further Evidence," *AH* 59 (Apr., 1975): 445–47.

54. Joseph D. Reid, Jr., "Sharecropping as an Understandable Market Response: The Postbellum South," *Journal of Economic History* 33 (Mar., 1973): 106–30; Joseph D. Reid, Jr., "Sharecropping and Agricultural Uncertainty," *Economic Development and Cultural History* 24 (Apr., 1976): 549–76; Joseph D. Reid, Jr., "Sharecropping in History and Theory," *AH* 59 (Apr., 1975): 426–40; Stephen J. DeCanio, *Agriculture in the Postbellum South: The Economics of Production and Supply* (Cambridge, Mass.: MIT Press, 1974).

has been recently struck. Regional labor forces in the South came into prominence after the Civil War. Both the farm and the industrial labor forces were unskilled, and poor schools and isolation kept them so. The elite classes benefited from the low wages, and it was in their interests to keep them so. Economic catastrophes created by the invasion of boll weevils, the migrations during the cotton depressions of the early 1920s, and finally the New Deal created labor shortages that drove wages up during the defense expansion of World War II. By inference these assumptions make agrarian protests valid, sharecropping a serious but not a conspiratorial problem, and southern poverty partially a result of the South's colonial economic status created by a low wage base.[55]

These theses may or may not apply to Texas. Scholars have demonstrated that tenancy probably preceded the Civil War. But work by Cecil Harper, Jr., draws a clear distinction between postbellum and antebellum tenancy. In pre–Civil War tenancy, whites anxious to acquire land moved from spot to spot in the hope of acquiring cheap land. These mobile tenants were younger than the male population at large, and tenancy was considered a way station en route to the acquisition of a farm. After the Civil War, white landowners carefully supervised blacks, who lacked white tenants' mobility. The nature of tenancy thus changed. By 1880, with the decrease in Texas' fertile public lands and changing attitudes about sharecropping, whites lost mobility and their tenant arrangements resembled that of blacks.[56]

Harper's conclusions, although he suggested that they were but tentative ones, would seemingly imply that racism did indeed stifle black agricultural advancement. Another possible inference, and one not suggested by Harper's judicious observations, could be that low wages would be to the landlord's advantage, and that increased agrarian demands might well follow the loss of opportunity for whites as

55. Gavin Wright, *Old South, New South: Revolutions in the Southern Economy since the Civil War* (New York: Basic Books, 1986). See also comments on the emergence of the New South by Numan V. Bartley, "Another New South?" *Georgia Historical Quarterly* 65 (summer, 1981): 125–37.

56. Cecil Harper, Jr., "Farming Someone Else's Land: Farm Tenancy in the Brazos River Valley, 1850–1880," Ph.D. diss., University of North Texas, 1988; Frederick Bode and Donald Ginter, *Farm Tenancy and the Census in Antebellum Georgia* (Athens: University of Georgia Press, 1986). Bode and Ginter saw more similarities between antebellum and postbellum tenancy in Georgia than Harper found in Texas.

the nature of tenancy changed in the 1880s. The clash between the elites and nonelites might not be so clear as the Marxists believed, but certainly reduced opportunity would engender the potential class conflict manifested by Populism.

In addition to a study of tenancy, some historian should write a history of labor in the late nineteenth century. Historians have pondered the political relationship, if any, between labor unions and Populists. Critics have charged Goodwyn with building a political sketch of a radical political party that unfairly left labor out. The Texas Farmers' Union endorsed labor boycotts, supported striking workers, and labeled goods produced by their organization as union made. The State Labor Federation urged its members in turn to purchase products that the Texas Farmers' Union sanctioned.[57] Whether a like arrangement occurred in Populism is questionable, but Goodwyn did catalog cooperation between the Knights of Labor and some alliancemen during the Great Southwestern strike.

The extent of this cooperation remains open to debate. Scholarly studies of labor unions during this period (and this is true for almost any other period in Texas history) are spotty in coverage and not very informative about rural attitudes toward unions. Spratt has a brief but inadequate chapter in *The Road to Spindletop* on labor unions. Ruth Allen has written a good and sympathetic account of the Knights of Labor in her book on the sometimes violent railroad strike of 1886, and she has sketched out some of the origins of the Texas Federation of Labor in *Chapters in the History of Organized Labor in Texas*. There have also been some interesting but not comprehensive studies of specific unions in Galveston and of workers in Houston.[58] Until there

57. David Montgomery, "On Goodwyn's Populist," *Marxist Perspectives* 1 (spring, 1978): 169–71; Dewey W. Grantham, *Southern Progressivism: The Reconciliation of Progress and Tradition* (Knoxville: University of Tennessee Press, 1982), pp. 294–97.

58. Ruth Alice Allen, *Chapters in the History of Organized Labor in Texas*, Bureau of Research in the Social Sciences, University of Texas, Bulletin no. 4143 (Austin: University of Texas, 1941); Ruth Alice Allen, *The Great Southwest Strike*, Bureau of Research in the Social Sciences, University of Texas, Bulletin no. 4214 (Austin: University of Texas Press, 1942); Ruth Alice Allen, *East Texas Lumber Workers; an Economic and Social Picture, 1870–1950* (Austin: University of Texas Press, 1961). See also such studies as Robert Edward Ziegler, "The Workingman in Houston, Texas, 1865–1910," Ph.D. diss., Texas Tech University, 1972; James V. Reese, "The Evolution of an Early Texas Union: The Screwmen's Benevolent Association of Galveston," *SHQ* 72 (July, 1968): 158–85; Allen Clayton Taylor, "A History of the Screwmen's Benevo-

is a general history of unions in the period, it is best to assume that agrarian revolts did not recruit laborers.

It may be doubtful that sources can be found to complete a history of trade unions in Texas during the Gilded Age. An alternative approach to labor history would be possible for the state and very helpful to the understanding of the late nineteenth-century work force. Herbert Gutman, a well-known and imaginative social historian, issued a call in 1968 that historians abandon trade union history and undertake an analysis of the working class.[59] He charged historians to draw upon other intellectual disciplines and use their methodologies to describe workers and their value systems. He argued that through the use of statistics and anthropology one could describe the working class as it emerged at the moment of contact between a preindustrial, agricultural society and an industrial one. Twenty years later, labor historians have refined and expanded his questions.[60]

An approach that used censuses and other sources to describe the daily work of late nineteenth-century Texans would open a vista to a little-known history. Texas in the late nineteenth century was moving in most of its regions from a preindustrial society to a more sophisticated economy. There are no specialized studies, for example, of farm laborers in Texas. Yet at one time over four hundred thousand full- or part-time workers did agricultural labor. Historians have dealt with casual impressions of farm labor and have worked on the issue of migrant workers.[61] Systematic studies of wages paid to casual laborers, sources of migrant workers other than Texas Mexicans, and the

---

lent Association from 1866–1924," M.A. thesis, University of Texas, 1968. Melton Alonza McLaurin, *The Knights of Labor in the South* (Westport, Conn.: Greenwood, 1978), considered southern labor to be mostly in textile mills and thus not in Texas.

59. The 1968 London speech was expanded upon by Gutman and published in "Work, Culture and Society," *AHR* 78 (June, 1973): 531–87. This essay was included in Herbert Gutman, *Work, Culture, and Society in Industrializing America: Essays in American Working-Class and Social History* (New York: Knopf, 1976).

60. For a brief introduction to this type of history see David Brody, "The Old Labor History and the New: In Search of an American Working Class," *Labor History* 20 (winter, 1974): 110–26. An excellent introduction to the current state of the art in labor history is David Montgomery, *The Fall of the House of Labor: The Workplace, the State, and American Labor Activism, 1865–1925* (Cambridge, England: Cambridge University Press, 1987).

61. See the essay by Arnoldo De León, "Texas Mexicans: Twentieth-Century Interpretations."

utilization of women and children in farm work are just a few of the topics worth consideration.

Studies of the transition of women into nineteenth-century industrial jobs could add to Texas women's history. Southern historians have suggested that because of textile mills and agricultural labor the South industrialized on the backs of women and children. Is a similar story true for this state, only with other raw material–based industries? Did changes in the workplace relegate women's work to an inferior position, as some have charged, because wage earning supported the capitalist system, which devalued homemaking and parenting?[62] The new labor history also lends itself to questions of ethnic Texans in the workplace. Did they bring different values than did those who came from Anglo farms to semi-industrial jobs? Did the blend of cultures give workers more or less control of the workplace? Recent studies have indicated that economic pressure from employers eroded conflicts between ethnic groups and encouraged class consciousness.[63] No one knows if a like assumption applies to the Texas workplace.

Other assumptions based on class interest merit exploration. Middle-class farmers and their poorer colleagues may have been divided upon any number of topics. In the matter of education, did they both wish for the same education from the public schools? There has been no adequate history of the common schools. Stewart Dean Smith wrote a general description of them from 1870–1900 as a yet unpublished dissertation. There has also been a rather impressionistic history of common school education done recently. Although Smith's work was very promising, neither of these books fills the need for a description and analysis of rural schools. Before an evaluation of class interest and the public schools can be made, Texans need to know just what the common schools did and who sought reforms for what reason. The usual assumptions were that farmers expected their public schools to nurture the children and to give them enough of an education to work on the farm. When the Progressives undertook school reform, they

62. For an analysis of this assumption and its critics see Anne M. Boylan, "Women's History: Some Axioms in Need of Revision," *Reviews in American History* 7 (Sept., 1978): 340–47.

63. These questions are explored in Richard L. Erlich, ed., *"Immigrants in Industrial America* (Charlottesville: University of Virginia Press, 1977). In particular look at the work of Virginia Yans-McLaughlin, "A Flexible Tradition: South Italian Immigrants Confront a New Work Experience," pp. 67–84.

intended that public schools train an efficient work force. The goals of both groups and the inherent conflict between them would be a possible theme around which to structure a history of rural education. It was also possible that Progressive farmers thought that scientific farming would bring an efficient work force to extensive agriculture. There could then have been conflicts within the agricultural community over what was the purpose of education for farmers.[64]

We know more about agrarian goals for higher education than for public schools. Henry Dethloff has written almost a model study of Texas A&M University, and he explored the values farmers wanted their college to impart to their children.[65] They were ambivalent early on about the advantages offered by scientific farming, suspected a liberal arts education, and wanted the college to return children to farms after graduation. There are rather startling gaps in the historical accounts, however, of other formal contacts that farmers had with education. A history of Texans in the country life movement, the corn and tomato clubs, and other volunteer activities to encourage scientific agriculture merit study. Those farmers who participated in such endeavors were middle-class farmers. There may have been a division between the poorer Texas farmers and their more affluent counterparts in the value of such clubs to their members. The study of agrarians and rural reforms would undoubtedly push forward the study of Texas women.

For that matter, a history of Texas agriculture should be pushed forward through the New Deal years. Others than simple political accounts, the New Deal in Texas remains almost virgin territory. Standard histories of New Deal agricultural policy usually discuss southern states, with a few references to Texas, and then move to the Midwest. If historians write of the New Deal in the West they have ignored the Lone Star State, with the exception of the dust bowl. The same has been true of standard studies of Progressive reforms aimed

64. Stewart D. Smith, "Schools and Schoolmen: Changes in Texas Education, 1870–1900," Ph.D. diss., University of North Texas, 1974; Thad Sitton and Milam C. Rowold, *Ringing the Children in: Texas Country Schools* (Texas A&M University Press, 1988). A good model to begin the study of education is William A. Link, *Schooling, Society and a Hard Place: Schooling, Society and Reform in Rural Virginia, 1870–1920* (Chapel Hill: University of North Carolina Press, 1986).

65. Henry C. Dethloff, *A Centennial History of Texas A&M University, 1876–1976*, 2 vols. (College Station: Texas A&M University Press, 1976).

at the rural population. Texans are mentioned but not given an extensive discussion.[66]

The problem with fitting Texans into any national or regional framework has limited sharply the study of rural Texans other than with regard to the topics that have drawn national scholarly interest. The very diversity of the state, which makes it an historically interesting one, has discouraged specialized studies of agriculture. The aversion of most Texas historians to social history has further limited our knowledge of rural Texas. Agrarian Texas then should be broadly conceived for the purpose of historical research. Problems and puzzles that began in the late nineteenth century can be traced well into the middle of the twentieth. Models drawn from new social history and from histories of the South should be very valuable in helping historians shape questions about rural Texas. Despite the work already done on the late nineteenth century, rural Texans await their historians.

66. See, for example, Dewey Grantham, *Southern Progressivism: The Reconciliation of Progress and Tradition* (Knoxville: University of Tennessee Press, 1984); Theodore Saloutos, *The American Farmer and the New Deal* (Ames: Iowa State University Press, 1982); Richard Lowitt, *The New Deal and The West* (Bloomington: University of Indiana Press, 1984).

⚘ Texas Progressivism:
A Search for Definition
Larry D. Hill

Beginning in the 1890s reform movements swept across America, and by 1910 many of the crusading men and women active in those movements were calling themselves "progressives." Ever since, historians have used the term *progressivism* to describe the many reform movements of the early twentieth century. In the goals they sought and the remedies they tried, the reformers were a varied and contradictory lot. Certainly there was no unified movement, and even the term *progressivism* defies rigorous definition.[1] Yet most scholars agree that if it was nothing more tangible than the "spirit of an age," progressivism was a vital, significant phenomenon, one that contemporaries recognized and talked about and fought about. In the broadest sense, progressivism was the way in which a whole generation of Americans defined themselves politically and responded to the nation's problems. Progressives made the first comprehensive efforts to grapple with the ills of a modern urban-industrial society.

And so it was in Texas. Yet the Lone Star State was not a leading progressive state. No one interpreting Texas progressivism has suggested that Texas marched in the same rank as Wisconsin. No Texas leader is enshrined in the pantheon of progressive reformers—there were no Texan equivalents of Tom L. Johnson, Golden Rule Jones, Robert La Follette, or Charles Evans Hughes. Moreover, most of the earliest historical accounts of Texas in the early twentieth century

---

1. The most cogent analysis of the difficulties in defining progressivism may be found in Peter G. Filene, "An Obituary to the 'Progressive Movement,'" *American Quarterly* 22 (spring, 1970): 20–34. Filene argues convincingly against there being an identifiable movement and even suggests that scholars abandon the use of the term *Progressive Era,* since its parameters cannot be defined with any precision.

never mention the term *progressivism*.[2] But many or most of the reforms advocated by the nation's progressive leaders became part of the Texas system during the three decades between 1900 and 1930.

In *Progressives and Prohibitionists: Texas Democrats in the Wilson Era*, Lewis L. Gould noted that "the impact of progressivism on Texas has remained largely an unresolved question. Less flamboyant than the era of James S. Hogg and militant Populism, less immediate than the New Deal and Lyndon Johnson, the reform period of the early twentieth century has received respectful but only passing attention."[3] It is true that the big synthesis is yet to be written, but Robert S. Maxwell has written a perceptive essay chronicling the changes in Texas during the period 1900–1930. Indeed, his treatment may be unique in referring to this thirty-year period as the "Progressive Era" in Texas, since most historians bring this era to a conclusion at the end of World War I. Also characterizing 1900–1930 as the period of "Progressivism in Texas," in their college textbook Robert A. Calvert and Arnoldo De León provide the most comprehensive treatment of the era's reforms, yet they have not honed the definition of progressivism.[4]

Maxwell provided a valuable service in suggesting a new time frame for the study of Texas progressivism, but there is no equivalent work that defines its full parameters. Nor is there a unifying work setting forth a common theme upon which to build a synthesis. What we have, then, is a collage, bits and pieces pasted together only by the application of the term *progressivism*. Thus we must rely upon the periodical and monographic literature to develop a composite picture. In addition, reliance upon broader works of southern history provides one regional perspective from which to interpret Texas progressivism.

For example, any historian who attempts to interpret Texas progressivism must take into account the writings of C. Vann Woodward,

2. Ralph W. Steen, *Twentieth Century Texas: An Economic and Social History* (Austin: Steck, 1942); Seth Shepard McKay, *Texas Politics, 1906–1944, with Special Reference to the German Counties* (Lubbock: Texas Tech Press, 1952); Seth S. McKay and Odie B. Faulk, *Texas after Spindletop, 1901–1965* (Austin: Steck-Vaughn, 1965).

3. Lewis L. Gould, *Progressives and Prohibitionists: Texas Democrats in the Wilson Era* (Austin: University of Texas Press, 1973), pp. 284–85.

4. Robert S. Maxwell, "Texas in the Progressive Era, 1900–1930," in *Texas: A Sesquicentennial Celebration*, ed. Donald W. Whisenhunt (Austin: Eakin, 1984), pp. 173–200; Robert A. Calvert and Arnoldo De León, *The History of Texas* (Arlington Heights, Ill.: Harlan Davidson, 1990), pp. 253–89.

230

in part because his works ascribe to the Lone Star State many of the characteristics that he viewed as typically southern. In *Origins of the New South, 1877-1913,* Woodward maintained that there was an "indigenous" southern progressivism that was not "derivative" of its northern counterpart but was "touched lightly here and there by crossfertilization from the West." Southern Progressivism was a one-party—that is, Democratic party—variety that benefited when the collapse of Populism removed the stigma from reformism. The disaffected left wing, abandoning the Populists, returned to the Democratic party, bringing with them their ideological baggage. As Woodward made clear, southern, hence Texas, progressivism was progressivism for white men only. Gripped by the racist contempt and cultural anxiety common to most white southerners, progressives joined with conservatives in implementing the Jim Crow system and disfranchising blacks, justifying their actions as the best means of reducing political corruption and social conflict.[5]

The broad studies of Alwyn Barr and James A. Tinsley owe much to Woodward. In *Reconstruction to Reform: Texas Politics, 1876-1906,* Barr demonstrates how Governor James M. Hogg's administrations (1891-95), by following a troubled path between the right and left wings of the Democratic party and promoting moderate reforms, abetted a reconciliation after the Populist upheaval and paved the way for later reforms. In pumping life into the Texas Railroad Commission and pursuing a vigorous antitrust policy, Hogg's regime was an important precursor of twentieth-century progressivism. Moreover, Barr explains how limited progressive reforms were accomplished during the conservative administrations of Joseph Sayers (1899-1903) and Samuel W. T. Lanham (1903-1907). As have historians of progressivism in other states and regions, Barr maintains that a wide variety of pressure groups increased the public's awareness of specific problems and lobbied successfully for legislation to promote amelioration. Thus, the Democratic party by 1904 had to take note of the myriad reforms being promoted by these private groups.[6]

In a 1986 article, Worth Robert Miller agreed with Barr in crediting

5. C. Vann Woodward, *Origins of the New South, 1877-1913* (Baton Rouge: Louisiana State University Press, 1951), pp. 371-74.

6. Alwyn Barr, *Reconstruction to Reform: Texas Politics, 1876-1906* (Austin: University of Texas Press, 1971), pp. xiii, 229-35.

former governor Hogg with paving the way for later reforms, but Miller contended that more significant was the pragmatic response of former Farmers' Alliance men in aligning themselves with Reform Democrats, whom they formerly had shunned in favor of the Populists. The farmers' rapprochement with Hogg's Reform Democrats produced a coalition whose efforts culminated in the 1906 election of a progressive governor, Thomas M. Campbell, and the Thirtieth Legislature.[7]

James A. Tinsley, in his excellent yet still unpublished doctoral dissertation, views progressivism as emanating primarily from an effort on the part of farmers and unionized workers to break the dominance over the state's politics and economy by an alliance of northern business interests and conservative Democratic politicians. More than Barr he chronicles the adoption of the wide range of reforms that emerged from the Texas legislature. His detailed accounting stresses that the passage of reform measures, already significant under the conservative Sayers and Lanham administrations, accelerated dramatically under progressive governor Thomas M. Campbell (1907–11), as the Thirtieth Legislature gained the reputation of being the most reform minded in the state's history.[8]

A useful synthesis, one that refines and embellishes C. Vann Woodward's earlier interpretations, is Dewey Grantham's *Southern Progressivism*. Accounting for the similarities as well as differences among the southern states, Grantham maintains that the social, economic, and political conditions of Texas during this period determined that its progressivism would have a western as well as southern cast. He notes that Texas, like most of the South, was rural and agricultural, but that the state's economy was more diversified than in most other states of the region. Although more diversified, the economy was "scarcely less colonial in nature." How to handle corporate wealth and how to restrain the power of railroads, lumber companies, and oil corporations was the central issue for progressives in the first ten years of the twentieth century. The central dilemma for Texas progressives was to satisfy the state's pervasive yearning for economic development and at the same

7. Worth Robert Miller, "Building a Progressive Coalition in Texas: The Populist-Reform Democratic Rapprochement, 1900–1907," *Journal of Southern History* (*JSH*) 52 (May, 1986): 163–82.

8. James Aubrey Tinsley, "The Progressive Movement in Texas," Ph.D. diss., University of Wisconsin, 1953.

time restrain the power of out-of-state capitalists. Thus Grantham maintains that in economic matters, Texas progressivism was essentially anticolonial, and he cites as evidence the Texas Railroad Commission's setting intrastate railroad rates well below interstate rates and the passage of the Robertson Insurance Act of 1907, which required companies to invest within the state at least 75 percent of their reserves devoted to policies on the lives of Texans. Thus, many of Texas' progressive reforms sought advantages for Texans over outsiders.[9]

Even Lewis Gould's work, which concentrates on other sources of progressivism, acknowledges the anticolonial orientation of the state's reformers. Yet Gould contends that there was no overriding corporate threat to the well-being of the state and that Texas' progressivism emanated from an entrenched Texan culture which derived from the state's rural roots, the homogeneity of its white majority, and an intense study of the state's history. Generally democratic in their relations with one another, white Texans were chauvinistic, provincial, and ethnocentric when looking across the state's boundaries. It was this faith in their uniqueness and superiority, Gould contended, rather than concern over domination by outside corporations, that caused reformers to come to grips with their state's economic and social problems. The very success of their campaigns to reform politics and the economy, Gould suggested, led naturally to an emphasis on a cultural issue like Prohibition.[10]

Gould also highlighted what was, perhaps, the greatest impact of all the progressive policies and legislation of the first two decades of the twentieth century. "The greatest effect in these areas," he wrote, "was on attitudes toward the power of government. As legislation and bureaucratic action demonstrated the benefits the state could convey, the old Democratic faith in localism and obstruction perceptibly relaxed." By 1921, Texas Democrats were thoroughly "Wilsonized." During Woodrow Wilson's presidency Texans emerged as a powerful force within the councils of the national Democratic party. Three Texans served in the Wilson cabinet and a fourth, Edward M. House, was the president's closest confidential adviser. The benefits that the state received from a sympathetic administration in Washington provided

9. Dewey W. Grantham, *Southern Progressivism: The Reconciliation of Progress and Tradition* (Knoxville: University of Tennessee Press, 1983): 150–53.
10. Gould, *Progressives and Prohibitionists*, pp. 28–57.

an impetus for weaning Texans from their negative past. Gould stressed that by 1921 Democrats were advocating programs and tolerating federal action that would have been viewed as intolerable as late as 1910. And the issue of Prohibition provided the bridge that allowed most Texas progressives to pass from their traditional negativism and adherence to weak government to acceptance of an activist government. Their failures to secure a Prohibition amendment in the state predisposed them to seek a national solution. Having passed over the bridge it was easier to accept future government activism.[11]

Historians of Texas progressivism at the local and municipal level have come to rely heavily upon the interpretations of Samuel P. Hays. According to Hays, the progressive impulse was fostered by a business elite who sought to apply to politics and government the lessons of economy and efficiency gleaned from experience in corporate enterprise. Their reliance upon Democratic rhetoric, he contended, masked their drive for structural changes in government, restrictions on political participation by the lower classes, and the advancement of their own economic interests. The self-styled progressives described in Evan Anders's *Boss Rule in South Texas: The Progressive Era* conform to the Hays model. The reformers represented an upwardly mobile group of entrepreneurs whose advancement was frequently thwarted by corrupt political bosses such as James B. Wells of Cameron County. Employing the rhetoric of democracy, the self-styled progressives nonetheless sought to disfranchise the working-class Hispanics as a means of breaking the power of the bosses, demonstrating that they were moved as much by prejudice as by moral indignation. In *Progressive Cities: The Commission Government Movement in America, 1901–1920,* Bradley Robert Rice maintains that contrary to the popularly held view, the adoption of the commission form of government in Galveston did not result primarily from the city fathers' inability to cope with the crisis wrought by the hurricane of 1900. Rice contends that an increasingly influential business elite succeeded as early as 1891 and 1893 in securing amendments to the city charter that accomplished structural changes. Well before the establishment of commission government, these reformers had succeeded in altering the system so that the separate wards were represented by aldermen who were elected at large by the entire city electorate. The result was the elimination of black and working-class

11. Ibid., pp. 287–91.

234

representatives from the city government. Already well organized and gaining in influence, this group — the Deep Water Committee — used the hurricane disaster as a means of securing "a more businesslike system" in Galveston. Houston, Dallas, Fort Worth, and El Paso soon followed Galveston's example. In each case the initial support for the commission form of government came from local business leaders. Yet Rice argued that the adoption of commission government was not the result of class conflict. It was, he maintained, more a product of modernization and the affirmation of corporate values.[12]

Two other studies of municipal reform in Texas suggest, on the other hand, that class considerations were uppermost on the minds of the reformers. In his study of reform in Beaumont, Paul E. Isaac found that "the movement . . . was led by well-to-do businessmen who believed that they should run the city for its own good." In *City Building in the New South: The Growth of Public Services in Houston, 1830–1910,* Harold L. Platt came to conclusions similar to those of Anders and Isaac. Progressive reformers in Houston sought a structure of municipal government that would parallel a board of directors of a modern corporation. And in supporting the poll tax, white primary, and Jim Crow system, as well as in the public services they inaugurated, Houston's city fathers, with little concern for the well-being of the working class, sought to create a more hospitable metropolitan environment for business leaders.[13]

Historians generally agree that Texas progressivism encompassed the reform tendencies that were present throughout the South. The most comprehensive cataloging of reforms in Texas may be found in Tinsley's dissertation. But George B. Tindall has provided the most

12. Samuel P. Hays, "The Politics of Reform in Municipal Government in the Progressive Era," *Pacific Northwest Quarterly* 55 (Oct., 1964): 157–69; Samuel P. Hays, *The Response to Industrialism, 1885–1914* (Chicago: University of Chicago Press, 1957), pp. 188–93; Evan Anders, *Boss Rule in South Texas: The Progressive Era* (Austin: University of Texas Press, 1982), pp. vii–ix, 280–83; Bradley Robert Rice, *Progressive Cities: The Commission Government Movement in America, 1901–1920* (Austin: University of Texas Press, 1977), pp. xi–xii, 3–12, 19–33, 110–11. See also Bradley Robert Rice, "The Galveston Plan of City Government: The Birth of a Progressive Idea," *Southwestern Historical Quarterly* (*SHQ*) 78 (Apr., 1975): pp. 365–408.

13. Paul E. Isaac, "Municipal Reform in Beaumont, Texas, 1902–1909," *SHQ* 78 (Apr., 1975): 429; Harold L. Platt, *City Building in the New South: The Growth of Public Services in Houston, Texas, 1830–1915* (Philadelphia: Temple University Press, 1983): 155–208.

succinct description of the "salient tendencies" of southern progressivism. In a 1963 article appearing in the *South Atlantic Quarterly*, he identified them as:

1. Democracy: reforms such as the party primary and regularizing voting procedures to enhance the power of the voters.
2. Efficiency: reorganizing government to eliminate waste.
3. Corporate regulation: government action against corporate abuses and the threat of monopoly.
4. Social justice: involving a variety of reforms from labor legislation to Prohibition to women's suffrage.
5. The public service concept of government: the extension of governmental responsibilities into such direct services to the people as good roads, education, public health, and conservation.[14]

There is considerable disagreement on what constituted the heyday and death knell of Texas progressivism. For Tinsley the policies of the Thomas M. Campbell administration (1907–11) and legislation passed concurrently by the Thirtieth Legislature represented the zenith. Its decline occurred when the middle class shifted the focus of reform to Prohibition. In 1914, the support of reform measures by the Wilson administration in Washington reflected credit upon those who engineered his capture of the state's delegation during the presidential campaign two years before. Yet their Prohibitionist gubernatorial candidate of 1914, Tom Ball, presented little in the way of a positive appeal for reform, opening the way for the demagoguery of Jim Ferguson to put the progressive forces on the defensive. By this time, also, Tinsley noted, organized opposition pressure groups were exercising influence in the legislature and chipping away at reforms, some of which were only months old.[15]

To the contrary, Lewis Gould insisted that not only was Prohibition a legitimate progressive reform but that by 1911 it had supplanted all others in importance and that it led reformers to abandon their states' rights orientation and embrace federal government action. Indeed, Texas progressives applauded Woodrow Wilson's vigorous leadership and embraced the reforms he sponsored. Wilson's patronage gave Texas a powerful position in the national Democratic party. To Gould

14. George B. Tindall, "Business Progressivism: Southern Politics in the Twenties," *South Atlantic Quarterly* 62 (winter, 1963): 93.
15. Tinsley, "The Progressive Movement in Texas," pp. 315–20.

these developments represented the apogee of Texas progressivism. He acknowledged that the breakup of the Wilson administration after World War I and the intensification of regional divisions in the party during the 1920s resulted in a diminution of Texas' influence in national affairs, but suggests that a regional variety of progressivism persisted within the state.[16]

George Brown Tindall maintained that the progressive urge "did not disappear but was transformed through greater emphasis upon certain of its tendencies and the distortion of others." More commonly, chambers of commerce and other business groups defined what constituted progress, so much so that Tindall applied the label "business progressivism" to the variety that survived into the 1920s and 1930s. The urge for social justice was muted and the drive for corporate regulation all but disappeared, but reliance upon the public service function of government was consolidated and intensified. Efficiency and development took precedent over reform. From this perspective the twenties were a time of "fruition and harvest" for progressivism.[17]

Norman D. Brown's marvelously detailed account of Texas politics in the 1920s, entitled *Hood, Bonnet, and Little Brown Jug,* is a faithful application of Tindall's thesis. His analysis of the business progressivism of the 1920s offered a model for the kind of comprehensive treatment so badly needed for the first twenty years of the century. Brown chronicled the administrations of business progressive governors Pat Neff (1921–25) and Dan Moody (1927–31). Both men sought to bolster government agencies so as to provide Texas with better services, including an effective penal system, good roads, higher-quality schools, and more legitimate auditing of state accounts. Each man made a fetish of law enforcement and honest, efficient government, Moody all the more so because the administration of his predecessor, Miriam Ferguson (1925–27), was besmirched by scandals involving her husband, Jim. Dan Moody's administration was characterized by the national press as a model of progressivism.[18]

Brown also identifies another strain of progressivism, social con-

16. Gould, *Progressives and Prohibitionists,* pp. 278–91.

17. Tindall, "Business Progressivism," pp. 94–96. Tindall's fullest exposition of "business progressivism" may be found in his *The Emergence of the New South, 1913–1945* (Baton Rouge: Louisiana State University Press, 1967).

18. Norman D. Brown, *Hood, Bonnet, and Little Brown Jug* (College Station: Texas A&M University Press, 1989).

trol, which thrived in the 1920s. Most progressives saw no incompatibility between social justice and social control. Indeed, many of their reforms were designed to accomplish both. In the 1920s, the goal of social control gained ascendancy. As both Brown and Gould have demonstrated, Prohibition was designed as much to mitigate the unruly tendencies of the lower classes as it was to reduce their influence in politics. During World War I, under the leadership of Governor William P. Hobby (1917-21), the state, at the same time it adopted generous social justice legislation to benefit servicemen and veterans, fostered an enforced superpatriotism which proved repressive to those who held dissenting opinions. Even when Governor Hobby gave his support to women's suffrage, he attempted at the same time to deny aliens the right to vote.[19]

Just as surely as some progressives could cite the preservation of certain cultural values as justifying Prohibition, so others could endorse the Ku Klux Klan's efforts to regulate personal behavior. As Norman Brown and Charles C. Alexander have demonstrated, the Klan of the 1920s professed to be the keeper of acceptable community morals. Antiblack prejudice seems to have given little impetus to the Klan's growth in most parts of Texas. Although it committed acts of violence against blacks, in Texas the Klan portrayed itself as a crusader for law and order, including Prohibition enforcement, and the protector of virtuous womanhood and orthodox morals, including premarital chastity, marital fidelity, and respect for parental authority. Proselytizing such values, Klansmen and Klan-supported officials gained substantial political power at all levels of government. However much progressives supported the values espoused by the Hooded Empire, they could not condone its campaign of systematic terror. Thus the Klan's excesses resulted in the diminution of its political influence, but not before it inspired such morality campaigns as the censorship of books and films, the establishment of codes for the dress and behavior of women, and the adoption of blue laws.[20]

As John W. Storey and others have demonstrated, the compul-

19. Gould, *Progressives and Prohibitionists*, pp. 42-57, 223-35; James A. Clark, with Weldon Hart, *The Tactful Texan: A Biography of Governor Will Hobby* (New York: Random House, 1958); James R. Green, *Grass-Roots Socialism: Radical Movements in the Southwest, 1895-1943* (Baton Rouge: Louisiana State University Press, 1983), pp. 381-82.

20. Brown, *Hood, Bonnet, and Little Brown Jug*, pp. 49-87, 211-52; Charles C. Alexander, *Crusade for Conformity: The Ku Klux Klan in Texas, 1920-1930* (Houston: Texas

sion to preserve cultural values, a basic characteristic of southern progressivism, became more defensive and negative in the 1920s with the intensification of Protestant Fundamentalism. Southern social Christianity, which had earlier concentrated on the issue of Prohibition, broadened its goals to the creation of a restrictive, enforced community based on its own standards. Dewey Grantham suggested that the crusades of the Klan and Protestant Fundamentalists produced a "kind of 'political fundamentalism,'" in which defenders of traditional morality sought to deny divisions in southern society by appealing to regional loyalties and coercing a sense of unity."[21]

Business progressivism was shaken by the Great Depression. Boosterism and confidence in enterprise seemed out of place as the economy plunged into the abyss. Ill equipped to alter a system that he had helped to create, business progressive governor Ross Sterling (1929–33) did little to assist Texans in meeting the crisis. By all accounts Governors Ferguson (1933–35) and James Allred (1935–39) met the challenges of the depression in a humane manner. In the face of renewed charges of corruption against her husband Jim, Miriam Ferguson's administration expanded relief efforts to the destitute and secured federal public works projects. Allred cooperated with the relief and recovery agencies of the New Deal. He helped to set up assistance programs for the aged, the needy blind, and indigent children, but could not persuade the legislature to fund them. He supported tax reform, but opposed the sales tax because it would fall disproportionately on poor consumers. Unlike the business progressive governors of the 1920s, he earned the hatred of business corporations.[22] Texas regained considerable influence in national Democratic party affairs,

Gulf Coast Historical Association, 1962); Charles C. Alexander, *The Ku Klux Klan in the Southwest* (Lexington: University of Kentucky Press, 1965), pp. vi–vii, 18–21, 27.

21. John W. Storey, *Texas Baptist Leadership and Social Christianity, 1900–1980* (College Station: Texas A&M University Press, 1986), pp. 39–69; Jeanne Bozzell McCarty, *The Struggle for Sobriety: Protestants and Prohibition in Texas, 1919–1935* (El Paso: Texas Western Press, 1980); Patsy Ledbetter, "Defense of the Faith: J. Frank Norris and Texas Fundamentalism, 1920–1929," *Arizona and the West* 15 (spring, 1973): 45–62; C. Allyn Russell, "J. Frank Norris: Violent Fundamentalist," *SHQ* 75 (Jan., 1972): 271–302; Kenneth K. Bailey, *Southern White Protestantism in the Twentieth Century* (New York: Harper and Row, 1964), pp. 44–71; Grantham, *Southern Progressivism*, p. 415; Brown, *Hood, Bonnet, and Little Brown Jug*, pp. 147–49.

22. Lionel V. Patenaude, *Texans, Politics and the New Deal* (New York: Garland, 1983), pp. 86–108; Donald W. Whisenhunt, *The Depression in Texas: The Hoover Years*

which had declined drastically after the breakup of the Wilson administration. Not only did John Nance Garner serve two terms as vice-president in the Franklin D. Roosevelt administration, but the New Deal assisted the rise to influence of Sam Rayburn, Wright Patman, and Marvin O. Jones in the House of Representatives and Tom Connally in the Senate. But Texans chafed at the even greater influence of northern urban liberals. As Texans witnessed what they perceived to be the leftward drift of the New Deal, the president's efforts to pack the Supreme Court, and a bitter debate over an antilynching bill, the New Deal's prestige diminished in the state and hastened the decline of progressivism itself. As George Norris Green has demonstrated in *The Establishment in Texas Politics: The Primitive Years, 1938–1957,* the enemies of progressivism regained ascendancy after 1938, with the result that Texans have elected an unbroken line of conservative governors and legislatures since 1939. Numerous and harsh antilabor laws, a regressive tax structure, and extreme reluctance to expand state services have all been typical of this conservative establishment.[23]

The periodical and monographic literature does give us valuable insights into the character of Texas progressivism, but this composite view is just that—many pieces, but no whole. Moreover, there are not even enough pieces. There are significant gaps in our knowledge of Texas progressivism. What is more, important questions that historians have posed about the progressivism elsewhere have not been raised within the context of Texas reform. For example, in his pioneering work on California progressivism, George E. Mowry contended that the reformers in that state were primarily urban, native-born, high-status, middle-class Protestants who viewed society's ills as emanating from the influences of monopolistic corporations, organized

(New York: Garland, 1983), pp. 99–101, 141, 149, 168–82; William Eugene Atkinson, "James V. Allred: A Political Biography," Ph.D. diss., Texas Christian University, 1978.

23. Patenaude, *Texans, Politics and the New Deal,* pp. 30–85; George Norris Green, *The Establishment in Texas Politics: The Primitive Years, 1938–1957* (Westport, Conn.: Greenwood Press, 1979), pp. 13–17; Lionel V. Patenaude, "Texas and the New Deal," in *The Depression in the Southwest,* ed. Donald W. Whisenhunt (Port Washington, N.Y.: Kennikat, 1980), pp. 89–101; Richard B. Henderson, *Maury Maverick: A Political Biography* (Austin: University of Texas Press, 1970), pp. 63–183; Irvin M. May, *Marvin Jones: The Public Life of an Agrarian Advocate* (College Station: Texas A&M University Press, 1980); James T. Patterson, *Congressional Conservatism and the New Deal* (Lexington: University of Kentucky Press, 1967), pp. 129–63.

labor, and socialism. In his brilliant and provocative work, *The Age of Reform*, Richard Hofstadter embellished upon Mowry's findings in suggesting that progressives were motivated by status anxiety.[24]

The Mowry-Hofstadter thesis stimulated a generation of scholarship, much of which tended to refute their findings. For example, J. Joseph Huthmacher demonstrated that in Massachusetts and New York the reformers would not have succeeded without the support of machine politicians and the supporting votes of the urban masses. Studies of progressive leadership in other states demonstrate that the reformers and their opposition came from the same social strata. Thus, status anxieties did not necessarily explain the reformers' motivation.[25] Michael Rogin took a second look at the California progressives, and applying quantitative methods found that after 1910 the success of progressive reforms was dependent more upon working-class than middle-class support. This is not to suggest that scholars should duplicate for Texas the debate over status anxieties as it was carried out for other states. On the other hand, George B. Tindall has suggested a new application of the thesis. In one of his Walter Lenwood Fleming Lectures of 1973 he suggested that "it may well be that some element of status anxiety governed southern reactions to the invasions of northern capital and the perceived threat that it would gobble up small businessmen."[26] If anticolonialism was a major factor in the adoption of Texas' railroad, insurance, banking, and other corporate regula-

---

24. George E. Mowry, *The California Progressives* (Berkeley: University of California Press, 1951), pp. 86–91; Richard Hofstadter, *The Age of Reform* (New York: Alfred A. Knopf, 1955), pp. 131–73. It should be noted that Alfred Chandler, Jr. arrived at conclusions similar to those of Mowry and Hofstadter in describing the leadership of the Progressive party. See "The Origins of Progressive Leadership," *The Letters of Theodore Roosevelt*, 8 vols. ed. Elting E. Morison (Cambridge, Mass.: Harvard University Press, 1954), 8:1962–65.

25. David P. Thelen, "Social Tensions and the Origins of Progressivism," *Journal of American History* (*JAH*) 56 (Sept., 1969): 323–41; William T. Kerr, Jr., "The Progressives of Washington, 1910–1912," *Pacific Northwest Quarterly* 55 (Jan., 1964): 16–27; E. Daniel Potts, "The Progressive Profile in Iowa," *Mid-America* 67 (Oct., 1965): 257–68. Jack Tager demonstrated that social tensions could not explain differences between Progressives and conservatives in Toledo, Ohio. See "Progressives, Conservatives, and the Theory of the Status Revolution," *Mid-America* 68 (July, 1966): 162–75.

26. Michael Rogin, "Progressivism and the California Electorate," *JAH* 55 (Sept., 1968): 297–314; George Brown Tindall, *The Persistent Tradition in New South Politics* (Baton Rouge: Louisiana State University Press, 1975), p. 52.

tory measures, perhaps status anxiety was an operative factor. It bears consideration.

Also needing further consideration are the interpretations of Samuel P. Hays and Robert H. Wiebe. As noted above, Rice, Isaac, Platt, and Anders have drawn from Hays in explaining how local elites employed the goals, more particularly the rhetoric, of progressivism in their attempts to establish control in local political affairs. But the larger implications of Hays's work have hardly been considered. Hays was concerned with the evolution of political structure in modern America. He contended that during the Progressive Era "the direction of change was toward centralization." New forms of organization arose that "tended to shift the location of decision-making away from the grass roots, the smaller contexts of life, to the larger networks of human interaction." Within this context the ward system gave way to citywide systems of executive action and the management of schools and roads passed from the township to the county and then to state departments of public instruction and highway commissions.[27]

Wiebe built upon Hays's themes in developing a new general interpretation of progressivism. Like Hays, Wiebe found that progressives sought identity less from local community than from business or profession. They represented a new middle class which derived its power from neither inherited wealth nor status but from its ability to wield the tools of science, technology, and organizational skills. Efficiency and rationalization were their gods. They were young men "with a passion for the future." For Wiebe, "the heart of progressivism was the ambition of the new middle class to fulfill its destiny through bureaucratic means."[28]

If one looks past the efforts by political and economic elites at the

27. Samuel P. Hays, "Preface to the Atheneum Edition," in *Conservation and the Gospel of Efficiency: The Progressive Conservation Movement, 1890–1920* (New York: Atheneum, 1975). In the edition herein cited Hays decries the fact that most readers of the original edition did not grasp its primary significance. They concentrated primarily upon his treatment of the evolution of conservation policies. He had hoped that they would recognize that he was more concerned with the evolution of political structures. Similarly, it may be stated that scholars who have drawn upon his work in interpreting certain tendencies of Texas progressivism have used it primarily to explain the rise of new local political elites.

28. Robert H. Wiebe, *The Search for Order, 1877–1920* (New York: Hill and Wang, 1967), pp. 113, 119, 166.

local level to what was happening in Austin, the larger implications of Hays's and Wiebe's writings offer tantalizing possibilities for a re-interpretation of Texas progressivism. For example, the Texas legisla-ture adopted laws that gave the attorney general greater power to ex-amine the books and records of corporations, which strengthened the state's hand in antitrust suits, protected potential buyers from fraudu-lent stock sales, insured bank deposits, and created such regulatory agencies as the State Tax Board, the State Bank Board, the Markets and Warehouses Commission, and the State Highway Commission, as well as a commissioner of insurance and banking. Other examples of state efforts to centralize, bureaucratize, and modernize abound.

Hays contends that the political struggles of the Progressive Era resulted less from the battle of good versus evil than from the "tension between centralizing and decentralizing forces." Tinsley demonstrated painstakingly that for every group that advocated a progressive re-form in Texas there was an organized opposition, but he cast these conflicts in terms of the people versus the interests.[29] It is time that they be viewed otherwise. The Hays-Wiebe thesis on the origins and parameters of progressivism has stood the test of time better than any other interpretive framework. Applying its greater implications may lead to a synthesis of Texas progressivism.

On the other hand, there are several developments in recent his-toriography that militate against such a synthesis. In his study of pro-gressivism in Wisconsin, David P. Thelen found the roots of progres-sivism in the myriad groups and individuals of the Gilded Age who "envisioned some change that would improve society." Yet those who sought reform remained fragmented during the Gilded Age because they "were generally stereotyped as cranks who were blind to the vast blessings and bright future of industrialism." Thelen maintained that the depression of 1893–97 changed this attitude. It "dramatized the failures of industrialists and demonstrated that the nation's business and political leaders were "utterly incapable of comprehending, let alone relieving, the national crisis." The depression aroused those "uni-versal emotions — anger and fear — which possess all men regardless of their backgrounds" and "posed dramatic and desperate enough threats to men of all types" to make them agree that drastic changes were needed. Thelen found that in Wisconsin previously divided reform-

29. Hays, "Preface"; Tinsley, "The Progressive Movement in Texas," pp. 75ff.

ers now coalesced in groups that cut across class lines. Thus, response to the depression created the kind of broad-based support that was necessary to accomplish reform.[30]

Tinsley confirmed that reform cut across class lines in Texas, but he did not really see the depression of the 1890s as a motivating factor. In a brief study of Texas' attitudes toward labor unions, Thomas B. Brewer maintained that early in the Progressive Era there was a working-class consciousness among farmers and laborers and that it created the favorable sentiment for legislation beneficial to labor. Yet like others he did not explain the process by which a reform movement that cut across class lines was accomplished.[31] An organizational synthesis along the lines projected by Hays and Wiebe does not readily accommodate the working class as a major player in the reform process, except as an object to be controlled by the middle class.

Richard L. McCormick also found fault with the prevalent Hays-Wiebe thesis because it largely ignored the progressives' "moral intensity" and "their surprise and animation upon discovering political and social evils." In fact, he contended that this "discovery of politico-business corruption" was the "central, transforming" factor in launching the era of Progressive reform. As did Thelen, McCormick viewed the depression of the 1890s as an initial catalyst. Disclosures followed in the press (particularly by the muckrakers) and from investigations by interest groups and legislative committees. By 1906, the enactment of remedies was in full swing. This timetable seems to fit squarely into the chronology of Texas progressivism. But was it the discovery of politico-business corruption that set the timetable in motion and drove it thereafter? Only the work of Tinsley seems to support this thesis. In a brief study on forestry and politics, Marilyn D. Rhinehart acknowledged the impact of publicity on reform. She concluded that progressives, including Campbell, gave a low priority to forest conservation before President Theodore Roosevelt's 1908 Governors' Conference on Conservation spurred the state into action. Ultimately, it was not indignation over corruption, but fear over the potential loss

---

30. Thelen, "Social Tensions and the Origins of Progressivism," pp. 335–41.

31. Tinsley, "The Progressive Movement in Texas," pp. 4–12, 62–65; Thomas B. Brewer, "State Anti-Labor Legislation: Texas—A Case Study," *Labor History* 18 (winter, 1970): 58–59.

of one of the state's sources of wealth that sustained the forest conservation movement.[32]

Juxtaposing the works of Tinsley and Rhinehart offers just one example of the perils one faces in attempting to create a synthesis from the existing literature of Texas progressivism. Clearly this body of work does not yet even define its parameters. Normally the quests for women's suffrage and conservation, for example, are viewed as firmly within the mainstream of progressivism. Yet A. Elizabeth Taylor wrote about the women's suffrage movement in Texas without linking it in any way to the reform trends of the day. When Robert S. Maxwell wrote of the legacy of W. Goodrich Jones, the "Father of Texas Forestry," he makes no links to progressivism. Darlene Clark Hine dealt with an issue as basic to southern progressivism as the disfranchisement of blacks, also without drawing any links.[33] While these works are not without their merits, they are nonetheless typical of the provincialism that pervades so much of historical literature dealing with the Lone Star State. Thus, too much basic monographic literature dealing with the specific issues of Texas progressivism remains to be researched and written before any scholar is likely to take on the task of producing a credible synthesis.

Given the current proclivities of historiography, one aspect of Texas' past is woefully in need of development—social history. That the new social history has been the vogue of the profession in this country for the past twenty years could not be confirmed by references to the literature on Texas. As Robert A. Calvert and Walter L. Buenger have noted, most of the literature, written in a classic heroic mode, has perpetuated myths about Texas' past that allowed the Anglo

32. Richard L. McCormick, "The Discovery That Business Corrupts Politics: A Reappraisal of the Origins of Progressivism," *American Historical Review* 86 (Apr., 1981): 247–74; Tinsley, "The Progressive Movement in Texas"; Marilyn D. Rhinehart, "Forestry and Politics in Texas, 1915–1925," *East Texas Historical Journal* 20 (1982): 6–17.

33. A. Elizabeth Taylor, "The Woman Suffrage Movement in Texas," *JSH* 17 (May, 1951): 194–215; A. Elizabeth Taylor, *Citizens at Last: The Woman Suffrage Movement in Texas* (Austin: Ellen C. Temple, 1987); Robert S. Maxwell, "One Man's Legacy: W. Goodrich Jones and Texas Conservation," *SHQ* 77 (Jan., 1974): 355–80; Robert S. Maxwell and James W. Martin, *A Short History of Forest Conservation in Texas, 1880–1940*, School of Forestry Bulletin no. 20 (Nacogdoches, Tex.: Stephen F. Austin State University, 1970); Darlene Clark Hine, *Black Victory: The Rise and Fall of the White Primary in Texas* (Millwood, N.Y.: KTO Press, 1979), pp. 33–49.

male to dominate. What is needed, they claimed, is a new synthesis that treats effectively the state's economic and cultural pluralism and leads to new ways of looking at ourselves.[34] If such a synthesis is desirable, we do not yet even have the building blocks—the microstudies—upon which to build such a synthesis. We still know very little about the social history of Texas in the Progressive Era.

This is the more unfortunate since through social history we may be able to gain valuable insights into factors militating for and against progressive reform. At a 1989 conference honoring his father, William L. Link called for historians to give more attention to the "social context of southern progressivism." He noted that it was time to turn away from our preoccupation with political and biographical studies of reformers and look instead at the preexisting conditions that compelled those reformers to see that personal and family-oriented social policy was inadequate for an industrial society. Southern progressives, he contended, demonstrated that their section's entrenched patterns of individual and community conduct needed to change. He was convinced that by concentrating on the social context historians will demonstrate that ordinary southerners, including the rural masses, were dynamic players—supporting and opposing—in the reform process. Among other things, Link demonstrated why the technique of religious revival was effective in accomplishing reforms in education, child labor, and public health, as well as Prohibition and women's suffrage. With evangelical crusades reformers changed public opinion to the extent that they were able to convince legislators in state capitals that a consensus existed in favor of sweeping reforms which, when enacted, interjected a much greater degree of government intervention into the affairs of individuals and local communities. The social context also helped to explain opposition to reform. It did not come just from the plutocracy; in the South resistance was strongest wherever reform challenged local autonomy.[35]

Our understanding of the social context in Texas is still incomplete, but as evidenced by other essays in this collection, knowledge

34. Walter L. Buenger and Robert A. Calvert, *Texas History and the Move into the Twenty-First Century*, vol. 2, *Preparing Texas for the 21st Century: Building a Future for the Children of Texas* (Austin: Texas Committee for the Humanities, 1990).

35. William L. Link, "The Social Context of Southern Progressivism," paper presented at Conference in Honor of Arthur S. Link, Princeton University, May 11–12, 1989.

of the lives of elite and ordinary Hispanic and black Texans has been enhanced by the growing number of high-quality studies.[36] Terry G. Jordan demonstrated that the ethnic mix of the state changed dramatically in the years 1890–1910. For example, during that period approximately one hundred thousand immigrants came from Mexico, producing a 300 percent increase in the Mexican population, while the total number of inhabitants of the state increased by only 75 percent. This increase in the Hispanic population was accompanied by a proportional (although not numerical) decrease in the black population and, Jordan contended, may have assisted the Anglo host culture in perceiving itself as more western than southern. Even the Anglo culture was far from homogeneous. The dominant element, the southern Anglos, were a blend of "English, Scotch-Irish and Welsh, with elements of Pennsylvania Germans, Hudson Valley Dutch, French Huguenots, Delaware Finns and Swedes, and others." Yankee Anglos functioned much like a separate ethnic group in Texas. To this mix must also be added the Cajuns, Germans, Czechs, Silesian Poles, Wends, Scandinavians, Italians, Orientals, and Jews from various countries.[37] Historians have not even begun to come to grips with the implications of this ethnic mix for progressive reform.

While the greatest proportion of the writings on Texas women concentrates on the nineteenth century and upon life on the frontier, the farm and the cattle kingdom, various forms of feminism in the twentieth century are receiving the attention of scholars. For the most part these studies concentrate upon the suffrage and Prohibition movements, the so-called petticoat lobby, and women officeholders, and to a lesser extent on the activities of women's organizations. As noted above with reference to the work of A. Elizabeth Taylor, these studies rarely make more than passing reference to progressivism. They tell us little about the lives of ordinary women, including the impact of the various forms of protective legislation (limited working hours, safety regulations) growing out of social feminism. In fact, the history of all kinds of Texas working people and labor organizations of this period is yet to be written.[38] The general treatments of Texas progressiv-

36. See the essays in this volume by Arnoldo De León and Alwyn Barr.
37. Terry G. Jordan, "A Century and a Half of Ethnic Change in Texas, 1836–1986," *SHQ* 89 (Apr., 1986): 385–417.
38. See the essays in this volume by Fane Downs and Walter L. Buenger.

ism, including those cited above by Maxwell, Calvert, De León, Tinsley, Gould, and Brown, all deal with issues relating to reform in education, but there is no study concentrating on the changes and improvements accomplished during this era; indeed, the last comprehensive study of the development of the Texas educational system was published in 1925. The impact of the progressive philosophy of education in Texas has received scant attention.[39]

The new social history has had little impact on the study of Texas' past. To write a history of progressivism in the state based on its social contexts will require numerous microhistories of communities and cultures within communities, or studies of particular reforms will have to be developed within their own peculiar social contexts. As my colleagues Calvert and Buenger contend, it is a worthwhile task, but one that is likely to daunt the resolve of more than one generation of scholars, and even if accomplished is likely to result in an even greater fragmentation of our understanding of progressivism. When we study a group we are likely to find a diversity of groups or an amalgam of groups. Concentration on a cultural group within a community may well uncover several subcultures that have developed over time. This is not the stuff of which syntheses are made, but it will stretch our understanding of the pluralism that may have molded some forms of progressivism and assist us in ridding ourselves of established falsehoods about our past.

Concentrating upon the social context of reform may also cause historians to come to grips more effectively with James E. Ferguson's place in this era of reform. Historians generally agree that southern progressives were not primarily concerned with the great social problems such as the increase in farm tenancy, or with the economic uplift of the masses.[40] In the campaign preceding his election in 1914, and early in his first term as governor, Ferguson evinced an abiding interest in the poor farmers of the state and successfully supported reforms to promote their uplift. In chronicling the political careers of her father and her mother, Miriam A. Ferguson, Ouida F. Nalle as-

39. Frederick Eby, *The Development of Education in Texas* (New York: Macmillan, 1925); Larry D. Hill and Robert A. Calvert, "The University of Texas Extension Service and Progressivism," *SHQ* 86 (Oct., 1983): 231–54.

40. Arthur S. Link, "The Progressive Movement in the South, 1870–1914," *North Carolina Historical Review* 23 (Apr., 1946): 172–95; Woodward, *Origins of the New South*, pp. 369–95; Grantham, *Southern Progressivism*, pp. xv–xxii.

cribes legitimate reformer's credentials to her father. The biographer of William P. Hobby, the lieutenant governor who succeeded Ferguson following his impeachment and removal from office, acknowledges that Hobby viewed the besieged governor as a reformer. Hobby supported Ferguson for reelection in 1916, then saw his own program as building upon his predecessor's legacy. Despite Ferguson's notorious war with the University of Texas, Ralph W. Steen viewed Ferguson as a genuine supporter of education for the masses of Texans.[41]

Even while hastening to brand him as a self-serving corruptionist, Ferguson's detractors acknowledge that he advanced the cause of reform.[42] Among the scholars of Texas progressivism, perhaps Lewis L. Gould has presented the strongest indictment of Ferguson's political character. "He had no fixed policy positions other than personal advantage, no real values save his own profit." The best treatments of the Ferguson administration, as well as the role he played in the political career of his wife Miriam, may be found in broad studies such as those cited above. V. O. Key has written that "Jim Ferguson was perhaps the most important leader in the state's politics for two decades." Although there is no great body of Ferguson papers, his career deserves a thorough study.[43]

As the foregoing essay demonstrates, historians have had only limited success in defining Texas progressivism. We have a clearer understanding of changes in progressivism that occurred after World War I than we do of the origins and spirit that drove the forces of reform during the first two decades of the century. The war years themselves have scarcely been touched upon by scholars. Nor do we have an adequate understanding of the social forces that partially changed pro-

41. Ouida F. Nalle, *The Fergusons of Texas* . . . (Austin: Naylor, 1946); Clark, *The Tactful Texan*, pp. 50–79; Ralph W. Steen, "Ferguson's War on the University of Texas," *Southwestern Social Science Quarterly* 35 (Mar., 1955): 356–62.

42. Maxwell, "Texas in the Progressive Era," pp. 187–88; Gould, *Progressives and Prohibitionists*, pp. 156–57, 185–88; Grantham, *Southern Progressivism*, p. 102; Brown, *Hood, Bonnet, and Little Brown Jug*, pp. 95–98; V. O. Key, Jr., *Southern Politics* (New York: Alfred A. Knopf, 1949), pp. 261–65.

43. Lewis L. Gould, "The University Becomes Politicized: The War with Jim Ferguson, 1915–1918," *SHQ* 86 (Oct., 1982): 261; Key, *Southern Politics*, p. 265. The first gubernatorial administration of Miriam A. Ferguson receives a full analytical treatment in Brown, *Hood, Bonnet, and Little Brown Jug*, pp. 253–339. A sequel by Norman D. Brown, currently in preparation, promises to do the same for her second administration, as well as for her other efforts to attain elective office.

gressivism from an early preoccupation with institutions and economic and political processes to a concern for the morality of individuals. Except in its shortcomings in race and minority relations, the legacy of progressivism for the state remains unclear.

Historians of Texas progressivism have been less successful than their counterparts in several other states in applying the lessons of recent trends in historiography. This is a paradox since Texans are alleged to give greater attention to the study of their state than do the peoples of other states. Witness the multimillion-dollar *Handbook of Texas* project which is currently drawing upon the talents and energies of literally hundreds of scholars. As noted above, this intense study of the state's past accounts partly for the infamous Texas chauvinism. If Calvert and Buenger are correct, this preoccupation may have impeded as much as it has increased historians' use of recent trends in historiography. Only a few studies of Texas progressivism place developments in Texas in a national context. No one has come up with a broad thematic synthesis that draws upon the experiences of other states and the nation or develops a significant new interpretation upon which studies of other states may build. Perhaps it is time to think of the study of twentieth-century Texas in general, and of progressivism in particular, as an historiographical frontier; then the spirit that drove past generations of scholars to perceive a unique state character may compel a new generation to define our more recent past in a broader context.

ৈ Texas Politics since the New Deal

Kenneth E. Hendrickson, Jr.

The major issues in Texas politics since the 1930s have been factional disputes between liberals and conservatives in the Democratic party, the rise and fall of numerous colorful and occasionally highly important individuals, the rise of the Republican party, and corruption. There are other issues, of course, but since this essay deals only with the literature of politics, they are not considered here.

What this essay does attempt to do is to show that recent Texas politics is a wide-open field for enterprising scholars. There is very little literature in the field and much of what exists is poor. Some of it is flawed by inept methodology or bias and much of it fails to put Texas into the context of national events. Biographical studies of such monumental figures as Johnson or Rayburn are exceptions to this criticism, but even on them the last word has yet to be said. On the other hand, some important issues and personalities have not been explored at all.

A good place to begin an exploration of the literature on Texas politics during the last fifty years is *Texas Politics, 1906–1944,* by Seth S. McKay. While strictly political and strictly objective, almost painfully so, it provides adequate background information. McKay outlines the major issues of the period and provides personality sketches of most of the leading politicians. Of great importance is his discussion of the issues that tended to fracture the solidarity of the Democratic party; issues like "Baileyism" and Prohibition, "Fergusonism," and finally the Great Depression and the New Deal, which contributed significantly to the growing animosity between the Texas Regulars and the liberals.[1]

The New Deal was indeed a watershed period in Texas politics,

---

1. Seth S. McKay, *Texas Politics, 1906–1944* (Lubbock: Texas Tech Press, 1952).

for the cracks produced earlier in Democratic solidarity now developed into major fissures. Here is a topic that desperately needs a first-rate analysis, but thus far we have only Lionel V. Patenaude's pioneering work, *Texans, Politics and the New Deal*. Patenaude deals reasonably well with the influence of Vice-President John Nance Garner, but he fails to devote sufficient attention to such issues as "hot oil" and he does not properly analyze the decline of the New Deal in Texas late in the decade.[2]

Among the major political figures in Texas during the New Deal period were Garner, Maury Maverick, James V. Allred, and W. Lee O'Daniel. There are several studies of Garner, but none is very good and there will probably never be a good biography of "Cactus Jack" because he burned his papers in 1948. So what we are left with are tomes like *Mr. Garner of Texas* and *Garner of Texas: A Personal History*. Both of these works are almost slavishly sympathetic. Moreover, they have no notes, no index, and no bibliography. Neither has much value for the serious student of history. Slightly better is *Cactus Jack*, by O. C. Fisher. Fisher succeeded Garner in Congress and knew the old man well. His book, while it is brief, superficial, and sympathetic to Garner, at least reflects some research and a little insight. Best of all, it contains many interesting photographs.[3]

There is no published study of Allred's career, but there is one good dissertation available by Gene Atkinson. On the other hand, Maverick is the subject of one decent work, *Maury Maverick: A Political Biography*, by Richard B. Henderson, and there is an older study of O'Daniel by Seth McKay. Henderson's biography of Maverick is a workmanlike job, and so is McKay's study of O'Daniel, except that it is so maddeningly objective. From reading it one would never guess that "Pappy" has been the subject of bitter criticism for being a "tool" of the "interests" and for betraying the poor and the old who trusted him.[4]

2. Lionel V. Patenaude, *Texans, Politics and the New Deal* (New York: Garland, 1983); George Norris Green, review of Lionel V. Patenaude, *Texans, Politics and the New Deal*, in *Southwestern Historical Quarterly* (*SHQ*) (Oct., 1984): 219–20.

3. Marquis James, *Mr. Garner of Texas* (New York: Bobbs-Merrill, 1939); Bascom Timmons, *Garner of Texas: A Personal History* (New York: Harper's, 1948); O. C. Fisher, *Cactus Jack* (Waco: Texian, 1978).

4. Gene Atkinson, "James V. Allred," Ph.D. diss., Texas Christian University, 1979; Richard B. Henderson, *Maury Maverick: A Political Biography* (Austin: University

Other Texas leaders of this period who could be studied with profit are Tom Connally, Martin Dies, Jesse Jones, and Morris Sheppard. *My Name Is Tom Connally*, by Tom Connally as told to Alfred Steinberg, is the best thing we have on the senator, but aside from the anecdotes it has little of real value to offer. On Dies there is *Martin Dies*, by William Gellerman. This was part of a series entitled "Civil Liberties in America." Chapter one begins: "There is little evidence in this man's career to indicate that he either understood or believed in American democracy." Needless to say, what follows is not very complimentary to the congressman. As for Jones, we find only *Jesse Jones*, by the ubiquitous Bascom Timmons, a friendly book that touches only ever so slightly on Texas politics. Finally, Sheppard has been the subject of two unpublished works. The first, by the senator's daughter Lucille Sheppard Keyes, is an excessively laudatory account of his career which has little to offer save chronology. It cannot be classified as serious history. The other is a dissertation by Richard R. Bailey. It is a brief but well-documented account of Sheppard's career which focuses mostly on his role as sponsor of the Eighteenth Amendment.[5]

Clearly, a survey of the literature on Texas politics for the New Deal period presents a sorry view. On the other hand, it presents many opportunities for historians and biographers who really want to make valuable contributions. Despite the fact that some collections of papers and documents are unavailable or do not exist, there are lots of big gaps that can be filled by intrepid scholars willing to dig for buried treasure. Certainly, the definitive histories of New Deal politics in Texas remain to be written.

Most observers would agree that the Great Depression, the New Deal, World War II, and the socioeconomic changes that accompanied them dramatically transformed Texas and its politics. Here was a state and a people deeply attached to nineteenth-century southern rural values, now suddenly faced with demands they were reluctant to meet. These demands came from various sources like the cities, mi-

---

of Texas Press, 1970); Seth S. McKay, *W. Lee O'Daniel and Texas Politics* (Lubbock: Texas Tech Press, 1945).

5. Tom Connally, as told to Alfred Steinberg, *My Name Is Tom Connally* (New York: Crowell, 1954); William Gellerman, *Martin Dies* (New York: John Day, 1944); Bascom Timmons, *Jesse Jones* (New York: Holt, 1956); Lucille Sheppard Keyes, *Morris Sheppard* (Washington, D.C.: Privately printed, 1950); Richard R. Bailey, "Morris Sheppard of Texas," Ph.D. diss., Texas Christian University, 1980.

norities, women, and the poor and were brought on by forces put in motion by rapid industrialization, technology, more rapid communications, the imperatives of the revolution of rising expectations, and the expanding role of the federal government. The New Deal and the Fair Deal laid out an agenda for handling many of these problems, but the agenda did not conform to Texans' traditional approach, which was to keep the cost of government low and the activities of government at a minimum. This is probably why George N. Green subtitled his book "The Primitive Years." With *The Establishment in Texas Politics,* Green clearly established himself as the premier historian of recent Texas politics. Unlike Seth McKay, Green is very analytical and judgmental. He is clearly on the side of liberalism, and his work has not set well with those Texans who like to think of themselves as conservative, who like people like Governor O'Daniel and Allan Shivers, who admire people like J. Evetts Haley and Martin Dies, and who dislike the word *liberal* and everything for which it stands.[6]

In no uncertain terms Green indicts those who ruled the state from 1938 to 1957 and with the skill of an experienced historian he supports his case with mountains of evidence concerning all sorts of political skullduggery. He defines his target, "the Establishment," as a loosely knit plutocracy of the Anglo upper classes. Then he goes ahead with specific attacks against Governor O'Daniel for betraying the common man as he became more and more of a right-wing extremist, and Martin Dies for constantly attempting to smear various people with charges of being "Nazis" or "Communists" without any proof. He says Coke R. Stevenson appointed anti-intellectuals to the board of regents of the University of Texas, thus stimulating a series of events that nearly destroyed academic freedom in the state, and he states flatly that Lyndon Baines Johnson was elected to the United States in 1948 quite simply because he was able to buy more votes than Stevenson. He also argues that Allan Shivers became a racist and a labor-baiter in his momentous struggles with his liberal adversary Senator Ralph Yarborough.[7]

There are several books concerning specific events, developments,

6. George N. Green, *The Establishment in Texas Politics: The Primitive Years, 1938–1957* (Westport, Conn.: Greenwood, 1979).

7. For a good summary, see Ben Procter, review of George Norris Green, *The Establishment in Texas Politics: The Primitive Years, 1938–1957,* in *SHQ* (Jan., 1980): 331–32.

and people mentioned by Green. The first of these is *Texas and the Fair Deal*, by Seth S. McKay. This volume deals mostly with elections, specifically those of 1946, 1948, 1950, and 1952. Like all McKay's works it is based largely on secondary sources, mostly newspapers. It is very detailed, that is, it is a sort of blow-by-blow history, and it contains almost no analysis, interpretation, or judgment. As a pure source of information, however, it is hard to beat.[8]

Oddly, the tidelands oil dispute, which contributed to major shifts in Texas politics, has received little attention. There was one important book on the subject published in 1953 entitled *The Tidelands Oil Controversy: A Legal and Historical Analysis.* Here Ernest R. Bartley offers a comprehensive and dispassionate treatment of the entire explosive topic. The reader comes away from this work with a thorough understanding of the complex relationship between the state and the federal government that produced the dispute about title to offshore lands after their value was enhanced by the discovery of oil. This book was reprinted in 1979.[9]

The only other major work on tidelands is a doctoral dissertation by Lindsy Escoe Pack. This is a very effective treatment and probably should be published. Pack shows how the tidelands controversy further divided an already disjointed Democratic party. When Adlai Stevenson forced the Texas Democrats to choose between the tidelands and party loyalty in 1952, the majority chose the tidelands. As a result the regular and loyalist factions of the party moved even further apart, providing an opportunity for the Republicans. Eisenhower's only political handicap in Texas was that he was a Republican, but counterbalancing this difficulty were the facts that he was a Texan by birth, a war hero, and most important of all, an advocate of state ownership. His victory was one of the significant developments marking the beginning of a new direction for the state's Republican party.

The politicians whose careers were most affected by the tidelands controversy were Allan Shivers and Price Daniel, Sr. In 1952, Shivers achieved a national reputation for his support of Eisenhower, but his actions forced him into a runoff election in his bid for an unprecedented third term as governor in 1954. Even greater was the effect on

8. Seth S. McKay, *Texas and the Fair Deal* (San Antonio: Naylor, 1954).
9. Ernest R. Bartley, *The Tidelands Oil Controversy: A Legal and Historical Analysis* (Austin: University of Texas Press, 1953).

K. E. HENDRICKSON, JR.

Daniel. His one objective in running for the United States Senate in 1952 was to regain the tidelands. Texas' ultimate success can be largely attributed to his determination.[10]

There were four governors during the "primitive era": Coke Stevenson, Beauford Jester, Allan Shivers, and Price Daniel. Stevenson was in office at the end of the war and he continued to serve until 1946. His administration is outlined by Green and, until some serious biographer finds "Calculatin'" Coke a worthy topic, this is all most students will need. There is one catastrophically bad book on Stevenson's life which was rushed into print by some of his admirers shortly after his death in 1976. Written by Frederica Burt Wyatt and Hooper Shelton and published by Shelton Press, the book's historiographical value can be summed up in the title of chapter one: "Genesis of a Genius."[11]

Beauford Jester was an important figure. Elected in 1946, over former University of Texas president Homer Rainey, he served until his untimely death in 1949, and during that period he faced a number of major issues such as labor unrest, minority rights, academic freedom, and the liberal-conservative clash within the Texas Democratic party. Jester tried with some success to get the state legislature to deal realistically with these problems and other matters like improving education, building better roads, and improving the state's charitable institutions. Again, Green deals nicely with the Jester years in summary fashion, but much more could be done. The governor has been the subject of one master's thesis by Ronald Lee McBee, but it is not nearly complete.[12] Here is a man whose career cries out for study by a serious scholar.

Allan Shivers followed Jester into the governor's mansion. He was profoundly significant in modern Texas politics and hence has received more attention than most other governors. Green, for example, devotes two full chapters to the Shivers era. But the only complete biography of Shivers was written by two journalists, Sam Kinch and

10. Lindsy Escoe Pack, "The Political Aspects of the Texas Tidelands Oil Controversy," Ph.D. diss., Texas A&M University, 1979. For a good summary see *Dissertation Abstracts International* 40, no. 12: 6394–A.

11. Frederica Burt Wyatt and Hooper Shelton, *Coke Stevenson . . . : A Texas Legend* (Junction, Tex.: Shelton Press, 1976).

12. Ronald Lee McBee, "Beauford Jester," M.A. thesis, University of Houston, 1952.

256

Stuart Long, who titled their work *Allan Shivers: The Pied Piper of Texas Politics*. It is a nice, readable book, but is certainly not the last word on the subject.[13] The definitive biography of Allan Shivers has yet to be written, and someday soon it should be done, for Shivers was an active governor. Among other things he reformed the budgetary system of the state and called for further reform in education, care for the ill and mentally handicapped, and further improvement of the highways. He also widened the split in the Democratic party by supporting President Eisenhower, and faced his share of controversy because of major scandals in the insurance industry during his administration.

Following Shivers came Price Daniel, Sr. There are no decent published studies of his career, so here is another biographical target that needs to be attacked. Daniel thought of himself as a resourceful and successful governor, and he probably was. When he left office in 1962, he claimed responsibility for such achievements as a long-range plan for water resources, improved roads and public schools, better law enforcement, and improved aid to the elderly. These are all matters worthy of consideration and analysis. A good starting place for anyone interested in pursuing Daniel as a research topic is "The Role of Governor Price Daniel as a Legislative Leader," by James R. Green. The author assessed Daniel's leadership efforts through the use of such techniques as special messages, the press conference, and the media, and concluded that he was quite effective, since 80 percent of his recommendations to the legislature between 1957 and 1963 became law. Green's work certainly leaves much to be desired, since it is based entirely on secondary sources and lacks depth, but on the other hand reading it whets the appetite for more Daniel scholarship.[14]

One of the most unpleasant aspects of the political scene in Texas during the primitive years was the reaction to the Communist terror as conjured up by Senator Joseph R. McCarthy of Wisconsin. The best source on this problem is the work of Don E. Carleton. In *Red Scare!: Right Wing Hysteria, Fifties Fanaticism and Their Legacies in Texas*, Carleton argues that the reaction to the "Red menace" was rooted in

---

13. Sam Kinch and Stuart Long, *Allan Shivers: The Pied Piper of Texas Politics* (Austin: Shoal Creek Publishers, 1973).

14. James R. Green, "The Role of Governor Price Daniel as a Legislative Leader," M.A. thesis, North Texas State University, 1967.

fear of the unknown—a disease that is sometimes active and sometimes in remission, but never goes away. Carleton focuses on the anti-
Communist movement in Houston where the American Legion, the
Society for the Preservation of Methodism, the Minute Women, and
other groups sought to root out and banish the local commies. They
did not find any, but they did ban school books, harass and intimidate
teachers, and force the resignation of assistant superintendent of schools,
Dr. George W. Ebey.[15]

Before the publication of his book, Carleton published an article
entitled "McCarthyism in Houston." This piece is based on his master's thesis and both works are worth examining.[16]

Closely related to this topic is George N. Green's "Some Aspects
of the Far Right Wing in Texas Politics." While not particularly analytical, it offers numerous important insights to explain the right-wing
mentality. Green argues forcefully that a viable two-party system is
the best way to achieve balance on the Texas political scene. Hence,
the resurrection of the Republican party in the state is a highly significant matter.[17]

Two books on the two-party question appeared in the fifties, both
the work of O. D. Weeks of the University of Texas Department of
Political Science. The first, *Texas Presidential Politics, 1952,* objectively
discusses the role played by Texans in the election of 1952. It points
out that splits occurred in both major parties in Texas and that these
proved to be significant in the national arena. Events in Texas were
thought to be important not only in the history of state politics but
also the politics of the South because many observers argued that these
events signified the beginning of the two-party system—an argument
with which Weeks disagreed. Weeks's second book, published four
years later, was intended as a sequel to his earlier work. Here, in *Texas
One-Party Politics, 1956,* he argues that little progress was made between

15. Don E. Carleton, *Red Scare!: Right Wing Hysteria, Fifties Fanaticism and Their
Legacies in Texas* (Austin: Texas Monthly Press, 1985). For a good summary see David
McComb, review of Carleton, *Red Scare!* in *SHQ* (Jan., 1986): 359–60.

16. Don E. Carleton, "McCarthyism in Houston," *SHQ* 80 (Oct., 1976): 163–76;
Don E. Carleton, "The Minute Women and the George W. Ebey Affair: A Case
Study of McCarthyism in Houston," M.A. thesis, University of Houston, 1974.

17. George N. Green, "Some Aspects of the Far Right Wing in Texas Politics,"
in *Essays on Recent Southern Politics,* ed. Harold M. Hollingsworth (Austin: University
of Texas Press, 1970), pp. 58–94.

1952 and 1956 toward the realization of a two-party system in Texas. The small gains made by the Republicans during that period were insignificant to the overall picture. Texas might eventually become a two-party state, but, concluded Weeks, it would take much longer than most observers predicted.[18]

Examining the rise of the Republican party in Texas from a broader perspective are two later books. The first of these is *A History of the Republican Party in Texas, 1865–1965,* by Paul Casdorph. Of course, much of this book deals with subject matter outside the scope of this essay, but to understand modern Texas Republicanism one has to know the background. Moreover, approximately one-half of the book is devoted to the period since World War II. This material contains little analysis or interpretation, but it is a very useful chronicle.[19]

Somewhat more interpretive is *From Token to Triumph: The Texas Republicans Since 1920,* by Roger Olien. Olien traces the evolution of Texas into a two-party state, showing how the Republican party developed from the days when it served only to distribute patronage when there happened to be a Republican president, to the recent period when the party has become a powerful force boasting a long-time U.S. senator, a two-term governor, and a singularly outspoken turncoat congressman-turned-senator. Olien deals effectively with the history of the party during the long period from the twenties to the fifties when it was dominated by Rentfro B. Creager, but he is at his best when describing the history of the party during the fifties and sixties when the Republicans' hopes and chances dramatically expanded.[20] Reading this book will stimulate interest in a number of related topics such as the career of Senator John Tower. Here is a fascinating character, a man who served for a quarter of a century in the Senate and possessed great power and influence and yet whose name is associated with not one single piece of important legislation.

---

18. O. D. Weeks, *Texas Presidential Politics, 1952* (Austin: University of Texas, Institute of Public Affairs, 1953); O. D. Weeks, *Texas One-Party Politics, 1956* (Austin: University of Texas, Institute of Public Affairs, 1957).

19. Paul Casdorph, *A History of the Republican Party in Texas, 1865–1965* (Austin: Pemberton, 1965).

20. Roger Olien, *From Token to Triumph: The Texas Republicans since 1920* (Dallas: Southern Methodist University Press, 1982). For a good summary see Dave McNeely, review of Roger M. Olien, *From Token to Triumph: The Texas Republicans since 1920,* in *SHQ* (Oct., 1985): 228–29.

Related to the rise of the Republican party in Texas, of course, is the problem of factionalism in the Democratic party. While it is touched upon in many monographs and biographical studies, little of real significance has yet been written to explain the titanic struggle between liberals and conservatives for control of the Democratic party since World War II. Among the few good items available is *Party and Factional Division in Texas,* by James R. Soukup, Clifton McCleskey, and Harry Holloway. Picking up on the argument of V. O. Key, who in 1949 said that in Texas as contrasted to other parts of the South political behavior revolved more around economics and ideology than around race and personality, these authors set out to test Key's thesis by studying fourteen elections between 1946 and 1962. They concluded that the trends detected by Key had become even more pronounced, that in 1964 liberal and conservative Democrats were squabbling mainly over economic policy, and that the resulting polarization was helping the Republicans. This book, even though now out of date, is an excellent source for anyone wishing to study the major political trends in Texas during the first two decades following World War II.[21]

Of related interest is an unpublished work by Martha Kay Dickenson, in 1973 a graduate student in political science. This study offers a number of interesting conclusions that might be productively re-examined today. It says that a pattern of conflict between liberal and conservative Democrats over economic issues was evident between 1944 and 1956, but not thereafter. After 1956 the Texas electorate was in a state of flux, the area offering most support to the liberals shifted continuously, and there was no pattern except for ethnic group alignment. From 1956 to 1972 personalism and candidate appeal were the most important factors in Texas elections.[22]

There is also tucked away another master's thesis by Charles W.

21. James R. Soukup, Clifton McCleskey, and Harry Holloway, *Party and Factional Division in Texas* (Austin: University of Texas Press, 1964). For a good summary see James A. Tinsley, review of James R. Soukup, Clifton McCleskey, and Harry Holloway, *Party and Factional Division in Texas,* in *SHQ* (Apr., 1965): 538–39. For another attempt to test Key's thesis see Chandler Davidson, *Biracial Politics: Conflict and Coalition in the Metropolitan South* (Baton Rouge: Louisiana State University Press, 1972). Urban politics are covered more fully in the essay by Char Miller elsewhere in this volume.

22. Martha Kay Dickenson, "Electoral Behavior in Texas from 1944 Through 1972," M.A. thesis, North Texas State University, 1973.

Stephenson that touches on the subject from a different perspective.[23] Additionally, Stephenson has written a book-length manuscript on the subject, but it has yet to be published. This is a story that needs to be told. It is the story of the Democrats of Texas (DOT), an organization within the Democratic party, that existed from 1956 to 1961 and whose presence marked the end of the "primitive era" in Texas politics. It is a story of practical politics describing how the liberals attempted — and failed — to gain control of the Democratic party organization. The DOT was formed in response to what its leaders considered a betrayal by Lyndon Johnson in 1956 when, after cooperating with them to block Allan Shivers's control of the state's presidential nominating machinery in the spring, he allied with the governor to ensure conservative control of the party in the fall. From then until its demise in 1961, the DOT pursued the liberal agenda of the national Democratic party in state politics, and twice helped to elect Ralph Yarborough to the Senate. The DOT tried to shape a liberal movement in a state that is not liberal. This required the forging of a coalition with the more moderate elements in the party, but these, as well as many liberals, were becoming increasingly committed to Lyndon Johnson's ambitions. In the end, the DOT leaders had to decide whether to join with Johnson, whom they distrusted, or as principled liberals to stand against him. When they chose the latter course their organization went almost at once into decline. It was destroyed by Johnson's election to the vice-presidency.[24]

If Stephenson's book is ever published, it promises to be one of the best yet on the Texas political scene. On the other hand, some rather poor books are already in print. One of these is *Money, Marbles, and Chalk: The Wondrous World of Texas Politics,* by Jimmy Banks. Banks was a reporter for the *Dallas Morning News* and his work is really nothing more than a collection of anecdotes and news clippings strung together in book form. There is virtually no scholarship involved, nor is there any useful analysis or interpretation. The author was apparently motivated largely by a desire to heap praise on the establishment — conservative Democrats, particularly those he worked for from

23. Charles W. Stephenson, "The Democrats of Texas and Liberalism, 1944–1960: A Study in Political Frustration," M.A. thesis, Southwest Texas State University, 1967.

24. Charles W. Stephenson to the author, Feb. 4, 1987.

time to time. Hence the reader of this tome will be treated to a very generous view of people like Allan Shivers, Price Daniel, Lloyd Bentsen, John Connally, Ben Barnes, and Dolph Briscoe. Indeed, there is a whole chapter on Governor Briscoe. The book is not significant and, to make matters worse, it is poorly written.[25]

Approximating Banks's work in quality is *Fifty Years in Texas Politics*, by Richard Morehead. Morehead, an outspoken conservative, was also a reporter for the *Dallas Morning News* for many years. His book is a roughly chronological view of state elections from 1933 to 1982, coupled with brief sketches of the governors of the state for that period. The style is journalistic and reflects almost no research. Morehead's paper and his memory served as his main source. His view of important events is quite different from that of a liberal observer — or that of an unbiased scholar, for that matter. The reader gets from the book no sense at all of the importance of the issue of party loyalty caused by Allan Shivers's endorsement of President Eisenhower, little on the important battles within the Democratic party, and almost nothing on the role played by Lyndon Johnson in these struggles.[26]

Johnson is the overwhelming figure in Texas politics during the postwar era and he has already been the subject of many biographies, most of which touch upon the state political scene to some degree. Therefore, no essay such as this would be complete without a review of the literature on that remarkable man and his influence. Among the first serious biographies of Johnson to be written were those of Eric Goldman and Doris Kearns. Goldman was a Princeton professor who was given certain peripheral functions at the Johnson White House. He was a sort of intellectual-in-residence from 1963 to 1966. After leaving he wrote *The Tragedy of Lyndon Johnson*. The book was, and is, good reading, but it is not good history, and for obvious reasons. The author's focal length was much too short and his access to substantial evidence much too limited.[27]

25. Jimmy Banks, *Money, Marbles and Chalk: The Wondrous World of Texas Politics* (Austin: Texas Publishing, 1971). For a useful summary see David Hearne, review of Jimmy Banks, *Money, Marbles, and Chalk: The Wondrous World of Texas Politics,* in *SHQ* (July, 1972): 95–96.

26. Richard Morehead, *Fifty Years in Texas Politics* (Burnett, Tex.: Eakin, 1982). For a useful summary see Robert H. Peebles, review of Richard Morehead, *Fifty Years in Texas Politics,* in *SHQ* (Apr., 1984): 442–43.

27. Eric Goldman, *The Tragedy of Lyndon Johnson* (New York: Knopf, 1968).

More interesting and much more controversial than Goldman's book was *Lyndon Johnson and the American Dream*. Kearns enjoyed Johnson's trust and confidence from 1967, when she was appointed a White House Fellow, until the president's death in 1973. Her work is a combination of psychobiography, memoir, and political history. Based largely on her lengthy conversations with Johnson, it reviews and assesses his life and career, trying to show how his behavior patterns, style of leadership, and political beliefs led to the Vietnam debacle and the erosion of his benevolent vision of a Great Society. Some readers found this book, and still find it, useful and fascinating because Kearns skillfully absorbed and reflected Johnson's version of his life and the problems of his time.[28] Said one reviewer, "She has succeeded in letting him reach us through her." Historian Gary Wills, on the other hand, commented that buried in this huge book was perhaps the material for one perceptive essay. Kearns, he concluded, had nothing useful to say about the Johnson presidency.[29] That is probably overstating the case, but in any event, there is much more from which the discriminating reader may choose.

One of the best early works is *Lyndon Baines Johnson: The Formative Years*, by William C. Pool, Emmie Craddock, and David Conrad. It is scholarly and is an excellent source on Johnson's early life. It does not touch upon his later career. Among the very bad Johnson books are two others that appeared early. These are *Lyndon Baines Johnson: A Biography*, by Harry Provence, and *A Texan Looks at Lyndon: A Study in Illegitimate Power*, by J. Evetts Haley. The former literally reeks with admiration while the latter was designed specifically to hurt Johnson's chances in the election of 1964.[30]

Much better is *Exploring the Johnson Years*, edited by Robert A. Di-

28. Doris Kearns, *Lyndon Baines Johnson and the American Dream* (New York: Harper, 1976).

29. Charles DeBenedetti, review of Doris Kearns, *Lyndon Baines Johnson and the American Dream*, in *Library Journal* (June 1, 1976): 1293; Gary Wills, review of Doris Kearns, *Lyndon Baines Johnson and the American Dream*, in *New York Review of Books* (June 24, 1976): 8.

30. William C. Pool, Emmie Craddock, and David Conrad, *Lyndon Baines Johnson: The Formative Years* (San Marcos: Southwest Texas State College Press, 1965); Harry Provence, *Lyndon Baines Johnson: A Biography* (New York: Fleet, 1964); J. Evetts Haley, *A Texan Looks at Lyndon: A Study in Illegitimate Power* (Canyon, Tex.: Palo Duro Press, 1964).

vine. This volume is a series of essays by top scholars on such issues as the Vietnam War, Latin America, civil rights, the war on poverty, federal education policy, the White House staff, and the media. There is nothing on the Texas years or Texas politics as such, but the quality of this book led at least one reviewer to wish for a second volume.[31]

Probably the two best-known books on Johnson are *The Politician: The Life and Times of Lyndon Baines Johnson*, by Ronnie Dugger, and *The Years of Lyndon Johnson: The Path to Power*, by Robert Caro.[32] Dugger's book focuses upon Johnson's life from his boyhood until the time he became Senate majority leader. Although it contains some exaggerations, and inaccuracies, and is entirely too emotional and psychoanalytical, it is still one of the best biographies to date. The author was well qualified for his task. A Texan with training in history and experience in journalism, Dugger was able to research his topic effectively and present his findings in an attractive and readable fashion. Dugger's picture of Johnson is complex. He recognizes the president's capacity for charm, compassion, and generosity, but he emphasizes, perhaps to the extent of distortion, Johnson's ruthlessness, crassness, opportunism, crudeness, vindictiveness, and viciousness. Exaggerated though it may be, this work surpasses most of its peers in richness of language, use of sources, and the exhaustive detail with which many of the events of Johnson's life are explored. Here, for example, is the best account of the disputed election of 1948. It is not particularly kind to Johnson, but it is thorough and judicious and even reports some evidence that runs counter to the author's own interpretation. Dugger's volume ends when Johnson becomes majority leader of the Senate; however, there are some sections that discuss later events which will be fully developed in the second volume, presumably soon to be published. Given the literary quality of Dugger's work and the controversy that surrounds it, it will be interesting to see if he alters his approach in volume two. Whatever the case, it is probably fair to say

31. Robert A. Divine, ed., *Exploring the Johnson Years* (Austin: University of Texas Press, 1981). For example, see William E. Leuchtenburg, review of Robert A. Divine ed., *Exploring the Johnson Years*, in *SHQ* (Oct., 1983): 221–22.

32. Ronnie Dugger, *The Politician: The Life and Times of Lyndon Baines Johnson: The Drive for Power from the Frontier to Master of the Senate* (New York: W. W. Norton, 1982); Robert Caro, *The Years of Lyndon Johnson: The Path to Power* (New York: Knopf, 1982).

that Dugger's work will only be bettered by a great historian writing at a later date.[33]

Robert Caro's book is easily the most controversial work on Lyndon Johnson. Met at first with overwhelming praise and honored with several literary awards, it has more recently been shown to be somewhat less than perfect. As Lewis Gould has written, it is not the definitive historical verdict on Johnson. It is instead a transitional study that has some value as Johnson studies move inevitably toward more measured appraisals by the academic community. To quote Gould, "on matters of research, Caro's command of the primary sources on Texas and American history is thin. Moreover, his handling of the substance of Johnson's political environment and his emergence as a leader is suspect and often slippery." Gould concludes that Caro's work is too long, is tasteless in places, and is misleading and flawed in its analysis. He argues that what Johnson scholarship requires is the attention of a writer who can address his subject dispassionately, sort out fact from legend, measure the influences that shaped Johnson, and draw up a judicious evaluation.[34]

The closest things we have right now to the filling of Gould's prescription are the recent *Big Daddy from the Pedernales: Lyndon Baines Johnson,* by the eminent historian Paul Conkin, and an earlier work by Vaughn D. Bornet. The title of Conkin's book sounds like it might be an effort to trivialize Johnson, but it definitely is not. It is a straightforward narrative replete with shrewd though cautious judgments. Conkin skillfully explains how Johnson's background molded his views and his career and argues that, ideologically, Johnson was "somewhere in the middle," yet always ready to move to the left or right in order to get something done. Conkin avoids many of the pitfalls that have entrapped other authors and is particularly critical of Caro and Dugger for their psychoanalytical speculations and their naive acceptance of some of the more bizarre Johnsonian anecdotes related to them by their interviewees.[35]

---

33. For a good summary of Dugger's book see Monroe Billington, review of Ronnie Dugger, *The Politician: The Life and Times of Lyndon Baines Johnson,* in *Journal of American History* (Mar., 1983): 1037–38.

34. Lewis L. Gould, "Robert Caro and George Reedy on Lyndon Johnson: An Essay Review," *SHQ* (July, 1983): 57–68, quotation on p. 59.

35. Paul Conkin, *Big Daddy from the Pedernales: Lyndon Baines Johnson* (Boston:

Bornet's effort is also well balanced. With wit and style he addresses both Johnson's great achievements and his failures and unapologetically offers numerous editorial judgments that appear to be sound. His annotated bibliography is in some ways the best part of the book, especially the section where he challenges Robert Caro for his sloppy methodology and questionable manipulation of evidence.[36]

There are a few more items on President Johnson that must be mentioned in order to make this survey complete. The best of these lesser works is *Lyndon: An Oral Biography,* by Merle Miller. It is pieced together from literally hundreds of taped interviews with people who lived and worked with Johnson. The result is a coherent and fascinating biographical study that is at once entertaining and informative. On the other hand, it suffers because it is based almost entirely on a form of evidence that by its very nature is complex, controversial, unbalanced, unverified, and unevaluated.[37]

Worse is *Sam Johnson's Boy: A Closeup of the President from Texas,* by Alfred Steinberg. This author's purpose was to show how, by ruthless and self-seeking determination, an obscure Texas boy enriched himself and rose to political heights beyond his capacities. The book is packed with anecdotes and human interest and is quite readable, but it does not qualify as serious history or serious biography and is therefore of little use of scholars. Much of it is simply a rehash of material that was already old in 1968 and its closing chapters are marred by a number of assertions so vicious that they would have to be categorized as "cheap shots" even by Johnson's sternest critics.[38]

Least useful of all the Johnson books is *The Compassionate Samaritan,* by Phillip R. Rulon. Whereas many of the Johnson biographies are flawed by an overemphasis on anti-Johnson bias and harsh criti-

---

Twayne and G. K. Hall, 1986); Vaughn D. Bornet, *The Presidency of Lyndon B. Johnson* (Lawrence: University of Kansas Press, 1983). For a corresponding assessment see Jim F. Heath, review of Paul Conkin, *Big Daddy from the Pedernales: Lyndon Baines Johnson,* in *American Historical Review* (Dec., 1978): 1302–3.

36. This assessment appears in Glen E. Lich, review of Vaughn D. Bornet, *The Presidency of Lyndon B. Johnson,* in *SHQ* (Oct., 1984): 338–40.

37. Merle Miller, *Lyndon: An Oral Biography* (New York: Putnam, 1980).

38. Alfred Steinberg, *Sam Johnson's Boy: A Closeup of the President from Texas* (New York: Macmillan, 1968). For this assessment see Patrick Anderson, review of Alfred Steinberg, *Sam Johnson's Boy: A Closeup of the President from Texas,* in *New York Times Book Reviews* (July 28, 1968).

cisms, this one reflects just the opposite view. It concocts a vision of the former president that is utterly fantastic. To read it is to discover that Johnson was the perfect son, the perfect student, the perfect friend, and the perfect politician. The stated purpose of the volume is to assess Johnson's major contributions to education, and that is certainly a legitimate goal, but in view of the author's incomplete research, bias, and poor writing style, his work is rendered practically valueless.[39]

In recent years a number of former Johnson aides have begun to publish their memoirs. One of these is *Lyndon B. Johnson: A Memoir,* by George Reedy. Reedy, who worked for Johnson for many years, offers a number of interesting insights into why Johnson both succeeded and failed as a political leader, but beyond that he has little to contribute. More recent and almost certain to be more controversial is *Remembering America: A Voice from the Sixties,* by Richard N. Goodwin. Here Goodwin discusses his years of service to Presidents Kennedy and Johnson and writes that Johnson's great social programs—and Johnson himself—were destroyed by the Vietnam War. Johnson escalated the war, says Goodwin, partly because he was the victim, as early as 1965, of intermittent instabilities and irrationalities which rendered him incapable of distinguishing between the reflections of his imagination and reality. Goodwin deals little if at all with Texas state politics, but nevertheless here is a book to be considered by anyone working on Texan and Johnsonian historiography.[40]

Almost everything written to date on Lyndon Johnson, except for the works of Bornet and Conkin, was produced by Johnson lovers or Johnson haters, or writers who are not professional historians. As Lewis Gould has said, it is now time to pass Johnson into the hands of serious historians who will go beyond painful memoirs and exaggerated characterizations to assess and fix Johnson's real place in American history.[41]

Close to Johnson in his importance to Texas politics is Sam Rayburn. His career was long and spilled over into the postwar years. Hence it must be considered here. Among the published Rayburn

---

39. Phillip R. Rulon, *The Compassionate Samaritan* (Chicago: Nelson-Hall, 1982).

40. George Reedy, *Lyndon B. Johnson: A Memoir* (New York: Andrew and Mc-Meel, 1982); Richard N. Goodwin, *Remembering America: A Voice from the Sixties* (New York: Little, Brown, 1988).

41. Gould, "Robert Caro and George Reedy on Lyndon Johnson," p. 67.

studies, the most useful to students of Texas state politics is by Anthony Champagne. The author describes how Rayburn maintained his ties with his constituents during his long career in Washington, and argues that the ingredients for Rayburn's success were to be found in the nature of the Fourth Congressional District, Rayburn's style, his organization, his campaign tactics, and his efforts to balance the interests of his district with those of the party and the nation. There are chapters on each of these topics. This is a good book. It is based on thorough research in the Rayburn Papers and other materials plus a large number of interviews. It presents a balanced view of Rayburn, highlighting his weaknesses as well as his strengths, and best of all, it is well written.[42]

Less useful is *Sam Rayburn: A Biography*, by Alfred Steinberg. Although Steinberg approaches his subject uncritically, offers little interpretation, and perpetuates certain historical inaccuracies, he does chronicle the events of Rayburn's career rather nicely. The biggest problem with this book from the viewpoint of the student of Texas politics is that the work has almost nothing to say on that subject.[43]

Least attractive is *Mr. Sam*, by C. Dwight Dorough. Dorough was a great admirer of Rayburn and his work reflects that admiration. In fact, it literally drips with adulation, and it omits almost all aspects of Rayburn's career that would be unflattering to his memory. Hence it is quite unbalanced even though it is a reasonably accurate outline. Perhaps the most damning thing to be said is that it is dreadfully dull.[44]

The most recent work is *Rayburn: A Biography*, by D. B. Hardemann and Donald C. Bacon. Hardemann was a longtime aide to Rayburn who began the project years ago but died in 1981 with the manuscript only barely started. Bacon, assistant managing editor of *U.S. News and World Report*, completed it. The resulting book is quite long, with over five hundred pages of text and notes, but it is somewhat shallow. Even though it reflects an awesome amount of research it con-

42. Anthony Champagne, *Congressman Sam Rayburn* (New Brunswick, N.J.: Rutgers University Press, 1984).

43. Alfred Steinberg, *Sam Rayburn: A Biography* (New York: Hawthorn, 1975). For a brief summary see *Choice* (Dec., 1975): 1374.

44. C. Dwight Dorough, *Mr. Sam* (New York: Random House, 1962). For a good summary see W. H. Stringer, review of C. Dwight Dorough, *Mr. Sam*, in *Christian Science Monitor* (Aug. 31, 1962).

tains little analysis of important aspects of Rayburn's career, especially his legislative techniques. Also, it is too sympathetic, but that is probably to be expected in a work widely viewed as an "official biography."[45]

There is one doctoral dissertation of Rayburn by Edward O. Daniel. This writer's main purpose was to trace the events that led Rayburn to his position as Speaker of the House. It also offers the interesting thesis that because of his consistently deferential attitude toward the president, Rayburn bears much of the responsibility for the rise of presidential government and the emasculation of congressional autonomy. Through years of submissiveness to the president which he enforced among his own subordinates, Rayburn may have permanently damaged the constitutional restraints regarding the separation and balance of powers among the three branches of government. Tantalizing as that argument may be, it is somewhat off course for a study of the literature on Texas state politics. Daniel actually has little to say about that.[46]

Of all the political controversies surrounding Lyndon Johnson's career perhaps the most famous is that concerning the Senate election of 1948. It is mentioned, of course, in almost all the Johnson literature and elsewhere as well. McKay, for example, devoted ninety-one pages to it in *Texas and the Fair Deal*. Still, there is only one published monograph on the subject and it is a very poor one entitled *Ballot Box 13: How Lyndon Johnson Won His 1948 Senate Race by 87 Contested Votes*, by Mary Kahl. It is the story of how the "venerable" Coke Stevenson, "homespun, quiet and dignified," was defeated for the United States Senate by a weak mother's boy who "calculated every friendship" with no regard for political philosophy. What seems at first glance to be a complete treatment of the topic soon proves to be flawed. There is no compelling explanation of how a statewide election could be decided by one ballot box, there is no adequate discussion of why Stevenson lost the support of the powerful Parr machine, and the book fails utterly to place the election in perspective by describing the nature

45. D. B. Hardemann and Donald C. Bacon, *Rayburn: A Biography* (Austin: Texas Monthly Press, 1987). For a summary of these views see William Murchinson, review of D. B. Hardemann and Donald C. Bacon, *Rayburn: A Biography*, in *National Review* (Nov., 1987): 58–60.

46. Edward O. Daniel, "Sam Rayburn: Trials of a Party Man," Ph.D. diss., North Texas State University, 1979. For a summary see *Dissertation Abstracts International* 40, no. 3A: 1647.

of Texas politics in general. Moreover, the research is weak. There is no indication that the author examined any material in the Johnson Library, the Barker Texas History Center in Austin, or the Truman Library in Missouri. It is fair to assume that material in these depositories would have thrown more light on the subject. It is also fair to say that here is a subject still open to definitive treatment by a serious historian.[47]

By the late 1950s, certain trends were apparent in Texas politics. The liberals were on the move, as can be seen in the activities of the DOT, and even though they would never gain permanent control of the Democratic party machinery, neither would they ever completely disappear. Likewise, the Republican party was changing and growing. Creager was gone and new leaders were emerging. Conservative Democrats thought seriously of changing their labels if not their allegiance. Even though the assassination of John Kennedy in Dallas in November, 1963, gave the Republicans a jolt and a severe setback, they too were not about to disappear. It was probably for these reasons, as well as others, that Green chose to argue that the "primitive era" in Texas politics ended in 1957. One supposes that that would make the period since 1957 the "post–primitive era," and yet there have been many "primitive" developments during the last three decades. So one wonders.

With these thoughts in mind let us consider the literature of the "post–primitive era." There have been five governors since Price Daniel, Sr.: John Connally, Preston Smith, Dolph Briscoe, Mark White, and Bill Clements twice. Only John Connally has been the subject of a biography: *John B. Connally: A Portrait in Power,* by Ann Fears Crawford and Jack Keever. Though now quite out of date, this is not a bad book. It argues that Connally's rise to wealth and power from his humble beginnings is the result of a combination of hard work, luck, and the shrewd use of fortuitous relationships with powerful people. Connally also benefited from good looks, "charisma," and an astute and cynical nature. The authors carefully chart Connally's ascendance to power and give some good insights into how he used that power

---

47. Mary Kahl, *Ballot Box 13: How Lyndon Johnson Won His 1948 Senate Race by 87 Contested Votes* (Jefferson, N.C.: McFarland, 1983). For an elucidation of these views see G. L. Seligmann, review of Mary Kahl, *Ballot Box 13: How Lyndon Johnson Won His 1948 Senate Race by 87 Contested Votes,* in *SHQ* (Oct., 1986): 208–9.

to better his own personal and political needs. All in all, this is not a flattering portrait, but on the other hand neither is it definitive.[48] John Connally likely will be the subject of several more studies before his story is fully and accurately told. As for other governors of this period, they will probably not draw much attention unless someone decides to finance a "Governors of Texas" series.

Other leaders of the "post–primitive era" are as important as the governors, some much more so. Among them are Frances Farenthold, Barbara Jordan, George Parr, John Tower, Henry B. Gonzalez, and Ralph Yarborough. Of these only Yarborough has been the subject of the biographer's pen in *Yarborough of Texas,* by William G. Phillips. But this thin volume is not really a full-scale biography. It is part of a group called the "Congressional Leadership" series and it was designed to summarize Yarborough's career in highly complimentary fashion. It speaks of Yarborough as the people's senator and argues that he symbolized the spectacular influence that Texas and Texans have had on American society. In Texas, says the author, Yarborough drew his support from small farmers, small businessmen, workers, the poor and underprivileged, the intellectual community, teachers, labor, and other professional groups. These were the elements of the so-called Yarborough coalition. They sent him to the Senate and enabled him to assert his decisive leadership in such vital areas as conservation, health, veterans' welfare, antipoverty, minimum wage, Social Security, Medicare, the aged, economic developments, and others. All this is very interesting and if nothing else points up the urgent need for a serious scholarly study of Senator Yarborough.[49]

There have been some bizarre events in Texas in recent years that belie the sophistication of modern Texas politics proclaimed by some observers, and most of these events have been chronicled by historians, journalists, or participants. Take, for example, the stock fraud scandal commonly known as the "Sharpstown affair" which stunned nearly all Texans in early 1971. It inspired *Texas under a Cloud,* by Sam Kinch, Jr., and Ben Procter. The scandal broke in January when it

48. Ann Fears Crawford and Jack Keever, *John B. Connally: A Portrait in Power* (Austin: Jenkins, 1973). For a summary see Harvey Kleaver, review of Ann Fears Crawford and Jack Keever, *John B. Connally: A Portrait in Power,* in *SHQ* (Oct., 1974): 225–26. A new release on Connally is James Reston, Jr., *The Lone Star: The Life of John Connally* (New York: Harper and Row, 1989).

49. William G. Phillips, *Yarborough of Texas* (Washington, D.C.: Acropolis, 1969).

was revealed that two bills promoted by Houston financier Frank W. Sharp had passed the legislature about the time that Sharp arranged some profitable bank loan–financed stock purchases for several leading politicians including Governor Preston Smith, state Democratic party chairman Elmer Baum, Speaker of the House Gus Mutscher, and others. Determined to show the magnitude and significance of influence peddling in Texas government and politics and to suggest reforms, Kinch and Procter rushed into print with an unfootnoted volume designed more to influence the elections of 1972 than to provide historical insight. Whether the book really was a factor in the elections is impossible to say, but the voters reacted to the scandal with vigor. No candidate running for state office who was even remotely connected with the affair survived the Democratic primaries of May and June, 1972. Overall, about half of the incumbents lost to their opponents. But the liberal Democrats did not profit much. Most of the winners were from the conservative-moderate wing of the party and many, like Dolph Briscoe, who swamped Frances Farenthold in the gubernatorial runoff, represented the same rural-oriented conservative philosophy as Preston Smith.[50]

A second book on the same subject is *The Year They Threw the Rascals Out,* by Charles Deaton. More limited in its historical value than *Texas under a Cloud,* this book is highly journalistic and poorly written. It is riddled with clichés. Moreover, its title is misleading since it implies a philosophical change in Texas politics that did not occur.[51] Finally, there have been two studies of the Sharpstown scandal by graduate students. These are by Tony Allison and Richard Stark. They are both mere chronicles written shortly after the event, but nevertheless they are useful as a starting point for anyone who might wish to reexamine this dreadful affair.[52]

By 1973, most people agreed, Texas needed a new constitution.

50. Sam Kinch, Jr., and Ben Procter, *Texas under a Cloud* (Austin: Pemberton, 1972). These views are reflected in Norman D. Brown, review of Sam Kinch, Jr., and Ben Procter, *Texas under a Cloud,* in *SHQ* (Oct., 1972): 227–28.

51. Charles Deaton, *The Year They Threw the Rascals Out* (Austin: Shoal Creek Publishers, 1973). See Ben Procter, review of Charles Deaton, *The Year They Threw the Rascals Out,* in *SHQ* (July, 1974): 107–8.

52. Tony Allison, "Governor Preston Smith and the Sharpstown Stock Scandal," M.A. thesis, Southwest Texas State University, 1972; Richard Stark, "House

That need produced the next bizarre event of recent years, the Constitutional Convention of 1974. After extensive preparations the Texas state legislature declared itself a constitutional convention and spent seven months preparing a document that would have been infinitely superior to the 1876 constitution. But, largely because of an effort to insert a "right to work" clause, the legislature found it impossible to approve its own work and on July 30, 1974, the convention ended in failure. The only book thus far produced on this strange event is *Challenge of Change*, by Nelson Wolff. Wolff, a convention delegate and legislator from San Antonio, tries to explain what happened and why, but the book is a poor effort. Wolff is neither a historian nor a very good writer and his work lacks depth and analysis. Moreover, it is dull. One comes away from reading it without any sense at all of having encountered an intense political struggle fought out by real people. Most of Wolff's characterizations are one-dimensional and virtually lifeless. Certainly there is room for another, better account.[53]

Yet another legendary incident in recent Texas politics was the flight of the so-called killer bees in 1979. In May of that year, toward the end of the one-hundred-and-forty-day legislative session of the Sixty-Sixth Legislature, Lieutenant Governor Bill Hobby resorted to some questionable, if not unethical, parliamentary maneuvers as he attempted to force passage of a separate-day presidential primary bill. In response, twelve senators, dubbed the "killer bees" by Hobby because, he said, "You never know where they'll strike next," refused to participate and went into hiding, hoping to remain undetected until the statutory end of the session. Their story is told in *The Miracle of the Killer Bees: Twelve Senators Who Changed Texas Politics*, by Robert Heard. Heard produced a creditable account of this incident. He was personally acquainted with the people involved, did a thorough job of research, and demonstrated thorough knowledge of Texas government and politics. Best of all, Heard is a good writer and his work is both entertaining and insightful. Perhaps the only major problem with this

---

Speaker Gus Mutscher and the Sharpstown Scandal," M.A. thesis, Baylor University, 1972.

53. Nelson Wolff, *Challenge of Change* (Austin: Naylor, 1975). For a good summary see Ben Procter, review of Nelson Wolff, *Challenge of Change, SHQ* (Apr., 1976): 487–89.

K. E. HENDRICKSON, JR.

book is its misleading title. The "killer bees" did not change Texas politics all that much.[54]

A book of general interest to the student of recent Texas politics is *The Chief Executive of Texas,* by Fred Gantt, Jr. In this excellent piece of work, which is thoughtfully researched, well organized, and clearly written, the author presents a thorough study of the Texas governorship. It covers the period from 1876 to 1963, so only selected portions relate to the New Deal and postwar era, but having all these dates in one handy reference enables the student to make valuable comparisons. One comes away from this book with a realistic feel for the operations of Texas government. It would be nice if someone could produce an update of equal quality.[55]

Also useful in *Texas Precinct Votes '68: 1968 General Election Precinct Analysis and Maps,* by V. Lance Tarrance. Pointing up the fact that for the study of local elections, precinct rather than county data are essential, especially for urban areas, Tarrance presented the figures in readable, well-organized form along with registration totals, total vote cast, and the vote by candidate for the three races he included. This study is enough to titillate any historian. How wonderful it would be if we had references like this for all elections.[56]

Two final items will complete our survey of the works on Texas political history that have appeared in book form. These are: *Texas: All Hail the Mighty State,* by Archie P. McDonald, and *Texas: A Sesquicentennial Celebration,* edited by Donald W. Whisenhunt. Professor McDonald's book, first written in segments for the *Dallas Morning News,* was later compiled in book form. It covers the entire sweep of Texas history, but the final two chapters contains discussions of the major political battles of the postwar era and the significant political changes of the past two decades. It is a good summary. Whisenhunt's book, a series of essays, contains one piece by the editor himself on recent politics. Again, it is a useful summary. There is little analysis or inter-

54. Robert Heard, *The Miracle of the Killer Bees: Twelve Senators Who Changed Texas Politics* (Austin: Honey Hill Publishing, 1981); Ben Procter, review of Robert Heard, *The Miracle of the Killer Bees: Twelve Senators Who Changed Texas Politics,* in *SHQ* (Jan., 1983): 458–59.
55. Fred Gantt, Jr., *The Chief Executive of Texas* (Austin: University of Texas Press, 1964).
56. V. Lance Tarrance, *Texas Precinct Vote '68: 1968 General Election Precinct Analysis and Maps* (Dallas: Southern Methodist University Press, 1970).

pretation in either of these works, but on the other hand it is clear that both authors are sympathetic to the liberal point of view.[57]

The scholarly periodical literature on postwar Texas politics is sparse and written mostly by nonhistorians. Still, there are some important and useful items that should be noted. Among these is "Development of a Party Role in a No-Party Legislature," by Robert Harmel and E. Keith Hamm. This article focuses on the development of legislative party organization and party voting in the Texas house of representatives. It describes the emergence of a Democratic caucus in response to growing Republican strength and it provides a roll call vote analysis which reveals a number of interesting behavioral changes. Voting has become less factionalized and more bifactional, liberal-moderate Democrats have increased in number, and Republicans have become more conservative as their numbers have grown.[58]

In another useful piece Kent L. Tedin and Richard W. Murray argue that in state and local elections the voters are extremely volatile. Using 1978 as a case study, the authors insist that parties played a minor role, and the candidates, ignoring issues and centering their campaigns on personalities, spent vast sums on advertising. A sizable number of voters were persuaded by these appeals. However, a contrary view is to be found in "Party Voting in Lower Level Electoral Contests," by Arnold Vedlitz and Richard W. Murray. This is a study of the influence of party labels in Harris County. A unique opportunity arose here because three candidates switched party affiliation during the period of the study. All were elected as Republicans but a breakdown of the vote showed that blacks gave overwhelming majorities to the three when they were Democrats and overwhelming majorities to their opponents when they were Republicans. Middle- and upper-class whites behaved in opposite fashion.[59]

"The Ideological Characteristics of Party Leaders: A Case Study

57. Archie P. McDonald, *Texas: All Hail the Mighty State* (Austin: Eakin, 1983); Donald W. Whisenhunt, ed., *Texas: A Sesquicentennial Celebration* (Austin: Eakin, 1984). For good summaries of these works see Jim B. Pearson, reviews of Archie P. McDonald, *Texas: All Hail the Mighty State,* and Donald W. Whisenhunt, ed., *Texas: A Sesquicentennial Celebration,* in *SHQ* (Jan., 1985): 347–48.

58. Robert Harmel and E. Keith Hamm, "Development of a Party Role in a No-Party Legislature," *Western Political Quarterly* 39, no. 1 (1986): 79–92.

59. Kent L. Tedin and Richard W. Murray, "Dynamism of Candidate Choice in State Elections," *Journal of Politics* 43, no. 2 (1981): 435–55; Arnold Vedlitz and Rich-

of Texas" surveys the ideologies of Democratic and Republican leaders in Texas and compares these to their counterparts at the national level and in other states. The conclusion is that variations in ideology are caused more by the influence of regionalism than by any other single factor. On the other hand, in "Amateur and Professional Democrats at the 1972 Texas State Convention," Joseph P. Nyitray argues that ideology is a better predictor of leadership preference among delegates than any other factor.[60]

Other items from the periodical literature that might be interesting to the historian include "Analyzing Factional Patterns in State Politics: Texas, 1944-1972," by John R. Todd and Kay D. Ellis; "How Texas Legislators Views News Coverage of Their Work," by John Merwin: "Political Attitudes of Political Party County Chairmen in Texas," by Charles P. Elliott; "Wallace Party Activists in Texas," by Robert Wrinkle and Charles P. Elliott, where it is argued that American Independent party supporters in Texas tended to come from the lower socioeconomic strata and to be conservative; and finally "The Shivercrat Rebellion: A Case Study in Campaign Speaking Strategies," by Jerry A. Hendrix, which analyzes the different strategies used by Lyndon B. Johnson and Allan Shivers in their race for the chairmanship of the Texas delegation to the Democratic National Convention in 1956.[61]

A summary of the historiography of recent Texas politics reveals some startling facts. There are few historians working on topics in this era who, judging by the works they have published thus far, are objective. No one the likes of Seth S. McKay has yet appeared to re-

ard W. Murray, "Party Voting in Lower Level Electoral Contests," *Social Science Quarterly* 59, no. 4 (1979): 752-57.

60. John J. S. Moon and Nancy Bowen Saunders, "The Ideological Characteristics of Party Leaders: A Case Study of Texas," *Western Political Quarterly* 32, no. 2 (1979): 209-14; Joseph P. Nyitray, "Amateur and Professional Democrats at the 1972 Texas State Convention," *Western Political Quarterly* 23, no. 4 (1975): 685-99.

61. John R. Todd and Kay D. Ellis, "Analyzing Factional Patterns in State Politics: Texas, 1944-1972," *Social Science Quarterly* 55, no. 3 (1974): 718-31; John Merwin, "How Texas Legislators View News Coverage of Their Work," *Journalism Quarterly* 48, no. 2 (1971): 261-64; Charles P. Elliott, "Political Attitudes of Political Party County Chairmen in Texas," *Rocky Mountain Social Science Journal* 11, no. 2 (1974): 78-83; Robert Wrinkle and Charles P. Elliott, "Wallace Party Activists in Texas," *Social Science Quarterly* 52, no. 1 (1971): 197-203; Jerry A. Hendrix, "The Shivercrat Rebellion: A Case Study in Campaign Speaking Strategies," *Southern Speech Journal* 33, no. 4 (1968): 289-95.

place that venerable chronicler. But at the same time it should be remembered that there are relatively few professional historians working in the field at all. Once one gets beyond the works of George N. Green, Roger Olien, Anthony Champagne, Don Carleton, and a few others there is little more to be found.[62] Much of the available material is by journalists and participants in the events described. Some of the work by journalists is quite useful — this is especially true of the work of Sam Kinch, Jr., and several of the biographers of Lyndon Johnson — but much has little value as historical literature.

Another interesting fact is that the serious (and best) work in this field, whether by historian or journalist, usually reflects a liberal bias, but this should not be surprising. Most historians and many journalists are people of the liberal persuasion and naturally tend to reflect this in everything they write. On the other hand, more than half of the literature, much of it not so good, reflects a conservative bias. Why, one might ask, are these biases so apparent? Probably it is because many observers view their subject through a special prism of emotion and pride which produces a distorted image of reality in their minds. For that reason events and people in Texas are often portrayed as far greater or far smaller than they really are. This distortion is partly the fault of Texans themselves. Not only have they contributed more than any other single group to the creation of their own image, but they have traditionally done little to smash myths and destroy stereotypes. They seem to love that sort of thing. But be that as it may, there are other factors to be considered. These include the unusual — in some ways unique — history of the state, its massive size, and the considerable contributions that Texans have made to the history of the nation at large. All these factors combined have produced a condition in which reality is blended with folklore, myth, and fantasy to produce a unique historiography. Texas, like the frontier, is more than a geographic location, more than a political entity; it is a state of mind.

That said, it is still necessary for serious researchers and writers to enter the wide-open field of recent Texas politics. There are no definitive studies, monographic or biographic, on any subject, and that includes Lyndon Baines Johnson. Many stories have either not been

62. Soon to be added to this list is Chandler Davidson, *Race and Class in Texas Politics* (Princeton: Princeton University Press, forthcoming), which examines Texas politics from the mid-1940s to the mid-1980s.

told well or have not been told at all. One thinks, for example, of the DOT, a vital episode in the recent political history of Texas, the careers of John Tower, John Connally, and many others, maybe even the recent governors. It is time for these and numerous other topics mentioned in this essay to be taken up by historians who will give us factual accounts written with wit and sound judgment. Then and only then will the recent political history of Texas begin its long journey out of the realm of myth and fantasy.

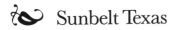 Sunbelt Texas

Char Miller

Enlightenment strikes at odd times and in strange places. It came for English essayist Stephen Brook, author of *Honkytonk Gelato: Travels through Texas,* at rush hour on the Dallas North Central Expressway. And it came in the form of a question: Why, he wondered, does Dallas exist?[1]

In part his was simply a rumpled commuter's response to a time of great stress. "Approaching the Expressway you must come to a complete halt," Brook wrote, "wait for a gap in traffic, and then hurl forward and pray that you accelerate quickly enough to prevent the car behind you from slamming into your rear." This, he concluded, was Dallas's contribution to "natural selection."

Brook's portrait of gridlock and freeway angst, when combined with the knowing laughter it provokes, testifies to an important cultural transformation: for late twentieth-century Texans the tales of pioneer wagon trains and cattle drives along the Chisholm Trail can have little meaning, a development of great significance in a state that has so long held the frontier to be its central symbol.

But Brook's query about Dallas's existence is important for another reason. His is, in part, a somewhat serious reflection on the nature of urban development itself. Peering out of his windshield, watching Dallas flash by, Brook was baffled by what he did *not* see. The geography in which the city was set, for instance, supplied few definitive clues to its emergence over time. "Built on a featureless prairie, it hugs a river, the Trinity, that's scarcely visible as it flows under highway interchanges," a river that as far as he could tell had no naviga-

---

1. Stephen Brook, *Honkytonk Gelato: Travels through Texas* (New York: Atheneum, 1985), pp. 10–11. All subsequent references to Brook come from these pages.

279

tional purpose. If land and water had not built this thriving metropolis, what had? Yet despite the lack of what Brook considered the normal signs of urban growth and evolution, Dallas was inescapably there, as an anxious glance into his rearview mirror confirmed.

Brook is not alone in his bewilderment. Citizens, politicians, even historians are struck by the sight of massive cities rising in the most unlikely places, in the marshlands of East Texas, the high prairies of the Panhandle, and in the arid flatlands of West Texas. Like Brook, we are grasping for ways to come to terms with the fact that Texas now contains three of the nation's ten largest cities; less than three decades ago it could not even claim one. And even its mid-sized cities have been growing at a brisk pace, one faster than comparable cities located elsewhere in the nation. All this in a state that used to boast more cattle than people.[2]

This demographic transformation, however bewildering, has not lacked for scholarly comment. Indeed, the study of Sunbelt Texas' evolution and fundamental characteristics, social costs, and political ramifications has emerged as one of the academic growth industries during the past decade. Not surprisingly, as an examination of this profusion of scholarship reveals, there is little agreement as to the initial causes of the Sunbelt phenomena, and even less as to its future course. This essay is not designed to resolve these disagreements, but rather seeks to set them in two interrelated contexts, one historical and the other historiographical. The experience of Texas, after all, must be set within that of the Sunbelt generally—therein lies one key to assessing the pace, timing, and significance of the urbanization of this once frontier state. But any assessment of this transformation in turn depends on the realization that the language and concepts historians have used to describe and analyze it have changed as markedly as have the cities about which they write. Only by weaving together these two contextual approaches—that of history and historiography—will the rich tapestry of the state's urban past more fully unfold.[3]

2. Carl Abbott, *The New Urban America: Growth and Politics in Sunbelt Cities*, rev. ed. (Chapel Hill: University of North Carolina Press, 1987), chap. 1.

3. Char Miller and David Johnson, "The Rise of Urban Texas," in *Urban Texas: Politics and Development*, ed. Char Miller and Heywood Sanders (College Station: Texas A&M University Press, 1990), pp. 3–29; David C. Perry and Alfred J. Watkins, eds., *The Rise of Sunbelt Cities* (Beverly Hills, Calif.: Sage, 1977); Richard M. Bernard and Bradley R. Rice, eds., *Sunbelt Cities: Growth and Politics since World War II* (Austin:

Sunbelt History

What then *is* the Sunbelt, and Texas' place within it? The region first had to be recognized *as* a region, of course, and that has
taken some doing. The term was initially employed in the late 1960s
and soon came to loom large in the popular imagination. Still, its
boundaries were and are inexact. Where is the Sunbelt? Some com-
mentators have adopted an all-inclusive definition which links together
those states south of the thirty-seventh parallel; an even more expansive version includes Virginia and the Pacific Northwest. Others rely
on more precise, but no less problematic descriptions which, depending on the source, focus exclusively on the Southwest or the Southeast
or the Gulf Coast states (or the Southwest plus Florida). Confusion,
in short, reigns.[4]

To clear up the confusion, historian Carl Abbott has proposed a
concise set of geographical limits and political borders, the delineation of which is based on historical patterns of economic change and
growth. For him, the "Economic Sunbelt" consists of a V-shaped wedge
of states that descends from Washington on the West and Virginia
on the East; note that his description carries well above the thirty-
seventh parallel and cuts out the central South. Those states included
in what he calls the Sunbelt-West and the Sunbelt-Southeast are held
together by a number of salient characteristics. They have each experienced rapid urban population growth between 1940 and 1980, growth
that especially in the 1960s and 1970s was attributable to in-migration.
One of the lures for these migrants to the Southeast and Southwest
was the steady increase there in the number of jobs in manufacturing, particularly in "high-tech" industries such as computers, communications, and electronics; this increase was further stimulated by
an expansion in defense and related industries. And then there has
been the arrival of the "snowbirds," whose movement from the inclem-
ent North in search of a warm-weather retirement, when linked to
the needs of an increasing number of tourists seeking leisurely vaca-
tion settings, has given birth to a new dimension in the regional econ-

---

University of Texas Press, 1985); Carl Abbott, *The New Urban America;* Bernard Weinstein et al., *Regional Growth and Decline in the United States* (New York: Praeger, 1985);
Steven Ballard and Thomas James, eds., *The Future of the Sunbelt* (New York: Praeger,
1983).

4. Abbott, *The New Urban America,* pp. 1–35.

omy. For these migrants, the very concept of a Sunbelt bespoke a place of bright promise.[5]

No place seemed to reflect these promises (and the social transformations that engendered them) more than Texas. Indeed, what geographer D. W. Meinig has called "Imperial Texas"—whose boundaries extend east through Louisiana, north to Oklahoma and the central Rockies, and west into New Mexico—is a pivot on which much of the Sunbelt turns. Between 1940 and 1980, for instance, the state's metropolitan growth jumped more than 8.8 million, far in excess of the national rate of growth. A sizable proportion of this was from inmigration, accounting for 70 percent of Houston's population growth between 1970 and 1983. This surge has enabled Texas to capitalize on the broader changes in the national economy in the post–World War II era, and it has since come to dominate in areas such as petrochemicals, biomedicine, and in research and development for the military-industrial complex. The Lone Star State has thus captured a disproportionate share of the wealth, prosperity, and status associated with the Sunbelt boom. It is no accident that these benefits themselves became the subject of the most successful nighttime television soap opera of the late 1970s and early 1980s, one set within the glass-walled canyons of Dallas; or that in the same historical moment that city's football team could proclaim itself to be "America's Team"—and get away with it. Texas was no longer just the archetype of the Sunbelt, it *was* the United States.[6]

Historians and other social scientists have made short work of such notions, generally dismissing the emphasis on Sunbelt glitz and glamor as so much imagineering. Rather than fall prey to urban booster mania, they instead have exposed the underside of the Sunbelt story, illuminating the lives of those who have been left out of the promise of prosperity. There is a methodological and thus historiographical reason for this perspective: the growing awareness of the importance of the Sunbelt in American politics and social discourse coincided with a sea change in the historical profession itself, one that altered the man-

5. Ibid.
6. Thomas R. Plaut, *Houston: Metropolitan Area Profile* (Austin: Bureau of Business Research, University of Texas, 1985), pp. 7–8; Miller and Johnson, "The Rise of Urban Texas"; on the Dallas Cowboys, see John F. Rooney et al., eds., *This Remarkable Continent* (College Station: Texas A&M University Press, 1982), p. 276.

ner in which this burgeoning region would be analyzed and interpreted. The key to this interpretive framework was the emergence in the 1960s of what came to be called the new social history. New because, in drawing upon the intense social criticism that was altering the American political landscape in the late 1960s, it validated the study of ordinary men and women. And so its practitioners began to probe the worlds these people inhabited and built, examined the tensions within their lives between work and family, tested the character of their political education and activism, and brought to light the communal institutions that gave life meaning in working-class neighborhoods. This was history from the bottom up, a nonelitist perspective in which the concepts of race, class, and ethnicity redefined how many historians reconstructed the past.[7]

This redefinition encountered an immediate challenge: How would historians gather data on those who tended not to leave literary evidence of their existence? Here a new approach to the past required the development of new research techniques. The resolution, if not revolution, came in the form of the computer, which enabled scholars to sift through vast quantities of information—building permits, federal census materials, financial records, and the like—to make intelligible lives once thought too obscure to merit attention. For a time these efforts were successful, and certainly some of the greatest gains were registered in urban history, a field that had its genesis in the postwar years. Its students were therefore particularly receptive to these developments in perspective, methodology, and technique, and employed them in one community study after another; these were almost exclusively designed to track the citizenry's employment patterns, wage scales, residential location, and social mobility, all with an eye to explaining the evolving context of the American urban experience.

What this heavy reliance on quantification ultimately demonstrated was the need for other, more broadly conceived organizing principles. Most of these in current use revolve around the idea of urbanization

---

7. The following paragraphs draw upon the insights of several authors. Bruce Stave, *The Making of Urban History: Historiography through Oral History* (Beverly Hills, Calif.: Sage, 1977), provides a solid overview of the new social history, as does Raymond Mohl, "New Perspectives on American Urban History," in *The Making of Urban America*, ed. Raymond Mohl (Wilmington, Del.: Scholarly Resources, 1988), pp. 293–316; Howard Gillette, Jr., and Zane L. Miller, eds., *American Urbanism: A Historiographical Review* (Westport, Conn.: Greenwood, 1987).

as *process,* and assume that any exploration of it must take into account the interaction among political authority, civic leadership, and spatial organization, between demography and topography—and that these are but some of the forces affecting the construction of urban environments. Only by adopting such a multifaceted approach could historians obtain a sharper picture of these cities and those who lived within them.

It is through this lens that historians and others now examine the Sunbelt in general and Sunbelt Texas in particular, an examination that contains a decidedly personal angle: not only are most of those who study recent urban Texas of the generation that experienced these historiographical shifts most directly, but also they have no less directly been a party to Sunbelt migration. An informal survey of those scholars who have written about recent Texas urban history, and who teach at the state's major four-year institutions, reveals that the vast majority of them were born and received their doctorates out of state; they then migrated to Texas in the post–World War II era, mostly during the 1970s and 1980s. These men and women, in short, were at once outsiders and participants. In them, biography and historiography are neatly intertwined.[8]

Out of this fusion has come some encouraging, if tentative, revisions of the narrative of the history of urban Texas. What follows is a survey of some of these revisions, research that not only challenges previous conceptions of the inner dynamics of city life in this largest of continental states, but that also tests the connections between the Texan and national experiences of urbanization.

Planning and Housing

Planning in Texas? Perish the thought. One need but view how its men are portrayed in countless westerns — images of stalwart

8. "Informal" means that the survey is not comprehensive. Although I have mined the American Historical Association's *Guide to Departments of History, 1987–1988* (Washington, D.C.: American Historical Association, 1987); and Terry Smart, ed., *Guide to Departments of History in Texas* (San Antonio: Texas Association for the Advancement of History, 1986), for relevant biographical material on the state's professional historians, and have supplemented these findings with my personal knowledge, there are no doubt those whom I have neglected to include. Still, informal or

and quiet men who, to succeed, must be disengaged from the very community they defend so heroically—to know that this is not a place that would cotton to communal restrictions on individual freedoms. These images are, of course, projections onto the past of closely held contemporary opinions, opinions that as well seem to govern the development of land in an urban society. Certainly in Houston life seems to have imitated art: the city's per capita expenditure for planning is considerably lower than for comparable northern cities, and citizens have repeatedly defeated the enactment of zoning ordinances. To have accepted such things, the political rhetoric has run, would have meant limiting entrepreneurial freedoms, limiting a sense of self that was hitherto unencumbered by modern urban constraints. Planning and zoning run against the grain of Texan individualism.[9]

But the lack of zoning does not mean that there has been *no* planning, no conscious demarcation of urban space to meet certain economic, political, and social needs. Houstonians may have opposed zoning, for instance, but that has in no way prevented the city from developing a highly planned environment. As Harold Platt has pointed out in his study of the Bayou City, by 1910, "the administrative machinery was in . . . place to generate bureaucratic solutions to the problems of environmental engineering and social management." The city's "growth-oriented plan of city-building" would unfold under the guidance of those whom Platt labels the "corporate experts," men who relied upon "business models of efficiency" to determine the extent of urban growth and to resolve any civic crises that might arise. To forestall the latter and stimulate the former governmental policy "hardened traditional patterns of racial and class discrimination into

---

not, the data strongly suggest the relationships between Sunbelt scholarship and migration is central to these historians' own lives.

9. Joe R. Feagin, *Free Enterprise City: Houston in Political-Economic Perspective* (New Brunswick, N.J.: Rutgers University Press, 1988); Don Graham, *Cowboys and Cadillacs: How Hollywood Looks at Texas* (Austin: Texas Monthly Press, 1984); Robert Fisher, "Protecting Community and Property Values: Civic Clubs in Houston, 1900–1970," in Miller and Sanders, *Urban Texas*, pp. 128–37; Barry Kaplan, "Houston: The Golden Buckle of the Sunbelt," in Bernard and Rice, *Sunbelt Cities*, pp. 200–201; Barry Kaplan, "Urban Development, Economic Growth and Personal Liberty: The Rhetoric of Houston's Anti-Zoning Movements, 1947–1962," *Southwestern Historical Quarterly (SHQ)* 84 (Oct., 1980): 133–68. Also see Joe T. Darden, ed., *Houston: Growth and Decline in a Sunbelt Boomtown* (Philadelphia: Temple University Press, 1989).

rigid lines of geographical segregation," a consequence that mocks Houstonians' ideological disdain for zoning: they simply have not needed it.[10]

This can be seen most clearly in the quality of housing available to the community. Throughout the twentieth century, middle-class whites have had access to an ever-increasing array of new houses, largely situated in the suburban tracts opening on the city's western, "vital fringe." Such opportunities, however, have not opened up for blacks and Hispanics in Houston. Until recently they have been locked into what one historian has called the city's "older sections," a euphemism for its historic ghettos and barrios located in the Third, Fourth, and Fifth wards. They have thus remained in areas in which the oldest housing stock exists, housing that has steadily deteriorated over time. And when in the 1950s upwardly mobile blacks and Hispanics sought to move up and out into nearby (and consequently older) white suburbs, their progress encountered sharp resistance from white residents. At times violence flared up, but more frequently whites developed neighborhood covenants to maintain demographic homogeneity and housing prices, covenants that the metropolitan government privately sanctioned. If these barriers were breached, then white flight to more distant tracts ensued. Again, zoning was not necessary to maintain the long-standing pattern of racial segregation and inequities in income and housing that have long plagued the community.[11]

10. Harold Platt, *City Building in the New South: The Growth of Public Services in Houston, Texas, 1830–1910* (Philadelphia: Temple University Press, 1983), pp. 208–209.

11. Kaplan, "Houston: The Golden Buckle of the Sunbelt," pp. 196–210; Cary Wintz, "Emergence of a Black Neighborhood: Houston's Fourth Ward, 1865–1915," in Miller and Sanders, *Urban Texas*, pp. 98–109; Fisher, "Protecting Community and Property Values"; Barry Kaplan, "Race, Income and Ethnicity: Residential Change in a Houston Community, 1920–1970," *Houston Review* 3 (winter, 1981): 178–203; Barry Kaplan, "Civic Elites and Urban Planning: Houston's River Oaks," *East Texas Historical Journal* 15 (1977); David McComb, *Houston: The Bayou City* (Austin: University of Texas Press, 1969). Franklin J. James, Betty I. McCummings, and Eileen A. Tynan, *Minorities in the Sunbelt* (New Brunswick, N.J.: Rutgers University Press, 1984), note that because housing in general in the Sunbelt is new, due to the region's rapid growth, "housing conditions of blacks and Hispanics in the Sunbelt are . . . better than those of minorities in the North." They find, for example, that only 6–8 percent of the housing in Houston and Dallas was constructed before 1940, but these are the exclusive domain of the city's minorities. For a discussion of these issues in San Antonio and elsewhere, see Michael J. White, *American Neighborhoods and Residential Differentiation*

Sunbelt Texas

This pattern is not markedly different in other Texas cities, including Austin, Dallas, Forth Worth, El Paso, and San Antonio, cities far more comfortable with the twin concepts of planning and zoning than is Houston. But except for San Antonio, most major cities in Texas historically have shied away from accepting federal outlays to resolve the housing problems, relying instead on private capital. Small wonder, then, that these cities' poor Hispanics and blacks live in segregated areas far distant from the locus of greatest growth and development, a separation that meets the needs of private developers. Jim Crow laws may have disappeared from the state's legal codes in the 1960s, but their impact on race relations continues: it is scored into the spatial organization and social geography of contemporary urban Texas.[12]

This legacy was reinforced by a shift in the idea of city planning that Robert Fairbanks has tracked in his studies of Dallas at midcentury. Throughout the first half of this century, American city planners conceived of cities as metropolitan wholes, ones in which the needs of *all* citizens must be acknowledged. In Dallas and in other parts of the nation, this resulted in the crafting of metropolitan plans designed to highlight the manifold problems the citizenry faced — in transpor-

(New York: Russell Sage, 1987), chaps. 4-5; Jack E. Dodson, "Minority Group Housing in Two Texas Cities," in *Studies in Housing and Minority Groups,* ed. Nathan Glazer and Dabis McEntire (Berkeley: University of California Press, 1960), pp. 84-109.

12. Michael J. White, *American Neighborhoods and Residential Differentiation,* chaps. 4-5; Robert D. Bullard, *Invisible Houston: The Black Experience in Boom and Bust* (College Station: Texas A&M University Press, 1987), chaps. 3-5; Richard A. Jones, "San Antonio's Spatial Economic Structure, 1955-1980," in *The Politics of San Antonio: Community, Progress and Power,* ed. David R. Johnson, John A. Booth, and Richard J. Harris (Lincoln: University of Nebraska Press, 1983), pp. 28-52; for maps that chart the persistence of discrimination, see Jerry Olson, *Austin Metropolitan Area Profile* (Austin: Bureau of Business Research, University of Texas, 1985), pp. 1-15; Susan M. Tully, *Dallas Metropolitan Area Profile* (Austin: Bureau of Business Research, University of Texas, 1985), pp. 1-14; Jym McKay, *El Paso Metropolitan Area Profile* (Austin: Bureau of Business Research, 1987), pp. 1-9; Bruce Renfro and Paula Cozort Renfro, *Fort Worth Metropolitan Area Profile* (Austin: Bureau of Business Research, University of Texas, 1985), pp. 1-11; Plaut, *Houston Metropolitan Area Profile,* pp. 1-15; Susan Goodman, *San Antonio Metropolitan Area Profile* (Austin: Bureau of Business Research, University of Texas, 1985), pp. 1-11; William N. Black, "Empire of Consensus: City Planning, Zoning and Annexation in Dallas, 1900-1960," Ph.D. diss., Columbia University, 1982; Robert B. Fairbanks, "Dallas in the 1940s: The Challenges and Opportunities of Defense Mobilization," in Miller and Sanders, *Urban Texas,* pp. 141-53.

287

tation and housing, in race relations and public services, in the basic infrastructure. These concerns reflected the plans' sweeping vision. According to *The Dallas Master Plan of 1943-45,* "the City is made up of many small parts, all interrelated and interdependent."[13]

Such interrelatedness did not mean that planners were advocating racial integration. When the Dallas planners discussed the dire housing needs of the local black community, for example, they proposed that those needs be resolved within the tight confines of the black ghetto. At that, when public housing was constructed in the Dallas metropolitan area most of the units were reserved for poor whites. That said, there remained at least a rhetorical commitment, however unfulfilled, to the commonweal. Without a sustained vision of "Greater Dallas," the planners recognized, fragmentation would occur, resulting in a "scattered, abnormally decentralized city with growing areas of slum and blighted districts in the central sections of the city."

By the 1950s, the planners accepted, even justified, the fragmentation of interests; the perspective of the city as an organism was fast fading. Instead, and in response to the concerns of a downtown business elite which thoroughly dominated the politics of Dallas — a situation not unique to that city — the city's planners narrowed their focus. Now the Central Business District (CBD) alone absorbed their energies. Now calls for the revitalization of the city began with the needs of this one district, and were couched in language that made its preeminence plain: "Keeping the downtown heart alive," the Dallas Central Business District Association declared, insured that "the rest of Dallas [would] remain alive." That, after all, is what the designation *central* was supposed to convey.

This did not bode well for those citizens on the economic and social periphery. As bulldozers and wrecking crews moved in to clear the central city slums, they forced out the area's impoverished inhabitants. Blacks in Dallas, in the wake of the construction of new expressways and the expansion of the CBD, were relocated to an area of west Dallas, formerly a site of garbage dumps, one set apart from white neighborhoods. In San Antonio, some Hispanics were pushed

13. Subsequent paragraphs also employ the arguments in Robert B. Fairbanks, "Metropolitan Planning and Downtown Redevelopment: The Cincinnati and Dallas Experiences, 1940-60," *Planning Perspectives* 2 (1987): 237-53; Fairbanks, "Dallas in the 1940s."

off from prime downtown real estate, and shunted into public housing on the west and south sides; and in Houston, CBD redevelopment and public housing for whites encroached upon historic black neighborhoods, leading many of their original residents to move to the city's eastern periphery. The politics of segregation and exclusion were now built into the planners' understanding of the idea of the central city.[14]

Suburbanization

These forces were and are no less integral to the idea of suburbs. Certainly that is the clear declaration of those meticulously planned, lavish country club environments that have come to shelter the Sunbelt elite. Built in the last twenty years, and located on the far edge of urban development, these enclaves not only include gated entrances for security and earth berms to screen views in and out, but are carefully landscaped with lakes or ponds to retain a semirural ambience. Preston Trail and Bent Twig in Dallas, the Dominion in San Antonio: their names alone speak to their natural beauty. The housing prices no less vocally reveal their inhabitants' status; as one commentator laconically noted about Preston Trail in the late 1970s, there "houses valued at less than half a million dollars tend to be the exception." Together, these developments offer eloquent testimony to the intense privatization of the American city, one badly split along lines of race, class, and age.[15]

That split was part of the initial conception and historic function of suburbs everywhere. Like suburbs in the rest of the United States, those that cropped up in Texas beginning in the late nineteenth century generally were situated along streetcar and rail lines that stretched out from the central core. They were later flung across a broader range

14. Wintz, "Emergence of a Black Neighborhood"; Bullard, *Invisible Houston,* chaps. 2–4; White, *American Neighborhoods and Residential Differentiation,* chaps. 4–5; Jack E. Dodson, "Minority Housing in Two Texas Cities," in Glazer and McEntire, *Studies in Housing and Minority Groups,* pp. 84–109.

15. Alan R. Sumner, ed., *Dallasights: An Anthology of Architecture and Open Spaces* (Dallas: AIA, Dallas Chapter, 1978), p. 135; Robert Fishman, *Bourgeois Utopias: The Rise and Fall of Suburbia* (New York: Basic Books, 1987). A recent sociological examination of the impact of this privatization on the American sense of community is Robert Bellah et al., *Habits of the Heart* (New York: Harper and Row, 1985).

of terrain in response to the automobile's greater lateral mobility and to the federal government's heavy investment in highways and mortgages that made distant suburbia at once accessible and affordable. From the start, developers emphasized the benefits of living at some remove from the city, luring the elite and middle classes who hoped thereby to avoid urban congestion, poor public services, and the vagaries of machine politics. The creation of Olmos Park in San Antonio in the 1920s — an automobile, incorporated suburb that found its parallels in Dallas and Houston — demonstrated additional advantages that such enclaves could provide those of considerable means. Prominent among these were racial and social homogeneity, which were reinforced by restrictive covenants, low taxes, and minimal government, which were achieved (and maintained ever since) through incorporation. These structures, among others, enabled the white elite in a very real way to escape paying for the pressing social problems that confronted a growing metropolis of the twentieth century, even as they profited from that growth. This pattern of suburbanization, like much of public life in Texas, was thus shaped by the interests and needs of one particular part of the private sector — the elites.[16]

This was not the only pattern of suburbanization, either in the nation or in Texas. Not all members of the civic elite who chose to live in suburbs did so to avoid bearing the burdens of urban growth. River Oaks in Houston, founded early in the century, was and continues to be a part of that city. Its developers deliberately refused to incorporate, believing that those who dominated the local economy had a responsibility to remain within the urban polity. This was not a matter of self-sacrifice: the community supplied many of its own public services, such as water, garbage pickup, and police protection,

16. There has been very little work done on the suburbanization of Texas, especially on the place and role of *incorporated* suburbs. See Char Miller and Heywood Sanders, "Olmos Park and the Creation of a Suburban Bastion," in Miller and Sanders, *Urban Texas,* pp. 113–27; for discussions of the national process, see Fishman, *Bourgeois Utopias;* Kenneth T. Jackson, *The Crabgrass Frontier: The Suburbanization of the United States* (New York: Oxford University Press, 1985); Jon C. Teaford, *City and Suburb: The Political Fragmentation of Metropolitan America, 1850–1970* (Baltimore, Md.: Johns Hopkins University Press, 1979); Henry Binford, *The First Suburbs: Residential Communities on the Boston Periphery, 1815–1860* (Chicago: University of Chicago Press, 1985); Michael Ebner, "Re-reading Suburban America: Urban Population Deconcentration, 1810–1980," *American Quarterly* 37, no. 3 (1985): 368–81.

that were in short supply in the larger metropolitan area. River Oaks served as inhabitants' self-interest in other ways, too. Only by participating in Houston's politics as citizens could they protect and extend their control of its economic development. Unincorporated Sunbelt subdivisions—of which Lakeway in Austin is an example—are but refinements of the River Oaks model.[17]

In their history and present configurations, Texas suburbs reflect larger national trends. But there are peculiarities to the Texas experience, the impact of which will require greater investigation. Suburbs emerged much later in Texas than they did in other parts of the United States. Henry Binford and other historians now suggest that the earliest American suburbs developed in the first years of the nineteenth century; in the Lone Star State they appeared toward the close of that century. The delay has much to do with the state's economic history. Significant evidence of urbanization and industrialization does not appear until well into the nineteenth century; the railroad did not enter San Antonio, for instance, until 1877, and mule-drawn streetcars only began to make their rounds there in 1878. "Streetcar suburbs," long a staple in northern urban history, consequently could not emerge in South-Central Texas until the late 1880s or early 1890s.[18]

This delay had an additional impact on the course of Texas urbanization: the automobile arrived almost as soon as the railroad and streetcar. This meant that fixed-line transit systems, and the suburbs that grew up along them, could not etch a radial pattern of urban expansion as deeply into the environment as had occurred in eastern and midwestern cities. Undifferentiated suburban sprawl, a gift of the automobile, became the norm more quickly in those places destined to be known as Sunbelt cities.[19]

This raises one final point about the suburbanization of Texas,

17. Kaplan, "Civic Elites and Urban Planning"; Joe R. Feagin, "The Social Costs of Houston's Growth: A Sunbelt Boomtown Reexamined," *International Journal of Urban and Regional Research* 9 (June, 1985): 164–85.

18. Donald Everett, "Monte Vista: The Gilded Age of an Historic District, 1890–1930," special supplement to the *North San Antonio Times,* (Jan. 28, 1988): 1–63. The development of Dallas and Houston streetcar suburbs followed a similar pattern, only slightly earlier. Sam Bass Warner, *Streetcar Suburbs: The Process of Growth in Boston, 1870–1900* (Cambridge, Mass.: Harvard University Press, 1962), offered the first exposition of this thesis on suburban development.

19. Jackson, *Crabgrass Frontier.*

a point that also may not precisely fit within contemporary historiography. Henry Binford, for one, has recently challenged the widely held belief that transit systems were the force behind the first suburbs. His studies of Cambridge and Somerville, Massachusetts, suggest that these were initially freestanding communities with independent economic activities; only later were they absorbed into the urban orbit as bedroom suburbs for Boston commuters. His argument may not hold in Texas for a number of reasons. The sheer size of the state, and the distances between its independent communities, reinforced the dispersal of population across the landscape, such that its first suburbs could not have been built up as was Cambridge; only now, in the late twentieth century, have the state's major metropolitan areas begun to reach the freestanding communities that have dotted the hinterland. That there have been few directly adjacent communities is due to another striking element in Texas politics: county government holds jurisdiction over unincorporated urban land, making superfluous the establishment of the independent polities that are influential in northeastern political life and, if Binford is correct, in the formation of its suburbs. Texas, in this sense, is not Massachusetts.[20]

Politics and Government

Nor are city politics in Sunbelt Texas exactly like those of its northern counterparts. Historian Carl Abbott has probed these regional differences and has identified three distinct stages in the Sunbelt's political evolution since World War II, an evolution that distinguishes the region from national norms. For Abbott, the first stage in the Sunbelt's growth, that of "urban initiative," witnessed the birth of political coalitions of reform-minded, downtown businessmen who came to power during the forties and fifties. Following their victories, these urban boosters streamlined governmental processes and began to manage the economic growth and physical expansion of the city to benefit the CBD. This central, or core, orientation would in time be checked during the second stage: as early as the 1950s vocal suburban politicians rose to confront downtown supremacy over the public interest. The ensuing battles led to compromises on such issues as highway construction, taxation, and the expansion of public ser-

20. Binford, *The First Suburbs.*

vices to outlying areas. Such city-suburban disputes themselves gave way to the third stage, one Abbot calls "the politics of community independence." Under this rubric fall those racial and ethnic conflicts, and interneighborhood confrontations, that increasingly spilled into the political arena in the 1960s and 1970s. In the communitarian tradition of new social history, Abbott grants these disputes, and especially the grass-roots organizations they spawned, a special insurgent role. Under pressures mounted by such organizations as Communities Organized for Public Services (COPS) in San Antonio, for example, the entrenched, Anglo business coalitions collapsed.[21]

Abbott's schema, like any good synthesis, is valuable in that it forces us to confront historical patterns, to perceive commonalities across time and place. One element in his theory, for instance, works particularly well: Abbot sets the context for the politics of annexation, a driving force in the growth of Sunbelt cities. Indeed, it was during the "urban initiative" period that annexation apparently mattered most. Through it the business reformers hoped to combat the "disease of deconcentration," a disease that "Frostbelt" cities could no longer fight, hemmed in as they had been by independent suburbs much earlier in the century. Only in the South and West was it still possible for a city to expand its political boundaries, and they have done so with a vengeance, nowhere more so than in Texas.[22]

Those who managed Texas cities in the years immediately surrounding World War II took full advantage of the generous Home Rule Charter that the state government granted to cities. Among other things, cities could annex unincorporated territory *without* a referendum. This facilitated the process of consolidation and of drawing in peripheral neighborhoods that showed marked growth. San Antonio, which in 1940 remained within the six-mile square the Spanish platted in the eighteenth century, embarked that year on an aggressive annexation campaign, going to court to challenge even incorporated suburbs' right to exist. By the mid-eighties, the city was nearly ten times larger than it had been four decades earlier. Dallas too has snapped up territory in advance or fast on the heels of an outward, suburban thrust. Starting at a mere 45 square miles in 1940, it had

21. Abbott, *The New Urban America,* pp. 235–38.
22. Abbott, *A New Urban History,* pp. 54–55, 181–82; Jackson, *Crabgrass Frontier,* pp. 138–56.

ballooned to more than 375 square miles by 1980. And Houston, as in many things, only pushed these trends to their extreme: its 556 square miles of territory in 1980, the vast bulk of which was annexed between the 1940s and the 1960s, made its physical limits the fifth largest in the nation. Abbott is thus correct to see annexation as a boon for urban Texas, a tactic the business coalitions employed to assert control over the local polity and to propel their cities into national prominence.[23]

In other ways, however, the match between Abbott's interpretation and historical reality is not as precise. His delineation of three stages in Sunbelt urban history makes each period seem more discrete than in fact it was, suggesting that each grew out of the other, when in fact they generally coexisted. Moreover, none of the issues that help define these stages of growth are intrinsic to the Sunbelt period. Dallas, Houston, and San Antonio had to various degrees seen the rise of chamber of commerce reformers throughout their histories. These cities had also experienced conflicts between CBD and suburban interests from the beginning of the twentieth century, and as early as the 1930s had resorted to annexation or its threat to bring the suburbs into line with metropolitan agendas. It is also clear that the conflict between the core and the periphery is overstated, at least for San Antonio, upon which Abbott draws extensively. As Heywood Sanders has demonstrated in his analysis of municipal bond issues that came before the River City's voters between the 1950s and 1970s, the Anglo suburbanites of the north side fully endorsed the political and fiscal agenda of the Good Government League, an endorsement that can not be explained by Abbott's model.[24]

Not fully explained either is the rise of Henry Cisneros, the mayor of San Antonio, who, Abbott contends, "has given [it] a new political center after the collapse of the Good Government League (GGL), the rise of Hispanics, and the city-suburban battles of the 1970s." His own

23. Black, "Empire of Consensus"; Arnold Fleischmann, "Sunbelt Boosterism: The Politics of Postwar Growth and Annexation in San Antonio," in Perry and Watkins, *The Rise of Sunbelt Cities*, pp. 151–68.

24. Fairbanks, "Dallas in the 1940s"; Robert B. Fairbanks, "The Good Government Machine: The Citizen's Charter Association and Dallas Politics, 1930–1960," in *Essays on Sunbelt Cities and Recent Urban America*, ed. Robert B. Fairbanks and Kathleen Underwood (College Station: Texas A&M University Press, 1990); Heywood Sanders, "Building a New Urban Infrastructure," in Miller and Sanders, *Urban Texas*, pp. 154–73.

evidence undercuts that contention, however. He describes Cisneros as "a state of the art civic entrepreneur" whose goal was "to link government and business," a link most obvious in the mayor's much bally-hooed Target '90 program for growth; it was, Abbott acknowledges, a "consensus . . . document involving several hundred civic leaders." Such consensus, hammered out among the community's leaders, had of course marked the GGL years and it is no wonder that its financial backers happily supported the young Hispanic politician. In him some of the GGL's most cherished principles would live on.[25]

Martial Metropoli

The politics of Sunbelt Texas, then, have made for some strange bedfellows, complicating scholars' efforts to fit them (both politics and fellows) into neat categories. This is no less true when one attempts to evaluate the impact of the military, especially since the dawn of World War II, on the political and economic fortunes of this, one of the most martial of states.

The relationship between war and urban development has only begun to draw scholarly attention, but early studies reveal that the impact was significant. Historian Roger Lotchin has been the lead theorist, and he has argued that beginning in the twenties and thirties a new and more enduring relationship between the military and some metropolitan areas unfolded, in the process changing the face of the local and national urban landscapes. Because of the extensive land requirements of military bases, for example, they were generally sited some distance away from downtown sectors, acting as magnets for nearby suburban development and consequently helping to damage the vitality of the core. This local ramification was magnified during the nation's military buildup of the late 1930s, and then intensified during the war itself. Many of the new bases and manufacturing plants designed to service the military's mobilization were constructed in the South and West, tilting the national process of urbanization away from the Northeast and Midwest, a crucial step in the postwar Sunbelt boom. Lotchin has concluded as a result that the so-called military-industrial complex is a misnomer: if anything the phenomenon should

25. Kemper Diehl and Jan Jarboe, *Cisneros: A Portrait of a New American* (San Antonio: Corona Press, 1984); Johnson et al., *The Politics of San Antonio,* pp. 3–27.

be known as the metropolitan-military complex. Nothing else so fully explains "the very direct relationship between war and defense on the one hand and urban geography and spatial relations on the other."[26]

But that relationship varied from one city to the next. Although in general city promoters "hoped that military investment would prime the pump of economic development," Lotchin observed, "and eventually turn their simple economies into complex ones through the process of economic diversification," things did not always turn out that way. As the record of Texas urban boosters suggests, success in this regard depended on how local elites reacted to the manifold opportunities before them, reactions that in turn were influenced by the economic climate and political context.[27]

The war was very good to the Texas economy, bringing with it a massive set of changes to Texas cities. There was a rapid influx of new residents to the state to find employment in its many war-related industries, or to be trained at one of the numerous military installations. To meet this demographic surge, federal, state, and local governments built new urban infrastructures — including water and sewer lines, streets and highways — and a new industrial and manufacturing base. And these developments did much to set the stage for Texas' explosive growth in the postwar years.

The benefits of this development were not spread evenly between the many Texas cities scrambling to get their share of military contracts and wartime prosperity. In this regard Dallas and Houston were the most successful in turning the war to their economic advantage. Dallas entrepreneurs, for instance, lobbied hard to obtain aircraft manufacturing plants, the construction of which the federal government would subsidize with funds from the Defense Plant Corporation (DPC). Although as a site Dallas was no more logical than anywhere else in the United States, the city aggressively pursued DPC monies, a campaign coordinated by the Dallas Chamber of Commerce, one that bore sweet fruit: North American Aviation constructed a massive, 855,000-square-foot plant in Dallas. Its equally large labor force and payroll pumped millions into the local economy, laying the

---

26. Roger Lotchin, *Martial Metropolis: U.S. Cities in War and Peace* (New York: Praeger, 1984), pp. x–xiii, 230–31.
27. Ibid.

groundwork for the city's continued involvement with airplane manufacturing.[28]

Houston too scored big, especially in the development of the petrochemical industry. Here logic was a factor. Close to the East Texas oil fields, it had the pipelines and transportation networks, the refining capacity and skilled labor necessary to develop the nation's first synthetic rubber. Building on these advantages, and a clear political one (native son Jesse H. Jones was head of the Reconstruction Finance Corporation that doled out the construction monies), Houston's industrial elite pushed hard to secure the necessary federal contracts; by the late 1940s these totaled nearly one billion dollars. Moreover, at war's end the Bayou City and its hinterland had a new and highly successful industry in place, one that would catapult the region into national prominence in succeeding years.[29]

The same could not be said for Austin or El Paso, San Antonio or Amarillo. These and other cities in Texas of course gained from wartime economic expansion. Their local military bases increased in size and function, and the resulting boost in payrolls had a dramatic impact on local economies and on the social mobility of their workers. In this, Kelly Airfield in San Antonio is typical. In 1938, its work force stood at 873, rising to 8,962 in 1941 and then mushrooming to 20,862 one year later. Among these civilian employees were an increasingly large number of Hispanics who over time would use their employment at the base to pull their way into the middle class, beginning in the 1960s. That important accomplishment aside, it is clear that Kelly and Lackland Field in San Antonio, Fort Bliss in El Paso, and Travis Field in Austin could expand only so far their host cities' economic and social horizons. Each base was a service center, providing

28. Fairbanks, "Dallas in the 1940s"; Miller and Johnson, "The Rise of Urban Texas"; Martin Melosi, "Dallas-Fort Worth: Marketing the Metroplex," in Bernard and Rice, *Sunbelt Cities*, pp. 162-95.

29. Jesse H. Jones, with Edward Angley, *Fifty Billion Dollars: My Thirteen Years with the RFC* (New York: Macmillan, 1952); Joe R. Feagin, "The Global Context of Metropolitan Growth: Houston and the Oil Industry," *American Journal of Sociology* 90, no. 6 (1985): 1204-30; Kelly Riddell and Joe R. Feagin, "Houston and Government: The Growth of the PetroChemical Industry and the War Production Board," paper presented to the Southwest Social Science Association meetings, Mar. 20, 1987; Miller and Johnson, "The Rise of Urban Texas."

training or maintenance. By themselves they did little to diversify the local economy, to increase industrial production, or to generate spin-off industries that would add to the communities' manufacturing capabilities. San Antonio may have become, in one historian's words, "a thoroughly military city," but in economic terms that was not necessarily a good thing. Servicing an airplane's engines, after all, does not have the same financial implications as does manufacturing them.[30]

But then it is not clear that San Antonio and other communities that became dependent upon the military services following the war could envision something other than what they became. Unlike Houston and Dallas, which already had developed diversified economies before the war, these others tended to be longtime regional service centers for agricultural hinterlands. Lacking a strong tradition of manufacturing, they thus also lacked an entrepreneurial elite skilled in the ways of modern, industrial city building; their past had narrowed their vision of future possibilities, something that was decidedly not true in Dallas or Houston. It should come as no surprise that it was these two cities that would power the state's economy in the Sunbelt years, an economic takeoff that was predicated on the ways they had managed their growth since the beginning of the century.[31]

Ethnicity, Class, and Race

It should come as no surprise, either, that not all citizens in Texas shared equally in the prosperity that the war generated or that the Sunbelt boom would accentuate. One's share, in fact, was closely linked to the color of one's skin, to the economic status of one's par-

30. David Johnson, "The Failed Experiment: Military Aviation and Urban Development in San Antonio, 1910–1940," in Lotchin, *Martial Metroplis*, pp. 89–108; David Johnson, "The Vicissitudes of Boosterism," in Bernard and Rice, *Sunbelt Cities*, pp. 235–54; Robert Landolt, *Mexican-American Workers of San Antonio, Texas* (New York: Arno, 1976), chap. 5; Abbott, *A New Urban America*, pp. 43, 47–48.

31. Miller and Johnson, "The Rise of Urban Texas"; Johnson, "The Failed Experiment," pp. 89–108; Olson, *Austin Metropolitan Area Profile*; McKay, *El Paso Metropolitan Area Profile*; and Goodman, *San Antonio Metropolitan Area Profile*, track the legacies of these decisions in the local economies. For a graphic demonstration of this argument, see Stanley Arbingast, *Texas Resources and Industries: Selected Maps of Distribution* (Austin: Bureau of Business Research, University of Texas, 1955).

ents, to the place of one's birth, a persistent theme writ large in analyses of Sunbelt cities.

That race, ethnicity, and class are subjects of historical scholarship at all is a testament to the influence of the new social history. These foci are perfect examples of its "bottom up" perspective, leading its proponents to direct their attention to society's least powerful and most oppressed, to those whose history has rarely been acknowledged. The story in Texas is everywhere the same: blacks and Hispanics are at a clear disadvantage from the start, a finding that holds up from city to city, regardless of ethnic composition or the sampling technique employed.

El Paso is a case in point. It is the westernmost city in the state, and is more properly part of the New Mexico and Arizona economic region; its economy and society are as well deeply interwoven with that of Ciudad Juarez, its sister city across the Rio Grande. By location and history, then, El Paso is different from other major Texas cities, a difference reflected in the city's ethnic balance. In the mid-eighties its population was approximately 60 percent Hispanic and 40 percent Anglo, with an infinitesimal number of blacks (0.3 percent, most of whom were in the military), proportions that have remained fairly stable since the 1940s.[32]

Stasis too marks the significant indices of social mobility and economic status of those living in El Paso, stasis that makes it like so many other Texas cities. In *Desert Immigrants,* an analysis of Mexican life in El Paso at the turn of the century, Mario García reports that those with Spanish surnames were crowded into the unskilled, semiskilled, and service sectors of the economy; by contrast, the city's large minority of Anglos, who were far better educated, dominated the low and high white-collar positions. Things had not changed much when a pair of sociologists conducted research on El Paso at midcentury. They found that 60 percent of those with Spanish surnames had less than seven years of formal education (64 percent of Anglos had four years of high school or more), they remained clustered in low-paying clerical and semiskilled jobs, and lived in the city's poorest neighborhoods. And in 1987, the Bureau of Business Research at the University of Texas, Austin, noted that in El Paso the lowest achievement levels in

32. McKay, *El Paso Metropolitan Area Profile;* Bradford Luckingham, *The Urban Southwest* (El Paso: Texas Western Press, 1982).

education are in the poorest areas, which are predominantly Hispanic, a result of Hispanics' concentration in blue-collar occupations. "The persistence of these differences between Mexicans and Americans over three-quarters of a century," Garcia concluded, "provides evidence of active and structural racial discrimination."[33]

A similar critique has been leveled at Houston, a city far to the east of El Paso, and one with a dramatically different ethnic and racial composition. According to the 1980 census, more than 27 percent of the population of the nation's fourth-largest city are black, somewhat less than 20 percent are Hispanic, and a bit more than half are Anglo. These important demographic differences aside, the minority populations of these two cities have fared similarly. Blacks and Hispanics in Houston are poorly housed and are locked into high-density, segregated environs; they are less well educated and earn considerably less income than their Anglo counterparts. Unemployment too follows race and ethnicity—blacks are unemployed at a rate double that of whites. These various discrepancies have been consistent across time. Certainly blacks and Hispanics are generally better educated than they were fifty years ago, and it is no less certain that the black community of Houston is collectively among the richest of the South. But it is also true that despite such advances, the Bayou City's minorities constitute the largest percentage of those employed in the blue-collar and service elements of its economy. And when the Sunbelt boom went bust in the early eighties, the historic gap between rich and poor, white and black (and Hispanic) widened, a widening that was manifest in Dallas, Fort Worth, and San Antonio, indeed the nation as a whole. Structural racism and economic dislocation: these remain the lot of minority peoples in America.[34]

Left here, the story would indeed be dreary. But new social his-

33. Mario T. García, *Desert Immigrants: The Mexicans of El Paso, 1880–1920* (New Haven, Conn.: Yale University Press, 1981), p. 88; Landolt, *Mexican-American Workers in San Antonio,* p. 37; McKay, *El Paso Metropolitan Area Profile,* pp. 4–5; William V. D'Antonio and William Form, *Influentials in Two Border Cities: A Study in Community Decision Making* (South Bend, Ind.: Notre Dame University Press, 1965); James W. Russell, "Class and Nationality Relations in a Texas Border City: The Case of El Paso," *Aztlán* 16, nos. 1–2 (1985).

34. Bullard, *Invisible Houston;* Plaut, *Houston Metropolitan Area Report;* Landolt, *Mexican-American Workers in San Antonio;* Richard J. Harris, "Mexican-American Occupational Attainments in San Antonio," in Johnson et al., *The Politics of San Antonio,*

tory is also charged with a more compelling vision: The victims of economic inequality and social injustice were active agents in the past. This too represents an important alteration in historians' perspectives. Once blacks and other minorities were largely perceived as *passive* victims of white oppression, the classic expression of which is Stanley Elkins's *Slavery*. This earlier emphasis on minorities as dependent variables, as but reflections of white society, only reinforced the social structures of racism. When the civil rights movement challenged these structures, beginning most visibly in the 1940s, so historians were confronted with the need to reevaluate their opinions. Increasingly they have come to acknowledge that despite the obvious difficulties, and often crushing burdens they bear, minorities in the United States have always helped define the contours of their own lives.[35]

The evidence for this is everywhere to be found. Historians have begun to assess the powerful role that the black church has played in the urban environment, for instance, leading one historian to argue that it is *the* "most important institution in the black American community." Not simply a spiritual and religious citadel, it has served, W. Marvin Dulaney has observed, as "a haven in a hostile world. Throughout American history, when society at large denied black Americans basic human, civil, and political rights, the black church was a beacon of hope, guiding black Americans through the mine field of racial oppression." Its centrality made it "a decisive instrument for bringing about social and political change."[36]

In Texas, the black church was crucial to the struggle to end public discrimination and voting disfranchisement. In the 1940s, churches in Houston and Dallas worked to organize voters to support candidates sympathetic to black needs and raised money for NAACP-filled court challenges to segregation. By the 1960s, the black ministry, and its language of brotherhood and nonviolence, lay at the heart of the boycotts, sit-ins, and other demonstrations designed to topple Jim

---

pp. 53–71; Goodman, *San Antonio Metropolitan Area Report;* Tully, *Dallas Metropolitan Area Report;* Renfro and Renfro, *Fort Worth Metropolitan Area Report.*

35. Stanley Elkins, *Black Slavery* (Chicago: University of Chicago Press, 1959); Michael Kammen, *The Past before Us: Contemporary Historical Writing in the United States* (Ithaca, N.Y.: Cornell University Press, 1980).

36. W. Marvin Dulaney, "The Black Church: An Agent of Social and Political Change," *Texas Journal of Ideas, History and Culture* 10 (fall/winter, 1988): 8–10; see also Bullard, *Invisible Houston,* chap. 10.

Crow statutes. Decades before these heady days, however, the church was also intimately involved in local politics. In San Antonio in the 1930s, for example, the churches on the predominantly black east side joined forces with Charles Bellinger, a black entrepreneur, gambler, and savvy politician, and with Hispanics on the west side, to cut a deal with the white-led political machine that controlled City Hall. In exchange for their votes, the east and west sides would receive increased public services — parks, water lines, and street paving among them. This exchange did not offer a profound challenge to the status quo: it was only a temporary alliance on the one hand and, on the other, reinforced the color barrier, since the new public parks were segregated. The alliance nonetheless demonstrates the ways blacks and Hispanics managed to carve a place for themselves in a largely hostile environment, actions that set the stage for larger victories in succeeding years.[37]

Labor organizing, always a tricky proposition in a state long opposed to unions, was another means available to those who sought to counter social inequities. Given the economic realities of Texas, in which blacks and Hispanics constituted the majority of those working in its sweat shops, pecan-shelling establishments, and garment industries, the task of organizing was complicated by intense racial and ethnic bias. And every study of this situation details the oppressive working conditions and the depressing income disparities, recounting too the shocking incidents of violent strike-breaking. Yet within these catalogs of gloom lie tales of small victories.[38]

37. Richard Henderson, *Maury Maverick: A Political Biography* (Austin: University of Texas Press, 1970), pp. 188–93; Landolt, *Mexican-American Workers in San Antonio,* chap. 9, contains other examples of black-Hispanic cooperation and of the early years of the Hispanic civil rights movement.

38. García, *Desert Immigrants,* pp. 89–109; Landolt, *Mexican-American Workers in San Antonio,* chaps. 4–5; Julia Kirk Blackwelder, *Women of the Depression: Caste and Culture in San Antonio, 1919–1939* (College Station: Texas A&M University Press, 1984); David Montejano, *Anglos and Mexicans in the Making of Texas, 1836–1986* (Austin: University of Texas Press, 1987); George Norris Green, *The Establishment in Texas Politics: The Primitive Years, 1938–1957* (Westport, Conn.: Greenwood, 1979); Don E. Carleton, *Red Scare: Right-Wing Hysteria, Fifties Fanaticism and Their Legacy in Texas* (Austin: Texas Monthly Press, 1985); Chandler Davidson, *Biracial Politics: Conflict and Coalition in the Metropolitan South* (Baton Rouge: Louisiana State University Press, 1972); Roger M. Olien and Diane Davids Olien, *Oil Booms: Social Change in Five Texas Towns* (Lincoln: University of Nebraska Press, 1982).

That at least is one lesson to draw from Julia Kirk Blackwelder's thorough study of women in San Antonio during the Great Depression. She admits that most of that era's strikes against the city's industries were failures and confirms that in "subsequent years the problems that had plagued union organizers in the 1930s continued to hamper the union movement." But out of these setbacks also came triumph, however delayed. Leading the strikes against local pecan processors and cigar manufacturers were the poor Hispanic women who were these sweat shops' main labor force. Their position and grievances made for a unique situation: more "women than men participated in protests against low wages and poor working conditions in San Antonio." Emboldened by their strike-making capacities, and making use of their new-found organizational skills, these women joined with non-Hispanic women and CIO organizers to form new labor organizations to challenge a broader range of shops and plants. Such struggles, replicated in El Paso and Crystal City, in Houston, Dallas, and Fort Worth, laid the groundwork for later, more militant challenges to the racial barriers and ethnic discrimination that had held sway for so long in Texas.[39]

The Future Before Us

One of the strengths of new social history is that it has re-fashioned our understanding of the past, in this case an urban past. Through such diverse but interrelated issues as planning and housing, race and ethnicity, politics and government, and the martial metropoli, our vision of the complex process of urbanization in Sunbelt Texas is expanded. Clearly it could be expanded further to include the impact of technology, transportation, and banking systems on, and the role of women and tourism in, the building of Lone Star cities. Indeed, the list of approaches one could employ seems infinite, a telling comment both on the flexibility of new social history and on why it has been so thoroughly embraced: it is the perfect democratic methodology for a pluralistic society.[40]

39. Blackwelder, *Women in the Depression*, pp. 150–51, and chaps. 6 and 8, passim. Landolt, *Mexican-American Workers in San Antonio;* and Montejano, *Anglos and Mexicans in the Making of Texas,* reach similar conclusions about labor organizing in the Rio Grande Valley and in El Paso in the 1960s. On blacks in Houston, see Bullard, *Invisible Houston,* chap. 10.

40. Perry and Watkins, *The Rise of Sunbelt Cities;* Bernard and Rice, *Sunbelt Cities;*

That strength may also be a weakness. One need not endorse Gertrude Himmelfarb's slashing attack on the political conceit and centrifugal quality of recent historiography to concede its fragmentary character. For all its interpretive power, the new social history has not yet generated a fully conceived narrative of the workings of the past. Synthesis is not its forte.[41]

This is strikingly obvious in the study of urban Texas (and no less obvious in the manner in which this essay was itself constructed). Of the state's major metropolitan areas, for example, only Galveston and Houston even have full-fledged urban biographies, a form of historical analysis that has all but disappeared beneath the waves of enthusiasm for newer methodologies. As such, the broad sweep of the histories of Dallas, Fort Worth, and El Paso, of Brownsville, San Antonio, Amarillo, and points in between have yet to be told. One important consequence of this is that specialized studies of men, women, and families, of collective behavior and ethnic culture, tend to operate in a contextual vacuum.[42]

This vacuum is not exclusively methodological in origin. In Texas, at least, it has also grown out of the general inattention to the state's rich urban past. Until very recently, in fact, there simply has not been enough research conducted to even hope to speak *of* an urban historiography; and it remains true that far more work needs to be done on a broad array of issues before we can construct a plausible picture of Texas urbanism. And there will always be gaps in our knowledge, thanks to the lamentable and cavalier attitude city governments have displayed toward public records, many of which have simply disappeared. Such invaluable primary source materials are impossible to replace, severely limiting future scholars' abilities to reconstruct the past.[43]

Mohl, *The Making of Urban America;* all testify to the variety of approaches possible in Sunbelt history. Michael Frisch, "American Urban History as an Example of Recent Historiography," *History and Theory* 18, no. 3 (1979): 350–77.

41. Gertrude Himmelfarb, "Denigrating the Rule of Reason: The 'New History' Goes Bottom Up," *Harper's* (Apr., 1984): 84–90; Thomas Bender, "Wholes and Parts: The Need for Synthesis in American History," *Journal of American History* 73 (June, 1986): 120–36; Eric Monkkonen, "The Dangers of Synthesis," *American Historical Review* 91 (Dec., 1986): 1146–57.

42. David McComb, *Galveston* (Austin: University of Texas Press, 1986); David McComb, *Houston.*

43. Abbott, *A New Urban America,* p. 301; Carleton, *Red Scare,* p. 317, makes simi-

These frustrations aside, there remains much that can be said, if only tentatively, about the present state and future directions of Texas urban history. As to the present, a couple of points need to be raised. The state's pattern of urbanization, for example, is similar to that which has governed the growth of cities throughout the United States. True, the United States was officially proclaimed an urban society by 1920, and Texas could not lay claim to the status until sometime between the 1940 and 1950 censuses. But this chronological lag should not mask the larger parallels. In matters of economic diversification and the expansion of public services, in the deconcentration of population to outlying residential tracts, and in the still rigidly segregated layout of metropolitan centers, Texas is much like California or Illinois or New York. This, it seems, is nothing new. As historian Lawrence Larsen has observed, little "was unique or new about the young cities of the west" in the late nineteenth century either; these frontier communities were simply "carbon copies of those constructed earlier in the older parts of the country."[44]

But they were and remain imperfect copies, as differences in the timing and pace of urbanization demonstrate. Moreover, the siting of Texas cities, which so confused Stephen Brook, *is* peculiar: neither navigable rivers nor transportation routes fully explain their placement, as they do so many other cities in American history. More contemporary differences also exist. The automobile has had a stronger influence on the spatial design of Houston and San Antonio than it has had on Boston and New York, for which the railroad was of paramount importance. This automobile dependency has led in turn to a wider dispersal of peoples, lower population density, and fewer multifamily dwellings, traits that link Texas more closely to other, newer southwestern cities. Through annexation, Texas has also been able to corral suburbanization, thus stalling the flight of tax monies that has been the death knell of northeastern and midwestern communities. And then there have been the periodic booms and busts that seem endemic to the state's oil and gas economy of the twentieth century.

---

lar points about recent Houston history as has Robert Fisher, University of Houston (Downtown), in conversations with me. The records of the GGL, arguably the single most important political organization in San Antonio's long history, were destroyed because no local repository recognized their historical significance.

44. Lawrence Larsen, *The Urban West and the End of the Frontier* (Lawrence: Regents Press of Kansas, 1978), p. ix.

They have contributed greatly to the expansion and contraction of
the economic power of Dallas, Houston, and the Permian Basin cities,
contributing as well to the growing disparities between the rich and
poor. Few other urban communities have experienced such cycles for
so sustained a period of time.[45]

Finally, there is the dramatic mass movement of northern Americans to the Sunbelt, a shift that the federal government facilitated with
its massive outlay of monies to the region during and subsequent to
World War II. It has been one of the most important migrations in
recent American history, a move from which the state of Texas has
profited mightily and by which its peoples and cities were forever transformed.

There is no little irony in this list of differences between the urban experiences of Texas and the northeastern and midwestern states.
The Sunbelt may have initially illuminated and intensified regional
discrepancies, but now, in the postboom era, these have begun to diminish, as the once glittering urban magnets are faced with declining
central cities, a slow rise in the number of multifamily homes and,
despite annexation efforts, a buildup of population beyond the metropolitan government's control. The future for Sunbelt Texas looks much
like the urban East's past.[46]

The infatuation with Sunbelt glitz, then, is simply that: an infatuation. This is particularly true when one recognizes that the full range
of the state's urban heritage has been ignored in the rush to succumb
to what one critic has labeled the "Sunbelt's snow job." Now perhaps
we can begin to build a historical framework for the study of urban
Texas in which the Sunbelt era will constitute only one, albeit an important, element. What follows is a first step in that direction.[47]

Any such framework must be grounded both in theory and historical context, the two playing off of each other. For the former, the
work of David Goldfield and other historians, which emphasizes a regional perspective, seems well suited to the fluid character of Texas
urbanism. These observers argue that one must determine how towns

45. Olien and Olien, *Oil Booms,* a study of the Permian Basin oil fields, is a
good introduction to the impact these cycles have had on some Texas cities.

46. Steven C. Ballard and Thomas E. James, eds., *The Future of the Sunbelt,* chaps.
9–10; Abbott, *A New Urban America,* pp. 260–61.

47. George B. Tindall, "The Sunbelt Snow Job," *Houston Review* 1 (spring, 1979):
3–13.

and cities function within the regional system of which they are a part, chart the timing and nature of regional development, and then assess the affected communities' responses to economic and social change. This analytical approach presumes as well that other factors — entrepreneurial skill, cultural receptivity to technological innovation, and government intervention among others — are crucial. Finally, regionalism deliberately acknowledges the active role that human beings, collectively and individually, play in the construction of social reality. In it, a wide range of historical methodologies and perspectives are fused together.[48]

The result, in the context of postindependence Texas history, is a three-stage chronology that focuses primarily on the major urban centers. The formative period runs between 1836 and the late 1880s. It was during this fifty-year period that San Antonio broke out of its status as an imperial outpost, a time when Dallas and Houston were born. The three compact cities generally operated independently of each other (a function of the vast distances between them), establishing their commercial bases and concentrating on bringing the surrounding hinterlands under control. The products and byproducts of these — agriculture and livestock for San Antonio and Dallas, cotton and later lumber for Houston and Galveston — were the economic bases that gave shape to these cities' present structure and design; from them, future growth would ensue.[49]

The future came with the railroad, as does the second stage in Texas urbanization, dating from the 1880s to 1930. That nineteenth-

---

48. David Goldfield, *Cottonfields and Skyscrapers: Southern City and Region, 1607–1908* (Baton Rouge: Louisiana State University Press, 1982); David Goldfield, "The New Regionalism," *Journal of Urban History* 10 (Feb., 1984): 171–86; Burton W. Folsom, *Urban Capitalists: Entrepreneurs and City Growth in Pennsylvania's Lackawanna and Lehigh Regions, 1800–1920* (Baltimore, Md.: Johns Hopkins University Press, 1981); Allan Pred, *Urban Growth and City-Systems in the U.S., 1840–1860* (Cambridge, Mass.: MIT Press, 1980); Miller and Johnson, "The Rise of Urban Texas."

49. Miller and Johnson, "The Rise of Urban Texas"; Elmer H. Johnson, *The Basis of the Commercial and Industrial Development of Texas: A Study of the Regional Development of Texas Resources,* Bureau of Business Research, University of Texas, Research Monograph no. 9 (Austin: Bureau of Business Research, University of Texas, 1933). This section was written before I read Christopher S. Davies, Life at the Edge: Urban and Industrial Evolution of Texas, Frontier Wilderness — Frontier Space," *SHQ* 89 (Apr., 1986): 443–554, which proposes some of the same arguments; our periodization and emphases within them differ, however.

century engine of progress, which arrived first in Houston before the Civil War and last in San Antonio in 1877, pulled the major urban areas together, changing their internal and external civic, economic, and political relations. Once a statewide transportation network was set in place in the late 1890s, the cities competed with one another for dominance of the larger Texas region, a competition with significant results. Using population as one indicator of success, San Antonio, Dallas, and Houston jockeyed for power until the 1920s when Houston, on the basis of the ship channel, petroleum discoveries, and other commercial ventures, became the preeminent urban center of the Southwest.[50]

The internal structures of the major urban areas were also altered during this second period. It was then that the first suburbs appeared, indicating the spread of population and the establishment of increasingly segregated communities; then that industrialization took hold of portions of local economies, changing production methods, labor relations, and the environment. The modern city had arrived in Texas.

Modernity came with a rush in the third and final stage, beginning in the 1930s and gathering force during and immediately after World War II. Each city experienced rapid population increases and explosive and outward residential development that drew upon and extended highway construction; each experienced strains on public services and the continued delineation of racial and ethnic discrimination in their spatial organizations. Even as each struggled to cope with these consequences of rapid metropolitan growth, they also endeavored to capitalize on their resource bases to garner a greater share of Sunbelt prosperity.

The close of this third period may be upon us, marked by the depression of the early 1980s, from which the state's urban areas have yet to fully recover. Moreover, the aftershocks of the crash have torn apart the urban banking system, changing the ways cities do business, quite possibly establishing a more obvious and formal dependence on northern financial centers and federal grants. Under revision, too, is the concept of city limits: there has been a gradual development of megalopoli, stretching between Dallas and Fort Worth, Houston and Galveston, and more gradually still between San Antonio and

50. Platt, *City Building in the New South*, chap. 8.

Austin; this may further indicate that a new level, a fourth stage in urbanization has been reached.[51]

This projection, as with every other element of this proposed framework, needs careful testing and refining, if not outright dismantling. Whatever form this evaluation takes, however, it cannot but help to deepen our sense of the urban texture in which ever larger numbers of Texans live. But that evaluation cannot happen unless and until the urban dimension of the Lone Star past receives the same painstaking excavation that has been undertaken on that nineteenth-century urban shrine of frontier liberty, the Alamo.

51. Recent estimates of urban populations in Texas are found in the *San Antonio Express,* Sept. 30, 1988, p. 1E.

❧ Flight from Modernity:

The Economic History of Texas since 1845

Walter L. Buenger

Much of the writing on Texas has been a flight from modernity: an attempt to recapture, defend, and celebrate a more romantic, primitive, and pristine past. Nowhere has this trend been more pervasive than in economic histories of the state. Shunning the complex for the simple, concentrating narrowly on the internal development of one firm or one industry, writers have lauded their heroic pioneer founders and builders. They have focused on brief and compelling epochs alleged to have changed the course of history. While filled with interesting and useful information these works include few links to the world outside the firm or industry and almost no analytical framework for evaluating long-term changes in the state's economy. Instead, growth and the profits of growth have been extolled as marks of success. The move into modern times that growth and wealth wrought has been ignored or deplored.[1]

Of course, there have been exceptions to this flight from modernity. John Stricklin Spratt posited that the changes in the Texas economy and in society that became apparent after the discovery of vast quantities of oil began with the establishment of a market economy in the last quarter of the nineteenth century. Instead of celebrating a romantic premarket economy, Spratt offered an analytical framework for understanding development. Yet by focusing on a brief period of time he obscured evidence of an extensive market economy

---

1. Among the more obvious examples of this pattern are T. R. Fehrenbach, *Lone Star: A History of Texas and Texans* (New York: Macmillan, 1968); Carl Coke Rister, *Oil! Titan of the Southwest* (Norman: University of Oklahoma Press, 1949); J. Evetts Haley, *The XIT Ranch of Texas, and the Early Days of Llano Estacado* (Chicago: Lakeside, 1929).

before 1875 and a semisubsistence economy in some areas of the state after 1901. Growth and decay occurred apace, not in tidy time frames.[2]

The purpose of this essay then is to explore the literature on the economic history of Texas. This literature falls into two rough categories: works devoted to industries, specific firms, and labor, and works devoted to particular epochs. Within both rough categories romanticism and a confining focus emerge as pervasive characteristics. Of course other motifs, such as a fascination with the colonial nature of the Texas economy, exist. This fascination, though, often springs from a desire to explain the decline of the firm, industry, or state from a "golden age." Thus colonialists become the villains in the melodrama. This fascination with a golden age and narrow focus on specific time slots has been self-limiting, for it has caused historians to neglect portions of the economic history of the state and to avoid advancing theories to explain long-running change. Understandably, the social milieu from which historians have emerged and the methods and philosophies in vogue within the historical profession helped solidify these limits. Still, past theories should not hamstring historians' future prospects.[3]

Industries, Firms, and Labor

Flights from modernity show up in the most concentrated dosages in popular histories such as T. R. Fehrenbach's *Lone Star* and novels like George Sessions Perry's *Hold Autumn in Your Hand.*[4] Nonetheless, almost every work done since the Great Depression on Texas industries, firms, and labor displays some evidence of distaste with the path of progress or a sentimental fondness for a long-past golden age. The nature of the industry under review and the amount of borrowing or comparison with other industries in other states seems to limit romanticism but not exclude it. Likewise, focusing on the inter-

2. John S. Spratt, *The Road to Spindletop: Economic Change in Texas, 1875–1901* (Dallas: Southern Methodist University Press, 1955).

3. For an overview of Texas history and comment on its historiography see Christopher S. Davies, "Life at the Edge: Urban and Industrial Evolution of Texas, Frontier Wilderness — Frontier Space, 1836–1896," *Southwestern Historical Quarterly (SHQ)* 89 (Apr., 1986): 443–554. Farmers and farming are explored more fully in "Agrarian Texas," by Robert A. Calvert, this volume.

4. George Sessions Perry, *Hold Autumn in Your Hand* (New York: Viking, 1941).

nal workings of the firms might diminish musings about a golden age for society but encourage emphasis on heroic pioneers.

Nostalgia drives studies of the cotton and livestock industries in particular. Perhaps this is to be expected of the oldest primary industries in the state. Of course, various other concerns have been bound up with nostalgia. The most important of them have been the erosion of traditional communities with the introduction of modern transportation and organization of the industry; an often contradictory attitude toward the relationship between man and machine; and outrage at the exploitation of labor. Important questions about the source of innovation are largely ignored.

Works by J. Frank Dobie, J. Evetts Haley, Tom Lea, and to some extent Walter Prescott Webb all convey the impression that life was somehow better on the open range of the nineteenth century when customs handed down from the Spanish blended with the energies of Anglo-Saxons to produce the flowering of a cattlemen's civilization.[5] Despite the work of Terry Jordan on the southern origins of ranching traditions, emphasis on the contributions of the romantic Spanish continues. Likewise even such fine studies of the internal development of the firm as those by William Curry Holden and Lester Fields Sheffy emphasize the heroic contributions of the patriarch and founder and lament the loss of local control of the company.[6]

5. On Dobie see Don Graham, "J. Frank Dobie: A Reappraisal," *SHQ* 92 (July, 1988): 1–15. Works by J. Evetts Haley include: *Charles Goodnight* (Boston: Houghton Mifflin, 1936); *Charles Schreiner, General Merchandise: The Story of a Country Store* (Austin: Texas State Historical Association, 1944); *The XIT Ranch; George W. Littlefield, Texan* (Norman: University of Oklahoma Press, 1943). Also see Tom Lea, *The King Ranch,* 2 vols. (Boston: Little, Brown, 1957); Walter Prescott Webb, *The Great Plains* (Boston: Ginn, 1931).

6. On the southern versus Spanish origins of ranching, see Terry G. Jordan, *Trails to Texas: Southern Roots of Western Cattle Ranching* (Lincoln: University of Nebraska Press, 1981); Paul Carlson, "The Texas Background—Spanish or American?" *West Texas Historical Association Year Book* (*WTHAYB*) 52 (1976): 61–70; John D. W. Guice, "Cattle Raisers of the Old Southwest: A Reinterpretation," *Western Historical Quarterly* 8 (Apr., 1977): 167–89; Jack Jackson, *Los Mesteños: Spanish Ranching in Texas, 1721–1821* (College Station: Texas A&M University Press, 1986); Sandra L. Myres, "The Ranching Frontier: Spanish Institutional Backgrounds of the Plains Cattle Industry," in *Essays on the American West,* ed. Harold M. Hollingsworth and Sandra L. Myres (Austin: University of Texas Press, 1969), pp. 19–39. For ranch histories, see William Curry Holden, *The Spur Ranch: A Study of the Inclosed Ranch Phase of the Cattle Industry in Texas* (Boston: Christopher, 1934); William Curry Holden, *The Espuela Land and Cattle Company: A*

Cotton has had its own purveyors of a golden age, but it has been far more difficult to obscure the sweat and tears inherent in the industry. Abigail Curlee Holbrook pointed to the heroic efforts of the pioneers of antebellum days. Lamar Fleming insisted that things were golden between the triumph of the U.S. financial system in World War I and the Smoot-Hawley Tariff of 1930. Authors readily acknowledge the primitive nature of the cotton industry before the 1940s, but some also convey a fascination for this primitiveness. Unlike cattle, cotton's golden age was not pristine, but its very brutishness seems to fascinate.[7]

Technological change or the advance of a market system made possible through improved transportation have been the usual, but not always explicit, explanations for the decline of a golden age or for any major economic change. In 1930 Holden and R. D. Holt examined the impact of improved transportation and fencing in the cattle industry. Decades later Jimmy H. Skaggs and E. C. Barksdale examined cattle trailing and meat packing with an eye for technological change. Recently J'Nell Pate has related how the changes in transportation and the market system caused the rise and fall of the Fort Worth Stockyards.[8] The marketing and processing of cotton and the changes

Study of a Foreign-Owned Ranch in Texas (Austin: Texas State Historical Association, 1970); Lester Fields Sheffy, *The Francklyn Land and Cattle Company: A Panhandle Enterprise, 1882–1957* (Austin: University of Texas Press, 1963); Lester Fields Sheffy, *The Life and Times of Timothy Dwight Hobart, 1855–1953* (Canyon, Tex.: Panhandle-Plains Historical Society, 1950). Also see A. Ray Stephens, *The Taft Ranch: A Texas Principality* (Austin: University of Texas Press, 1964).

7. Abigail Curlee Holbrook, "Cotton Marketing in Antebellum Texas," *SHQ* 73 (Apr., 1970): 456–78; Lamar Fleming, Jr., *Growth of the Business of Anderson, Clayton & Co.,* ed. James A. Tinsley (Houston: Texas Gulf Coast Historical Association, 1966); Col. William B. Bates, *Monroe D. Anderson: His Life and Legacy* (Houston: Texas Gulf Coast Historical Association, 1957); Ellen Clayton Garwood, *Will Clayton: A Short Biography* (Austin: University of Texas Press, 1958).

8. J'Nell L. Pate, *Livestock Legacy: The Fort Worth Stockyards, 1887–1987* (College Station: Texas A&M University Press, 1988); Jimmy M. Skaggs, *The Cattle Trailing Industry: Between Supply and Demand, 1868–1890* (Lawrence: University of Kansas Press, 1973); Jimmy M. Skaggs, *Prime Cut: Livestock Raising and Meatpacking in the United States, 1607–1983* (College Station: Texas A&M University Press, 1986); E. C. Barksdale, *The Meat Packers Come to Texas* (Austin: Bureau of Business Research, University of Texas, 1959; William Curry Holden, "The Problem of Maintaining the Solid Range on the Spur Ranch," *SHQ* 34 (July, 1930): 1–19; R. D. Holt, "The Introduction of Barbed Wire into Texas and the Fence Cutting War," *WTHAYB* 6 (1930): 65–79.

created by new technology have also drawn the attention of historians. In general their work deserves more widespread use. For example, L. Tuffly Ellis has given a detailed account of the evolution of the post–Civil War cotton trade. Lamar Fleming and others have highlighted changes in transportation and technology. Only the more general work by Harold D. Woodman is widely cited.[9]

Many studies of ranching and cotton indicate the advantages of greater size and more extensive organization. Man gave way to machine, the individual to the corporation. Greater size and scale demanded greater financial strength. Oftentimes the money to expand in cotton or cattle came from Europe or the Northeast. This in turn has raised the question of the growing dependence of Texas on the outside world — the loss of cherished self-reliance. Troubled by the implications of the loss of independence, authors have dealt in depth with colonialism and the implication of a market economy for cotton farmers. Robert Snyder, for example, examined the collapse of the 1931 cotton market and perforce often focused on Texas. He described this crisis as "a tragic last gasp by the family farmer."[10]

Colonialism has been of far less concern for writers on the livestock industry. For example, Pate missed an excellent opportunity to discuss the implications of outside ownership on the Fort Worth Stockyards. Did it matter that the stockyards were controlled by the Swift and Armour trusts? Likewise, Steffy gives scant space to the long-term impact of outside ownership. Instead, non-Texas owners tend to be viewed as white knights who brought progress to a capital-scarce re-

9. L. Tuffly Ellis, "The Texas Cotton Compress Industry: A History," Ph.D. diss., University of Texas, Austin, 1964; L. Tuffly Ellis, "The Revolutionizing of the Texas Cotton Trade, 1866–1885," *SHQ* 73 (Apr., 1970): 478–508; Fleming, *Anderson, Clayton;* Harold D. Woodman, *King Cotton and His Retainers: Financing and Marketing the Cotton Crop of the South, 1800–1925* (Lexington: University of Kentucky Press, 1968). See also Raymond E. White, "Cotton Ginning in Texas to 1861," *SHQ* 61 (Oct., 1957): 257–69; Raymond E. White, "The Texas Cotton Ginning Industry, 1860–1900," *Texana* 5 (winter, 1967): 344–45; Wilman H. Droze, "Rise of the Cotton Mill Industry in Texas, 1850–1933," *Cotton History Review* 2 (1961): 71–84.

10. Robert E. Snyder, *Cotton Crisis* (Chapel Hill: University of North Carolina Press, 1984), p. 135; Holden, *The Espuela Land and Cattle Company;* Sheffy, *Francklyn Land and Cattle Company;* Richard Graham, "The Investment Boom in British-Texan Cattle Companies, 1880–1885," *Business History Review* 34 (winter, 1960): 421–45; J. Fred Rippy, "British Investment in Texas Lands and Livestock," *SHQ* 58 (Jan., 1955): 331–41; Fleming, *Anderson, Clayton.*

gion. If there are villains in such works it is labor, not the community-wrenching capitalists.[11]

When writing of the decay of traditional communities or the impact of an expanded market, machines often seem the enemy of man. Growth in scale and complexity of organization increased the substitution of machines for human labor. That labor turned from doing a variety of tasks to one repetitive endeavor. It moved from the relative independence of country life to the dependence of an urban setting.[12] By the 1950s, the bond between land and man that so long typified Texas and the rest of the South was broken. The cities held out future promise of a higher standard of living, but the type of economic activity was to be far different. The work of Skaggs and Pate on the livestock and meatpacking industry are particularly telling concerning the role of cities in the evolution of that industry.[13]

Doubtless many of those laboring in the earth as cotton farmers or above the earth as cowboys were glad to trade country for city life. The history of labor, particularly black or Mexican labor, has been far from romantic. Instead the persistent theme since the 1930s has been exploitation of labor. Of interest is Randolph B. Campbell's new work on slavery in Texas. Alwyn Barr and Lawrence D. Rice have carried the story beyond the Civil War. Bob McKay gives another dimension to the impact of governmental regulations. Obviously much of the pain of dislocation and disruption of the cotton industry was felt by blacks and Mexicans. Joe Frantz has painted a more realistic image of the cowboy, but more needs to be done on the workers instead of the owners. If in these works there is a sense of regret for paths not taken there is also a bitterness for the path taken.[14]

11. Pate, *Livestock Legacy;* Sheffy, *Francklyn Land & Cattle Company.* One exception to this trend is Gene M. Gressley, *Bankers and Cattlemen* (New York: Knopf, 1966).

12. This topic has been treated for the South as a whole in Pete Daniel, *Breaking the Land: The Transformation of Cotton, Tobacco, and Rice Cultures since 1880* (Urbana: University of Illinois Press, 1985); Jack Temple Kirby, *Rural Worlds Lost: The American South, 1920–1960* (Baton Rouge: Louisiana State University Press, 1987); Gilbert C. Fite, *Cotton Fields No More: Southern Agriculture, 1865–1980* (Lexington: University of Kentucky Press, 1984).

13. Skaggs, *The Cattle Trailing Industry;* Skaggs, *Prime Cut;* Pate, *Livestock Legacy.* Also see David Galenson, "The Profitability of the Long Drive," *Agricultural History* (*AH*) 51 (Oct., 1977): 737–58.

14. Randolph B. Campbell, *An Empire for Slavery: The Peculiar Institution in Texas, 1821–1865* (Baton Rouge: Louisiana State University Press, 1989); Alwyn Barr, *Black*

Some of the paths taken in the cotton and ranching industries need further study. The relationship of sheep and goat ranching to cattle ranching remains neglected despite Paul Carlson and Douglas Barnett's recent efforts. Almost nothing has been written about other livestock, such as hogs.[15] Analyses of the role of the entrepreneur and innovator also have been slighted. Perhaps the work of Harwood Hinton on John Chisum will supplement a somewhat meager literature. Chisum seems to have been more a cattle broker or factor than a traditional rancher. He bought and sold others' cattle and continually moved from one area to another. Related questions about innovation require answers. Why did changes in marketing and the introduction of new products based upon Texas staples usually come from outsiders? What was the role of culture in the economy? What was the role of government at all levels? Unfortunately, a literature preoccupied with the heroic founders and builders has seldom had room for such analysis.[16]

Texans (Austin: Jenkins, 1973); Lawrence D. Rice, *The Negro in Texas, 1847–1900* (Baton Rouge: Louisiana State University Press, 1971); Bob McKay, "The Texas Cotton Acreage Control Law of 1931 and Mexican Repatriation," *WTHAYB* 59 (1983): 143–55; Karl E. Ashburn, "The Texas Cotton Acreage Control Law of 1931–1932," *SHQ* 61 (July, 1957): 116–24; Karl E. Ashburn, "Slavery and Cotton Production in Texas," *Southwestern Social Science Quarterly* 14 (Dec., 1933): 257–71; Cordia Sloan Duke and Joe B. Frantz, *6,000 Miles of Fence: Life on the XIT Ranch of Texas* (Austin: University of Texas Press, 1961).

15. Douglas E. Barnett, "Angora Goats in Texas: Agricultural Innovation on the Edwards Plateau, 1858–1900," *SHQ* 90 (Apr., 1987): 347–72; Douglas E. Barnett, "Mohair in Texas: Livestock Experimentation on the Edwards Plateau," M.A. thesis, University of Texas, Austin, 1983; Paul H. Carlson, *Texas Woollybacks: The Range Sheep and Goat Industry* (College Station: Texas A&M University Press, 1982); Paul H. Carlson, "Bankers and Sheepherders in West Texas," *WTHAYB* 61 (1985): 5–14; E. Karl Alf, "George Wilkins Kendall and the West Texas Sheep Industry," *WTHAYB* 58 (1982): 67–76; Winifred Kupper, *The Golden Hoof: The Story of Sheep of the Southwest* (New York: Knopf, 1945); Arnoldo De León, "Los Tasinques and the Sheep Shearers' Union of North America: A Strike in West Texas, 1934," *WTHAYB* 55 (1979): 3–16; Paul H. Carlson, "Sheepherders and Cowboys: A Comparison of Life-Styles in West Texas," *WTHAYB* 58 (1982): 19–28. On hogs, see Pate, *Livestock Legacy*, pp. 77–88.

16. For examples of missed opportunities for discussion of the source of entrepreneurship and innovation see Pate, *Livestock Legacy;* Bates, *Monroe D. Anderson;* Garwood, *Will Clayton;* Sylvia Stallings Morris, ed., *William Marsh Rice and His Institute: A Biographical Study* (Houston: Rice University Studies, 1972). More promising are Harold Hyman, *Oleander Odyssey: The Kempners of Galveston, Texas, 1854–1980s* (College Station: Texas A&M University Press, 1990); Harwood Hinton, *John Chisum* (forthcoming).

Romanticism and focus on a golden age are also common in studies of lumber and petroleum, which at the turn of the century joined cotton and cattle as dominant partners in the economy. Subthemes vary, however. In addition to the impact of technology on traditional communities and the relationship of man to machine, greater attention has been given to the colonial nature of the Texas economy brought about by the expansion of these two industries. Government's role is given increased emphasis. Labor exploitation in a resource-based economy remains a major concern.

Heroic pioneers walk the pages of histories of the oil industry with unabashed frequency. Titles such as *Oil! Titan of the Southwest* suggest this larger-than-life quality. Even industry regulators come in for their share of praise in *Three Stars for the Colonel.* Marquis James does for the founders of Texaco what he did for Sam Houston: creates an American legend. Such legends are particularly common in works concerning Spindletop and other early oil fields.[17] Despite the work of Roger and Diana Olien, the "blood and mud" school still dominates much of the literature on early oil pioneers. Indeed, even their work on wildcatters has some of the characteristics of hero worship. The work of C. A. Warner and the photographic collections of Walter Rundell, Jr., do add realism.[18]

The intensity of this romantic attachment has obscured the importance of other extractive commodities such as sulfur and other fa-

17. James A. Clark and Michael Halbouty, *Spindletop* (New York: Random House, 1952); James A. Clark, *Three Stars for the Colonel* (New York: Random House, 1954); Marquis James, *The Texaco Story: The First Fifty Years* (New York: Texas Co., 1953); Rister, *Oil! Titan of the Southwest*. Others that stress the epic rise of the firm or industry include Richard R. Moore, *West Texas after the Discovery of Oil: A Modern Frontier* (Austin: Jenkins, 1971); Samuel D. Myres, *The Permian Basin: Petroleum Empire of the Southwest,* 2 vols. (El Paso, Tex.: Permian, 1973, 1977). For additional titles see Walter Rundell, Jr., "Texas Petroleum History: A Selective Annotated Bibliography," *SHQ* 67 (Oct., 1967): 267–78.

18. Roger Olien and Diana Olien, *Wildcatters: Texas Independent Oilmen* (Austin: Texas Monthly Press, 1984); Roger M. Olien and Diana Olien, *Oil Booms: Social Change in Five Texas Towns* (Lincoln: University of Nebraska Press, 1982); C. A. Warner, "The Oil Industry in Texas since Pearl Harbor," *SHQ* 61 (Jan., 1958): 327–40; C. A. Warner, *Texas Oil and Gas since 1543* (Houston: Gulf Publishing, 1939); Walter Rundell, Jr., *Early Texas Oil Photographic History, 1866–1936* (College Station: Texas A&M University Press, 1977); Walter Rundell, Jr., *Oil in West Texas and New Mexico: A Pictorial History of the Permian Basin* (College Station: Texas A&M University Press, 1982).

cets of the petroleum industry such as natural gas and promoted the falsehood that Texas has a one-dimensional economy based upon oil. Older studies of natural gas and sulfur do exist, but they are seldom clearly focused on Texas. More promising are recently initiated studies of the natural gas industry and its relationship to insurance, banking, and law firms. Pipeline construction and financing has also received increased attention. It will probably be some time, however, before the romance of oil recedes from the public imagination.[19]

Studies of the lumber industry are not always couched in terms of a romantic epic, but the intrepid pioneers often get more praise than historians of labor would judge to be warranted. The biography of John Henry Kirby and the history of W. T. Carter and Brother are both filled with praise for their subjects. Again, even titles such as *Sawdust Empire* suggest the conceptualization of an industry in romantic terms.[20]

Such romanticism has been tempered by the treatment of both petroleum and lumber in more abstract terms. The focus has been on changing technology and the evolution of the industry. The impact on society in general has been another theme. For example, Harold Platt recently traced the relationship between energy and urban growth by comparing Houston and Chicago. Other works in this category include the study of the Gulf Coast refining region by Joseph A. Pratt, Edward W. Constant's study of the relationship between technology and regulation, and Henrietta Larson and Kenneth Porter's

19. R. H. Montgomery, *The Brimstone Game* (Austin: Privately printed, 1949); Alfred M. Leeston, John A. Crichton, and John C. Jacobs, *The Dynamic Natural Gas Industry: The Development of an American Industry* (Norman: University of Oklahoma Press, 1963); Richard W. Hooley, *Financing the Natural Gas Industry: The Role of Life Insurance Investment Policies* (New York: Columbia University Press, 1961); M. Elizabeth Sanders, *The Regulation of Natural Gas: Policy and Politics, 1938–1978* (Philadelphia: Temple University Press, 1981). Work in progress includes Don E. Carleton, "Fueling the Machines of War: J. R. Parten and the Oil Transportation Crisis of 1942–1944"; Chris J. Castaneda, "Politics, Power, and Money: Buying the Big and Little Inch Pipelines"; Joseph A. Pratt, "The Texas Eastern Transmission Corporation and the Post-War Development of the Big and Little Inch Pipelines," all given at the annual meeting of the Texas State Historical Association, Mar. 2, 1990.

20. Mary Lasswell, *John Henry Kirby: Prince of the Pines* (Austin: Encino, 1967); Robert S. Maxwell and Robert D. Baker, *Sawdust Empire: The Texas Lumber Industry, 1830–1940* (College Station: Texas A&M University Press, 1983); J. Lester Jones, *W. T. Carter & Bro.* (Houston: Privately printed, 1978).

history of Humble.[21] John O. King has also dealt extensively with the development of both the petroleum and lumber industries, but has maintained the human story that attracts the interest of those outside the academy. Robert Maxwell's work at times also bridges the gap between the evolution of the industry and biography.[22]

Studies of heroic pioneers are further tempered by the relatively high number of studies of labor in the lumber and petroleum industries. Perhaps this has been because labor unions have been most successful in petroleum and labor exploitation most severe in lumber. For whatever reason, works by Ruth Allen, Pratt, James C. Maroney, and others have dealt sympathetically with labor in the petroleum industry. George T. Morgan and Allen have written extensively on lumber workers.[23]

Labor unions have often been either positively or negatively affected by government, and the role of government has received con-

21. Harold L. Platt, "Energy and Urban Growth: A Comparison of Houston and Chicago," *SHQ* 91 (July, 1987): 1–18; Henrietta Larson and Kenneth Porter, *History of the Humble Oil and Refining Company: A Study in Industrial Growth* (New York: Harper and Row, 1959); Joseph A. Pratt, *The Growth of a Refining Region* (Greenwich, Conn.: JAI Press, 1980); Edward W. Constant II, "Cause or Consequence: Science, Technology, and Regulatory Change in the Oil Business in Texas, 1930–1975," *Technology and Culture* 30 (Apr., 1989): 426–55. Also see Arthur M. Johnson, "The Early Texas Oil Industry: Pipelines and the Birth of an Integrated Oil Industry, 1901–1911," *Journal of Southern History* (*JSH* 32 (Nov., 1966): 516–28.

22. John O. King, *Early History of the Houston Oil Company of Texas, 1901–1908* (Houston: Texas Gulf Coast Historical Association, 1959); John O. King, *Joseph Stephen Cullinan: A Study of Leadership in the Texas Petroleum Industry, 1897–1937* (Nashville: Vanderbilt University Press, 1970); Robert S. Maxwell, "Lumbermen of the East Texas Frontier," *Journal of Forest History* 9 (Apr., 1965): 12–16; Robert S. Maxwell, "One Man's Legacy: W. Goodrich Jones and Texas Conservation," *SHQ* 77 (Jan., 1974): 355–80; Robert S. Maxwell, "The Pines of Texas: A Study in Lumbering and Public Policy," *East Texas Historical Journal* (*ETHJ*) 2 (Oct., 1962): 77–86.

23. Ruth A. Allen, *Chapters in the History of Organized Labor in Texas* (Austin: University of Texas Publications, 1941); James C. Maroney, "The Texas-Louisiana Oil Field Strike," *Essays in Southern Labor History*, ed. Gary M. Fink and Merl E. Reed (Westport, Conn.: Greenwood, 1977); Clyde Johnson, "CIO Oil Workers' Organizing Campaign in Texas, 1942–1943," in Fink and Reed, *Essays in Southern Labor History;* F. Ray Marshall, "Independent Unions in the Gulf Coast Petroleum Refining Industry—The Esso Experience," *Labor Law Journal* 12 (Sept., 1961): 823–40; George T. Morgan, Jr., "No Compromise—No Recognition: John Henry Kirby, the Southern Pine Operators Association, and Unionism in the Piney Woods, 1906–1916," *Labor History* 10 (spring, 1969): 193–204; George T. Morgan, Jr., "The Gospel of Wealth Goes

siderable attention in studies of petroleum and lumber. This has been most true in the areas of conservation and regulation of production. Marilyn D. Rhinehart has traced the relationship of forestry and politics in Texas from 1915 to 1921. Robert Maxwell and James W. Martin have recounted the story of conservation in the timber industry. David Prindle has written of regulation and conservation in the petroleum industry. William R. Childs has begun a more extensive and systematic examination of regulation. The role of government runs through the work of Pratt and John G. Clark.[24]

State and local governments have often defended regional interests from colonial forces. State agencies such as the Texas Railroad Commission, the Forest Service, trade associations, and industry leaders have forged an alliance to battle for their own and the state's interest. These state agencies and industry leaders have repeatedly turned to the Texas legislature and Texas court systems for aid. They have responded in a variety of ways, but particularly important for oil and lumber have been its antimonopoly, conservation, and bankruptcy laws. Although some good work has been done, the means and ends of government regulation deserve further exploration.[25]

Another industry closely tied to government as well as to all other

South: John Henry Kirby and Labor's Struggle for Self-Determination, 1901–1916," *SHQ* 75 (Oct., 1971): 186–97; Ruth A. Allen, *East Texas Lumber Workers: An Economic and Social Picture, 1870–1950* (Austin: University of Texas Press, 1961).

24. Robert S. Maxwell and James W. Martin, *Forest Conservation in Texas, 1880–1940*, School of Forestry Bulletin no. 20 (Nacogdoches, Tex.: Stephen F. Austin State University, 1970); Marilyn D. Rhinehart, "Forestry and Politics in Texas, 1915–1921," *ETHJ* 20, no. 2 (1982): 6–17; John G. Clark, *Energy and the Federal Government: Fossil Fuel Policies, 1900–1946* (Urbana: University of Illinois Press, 1987); Pratt, *The Growth of the Refining Region;* Joseph A. Pratt, "The Petroleum Industry in Transition: Antitrust and the Decline of Monopoly Control in Oil," *Journal of Economic History* 40 (Dec., 1980): 815–37; David Prindle, *Petroleum Politics and the Texas Railroad Commission* (Austin: University of Texas Press, 1981); William R. Childs, "From Progressive to Personality Politics: The Transformation of the Railroad Commission of Texas, 1919–1940," paper presented at the Annual Meeting of the Texas State Historical Association, Mar. 2, 1990; William R. Childs, "Origins of the Texas Railroad Commission's Power to Control Production of Petroleum: Regulatory Strategies in the 1920s" (forthcoming).

25. Pratt, "Petroleum Industry in Transition"; Prindle, *Petroleum Politics;* King, *Cullinan;* Joseph A. Pratt, "Creating Coordination in the Modern Petroleum Industry: The American Petroleum Institute and the Emergence of Secondary Organizations in Oil," *Research in Economic History* 8 (1983): 179–215; York Y. Willbern, "Administration Control of Petroleum Production in Texas," in *Public Administration and Policy*

industries was transportation. The expansion of railroads made possible the expansion of the rest of the economy. They were also the first major enterprise with out-of-state owners to be found in Texas. As such they have been maligned as eroders of traditional communities and colonial oppressors, but they have also been lauded as great agents of progress. Among their enthusiastic defenders was S. G. Reed, one of the first to seriously study railroads or any other transportation industry in Texas. Reed set a pattern. Not only do railroads still draw more attention than any other facet of the transportation industry, but they are still often viewed as a progressive, modernizing force. Except for works like that by Charles P. Zlatkowich, railroad histories also attract the interest of those fascinated by the romantic image of the machine conquering nature.[26] With the completion of Don Hofsommer's study of the Southern Pacific, almost every major railroad company that operated in Texas now has a published history. While some, such as Keith Bryant's study of the Santa Fe, avoid exaggerated praise of the company, almost all are focused on the various business activities of the firm and not the impact of those activities. Bryant has also been among only a handful who consider the broader impact of the railroads on society.[27]

Formation: Studies in Oil, Gas, Banking, River Development, and Corporate Investigations, ed. Emmette S. Redford (Austin: University of Texas Press, 1956).

26. S. G. Reed, *A History of Texas Railroads* (Houston: St. Clair Publishing, 1941); Charles P. Zlatkowich, *Texas Railroads: A Record of Construction and Abandonment* (Austin: Bureau of Business Research, University of Texas, and Texas State Historical Association, 1981). See also Everett L. DeGolyer, Jr., "The Railroads: The End of an Era," *SHQ* 73 (Jan., 1970): 356–64; V. V. Masterson, *The Katy Railroad and the Last Frontier* (Norman: University of Oklahoma Press, 1952); F. Stanley, *The Story of the Texas Panhandle Railroads* (Borger, Tex.: Hess, 1976). For further bibliographic information on railroads see Don L. Hofsommer, *Railroads of the Trans-Mississippi West: A Selected Bibliography of Books* (Plainview, Tex.: Llano Estacado Press, Wayland College, 1976).

27. Keith L. Bryant, Jr., *History of the Atchison, Topeka, and Santa Fe Railway* (New York: Macmillan, 1974); Keith L. Bryant, Jr., *Arthur Stillwell: Promoter with a Hunch* (Nashville: Vanderbilt University Press, 1971); Don L. Hofsommer, *The Southern Pacific, 1901–1985* (College Station: Texas A&M University Press, 1986); Richard C. Overton, *Gulf to Rockies: The Heritage of the Fort Worth and Denver-Colorado and Southern Railways, 1861–1898* (Austin: University of Texas Press, 1953); H. Craig Miner, *The Rebirth of the Missouri Pacific, 1956–1983* (College Station: Texas A&M University Press, 1983); John C. Rayburn, "Count Telfener and the New York, Texas & Mexican Railway Company," *SHQ* 68 (July, 1964): 29–42; E. Dale Odom, "The Vicksburg, Shreveport

Other types of transportation seem to have fewer fans than railroads. They certainly have fewer histories. Marilyn Sibley has done an interesting history of the port of Houston. James Baughman has also done work on water transportation. Robert Thonhoff has written of the stage lines. Interurbans have received scattered attention. In general, these studies lack the lyric romanticism of works on railroads but in some ways celebrate the pioneer fathers and chastise their enemies.[28]

Something that clearly needs more attention is the impact of transportation changes on the towns and cities of Texas. Andrew Forest Muir, Earl Fornell, and others have focused on nineteenth-century Galveston and Houston. Baughman and Sibley's works extend that picture into the late nineteenth and early twentieth century. Houston and Galveston are also the only cities to have full-scale urban biographies that chronicle the impact of transportation. The other cities of Texas have been largely ignored.[29]

---

and Texas: The Fortunes of a Scalawag Railroad," *Southwestern Social Science Quarterly* 44 (Dec., 1963): 277–85; Robert S. Maxwell, *Whistle in the Piney Woods: Paul Bremond and the Houston, East and West Texas Railway* (Houston: Texas Gulf Coast Historical Association, 1963); Keith L. Bryant, Jr., "The Atchison, Topeka & Santa Fe Railway and the Development of the Taos and Santa Fe Art Colonies," *Western Historical Quarterly* 9 (Oct., 1978): 437–53; Harry Williams, Jr., "The Development of a Market Economy in Texas: The Establishment of the Railway Network, 1836–1890" Ph.D. diss., University of Texas, Austin, 1957.

28. Marilyn McAdams Sibley, *The Port of Houston: A History* (Austin: University of Texas Press, 1968); Judy Watson, "The Red River Raft," *Texana* 5 (spring, 1967): 68–76; James P. Baughman, "The Evolution of Rail-Water Systems of Transportation in the Gulf Southwest, 1836–1890," *JSH* 34 (Aug., 1968): 357–81; James P. Baughman, *Charles Morgan and the Development of Southern Transportation* (Nashville: Vanderbilt University Press, 1968); Robert H. Thonhoff, *San Antonio Stage Lines, 1857–1881* (El Paso: Texas Western Press, 1971); J. W. Williams, "The Butterfields Overland Mail Road across Texas," *SHQ* 61 (July, 1957): 1–19; Emmie Giddings Mahon and Chester V. Kielman, "George H. Giddings and the San Antonio–San Diego Mail Line," *SHQ* (Oct., 1957): 220–39; Pamela Ashworth Puryear and Nath Winfield, Jr., *Sandbars and Sternwheelers: Steam Navigation on the Brazos* (College Station: Texas A&M University Press, 1976); H. Roger Grant, "'Interurbans Are the Wave of the Future': Electric Railway Promotion in Texas," *SHQ* 84 (July, 1980): 29–48.

29. Earl W. Fornell, *The Galveston Era: The Texas Crescent on the Eve of Secession* (Austin: University of Texas Press, 1961); Andrew F. Muir, "Railroads Come to Houston, 1857–1861," *SHQ* 64 (July, 1960): 42–63; Vera L. Dugas, "A Duel with Railroads: Houston v. Galveston, 1866–1881," *ETHJ* 2 (Oct., 1964): 118–27; William D. Angel, Jr., "Vantage on the Bay: Galveston and the Railroads," *ETHJ* 22, no. 1 (1984): 3–18;

As was true of lumber and petroleum, transportation industries were attacked almost from their inception as the penetrating wedge of economic colonizers. This led to increased activism by the state and local governments, to the vilification of so-called "robber barons" like Jay Gould, and to persistent attention to these topics by historians. Railroad regulation and the creation of the Texas Railroad Commission have been the object of several studies, but more clearly could be done. Robert L. Peterson's 1960 dissertation focuses on the regulation of railroads at the turn of the century, but it should be updated and placed in the perspective of broad social and economic changes in the state. A decent book on the topic is yet to be published, although articles and unpublished works are fairly abundant. Perhaps the work in process by Childs on the railroad commissioner will fill the void.[30]

Heroes and villains abound in this literature. The main villain was Jay Gould and the principle heroes were James S. Hogg and John H. Reagan. The latest biography of Jay Gould has attempted to move beyond the old stereotypes, but the legend seems enduring. Perhaps the complex changes let loose by altered transportation called forth and continue to call forth a Manichean view of the world in which good battles evil.[31]

David G. McComb, *Houston: A History* (Austin: University of Texas Press, 1981); David G. McComb, *Galveston: A History* (Austin: University of Texas Press, 1986). Two exceptions to the focus on Houston and Galveston are Keith L. Bryant, Jr., "Arthur Stillwell and the Founding of Port Arthur: A Case of Entrepreneurial Error," *SHQ* 75 (July, 1971): 19–40; Michael Quinley Hooks, "The Struggle for Dominance: Urban Rivalry in North Texas, 1870–1910," Ph.D. diss., Texas Tech University, 1979.

30. Robert L. Peterson, "State Regulation of Railroads in Texas, 1836–1920," Ph.D. diss., University of Texas, Austin, 1960; Robert L. Peterson, "Jay Gould and the Railroad Commission of Texas," *SHQ* 58 (Jan., 1955): 422–32; J. R. Norvell, "The Railroad Commission of Texas: Its Origin and History," *SHQ* 68 (Apr., 1965): 465–80; Gerald Nash, "The Reformer Reformed: John H. Reagan and Railroad Regulation," *Business History Review* 29 (June, 1955): 189–96; Gerald Nash, "A Chapter from an Active Life: John H. Reagan and Railroad Regulation," M.A. thesis, Columbia University, 1952. For early activity by the state see Roger A. Griffin, "Governor E. M. Pease and Texas Railroad Development in the 1850s," *ETHJ* 10 (fall, 1972): 103–118. For an indication of Childs's early findings, see his "From Progressive to Personality Politics."

31. In addition to the works on Gould and Reagan already cited see Julius Grodinsky, *Jay Gould, His Business, 1867–1892* (Philadelphia: University of Pennsylvania Press, 1957); Maury Klein, *The Life and Legend of Jay Gould* (Baltimore, Md.: Johns Hopkins University Press, 1986); Robert C. Cotner, *James Stephen Hogg: A*

Shades of gray have been slowly added to this view of the world by increased attention paid to the men in the middle: those who acted as agents of outside capitalists while they insulated Texans from the worst onslaughts of their employers. A forthcoming history of Baker, Botts, a firm whose members long served as the principal Texas attorneys for the Southern Pacific Railroad, should be of great interest in this regard. Mid-nineteenth-century lawyers and merchants who profited from improved transportation such as William Pitt Ballinger, T. W. House, and William Marsh Rice deserve further study. More could be done with the bankers and real estate promoters of early twentieth-century Texas who so strenuously worked to link their cities to the outside world by improving rail and water transportation.[32]

Transportation workers needed all the defenders they could muster because the most spectacular of the nineteenth- and early twentieth-century strikes occurred in the transportation industries. While some excellent studies exist, the links between labor unions and local government lack adequate analysis. How did unions gain or lose the support of government? How did the union movement fit into the general anticolonial and antimonopoly political ideology? Like the history of firms, the history of labor unions needs to move away from too internal a focus.[33]

Bankers, insurance dealers, real estate promoters, and their regulators seemingly viewed labor unions with a jaundiced eye, but it is

---

Biography (Austin: University of Texas Press, 1959); Ben H. Proctor, *Not without Honor: The Life of John H. Reagan* (Austin: University of Texas Press, 1962).

32. J. S. Cullinan was another example of a man in the middle; see King, *Cullinan*. Also see Joseph A. Pratt and Kenneth Lipartito, *History of Baker, Botts* (Austin: University of Texas Press, forthcoming); Morris, *William Marsh Rice;* Henry C. Grover, "The Dissolution of T. W. House and Company," M.A. thesis, University of Houston, 1962; John A. Moretta, "William Pitt Ballinger: Public Servant, Private Pragmatist," Ph.D. diss., Rice University, 1985.

33. Ruth A. Allen, *The Great Southwest Strike* (Austin: University of Texas Publication, 1942); James V. Reese, "The Early History of Labor Organizations in Texas, 1838–1876," *SHQ* 72 (July, 1968): 1–20; James V. Reese, "The Evolution of an Early Texas Union: The Screwmen's Benevolent Association of Galveston," *SHQ* 75 (Oct., 1971): 158–85; Allen Clayton Taylor, "A History of the Screwmen's Benevolent Association from 1866–1924," M.A. thesis, University of Texas, Austin, 1968; James C. Maroney, "The Galveston Longshoremen's Strike of 1920," *ETHJ* 16 (1978): 3; Robert E. Zeigler, "The Workingman in Houston, Texas, 1865–1914," Ph.D. diss., Texas Tech University, 1972.

difficult to say anything conclusive about them. For depite their essential roles in the economic development of Texas the literature on these persons and their industries has been slight. As always, the literature reveals an emphasis on the "golden age" and romantic pioneers. Colonialism also comes in for considerable attention. The question most often asked has been if these local elites took part in the exploitation of their fellow Texans by outside forces. Did the money changers and promoters exploit the common man?

Bruce Palmer insisted that Texans issued a more radical critique of the social order than other southerners and that they "clung longest and most tenaciously to anti-monopoly greenbackism." Certainly, until the 1970s banking laws in Texas were more restrictive than in most states and bankers were viewed with some degree of popular disdain. Not surprisingly works on banking and the closely related insurance and real estate industries have been scarce. Despite efforts by the Texas Bankers Association, the industry has long had a clouded image in the state.[34]

Still, companies and the friends and family of company pioneers have generated a small literature. For example, William Kirkland wrote a brief history of his family's bank. H. Harold Wineburgh wrote a biography of his much admired friend, Fred Florence. Avery L. Carlson paid particular attention to his friend and patron, Khleber Miller Van Zandt, in his book on banking in Texas. As might be expected these works place the firm and its pioneers in the best possible light.[35] Neglected even in this type of literature have been prominent individuals and firms in real estate and insurance. Jesse Jones, one of the first large-scale real estate developers in the state, does have one book-

34. Bruce Palmer, *Man over Money: The Southern Populist Critique of American Capitalism* (Chapel Hill: University of North Carolina Press, 1975), p. 182; T. Harry Gatton, *The Texas Bankers' Association: The First Century, 1885-1985* (Austin: Texas Bankers' Association, 1984).

35. H. Harold Wineburgh, *The Texas Banker: The Life and Times of Fred Farrel Florence* (Dallas: H. H. Wineburgh, 1981); Nathan Adams, *The First National in Dallas* (Dallas: First National Bank, 1942); Avery L. Carlson, *A Monetary and Banking History of Texas* (Ft. Worth: Ft. Worth National Bank, 1930); William A. Kirkland, *Old Bank—New Bank: The First National Bank Houston, 1866-1965* (Houston: Pacesetter, 1975). Also see Sandra L. Myres, ed., *Force without Fanfare: The Autobiography of K. M. Van Zandt* (Ft. Worth: Texas Christian University Press, 1968); Sandra L. Myres, *The Fort Worth National Bank, Century One: 1873-1973* (Ft. Worth: Ft. Worth National Bank, 1973).

length biography, but in it the heroic pathbreaker can do no wrong and the businessman's day-to-day activities receive scanty coverage. There is also a laudatory biography of Jones's equivalent in Fort Worth, Amon Carter. The real estate and banking endeavors of Jones and Trammel Crow receive attention in a study of the Texas Commerce Banks, and Morton Keller provides a history of the life insurance industry at a pivotal time for Texas. Morgan and King's recently published study of the Woodlands perhaps gives notice of better things to come, for it ably recounts the growth of this planned community.[36]

Instead of individuals and firms the primary emphasis has been on regulation. The evolution of the state banking system has received some attention. So too has the famous Robertson Insurance Act of 1907 which restricted the business of out-of-state firms. Significant regulatory changes in banking in the 1950s and early 1970s have also been well documented. In this case, a good biography of the principal regulators, such as Thomas B. Love, would be most welcome.[37]

Recently, a few works have appeared that attempt to trace the evo-

36. Bascom N. Timmons, *Jesse H. Jones: The Man and the Statesman* (New York: Holt, 1956); Jerry Flemmons, *Amon: The Life of Amon Carter, Sr., of Texas* (Austin: Jenkins, 1978); Walter L. Buenger and Joseph A. Pratt, *But Also Good Business: Texas Commerce Banks and the Financing of Houston and Texas, 1886–1986* (College Station: Texas A&M University Press, 1986); Morton Keller, *The Life Insurance Enterprise, 1885–1910: A Study in the Limits of Corporate Power* (Cambridge, Mass.: Belknap, 1963); George T. Morgan, Jr. and John O. King, *The Woodlands: New Community Development, 1964–1983* (College Station: Texas A&M University Press, 1987). For a different view of Jones see Walter L. Buenger, "Between Community and Corporation: The Southern Roots of Jesse H. Jones and the Reconstruction Finance Corporation," *JSH* 56 (Aug. 1990): 481–510.

37. James Aubrey Tinsley, "The Progressive Movement in Texas," Ph.D. diss., University of Wisconsin, Madison, 1953; James Aubrey Tinsley, "Texas Progressives and Insurance Regulation," *Southwestern Social Science Quarterly* 36 (Dec., 1955): 237–47; Thomas A. Crosson, "A History of the Robertson Law and Its Effect Upon Life Insurance in Texas," M.A. thesis, University of Pennsylvania, 1951; John Roy Mitchell, "The Limits of Reform: Major Financial Legislation in Texas, 1904–1910," M.A. thesis, Texas A&M University, 1989; William Hubert Baughn, *Changes in the Structure of Texas Commercial Banking, 1946–1956* (Austin: Bureau of Business Research, University of Texas, 1959); Lawrence L. Crum, *Transition in the Texas Commercial Banking Industry, 1950–1965* (Austin: Bureau of Business Research, University of Texas, 1970); Joseph M. Grant and Lawrence L. Crum, *The Development of State-Chartered Banking in Texas: From Predecessor Systems until 1970* (Austin: Bureau of Business Research, University of Texas, 1978); Benjamin Klebaner, "The Bank Holding Company Act of 1956," *Southern Economic Journal* 24 (Jan., 1958): 313–26. On Love see Donna Lee Younker,

lution of a firm and its impact on society. Walter Buenger and Joseph Pratt have written about banking. Harold Hyman has written about the Kempner family and their varied business interests, including insurance. Focusing on the impact of banks, insurance companies, and related enterprises on the entire Houston/Galveston economy calls forth new questions. What has been the role of these firms and their owners and managers in the promotion and growth of the cities in which they did business? In turn, how has the larger society influenced the firm and its owners? What has been the impact of regulatory changes and population changes? How have specific cultures or values shaped a firm? How has technology changed an organization?[38]

Buenger and Pratt also focus on the strenuous efforts Texas bankers made to erect a financial system that could operate outside the shadow of the money center banks. This was probably the reverse side of the point Palmer made about Texas Populists' concern for monetary policy. All Texans, even bankers, sought greater local control and more plentiful sources of credit. Dewey Grantham points to this concern with resisting colonialism as a central feature of Texas Progressivism. Tinsley sees it as at the heart of insurance reform.[39]

Colonialism is part of a conundrum that has long troubled businessmen and historians: Just what has been and what should be the role of Texas in the regional, national, and international economy? As those in the cattle, lumber, and petroleum businesses discovered, finance was the wedge via which outsiders gained control. Local control of banking and insurance (one of the primary sources of long-term financing of real estate) allowed Texans to aspire to a more dominant role. As the case of the Texas Commerce Bank so vividly makes clear, such aspirations are now dead. Almost all major Texas banks are now owned by out-of-state interests. This perhaps will inspire some level of anticolonialism among future historians of Texas business.[40]

"Thomas B. Love's Service in the Texas Legislature and in State Government During the Lanham and Campbell Administrations," M.A. thesis, Southern Methodist University, 1958.

38. Buenger and Pratt, *But Also Good Business;* Hyman, *Oleander Odyssey.*

39. Buenger and Pratt, *But Also Good Business;* Tinsley, "The Progressive Movement in Texas"; Dewey Grantham, *Southern Progressivism: The Reconciliation of Progress and Tradition* (Knoxville: University of Tennessee Press, 1983), pp. 98–103. To place Texas in the national picture of insurance reform see Keller, *The Life Insurance Enterprise.*

40. See such examples already cited as King, *Cullinan;* Gressley, *Bankers and Cat-*

Law firms and control of the legal system were often married to the entering wedge of finance. For example, the most famous partner of Baker, Botts, Capt. James A. Baker, also chaired the board of a Houston bank and was for many years the glue that connected local businesses to credit.[41] More work should be published on other firms to establish whether Baker was an exception or the rule. Did lawyers play such a prominent role across the state?

Baker also spent a part of each year in the Northeast and through friendship and business ties was well connected to the largest corporations and their managers. He seems to have been one of those middlemen found in other industries. He gave outsiders improved access to Texas, but steered part of the wealth into his and other Texans' pockets. This is a variant on the anticolonialism theme that deserves much more work. A full-scale biography of Baker and others like him that avoids the pitfalls of hero worship is one path to this goal.[42]

Medical doctors were another group of professionals who played prominent roles in the economy. Not only did they provide a vital service, but like lawyers they often took part in other business activities. In the field of medicine we have a more extensive range of works on the heroic pioneers than in law. Medicine as an industry has also been studied. One important new study by Marilyn McAdams Sibley focuses on Houston's Methodist Hospital, but much more could be done on that city's dynamic Medical Center. Also lacking is emphasis on such common themes as anticolonialism. Did it play a part in the creation of the Medical Center?[43]

---

tlemen; Sheffy, *The Francklyn Land & Cattle Company;* Buenger and Pratt, *But Also Good Business.*

41. Pratt and Lipartito, *Baker, Botts;* Buenger and Pratt, *But Also Good Business,* pp. 82–83.

42. Some biographical work has been done on Baker by a member of his firm. See Jesse Andrews, "A Texas Portrait: Capt. James A. Baker, 1857–1941," *Texas Bar Journal,* (Feb., 1961): 110–11, 187–89. A history of other firms such as Vinson, Elkins has been discussed in the past.

43. P. I. Nixon, *A Century of Medicine in San Antonio* (San Antonio: privately published, 1936); P. I. Nixon, *A History of the Texas Medical Association, 1853–1953* (Austin: University of Texas Press, 1954); P. I. Nixon, *Pat Nixon of Texas: Autobiography of a Doctor,* ed. Herbert H. Lang (College Station: Texas A&M University Press, 1979); B. M. Jones, *Health Seekers in the Southwest, 1817–1900* (Norman: University of Oklahoma Press, 1967); Elizabeth Silverthorne, *Ashbel Smith of Texas: Pioneer, Patriot, Statesman, 1805–1886*

The Texas economy has usually been more varied than that of other southern states, but it has been the primary industries that have always received the scrutiny of historians. Among others, the food and beverage industry deserves to move out of the shadows. Hyman's study of the Kempners gives more information on Imperial Sugar and the sugar industry. Joe Frantz has studied one abortive attempt to establish the dairy industry. Henry Dethloff's recently published history of the American rice industry contains much information on Texas. Others have studied the evolution of the rice industry into one of the Gulf Coast's most significant economic activities, but more could be done on the state's rice-processing firms. Major breweries existed in the state by the close of the Civil War and the processing and distribution of coffee and wheat have long been a major part of the Houston economy. Yet no significant histories of specific firms or the industries as a whole exist. Wheat has played a role in the creation and growth of other cities and other regions of the state, but again has not been seriously studied. The wholesaling of commodities in general needs much more work.[44]

Another neglected area has been manufacturing. Studies of the impact of petroleum usually give space to the manufacturing related to that industry, but oil has not been the only reason for the growth of manufacturing capacity in Texas. Much more could be done on the defense-related industries and on the electronics industry. Automobile plants and their unions receive scant mention. These industries have been centered in the Dallas–Forth Worth region, an urban area whose economy has never been adequately studied. Perhaps that is why the region's specific industries have also been neglected.[45]

(College Station: Texas A&M University Press, 1982); Marilyn McAdams Sibley, *The Methodist Hospital: Serving the World* (Austin: Texas State Historical Association, 1989).

44. Joe B. Frantz, *Gail Borden: Dairyman to a Nation* (Norman: University of Oklahoma Press, 1951); William R. Johnson, *A Short History of the Sugar Industry in Texas* (Houston: Texas Gulf Coast Historical Association, 1961); Henry Dethloff, *A History of the American Rice Industry, 1685–1985* (College Station: Texas A&M University Press, 1988); Joseph Cannon Bailey, *Seaman A. Knapp: Schoolmaster of American Agriculture* (New York: Columbia University Press, 1945); Edward Hake Phillips, "The Gulf Coast Rice Industry," *AH* 25 (Apr., 1954): 91–96; Sister Francis Assisi Scanlon, "The Rice Industry of Texas," M.A. thesis, University of Texas, Austin, 1954; Robert Overvelt, *Val Verde Winery* (El Paso: Texas Western Press, 1985).

45. Pratt, *Growth of a Refining Region.*

Epochs

Along with industry studies, firms, and labor, particular time periods in the evolution of the state's economy have drawn attention. From the antebellum years through the Great Depression historians have divided and subdivided the economic history of the state. Usually these studies point out significant changes over the time period and contain fewer romantic nuances. They share a general concern with the growth and impact of a market economy, and they attempt to define what made that epoch unique. The better histories put forward a theory to explain change over time. Most problems with such works spring from the very periodization used or from rigid determination to use the history of that time period in an historiographical debate.

Antebellum Texans witnessed the rapid expansion of slavery and a plantation economy. They took part in the steady move westward of the Texas frontier. These two basic changes, the growth of slavery and plantations and the move west, have dominated the historical literature on the era's economy. The bulk of the recent work on slavery and the plantation has been done by Randolph B. Campbell and Richard G. Lowe. Using census data, tax records, and probate records they have painted a picture of an economy that was expanding rapidly while remaining self-sufficient in foodstuffs. Wealth was increasingly concentrated in the higher income brackets. Case studies have augmented this picture of general prosperity but growing disparity in wealth and power. Little romance tinges the pages of these works. Slavery is viewed as a flexible labor system employed by capitalists, not as a patriarchal, economically backward system that yielded more psychic than monetary return.[46]

46. Richard G. Lowe and Randolph B. Campbell, *Planters and Plain Folk: Agriculture in Antebellum Texas* (Dallas: Southern Methodist University Press, 1987); Randolph B. Campbell and Richard G. Lowe, "Some Economic Aspects of Antebellum Texas Agriculture," *SHQ* 82 (Apr., 1979): 351–78; Randolph B. Campbell and Richard G. Lowe, *Wealth and Power in Antebellum Texas* (College Station: Texas A&M University Press, 1977); Randolph B. Campbell and Richard G. Lowe, "Slave Property and the Distribution of Wealth in Texas, 1860," *Journal of American History (JAH)* 63 (Sept., 1976): 316–24; Campbell, *Empire for Slavery*; Randolph B. Campbell, "Intermittent Slave Ownership: Texas as a Test Case," *JSH* 51 (Feb., 1985): 15–30; Cecil Harper, Jr., "Slavery without Cotton: Hunt County, Texas, 1846–1864," *SHQ* 88 (Apr., 1985): 387–405. This view is supported by work on the South in general such as Robert E.

Studies of the importance of the frontier have easily surpassed in number works on the plantation. From early in this century to the present day, interest has been high in the antebellum western frontier. Soldiers, settlers, Indians, and Mexicans struggled for dominance. Meanwhile, the western frontier obscured the importance of other frontiers. Except for a pioneering work by Leroy Graf little has been done on the economy of South Texas. In the last twenty-five years the urban frontier has finally received increased notice. Kenneth Wheeler and others have begun to study the roots of urban economic development.[47] The focus of these works has seldom been simply the economy. This diffuse focus and the romanticism of the works on the western frontier in particular cloud our understanding of the antebellum economy.

Most regrettable has been the failure to ask pertinent questions. For example, what was the level of market activity and orientation in the state? In fact, until recently we have known little about the basic structure of the dominant agricultural sector of the economy. The work of Campbell, Lowe, and Cecil Harper indicates that Texans understood the workings of the market in cotton, land, and slaves. They were interested in maximizing their profits, but as case studies demonstrate, some farmers traded a bit of profit for greater security. Was this true of the broad range of Texas farmers?

If there are gaps in our knowledge of the antebellum economy there are chasms in our knowledge of the Civil War and Reconstruction era economy. This has not been for lack of interest. Instead it springs from the soap opera characteristics of the writing on this period. Good and evil are exaggerated. Events seem larger than life. Perhaps they were, because this was certainly a pivotal era in Texas history. It was pivotal for the economy as well because Texas went from

---

Gallman and Ralph V. Anderson, "Slaves as Fixed Capital: Slave Labor and Southern Economic Development," *JAH* 64 (June, 1977): 24–46.

47. Leroy P. Graf, "The Economic History of the Lower Rio Grande Valley, 1820–1875," Ph.D. diss., Harvard University, 1942; Kenneth W. Wheeler, *To Wear a City's Crown: The Beginnings of Urban Growth in Texas, 1836–1865* (Cambridge: Mass.: Harvard University Press, 1968); Fornell, *The Galveston Era;* Mary Susan Jackson, "The People of Houston in the 1850s," Ph.D. diss., Indiana University, 1975; Susan Jackson, "Movin' On: Mobility through Houston in the 1850s," *SHQ* 81 (Jan., 1978): 251–82; Larry Jay Gage, "The City of Austin on the Eve of the Civil War," *SHQ* 63 (Jan., 1960): 428–38; Earl F. Woodward, "Internal Improvements in Texas in the Early 1850s," *SHQ* 76 (Oct., 1972): 161–82.

being one of the wealthiest of states to one of the poorest. Most works on the period attempt to capture the drama and explain the impact of war and politics on the economy.

The point Randolph Campbell makes in another essay in this volume, that our understanding of historical continuities has been limited by the tendency to break studies of the years between 1845 and 1877 at the start and finish of the war, is equally valid for histories of the economy. What changed in 1861? Did the war retard or encourage economic growth? Was change permanent? Answers to all these questions require a broader vision. Vera Lea Dugas comes closest to this broad vision, but her work is unpublished, does not systematically cover the antebellum years, and is twenty-five years old. Other than this, little has been done on the wartime economy except several studies of the cotton trade across the Mexican border.[48]

Instead of the war, most economic studies focus on Reconstruction. Here the dangers of periodization and of fighting the historiographic battle comes clear. Suspended in time, the agents of the Republicans and Democrats fight old battles anew. Did Republican policy aid or retard growth? What about graft, corruption, and railroad construction? Indian fighting and the expansion of the frontier provide some relief from the battles of Reconstruction, but it is past time to put aside passion and come to grips with economic change in the era.[49]

More unanimity of opinion characterizes works on the closely related Populist and Progressive eras. Almost every study of the two decades on each side of 1900 includes extensive discussion of the theme developed in Spratt's *Road to Spindletop*. How did the expansion of the market change the lives of Texans, particularly Texas farmers? James R. Green, for example, highlighted the economic plight of the little man

---

48. Vera Lea Dugas, "A Social and Economic History of Texas in the Civil War and Reconstruction Periods," Ph.D. diss., University of Texas, Austin, 1963; Vera Lea Dugas, "Texas Industry, 1860-1880," *SHQ* 59 (Oct., 1955): 151-83; Ronnie C. Tyler, "Cotton on the Border, 1861-1865," *SHQ* 73 (Apr., 1970): 456-77; Fredericka Meiners, "The Texas Border Cotton Trade, 1862-1863," *Civil War History* 23 (Dec., 1977): 293-306.

49. Larry Earl Adams, "Economic Development in Texas during Reconstruction, 1865-1875," Ph.D. diss., University of North Texas, 1980; Samuel Lee Evans, "Texas Agriculture, 1865-1880," M.A. thesis, University of Texas, Austin, 1955; S. S. McKay, "Economic Conditions in Texas in the 1870s" *WTHAYB* 25 (1949): 84-127. One interesting exception is Winston Lee Kinsey, "The Immigrant in Texas Agriculture during Reconstruction," *AH* 53 (Jan., 1979): 125-41.

and his political response. The tragedy has been so well drawn and become so deeply etched in the minds of historians that it is perhaps time for a systematic study using quantitative methods that would determine just what farmers drifted down into poverty and what type of farmers prospered. If Reconstruction calls forth too turbulent a debate, then the debate over the economy during Populism and Progressivism has for thirty years lacked the energy provided by divergent points of view and systematic analysis. A different type of romanticism, an identification with the little guy, with the bygone age of the self-sufficient communal farmer, has obscured our understanding.[50]

This more specific work on the economy in the Populist and Progressive eras should include a detailed study of landholding patterns and the concentration of wealth. Other questions include: How did the status and function of labor change? What about the source of labor? Some work has been done on the upsurge in Mexican immigration to Texas after 1900, but much more could be done.[51]

Considerable scholarship exists on the rise of cities in the Populist and Progressive eras and the corresponding rise in an activist government. Harold Platt has done several interesting things on Houston which demonstrate that the city's economic elite gained control of urban government and used it to promote their prosperity. Urban rivalry in the period has also been a focus on attention. These same urban elites harnessed government to outstrip their rivals in nearby cities.[52]

50. The only study that attempts to analyze agriculture in a systematic way is unpublished and out of date. See Samuel Lee Evans, "Texas Agriculture, 1880–1930" Ph.D. diss., University of Texas, Austin, 1960. Also see James R. Green, "Tenant Farmer Discontent and Socialist Protest in Texas, 1901–1917," *SHQ* 81 (Oct., 1977): 133–54; James R. Green, *Grass Roots Socialism: Radical Movements in the Southwest, 1895–1943* (Baton Rouge: Louisiana State University Press, 1978). Calvert also covers this topic in greater detail in his essay.

51. Camilo A. Martínez, "The Mexican and the Mexican-American Laborers in the Lower Rio Grande Valley of Texas, 1870–1930," Ph.D. diss., Texas A&M University, 1987; Lawrence A. Cardoso, "Labor Emigration to the Southwest, 1916 to 1920: Mexican Attitudes and Policy," *SHQ* 79 (Apr., 1976): 400–16. Also see Zeigler, "The Workingman in Houston."

52. Harold L. Platt, "Urban Public Service and Private Enterprise: Aspects of the Legal and Economic History of Houston, Texas, 1865–1905," Ph.D. diss., Rice University, 1974; Harold L. Platt, *City Building in the New South: The Growth of Public Services in Houston, Texas, 1830–1910* (Philadelphia: Temple University Press, 1983); Harold L. Platt, "Houston at the Crossroads: The Emergence of the Urban Center of

As cities grew and the economy became more industrialized, state regulation of business increased. The four industries already discussed, petroleum, insurance, banking, and transportation, were particular objects of state regulation. But there was a strong antimonopoly movement that affected the entire economy. Besides regulation, government attempted to boost the economy by improving education and funding extension services. In other words, the state committed itself to providing the technical expertise needed in a more complex economy. Besides Tinsley's excellent but unpublished work on the progressive movement, little attempt has been made to draw all the pieces of the puzzle together. An obvious need is an updated study of economic and social change and their political ramifications that treats the period 1880–1930 as a whole. Such a work should explain any possible connections between the populists and progressives while it explores the validity of Spratt's thesis that the expansion of the market provoked a tumultuous political response. It should explain why the urge to regulate business seems to have been somewhat stronger in Texas than in other southern or western states.[53]

The 1920s have been as yet lightly studied in Texas history. Scholars seem unsure whether to treat this decade as part of the Progressive Era, as a separate entity, or as an introduction to the Great Depression. Certainly, some of the themes of business regulation continue and should be studied further.[54]

Paucity of literature at least links the 1920s to the 1930s. Still, the

---

the Southwest," *Journal of the West* 18 (July, 1979): 51–61; Hooks, "The Struggle for Dominance"; Thomas T. Barker, Jr., "Partners in Progress: The Galveston Wharf Company and the City of Galveston, 1900–1930," Ph.D. diss., Texas A&M University, 1979; James Weinstein, "Organized Business and the City Commission and Manager Movements," *JSH* 28 (May, 1962): 166–82.

53. One scholar has begun to link the populists and progressives. See Worth Robert Miller, "Building a Progressive Coalition in Texas: The Populist-Reform Democratic Rapprochement, 1900–1907," *JSH* 52 (May, 1986): 163–82. To compare Texas with other southern states see Grantham, *Southern Progressivism*. On the relationship between business and higher education see Larry D. Hill and Robert A. Calvert, "The University of Texas Extension Services and Progressivism," *SHQ* 86 (Oct., 1982): 231–54; Lewis L. Gould, "The University Becomes Politicized: The War with Jim Ferguson, 1915–1918," *SHQ* 86 (Oct., 1982): 255–76.

54. Almost nothing on the economy in the 1920s has been published. For a good grasp of the period see Norman D. Brown, *Hood, Bonnet, and Little Brown Jug: Texas Politics, 1921–1928* (College Station: Texas A&M University Press, 1984).

plight of cities and workers has attracted scholars. Specific industries already cited, such as cotton, experienced traumatic upheavals which displaced large numbers of workers. Mechanization, of course, played a major role in this dislocation. Kenneth Walker's story of the pecan-shelling industry in San Antonio is a classic story of the role of government and of mechanization. While seldom intentional the impact of government could be baneful as well as helpful for the lowest socio-economic groups.[55]

The most common work on the Great Depression in Texas focuses on specific cities. Typically these cities fared somewhat better than those in other parts of the nation because of the discovery of oil in East Texas. San Antonio, however, was relatively unaffected by petroleum and badly hit by the depression. Julia Blackwelder's study of women in San Antonio is an excellent start, but *only* a start, toward understanding the impact of the depression on the state's oldest major city.[56]

The function of government in the Texas economy during the depression also clearly needs further study. For the first time the national government played a major role in the day-to-day economic life of most Texans. State government, particularly in the area of regulation, also remained crucial. Texans did not always react with joy at the new rise in governmental activity. Indeed, the depression left Texans somewhat ideologically adrift. Their well-being demanded an active, interventionist government while their vaunted individualism led them to reject such a government.[57]

Post-1940 studies of the Texas economy have been virtually nonexistent. Some histories of companies or families such as those by

55. Kenneth P. Walker, "The Pecan Shellers of San Antonio and Mechanization," *SHQ* 69 (July, 1965): 44-58.

56. Robert C. Cotner, ed., *Texas Cities and the Great Depression* (Austin: Texas Memorial Museum, 1973); Dianne Treadway Ozment, "Galveston during the Hoover Era, 1929-1933," M.A. thesis, University of Texas, Austin, 1968; Marsha Grant Berryman, "Houston and the Early Depression: 1929-1932," M.A. thesis, University of Houston, 1965; William Edward Montgomery, "The Depression in Houston during the Hoover Era, 1929-1932," M.A. thesis, University of Texas, Austin, 1966; Julia Blackwelder, *Women of the Depression: Caste and Culture in San Antonio, 1929-1939* (College Station: Texas A&M University Press, 1984).

57. Donald W. Whisenhunt, "Texas in the Great Depression, 1929-1933: A Study of Public Reaction," Ph.D. diss., Texas Tech University, 1966; Donald W. Whisenhunt, ed., *The Depression in the Southwest* (Port Washington, N.Y.: Kennikat, 1980); Donald W. Whisenhunt, *The Depression in Texas: The Hoover Years* (New York: Garland, 1983).

Buenger and Pratt, Hofsommer, and Hyman carry the story into the recent past, but they are exceptions. Much more could be and should be written about the impact of World War II on the economy. The economic decline of the mid-1980s spawned a spate of books, but few, besides Joe R. Feagin's study of Houston, systematically considered the cause and effect of the decline. The long period of relative prosperity between World War II and the bust of the 1980s has been virtually ignored.[58]

In a way the absence of good studies of any period after the depression reflects the flight from modernity that typifies the economic history of Texas. As George Perry so graphically illustrated in his novel, *Hold Autumn in Your Hand,* the depression witnessed the last gasp of the yeoman farmer. The move from country to city, begun in force in the 1930s, accelerated in the 1940s. Mechanization spawned by the labor shortages and high demand for farm commodities of World War II almost universally changed even agriculture into a big business. Other enterprises in other sections of the economy grew in size and scope. Increasingly Texas was interconnected in obvious ways to a worldwide economy. While some Texans cultivated the image of rugged and eccentric oilmen, the reality was that more Texans came to be like their counterparts in New York. Loss of individuality and distinctiveness seemed to come with prosperity. Yet historians preserved distinctiveness by focusing on the years before 1940. Thus the Great Depression was a break point both in the economic history of the state and the treatment of that development by historians.

Past Theories and Future Prospects

Yet the Great Depression cried out for a theory to explain the sorry state of the economy, and that forced analysis of economic development over the long term. Usually theories that explain change

58. Although brief and of only marginal value one exception to the lack of focus on the modern economy is Mary Ann Norman, *The Texas Economy since World War II* (Boston: American Press, 1983). The rise and fall of Houston has attracted considerable attention. See Joe R. Feagin, *Free Enterprise City: Houston in Political Economic Perspective* (New Brunswick, N.J.: Rutgers University Press, 1988); Harold T. Gross and Bernard L. Weinstein, *Houston's Economic Development: Opportunities and Strategy* (Dallas: Southern Methodist University Center for Enterprising, 1985). Additional comment on the 1980s can be found in *Houston Business Journal; Houston Profile; Texas*

have come from historians of the entire South or from those outside the discipline of history. Gavin Wright, an economic historian, has pointed to the role of the external marketplace, the dominance of outside capital, and changes in the internal labor market as key determinants of economic change. The generally downward trend of cotton prices, the failure of investors to follow their money southward and create a more dynamic economy, low-wage industries, and the inability of workers to escape from those low-wage industries all locked the South in relative poverty. Most would agree that to some extent state and national governments could break the hold of outside capital, external markets, and low wages, and Pete Daniel and Jack Temple Kirby have made strong cases for the impact of federal policy on the South during the depression and World War II. Historians of Texas must decide if these theories apply to their subject of study. Was Texas' economic development retarded by low wage industries and a semi-colonial economy? Was it government spending and government policy that lifted Texas out of poverty?[59]

The structural weaknesses that caused the depression did not grow overnight. Each preceding era contributed to the structure of the economy. The greatest failing of the studies of each of the earlier eras was to ignore the long-term impact of change. Some scholars, however, have advanced, at least indirectly, an explanation for long-term change. For example, a theory expounded by Pratt and others is that growth always depended upon the progress of one primary industry. Growth sprang from cotton and related industries. Then it grew from oil and related industries. Obviously this meant that all industries were particularly vulnerable to commodity price swings. Thus, as Wright indicated, in a commodity-based economy the key factor was the world market. The question then becomes why industry remained focused in a narrow range. Was it colonialism? Was it lack of capital or was capital tied up in such seemingly profitable investments as slavery and petroleum? Did the climate, culture, or soil type limit diversity? Indeed, given the rather impressive array of industries that have oper-

---

Business Review; Texas Monthly. See in particular Paul Burka, "The Year Everything Changed," *Texas Monthly* 11 (Feb., 1983). Also of interest is Davies, "Life at the Edge."

59. Gavin Wright, *The Political Economy of the Cotton South* (New York: Norton, 1978); Gavin Wright, *Old South, New South: Revolutions in the Southern Economy since the Civil War* (New York: Basic Books, 1986). Also see Daniel, *Breaking the Land;* Kirby, *Rural Worlds Lost;* Pratt, *Growth of a Refining Region;* King, *Cullinan.*

ated in Texas, has it really been an economy focused in a very narrow range? Many questions remain to be answered.

The apparent variety but limited vitality of the economy between 1880 and 1940 suggests another possibility: something about the culture, ethnicity, or ideology of Texans set limits on economic development. What was most important was not market structure, the rise and fall of particular industries, or the inexorable advance of technology, but the human actors within this setting. Joe Feagin has recently pointed out how Houston elites' free-enterprise mentality retarded investment in education and public services. Harold Hyman gives us the example of what it meant to be Jewish and doing business in Texas. In contrast to southern whites, Jews seem to be much more community minded and farsighted. Did southern white male culture limit economic opportunities? In a recent article Walter Buenger focuses on one of the premier businessmen to spring from this culture: Jesse H. Jones. Jones at least combined a commitment to community service in order to gain status, a resentment of domination by Wall Street because it deprived his city of its rightful place, and a shrewd awareness that what was good for the city was good for his real estate, banking, and newspaper interests. He combined communalism with self-interest. The propensity for Texans to resent colonialism more than other southerners, a quality noted by numerous historians, might also be cultural in origin and the link between culture and anti-colonialism might help explain the particular path of economic development in Texas. The basic questions in need of answers are: Was Texas capitalism different? Why was it different and what effect did this have?[60]

That such questions have been asked or not asked stems from both the peculiar habits and perspectives of historians and the influence of the environment in which they wrote. Three rough historiographic eras have existed. From 1930 to about 1945, writers commemorated the uniqueness of Texas in order to resist the intrusion of the more bureaucratic and industrialized world. Likewise the urge to record the history of particular firms often grew from the impending demise of the firm or its incorporation into a larger, more nationally oriented entity. Naturally such histories typically highlighted the pioneer past.

60. Buenger, "Between Community and Corporation"; Feagin, *Free Enterprise City;* Hyman, *Oleander Odyssey.*

338

Research based upon the written word of elites and the popularity of the biographical method also encouraged filiopietism. It was the West, not the South, that was celebrated as an alternative to modernity by Texas intellectuals who came of age in the 1920s and who began publishing in the 1930s. Disillusioned by Confederate defeat and postwar southern poverty, they looked westward instead of southward. Like a country that turned to western movies to escape the woes of the depression, historians turned to western themes, and they struck out vigorously against the colonialism that kept their region poor. The most prominent of these was Walter Prescott Webb, but Haley, Holden, and others also sought a western alternative to their present. They created a functional past, a past in which the frontier was tamed, a past before the complexities of modern times.[61]

As times changed, the choice of topics and emphasis of historians of the economy also changed. The generation that won World War II and experienced sustained economic growth tended to view that growth with irreducible optimism. Technology would always provide the answer. From the late 1940s through the mid-1960s, the rising prosperity of the state gave the still existing concern with modernity a patina of inevitability. The engine of progress could not be derailed. The increased use of empirical analysis and the influence of trained business historians and economists abetted this trend. There is a mechanistic quality to the work of Spratt and to a lesser degree John O. King's work shares this sense of inevitability. The writings of Clark and Halbouty abound with optimism; one more big strike around the corner, one more Spindletop yet to be found in a never-ending continuum of prosperity.

61. Kenneth B. Ragsdale, *The Year America Discovered Texas: Centennial '36* (College Station: Texas A&M University Press, 1987); Walter Prescott Webb, *Divided We Stand: The Crisis of a Frontierless Democracy* (New York: Farrar and Rinehart, 1937); Walter Prescott Webb, "The South's Future Prospect," in *The Idea of the South*, ed. Frank E. Vandiver (Chicago: University of Chicago Press, 1964), pp. 67–78; James S. Payne, "Texas Historiography in the Twentieth Century: A Study of Eugene C. Barker, Charles W. Ramsdell, and Walter P. Webb," Ph.D. diss., University of Denver, 1972; Necah Stewart Furman, *Walter Prescott Webb: His Life and Impact* (Albuquerque: University of New Mexico Press, 1976); Gregory M. Tobin, *The Making of a History: Walter Prescott Webb and The Great Plains* (Austin: University of Texas Press, 1976); Joe B. Frantz, "Walter Prescott Webb and the South," in *Essays on Walter Prescott Webb*, ed. Kenneth R. Philip and Elliott West (Austin: University of Texas Press, 1976), pp. 3–15.

The 1960s marked another break point. The use of quantitative methods and of methods borrowed from the social sciences encouraged a look at society as a whole. Goals as well as methods changed. Influenced by antiestablishment movements in the 1960s, historians stressed the economic history of the plain folks, not elites. The economic activities of women, blacks, and Mexicans, of the middle and lower classes, became accepted topics. At the very least historians have compared elites and nonelites. Here *Planters and Plain Folk,* by Lowe and Campbell, might serve as the classic example. In like vein during the 1960s, the firm became important not because of its internal history and heroic leaders, but because of what it could tell us about the nature of business and its impact on society.

Even after the 1960s, however, notes of regret at the passing of a lost age remained common. Each new era has simply overlaid the past, not replaced it. Perhaps this was less true of historians who were not sons or daughters of the state. Judging from the work of most historians, however, it has been difficult to escape the function of an intellectual middleman: preserving the heroic and atypical, interpreting Texas to the nation, and explaining the place of Texas in a regional or national economy.

This being the case, what are our options? Here is a list of alternatives that will perhaps lead historians to push against their self-imposed limits.

First, Texas economic history, indeed all Texas history, could benefit from borrowing from the larger field of southern history. The romance of the ranching frontier has too long obscured the reality that Texas has an economy based on cheap labor and commodities, much like the rest of the South. Racism was one reason this was so. Except in the antebellum period no serious effort has been made to compare Texas' development with other southern states. The quantitative methods used to analyze the South's economic history have not always been used to evaluate Texas. Borrowing from other disciplines, a practice common in southern history, would also be useful. Simple comparison with other southern states might yield useful insights. These methods and questions should add greatly to our understanding of Texas.

Second, since the 1890s the Texas economy has been dominated by its urban areas and by the businesses of those cities. It is past time to look at the relationship between the growth of economic elites, firms, and cities. Each did not operate in a vacuum. How did they shape the development of each other? Did the firm lead toward or away from a resource-dominated economy? Did the culture of the city shape the firm? Was the reverse true? Why did some urban sites grow and others wither? The role of the elite men and women who stood between Texas and the world, the links to the outside culture and economy, are particularly interesting. How did they protect their cities from colonialism and lead them into participation in the dominant economy and culture?

Finally, new approaches require a new philosophy. The depression of the mid-1980s made it obvious that the economic history of the state has not been an uninterrupted stream of progress. Further, relative poverty had the blessing of easing the seeming encroachment of modernity. We learned that we need not flee the "soulless" modern life. It fled us. That experience left behind perhaps the ideal state of mind to write a long-running history of the state, one that laps over the traditional time periods, includes theories of change, and avoids excessive romanticism.

ॐ Contributors

ALWYN BARR, professor of history at Texas Tech University, is a former director of Ethnic Studies at that institution. His *Reconstruction to Reform* (1971) won the Coral Horton Tullis Award for the most important contribution to Texas history that year. Among his numerous publications on African American history are *Black Texans: A History of Negroes in Texas, 1528–1971* (1973) and co-editor (with Robert A. Calvert) *Black Leaders: Texans for Their Times* (1981). His most recent publication is *Texans in Revolt* (1990).

WALTER L. BUENGER, associate professor of history at Texas A&M University, won the Texas Historical Commission award for 1984 for his first book, *Secession and Union* (1984). His research interests have moved more into the twentieth century with the publication (with Joseph A. Pratt) of *But Also Good Business: Texas Commerce Banks and the Financing of Houston and Texas* (Texas A&M University Press, 1986). An article by him on Jesse Jones, Houston financier, recently appeared in the *Journal of Southern History*.

ROBERT A. CALVERT, associate professor of history at Texas A&M University, is the past president of the Texas State Historical Association and former Book Review Editor of the *Southwestern Historical Quarterly*. He has published several articles dealing with agriculture and reform in *Agricultural History* and the *Southwestern Historical Quarterly*. His most recent book is *A History of Texas* (with Arnoldo De León, 1990).

342

RANDOLPH B. CAMPBELL, Regents Professor, the University of North Texas, won the Coral Horton Tullis Award and the Friends of the Dallas Library Institute of Texas Letters Award for his most recent book, *An Empire for Slavery: The Peculiar Institution in Texas* (1989). He is the author or co-author of three other books dealing with antebellum Texas and has contributed prize-winning articles to the *Southwestern Historical Quarterly* and the *Journal of Southern History.*

DONALD E. CHIPMAN, a professor of history at the University of North Texas, has published extensively on New Spain, including a biography, *Nuno de Guzman and the Province of Panuco in New Spain* (1967). His recent research interest has turned to Spanish Texas, with a recent article on Cabeza de Vaca, *Southwestern Historical Quarterly* (1987) and a manuscript in the works on Spanish explorations of Texas.

RONALD L. DAVIS, professor of history and director of the Southern Methodist University oral history program on the performing arts, has published several books on opera and a three-volume history of American music. Recently his research interests have led him to work on Hollywood and film, and *The Glamour Factory: Inside Hollywood's Big Studio System* is currently in press. His newest project is a biography of Linda Darnell, a movie star from Texas.

ARNOLDO DE LEÓN, C. J. "Red" Davidson Professor of History at Angelo State University, is recognized as a leading authority on the history of Texas Mexicans. His significant works include *The Tejano Community, 1836–1900* (1982); *They Called Them Greasers: Anglo Attitudes toward Mexicans in Texas, 1821–1900* (1983); and *Ethnicity in the Sunbelt: A History of Mexican Americans in Houston, Texas* (1989). He recently published *Tejanos and the Numbers Game* (1989) with Kenneth Stewart.

FANE DOWNS, former president of the West Texas Historical Association, is a noted authority on the women's movement in Texas, and has published numerous articles and book chapters on the topic. She is the advisory editor on the history of women for the forthcoming *Handbook of Texas*. After twenty years of service at McMurry College, including chair of the history department and the division of social sciences, she recently acquired a degree in theology and is presently a Presbyterian minister in Dallas.

KENNETH E. HENDRICKSON, JR., Hardin Distinguished Professor of American History and chair of the department of history at Midwestern State University, began his career with a biography of Richard Pettigrew of South Dakota (1968). Among his recent publications are *The Waters of the Brazos: A History of the Brazos River Authority* (1981) and *Red River Uplift: A History of the Oil and Gas Industry in North Texas* (in press).

LARRY D. HILL, chair of the department of history at Texas A&M University, has specialized in foreign policy of the progressive years, 1901–21. His *Emissaries to a Revolution: Woodrow Wilson's Executive Agents in Mexico* (1974) began an interest in progressivism that has continued with articles in journals and current work on a manuscript that deals with the food administration in World War I. He serves as co-editor (with Robert A. Calvert) of the Texas A&M Southwestern Studies monographic series, published by Texas A&M University Press.

PAUL D. LACK, professor of history at McMurry, has published several articles on urban slavery in the *Southwestern Historical Quarterly*, *Arkansas Historical Quarterly*, and other journals. He serves as advisory editor on the Texas Revolution for the *Handbook of Texas* and has finished a book-length manuscript titled "The Texas Revolutionary Experience: A Social and Political History, 1835–1836."

CHAR MILLER, an associate professor of history at Trinity University, has done extensive work on the American mission movement. He published *Fathers and Sons: The Bingham Family and the American Mission* in 1982. After authoring numerous other articles and editing a book on similar topics, he has lately won

344

scholarly attention for his work on San Antonio. His most recent publication is as co-editor of *Urban Texas: Politics, Race, and Development* (Texas A&M University Press, 1989) in the Texas A&M Southwestern Studies series.

❧ Index to Authors

346

Bradburn, Juan Davis, 143
Brady, David W., 94n
Branch, Hettye Wallace: *The Story of "Bo
John"*, 60n
Branch, Mary, 71
Brand, Donald D., 129
Branda, Eldon S., 107nn, 108n, 110nn,
122
Braudel, Fernand: *The Mediterranean and
the Mediterranean World in the Age of
Philip II*, xxivn; *The Structures of Every-
day Life*, xxivn
Brenner, Judith Ann: *Sul Ross*, 213
Brewer, John Mason, 74; *Dog Ghosts*, 54;
Negro Legislators of Texas, 51n, 185
Brewer, Thomas B., 244
Bridges, Clarence A., 188nn
Briggs, Richard Lee, 182
Briggs, Ronald, xxxivn
Brindley, Anne A., 125
Briscoe, Betty Jane Slaughter, 179n
Brody, David, 225n
Brook, Stephen: *Honkytonk Gelato*, 279
Brophy, William J., 67, 68 and n, 69,
71n, 72nn, 76, 78
Brown, John Henry: *History of Texas
from 1685 to 1892*, 50n
Brown, Lawrence L.: *The Episcopal
Church in Texas*, 178n
Brown, Norman D.: *Hood, Bonnet and
Little Brown Jug*, 237, 238, 239n, 249
and n, 272n, 334n
Brown, Olive D., 71
Bryan, J. P., ed.: *The Texas Diary*, 136n
Bryant, Ira B., 71n; *Barbara Charline Jor-
dan*, 77
Bryant, Keith L., Jr.: *Arthur Stillwell*,
321; articles, 10, 211n, 321, 322n; *History
of the Atchison, Topeka, and Santa Fe Rail-
way*, 321; *History of the Santa Fe*, 321
Bryson, Conrey: *Dr. Lawrence A. Nixon
and the White Primary*, 77n
Buck, Samuel M.: *Yanaguana's Successors*,
119
Budd, Harrell, 210n
Buenger, Walter L.: articles, xxxi, 170,

Buenger, Walter L. (*cont.*)
189, 190, 247n, 326n, 338; *Secession and
the Union in Texas*, 39, 44n, 189
Buenger, Walter L., and Joseph A.
Pratt: *But Also Good Business*, 326n, 327,
328
Buenger, Walter L., and Robert A. Cal-
vert: *Texas History and the Move Into the
Twenty-First Century*, 245, 248, 250
Bugbee, Lester G., 117
Bullard, Robert D.: *Invisible Houston*,
69, 75, 76, 287n, 289n, 300n, 301n,
303n
Bullock, Henry Allen, 70n, 71n, 75
Burch, Marvin C., 119
Burka, Paul, 336n
Burns, Mamie Sypert: *This I Can Leave
You*, 96
Burran, James A., 69
Busby, Mark: *Preston Jones*, 14
Butterfield, Jack C.: *Clara Driscoll*,
95n
Byrd, James W.: *J. Mason Brewer*, 74
Bywaters, Jerry: *Seventy-Five Years of
Art in Dallas*, 9

Cabeza de Vaca, Alvar Núñez, 104
Cain, Jerry Berlyn, 52
Calderón, Roberto R., 29n; comp.,
South Texas Coal Mining, 35n
Calvert, Robert A., 204, 221n; articles,
xin, xxviii, 78n, 204, 311n, 312, 333n;
and Barr, 56n, 57n, 64n, 71n, 72n, 74n,
185n; and Baum, 210, 214n; and
Buenger, 245, 248, 250; and Hill, 248n,
334n; and Witherspoon, 205
Calvert, Robert A., and Arnoldo De
León, *History of Texas*, 230
Camarillo, Albert, 32n
Campbell, Randolph B., 184n; articles,
xxix, 53, 55n, 165, 166, 167, 175, 180n,
183n, 184n, 185n, 188, 216, 330, 331, 332,
340; *An Empire for Slavery*, xxxin, 53,
54, 55n, 130, 156, 159, 168, 169, 172, 178n,
315, 330; *A Southern Community in Crisis*,
xxvn, 165n

Johnson, David R., John A. Booth, and
Richard J. Harris, eds.: *Politics of San
Antonio,* 287n, 295n, 300n
Johnson, Elmer H.: *Basis of the Commer-
cial and Industrial Development of Texas,*
307n
Johnson, Roney, III, 175n
Johnson, William R.: *A Short History of
the Sugar Industry in Texas,* 329n
Johnstone, Paul H., xin
Jones, Billy Mac: *Health Seekers in the
Southwest,* 328n; *Search for Maturity,* 198
Jones, Everett L., 60n
Jones, J. Lester: *W. T. Carter & Bro.,* 318
Jones, Jesse H., 338; *Fifty Billion Dollars,*
297
Jones, Lamar B., 28n
Jones, Margo, 14, 95; *Theatre-in-the-
Round,* 13
Jones, Oakah L., Jr.: *Los Paisanos,* 129
Jones, Pauline, 185n
Jones, Preston, 14; *A Texas Trilogy,* 14
Jones, Richard A., 287n
Jones, Robert L., 185n
Jordan, Barbara, and Shelby Hearon:
Barbara Jordan, 77
Jordan, Terry G., articles, 167 and n,
219, 220n, 247; *German Seed on Texas
Soil,* 154n, 169, 220n; *Immigration to
Texas,* 219; *Texas Graveyards,* 74; *Texas
Log Buildings,* 54; *Trails to Texas,* 129,
312
Jordan, Terry G., John L. Bean, Jr.,
and William M. Holmes: *Texas: A
Geography,* 126, 219
Jordan, Winthrop: *White Over Black,* 51n
Joseph, Donald, 124
Juárez, José Roberto, 34n
Justice, Blair: *Violence in the City,* 76
Jutson, Mary Carolyn Hollers: *Alfred
Giles,* 11

Kahl, Mary: *Ballot Box 13,* 269
Kalil, Susie: *The Texas Landscape,* 9
Kammen, Michael: *The Past before Us,*
301n

Kanellos, Nicolas: *Mexican American
Theater,* 14
Kaplan, Barry J., 75, 285n, 286n, 291n
Kealing, H. T.: *History of African Method-
ism,* 50n
Kearns, Doris: *Lyndon Baines Johnson and
the American Dream,* 263
Keener, Charles V., 194n
Keever, Jack, 270
Keller, Morton: *The Life Insurance Enter-
prise,* 326n, 327n
Kenzer, Robert C.: *Kinship and Neigh-
borhood in a Southern Community,* 87,
220n
Kerr, Homer Lee, 168, 169, 219n
Kerr, William T., Jr., 241n
Key, Bettye Ann Showers, 215n
Key, V. O., Jr., 260; *Southern Politics,* 249
and n
Keyes, Lucille Sheppard, 253
Kibbe, Pauline: *Latin Americans in Texas,*
24n
Kielman, Chester V., 322n
Kilgore, Dan, 129; *How Did Davy Die?,*
149
Kinch, Sam, and Stuart Long: *Allan
Shivers,* 257
Kinch, Sam, Jr., and Ben Procter: *Texas
under a Cloud,* 271
King, Alma Dexta, 185n
King, Alvy L.: *Louis T. Wigfall,* 186n
King, C. Richard, 13
King, Irene M.: *John O. Meusebach,*
154n, 170n
King, John O., 326; *Early History of the
Houston Oil Company,* 319; *Joseph Stephen
Cullinan,* 319, 324n, 327n, 337n
King, Keith L., 204n
Kinnaird, Lawrence, ed.: *The Frontiers
of New Spain,* 121; *Spain in the Missis-
sippi Valley,* 122
Kinsey, Winston Lee, 332n
Kirby, Jack Temple: *Rural Worlds Lost,*
315n, 337
Kirkland, William: *Old Bank—New
Bank,* 325

367

Texas through Time was composed into type on a Compugraphic digital phototypesetter in eleven point Baskerville with two points of spacing between the lines. Baskerville was also selected for display. The book was designed by Jim Billingsley, typeset by Metricomp, Inc., printed offset by Thomson-Shore, Inc., and bound by John H. Dekker & Sons, Inc. The paper on which this book is printed carries acid-free characteristics for an effective life of at least three hundred years.

TEXAS A&M UNIVERSITY PRESS : COLLEGE STATION